Lecture Notes in Computer Science 1608

Edited by G. Goos, J. Hartmanis and J. van Leeuwen

T0223086

Springer

Berlin
Heidelberg
New York
Barcelona
Hong Kong
London
Milan
Paris
Singapore
Tokyo

S. Doaitse Swierstra   Pedro R. Henriques
José N. Oliveira (Eds.)

Advanced
Functional Programming

Third International School, AFP'98
Braga, Portugal, September 12-19, 1998
Revised Lectures

 Springer

Series Editors

Gerhard Goos, Karlsruhe University, Germany
Juris Hartmanis, Cornell University, NY, USA
Jan van Leeuwen, Utrecht University, The Netherlands

Volume Editors

S. Doaitse Swierstra
Utrecht University, Department of Computer Science
P.O. Box 80.089, 3508 TB Utrecht, The Netherlands
E-mail: doaitse@cs.uu.nl

Pedro R. Henriques
José N. Oliveira
University of Minho, Department of Informatics
Campus de Gualtar, 4709 Braga Codex, Portugal
E-mail: {prh,jno}@di.uminho.pt

Cataloging-in-Publication data applied for

Die Deutsche Bibliothek - CIP-Einheitsaufnahme

Advanced functional programming : third international school ;
revised lectures / AFP'98, Braga, Portugal, September 12 - 19, 1998.
S. Doaitse Swierstra ... (ed.). - Berlin ; Heidelberg ; New York ;
Barcelona ; Hong Kong ; London ; Milan ; Paris ; Singapore ; Tokyo
: Springer, 1999
   (Lecture notes in computer science ; Vol. 1608)
   ISBN 3-540-66241-3

CR Subject Classification (1998): D.1.1, D.3.2, D.2.2, D.2.10

ISSN 0302-9743
ISBN 3-540-66241-3 Springer-Verlag Berlin Heidelberg New York

Typesetting: Camera-ready by author
SPIN: 10704973   06/3142 – 5 4 3 2 1 0   Printed on acid-free paper

Preface

In this volume you will find the lecture notes corresponding to the presentations given at the 3rd summer school on Advanced Functional Programming, held in Braga, Portugal from September 12–19, 1998.

This school was preceded by earlier ones in Båstad (1995, Sweden, LNCS 925) and Olympia, WA (1996, USA, LNCS 1129). The goal of this series of schools is to bring recent developments in the area of functional programming to a large group of students. The notes are published in order to enable individuals, small study groups, and lecturers to become acquainted with recent work in the fast developing area of functional programming.

What made this school particularly interesting was the fact that all lectures introduced useful software, that was used by the students in the classes to get hands-on experience with the subjects taught. We urge readers of this volume to download the latest version of this software from the Internet and try to do the exercises from the text themselves; the proof of the program is in the typing.

The first lecture, on *Sorting Morphisms*, serves as a gentle introduction to the things to come. If you have always been afraid of the word "morphism", and you have been wondering what catamorphisms, anamorphisms, hylomorphims, and paramorphims were about, this is the paper to read first; you will discover that they are merely names for recursion patterns that occur over and over again when writing functional programs. The algorithms in the paper are all about sorting, and since you are likely to know those algorithms by heart already, seeing them structured and analyzed in a novel way should serve as a motivation to read on to the second lecture.

The second lecture, on *Generic Programming*, is almost a book in a book. The notes can be seen as the culminating point of the STOP-project, sponsored by the Dutch government at the end of the 80's and the beginning of the 90's. Its overall goal was the development of a calculational way of deriving programs. The project has provided deeper insight into real functional programming and into the theory behind many things commonly written by functional programmers. One of the main achievements of the project has been to make people aware of the fact that many algorithms can be described in a data-independent way. The PolyP system introduced in these notes is one of the translations to the Haskell-world of this theoretical underpinning.

The third lecture, on *Generic Program Transformation*, can also be seen as an application of the theory introduced in lecture two. Many efficiency-improving program transformations can be performed in a mechanical way, and these would not have been possible without insight into the correctness of such transformations gained in the lecture on Generic Programming.

The fourth lecture, on *Designing and Implementing Combinator Languages*, introduces an easy to write formalism for writing down the catamorphisms introduced in earlier chapters. It is shown how quite complicated catamorphisms, that at first sight seem rather forbidding by making extensive use of higher-order domains, can actually be developed in a step-wise fashion, using an attribute grammar view; it is furthermore shown how to relate this way of programming with concepts from the object-oriented world thus making clear what the strengths and weaknesses of each world are.

The fifth lecture, titled *Using MetaML: A Staged Programming Language*, introduces the concept of partial evaluation. It serves as another instance of the quest for "the most generic of writing programs at the lowest cost". The staging techniques show how costs that were introduced by adding extra levels of abstraction, may be moved from run-time to compile-time.

It has been common knowledge to users of modern functional languages that the type system can be a great help in shortening programs and reducing errors. In the extreme one might see a type as a predicate capturing the properties of any expression with that type. In the sixth lecture on *Cayenne – Spice up your Programming with Dependent Types* it is shown in what direction functional languages are most likely to develop, and what may be expected of the new type systems to be introduced.

The last lecture, titled *Haskell as an Automation Controller*, shows that writing functional programs does not have to imply that one is bound to remain isolated from the rest of the world. Being able to communicate with software written by others in a uniform way, is probably one of the most interesting new developments in current computer science. It appears that the concept of a monad together with the Haskell typing rules, is quite adequate to describe the interface between Haskell programs and the outer world.

Finally we want to thank everyone who contributed to this school and made it such a successful event: sponsors, local system managers, local organizers, students, and last but not least the lecturers. We are convinced that everyone present at the school enjoyed this event as much as we did, and we all hope that you will feel some of the spirit of this event when studying these lecture notes.

March 1999   Doaitse Swierstra
                                              Pedro Henriques
                                              José Oliveira

Sponsorship

The school has received generous sponsorship from:
FCT - Fundação para a Ciência e Tecnologia, Ministério da Ciência e Tecnologia

Adega Cooperativa de Ponte de Lima
Agência Abreu
CGD - Caixa Geral de Depósitos
CIUM - Centro de Informática da Universidade do Minho
DI - Departamento de Informática da Universidade do Minho
GEPL - Grupo de Especificação e Processamento de Linguagens
LESI - Direcção de Curso de Engenharia de Sistemas e Informática
Enabler
Lactolima
Laticínios das Marinhas, Lda
Novabase Porto - Sistemas de Informação SA
Primavera Software
Projecto Camila - Grupo de Métodos Formais
Sidereus - Sistemas de Informação e Consultoria Informática Lda
SIBS - Sociedade Interbancária de Serviços
Vieira de Castro

Local Committee:

José Almeida, Minho
Luís Barbosa, Minho
José Barros, Minho
M. João Frade, Minho
Pedro Henriques, Minho
F. Mário Martins, Minho
F. Luis Neves, Minho
Carla Oliveira, Minho
Jorge Pinto, Lix
Jorge Rocha, Minho
Cesar Rodrigues, Minho
João Saraiva, Minho
M. João Varanda, Minho

Table of Contents

Sorting Morphisms

Lex Augusteijn

Philips Research Laboratories, Eindhoven
lex@natlab.research.philips.com

Abstract. Sorting algorithms can be classified in many different ways. The way presented here is by expressing the algorithms as functional programs and to classify them by means of their *recursion patterns*. These patterns on their turn can be classified as the natural recursion patterns that destruct or construct a given data-type, the so called *cata-* and *anamorphisms* respectively. We show that the selection of the recursion pattern can be seen as the major design decision, in most cases leaving no more room for more decisions in the design of the sorting algorithm. It is also shown that the use of alternative data structures may lead to new sorting algorithms.

This presentation also serves as a gentle, light-weight, introduction into the various morphisms.

1 Introduction

In this paper we present several well known sorting algorithms, namely *insertion sort, straight selection sort, bubble sort, quick sort, heap sort* and *merge sort* (see e.g. [8,11]) in a non-standard way. We express the sorting algorithms as functional programs that obey a certain pattern of recursion. We show that for each of the sorting algorithms, the recursion patterns forms the major design decision, often leaving no more space for additional decisions to be taken. We make these recursion patterns explicit in the form of higher-order functions, much like the well-known map function on lists.

A different approach to the classification of sorting algorithms can be found in [3], where formal specifications of sorting functions are made more and more specific in a step-wise fashion, thus deriving the structure of merge sort, quick sort, insertion sort and selection sort.

In order to reason about recursion patterns, we need to formalize that notion. Such a formalization is already available, based on a category theoretical modeling of recursive data types as can e.g. be found in [4,9]. In [2] this theory is presented together with its application to many algorithms, including selection sort and quicksort. These algorithms can be understood however only after absorbing the underlying category theory. There is no need to present that theory here. The results that we need can be understood by anyone having some basic knowledge of functional programming, hence we repeat only the main results here. These results show how to each recursive data type a number of morphisms is related, each capturing some pattern of recursion which involve the

S.D. Swierstra et al. (Eds.): Advanced Functional Programming, LNCS 1608, pp. 1–27, 1999.
© Springer-Verlag Berlin Heidelberg 1999

recursive structure of the data type. Of these morphisms, we use the so called *catamorphism, anamorphism, hylomorphism* and *paramorphism* on linear lists and binary trees. The value of this approach is not so much in obtaining a nice implementation of some algorithm, but in unraveling its structure.

This presentation gives the opportunity to introduce the various morphisms in a simple way, namely as patterns of recursion that are useful in functional programming, instead of the usual approach via category theory, which tends to be needlessly intimida ting for the average programmer.

In this paper, we assume that all sorting operations transform a list 1 into a list s that is a permutation of 1, such that the elements of s are ascending w.r.t. to a total ordering relation <. Moreover, we assume the existence of an equivalence relation == on the elements, such that for all elements a, b, either a<b, a==b or b<a.

We express the sorting algorithms in the functional language Hugs [7], which is a dialect of Haskell [6]. We assume that the reader is familiar with, but not necessarily an expert in, functional programming.

This paper is organized as follows. In Sect. 2 we present the morphisms on the list data type and show that insertion sort, selection sort and bubble sort can be expressed in terms of these morphisms. In Sect. 3 we present the leaf tree data type and show how merge sort can be expressed as a morphism over that data type. In Sect. 4 we present the binary tree data type with its morphisms, which are used to express both quick sort and heap sort. In Sect. 5 paramorphisms on lists are presented, which can be used to express the recursion pattern of several auxiliary functions used by the different sorting algorithms. We show in Sect. 6 that rose trees form a generalization of lists, binary trees and leaf trees. This fact enables a derivation of pairing heap sort and reveals a novel generalization of quick sort. It also opens the door for a taxonomy of algorithms, based on a hierarchy of data structures and on recursion patterns over those data structures. Section 7 presents the conclusions of this paper.

2   Morphisms on Lists

The list data type can be described by the following pseudo data type definition in Haskell.

```
data [x] = []
         | x : [x]
```

In this section we present three recursion patterns over this data type, and show how *insertion sort, selection sort* and *bubble sort* can be expressed by means of these recursion patterns.

2.1   The List Catamorphism

A *catamorphism* on a type T is a function of type $T \to U$ that destruct and object of type T according to the structure of T, calls itself recursively of any

components of T that are also of type T and combines this recursive result with
the remaining components of T to a U.

A simple example is the function that computes the product of a list of
integers:

```
prod []    = 1
prod (x:l) = x * prod l
```

A *list catamorphism* can thus be characterized by two components (a,f),
corresponding to the two forms of the list type. The first is a part that maps the
empty list onto a U. This is just the constant a (for prod this is 1). A *non-empty
list* can be destructed into a head h and a tail t. The tail t is recursively mapped
onto a u by rec t and then combined with the head by means of the expression
f h (rec t), where f is the second part of the catamorphism. For prod this
is (*).

We can present this structure in a diagram where the nodes form the types of
the (intermediate) results and the edges the mappings between them.

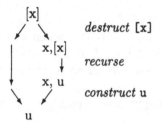

Recursive functions over lists that have this structure can be written by
means of a higher order function of (a,f) that captures this recursive patterns.
As this recursion pattern is generally called *catamorphism* ($\kappa\alpha\tau\alpha$ means downwards), we call this higher order function list_cata. As described above, it
returns a on the empty list and applies f to the head and the recursive call
on the tail. the more experienced reader will recognize this function as the well
known foldr.

The (a,f) is usually called an *algebra*, more specifically a *list algebra*. We
abbreviate its type by List_alg.

```
> type List_alg x u = (u, x->u->u)

> list_cata :: List_alg x u -> [x] -> u
> list_cata (a,f) = cata where
>    cata []    = a
>    cata (x:l) = f x (cata l)
```

With this definition we can rewrite prod as follows:

```
> prod = list_cata (1, (*))
```

It can be observed that this catamorphism replaces the empty list by **a** and the non-empty list constructor (:) by **f**. This is what a catamorphism does in general: replacing the constructors of a data type by other functions. As a consequence, recursive elements are replaced by the application of the catamorphism to them, i.e. l is replaced by **cata** l.

Exercise 1: Write the list reversal function as a list catamorphism.

2.2 The List Anamorphism

Apart from a recursion pattern that traverses a list, we can specify a converse one that *constructs* a list. A simple example is the function that constructs the list [n,n-1..1].

```
count 0 = []
count n = n : count (n-1)
```

An anamorphism over a type T is a function of type $U \to T$ that destructs the U in some way into a number of components. On the components that are of type U, it applies recursion to convert theme to T's. After that it combines the recursive results with the other components to a T, by means of the *constructor functions* of T.

The structure of this pattern for the list type can be obtained by inverting the catamorphism diagram above.

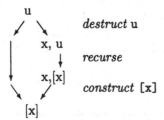

We need some destructor function of u that tells us whether to map u onto the empty list, or to destruct it, be means of some function f into the head of the resulting list x and another u. This other u can then recursively be mapped onto a list, which forms the tail of the final result.

To this end, we define use the type that represents the disjoint sum of to values.

```
data Either a b = Left a | Right b
```

Again, this pattern of recursion can be captured in a higher order function. As this recursion pattern is generally called *anamorphism* ($\alpha\nu\alpha$ means upwards), we call this higher order function list_ana.

The type u-> Either () (x,u) is usually called a *co-algebra*, more specifically a *list co-algebra*. We abbreviate this type by List_coalg.

```
> type List_coalg u x = u -> Either () (x,u)

> list_ana :: List_coalg u x -> u -> [x]
> list_ana a = ana where
>    ana u = case a u of
>             Left _         -> []
>             Right (x,l) -> x : ana l
```

The function count can be rewritten as:

```
> count = list_ana destruct_count
> destruct_count 0 = Left ()
> destruct_count n = Right (n,n-1)
```

Exercise 2: Write a prime number generator as a list anamorphism.

2.3   The List Hylomorphism

Given a general way to construct a list and to destruct one, we can compose the two operations into a new one, that captures recursion *via* a list. For some philosophical reason, this recursion patterns is called *hylomorphism* ($\acute{v}\lambda\eta$ means matter).

The list hylomorphism can be defined as

```
list_hylo (a,c) = list_cata c . list_ana a
```

As an example, we could define the factorial function as
`fac = prod . count`, or more explicitly as:

```
  fac = list_cata (1,(*)) . list_ana destruct_count
```

This straightforward composition forms an intermediate list, which appears to be unnecessary as the following diagrams exhibits.

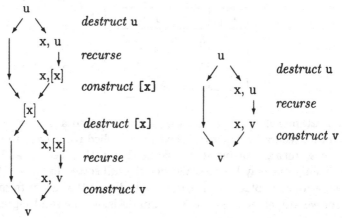

Instead of construction the list in the middle, we can immediately map the (x,u)-pair onto the (x,v)-pair by recursively applying the hylomorphism to the u.

The implementation is obtained from the list_ana by replacing the empty list by a and the list constructor (:) by f.

```
> type List_hylo u x v = (List_coalg u x, List_alg x v)

> list_hylo :: List_hylo u x v -> u -> v
> list_hylo (d,(a,f)) = hylo where
>    hylo u = case d u of
>             Left _     -> a
>             Right (x,1) -> f x (hylo 1)
```

Applying this to the factorial function, it can be written as:

```
> fac = list_hylo (destruct_count, (1,(*)))
```

Substitution of list_hylo and destruct_count then leads to the usual definition of fac:

```
fac 0 = 1
fac n = n * fac (n-1)
```

Exercise 3: Write the function x^n as a list hylomorphism.

2.4   Insertion Sort

We can use the list_cata recursion pattern to sort a list. In order to analyze the structure of such a sorting algorithm, we first draw a little diagram.

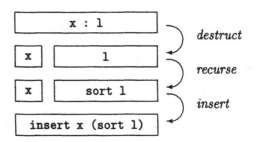

The catamorphism *must* destruct a list x:1 into a head x and a tail l, by virtue of its recursive structure. Next it is applied recursively to the tail, which in this case means: sorting it. So we are left with a head x and a sorted tail. There is only one way left to construct the full sorted list out of these: insert x at the appropriate place in the sorted tail. We see that apart from the recursion pattern, we are left with no more design decision: the resulting algorithm is an insertion sort.

```
> insertion_sort l = list_cata ([],insert) l where
>    insert x [] = [x]
>    insert x (a:l) | x < a      = x:a:l
>                   | otherwise = a : insert x l
```

Observe that insert x is a recursive function over lists as well. As it does not correspond to the recursive structures introduced so far, we postpone its treatment until Sect. 5.2.

2.5   Selection Sorts

In applying the anamorphism recursion pattern to sorting, we are faced with the following structure.

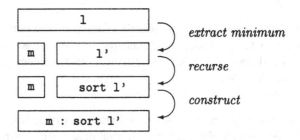

First of all, the unsorted list l is mapped onto an element m and a remainder l'. This remainder is sorted by recursion and serves as the tail of the final result. From this structure, we can deduce that m must be the minimum of l and l' should equal some permutation of l with this minimum removed from it. It is the permutation which gives us some additional design freedom. Two ways to exploit this freedom lead to a straight selection sort and a bubble sort respectively. Here we abstract from the way of selection and define the general selection sort as:

```
> selection_sort extract = list_ana select where
>    select [] = Left ()
>    select l  = Right (extract l)
```

Straight Selection Sort. When we first compute the minimum of l and then remove it from l, maintaining the order of the remaining elements, we obtain a straight selection sort. It has the following recursive structure.

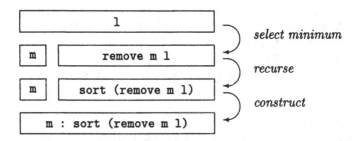

Its implementation as an anamorphism is as follows.

```
> straight_selection_sort l = selection_sort extract l where
>    extract l = (m, remove m l) where m = minimum l

> remove x [] = []
> remove x (y:l) | x == y     = l
>                | otherwise = y : remove x l
```

Observe that **remove x** is a recursive function over lists as well. As it does not correspond to the recursive structures introduced so far, we postpone its treatment until Sect. 5.3, where we also give an implementation of **minimum** as a catamorphism as well.

Bubble Sort. Selection sort seems a little too expensive as **select** traverses the list twice, once for obtaining the minimum and once for removing it. We can intertwine these to operations to let the minimum 'bubble' to the head of the list by exchanging elements and then split the minimum and the remainder.

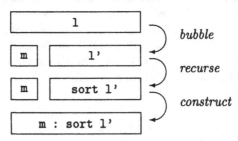

```
> bubble_sort l = selection_sort bubble l where
>    bubble [x]   = (x,[])
>    bubble (x:l) = if x < y then (x,y:m) else (y,x:m) where
>                       (y,m) = bubble l
```

Observe that **bubble** is a recursive function over lists as well. It appears to be a catamorphism, as the following alternative definition shows:

```
> bubble_sort' l = selection_sort bubble l where
>    bubble (x:l) = list_cata ((x,[]),bub) l
>    bub x (y,l) = if x < y then (x,y:l) else (y,x:l)
```

3 Leaf Trees

The sorting algorithms that can be described by list-based recursion patterns
all perform linear recursion and as a result behave (at least) quadratically. The
$O(n \log n)$ sorting algorithms like quick sort and merge sort use at least two
recursive calls per recursion step. In order to express such a recursion pattern
we need some binary data structure as a basis for the different morphisms. In
this section we concentrate on leaf trees with the elements in their leaves. The
next section treats binary trees with the elements at the branches.

One form of binary trees are so-called *leaf-trees*. These trees hold their elements
on their leaves. The leaf-tree data type is given by:

```
> data LeafTree x = Leaf x
>                 | Split (LeafTree x) (LeafTree x)
```

3.1 The Leaf-Tree Catamorphism

The structure of the leaf-tree catamorphism is completely analogous to that
of the list catamorphism. First destruct the tree, recurse on the sub-trees and
combine the recursive results.

An example is the sum of all elements in a leaf tree:

```
tree_sum Leaf x      = x
tree_sum (Split l r) = tree_sum l + tree_sum r
```

The leaf-tree catamorphism needs a function on the element, rather than a
constant, to construct its non-recursive result. This corresponds to the following
diagram, where T stands for `BinTree x`.

The recursion pattern diagram is:

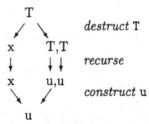

Capturing the recursion pattern in a higher order function `leaftree_cata`,
gives the following definition (again, just replace the tree constructors `Leaf` and
`Split` by other functions, `fl` and `fs` respectively).

```
> type Leaftree_alg x u = (x -> u, u -> u -> u)

> leaftree_cata :: Leaftree_alg x u -> LeafTree x -> u
> leaftree_cata (fl,fs) = cata where
>   cata (Leaf x)    = fl x
>   cata (Split l r) = fs (cata l) (cata r)
```

Using the function leaftree_cata, we can define tree_sum as:

```
> tree_sum = leaftree_cata (id, (+))
```

3.2   The Leaf-Tree Anamorphism

The structure of the leaf-tree anamorphism is analogous to that of the list anamorphism. First decide by means of a destructor d between the tree constructors to be used (Tip or Branch). This results in an element or in two remaining objects which are recursively mapped onto two trees. Then combine the element or these subtrees.

An example is the construction of a Fibonacci tree:

```
fib_tree n
  | n < 2     = Leaf 1
  | otherwise = Branch (fib_tree (n-1)) (fib_tree (n-2))
```

The anamorphism procedure corresponds to the following diagram.

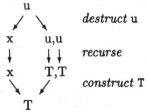

Capturing the recursion pattern in a higher order function leaftree_ana, gives the following definition.

```
> type Leaftree_coalg u x = u -> Either x (u,u)

> leaftree_ana :: Leaftree_coalg u x -> u -> LeafTree x
> leaftree_ana d = ana where
>   ana t = case d t of
>             Left l        -> Leaf l
>             Right (l,r) -> Split (ana l) (ana r)
```

Rewriting fib_tree with this higher order function gives:

```
> fib_tree = leaftree_ana destruct_fib
> destruct_fib n | n < 2     = Left 1
>                | otherwise = Right (n-1,n-2)
```

3.3   The Leaf-Tree Hylomorphism

As expected, the leaf-tree hylomorphism can be obtained by composing the ana-
and the catamorphism.

An example is the Fibonacci function
fib = tree_sum . fib_tree, or more explicitly as:

```
    fib = leaftree_cata (id,(+)) . leaftree_ana destruct_fib
```

Again the tree in the middle need not be constructed at all as the following
diagram illustrates. We can apply recursion to map the two u's into v's, without
constructing the trees.

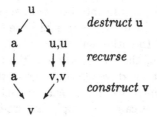

and its implementation with no further comment:

```
> type Leaftree_hylo u x v
>       = (Leaftree_coalg u x, Leaftree_alg x v)

> leaftree_hylo :: Leaftree_hylo u x v -> u -> v
> leaftree_hylo (d,(fl,fs)) = hylo where
>   hylo t = case d t of
>             Left l    -> fl l
>             Right (l,r) -> fs (hylo l) (hylo r)
```

Using this definition of leaftree_hylo we can define the Fibonacci
function as:

```
> fib = leaftree_hylo (destruct_fib, (id,(+)))
```

This can of course be simplified by substituting the functions leaftree_hylo
and destruct_fib into:

```
fib n | n < 2    = 1
      | otherwise = fib (n-1) + fib (n-2)
```

Exercise 4: Write the factorial function as a leaf-tree hylomorphism.

Exercise 5: Write the function x^n as a leaf-tree hylomorphism. What is its complexity? Can you write it as a hylomorphism with $\mathcal{O}(\log n)$ complexity?

3.4 Merge Sort

The leaf-tree hylomorphism can be used to sort lists via leaf-trees. The recursion pattern can be depicted as follows.

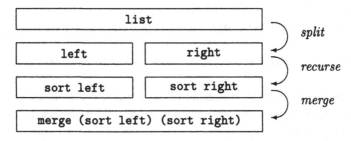

In the recursive case, the list is split into two sub-list, which are sorted, and then combined. The main choice left here is to make the sub-lists dependent or independent of the elements of the other sub-lists.

When we assume independence, the combination of the recursive results must merge two unrelated sorted lists, and we obtain merge sort.

The choice of two sub-lists which are dependent on each other does not buy us much. If we assume that we can only apply an ordering and an equality relation to the elements, we can't do much more than separating the elements into small and large ones, possibly w.r.t. to the median of the list (which would yield quicksort). We do not pursue this way of sorting any further here.

The implementation of merge sort as an hylomorphism from lists, via leaf-trees, onto lists is given below. The non-recursive case deals with lists of one element. The empty list is treated separately from the hylomorphism.

```
> merge_sort [] = []
> merge_sort l  = leaftree_hylo (select,(single,merge)) l
>   where
>     single x = [x]
>     merge (x:xs) (y:ys) | x < y      = x : merge xs (y:ys)
>                         | otherwise = y : merge (x:xs) ys
>     merge [] m = m
>     merge l [] = l
>     select [x] = Left x
>     select l   = Right (split l)
```

The function `split` splits a list into two sub-list, containing the odd and even elements. We present it here in the form of a list catamorphism.

```
> split = list_cata (([],[]),f) where
>    f x (l,r) = (r,x:l)
```

4   Binary Trees

Another form of binary trees are trees that hold the values at their *branches* instead of their leaves. This binary tree data type is defined as follows.

```
> data BinTree x = Tip
>                 | Branch x (BinTree x) (BinTree x)
```

4.1   The Tree Catamorphism

The structure of the tree catamorphism should be straight-forward now. First destruct the tree, recurse on the sub-trees and combine the element and the recursive results. This corresponds to the following diagram, where T stands for `BinTree x`.

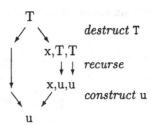

Capturing the recursion pattern in a higher order function `bintree_cata`, gives the following definition.

```
> type Bintree_alg x u = (u, x -> u -> u -> u)

> bintree_cata :: Bintree_alg x u -> BinTree x -> u
> bintree_cata (a,f) = cata where
>    cata Tip            = a
>    cata (Branch x l r) = f x (cata l) (cata r)
```

Observe again that a catamorphism replaces constructors (`Tip` by `a` and `Branch` by `f`) and recursive elements by recursive calls (`l` by `cata l` and `r` by `cata r`).

4.2 The Tree Anamorphism

The binary tree catamorphism is again obtained by reversing the previous one.

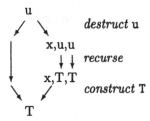

Capturing the recursion pattern in a higher order function `bintree_ana`, gives the following definition.

```
> type Bintree_coalg u x = u -> Either () (x,u,u)

> bintree_ana :: Bintree_coalg u x -> u -> BinTree x
> bintree_ana d = ana where
>    ana t = case d t of
>            Left _          -> Tip
>            Right (x,l,r) -> Branch x (ana l) (ana r)
```

4.3 The Tree Hylomorphism

The binary tree hylomorphism should be straightforward now. We present only its diagram

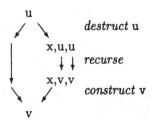

The implementation of the binary tree hylomorphism is obtained from the anamorphism by replacing `Tip` by `a` and the `Branch` constructor by `f`.

```
> type Bintree_hylo u x v = (Bintree_coalg u x, Bintree_alg x v)

> bintree_hylo :: Bintree_hylo u x v -> u -> v
> bintree_hylo (d,(a,f)) = hylo where
>    hylo t = case d t of
>            Left _          -> a
>            Right (x,l,r) -> f x (hylo l) (hylo r)
```

Exercise 6: Write the factorial function as a binary tree hylomorphism.

Exercise 7: Write the function x^n as a binary tree hylomorphism. What is its complexity?

Exercise 8: Write the towers of Hanoi as a binary tree hylomorphism.

4.4 Quicksort

We can apply the binary tree hylomorphism recursion pattern to sorting by sorting a list via binary trees (which are never really constructed of course). The following diagram exhibits the recursion pattern.

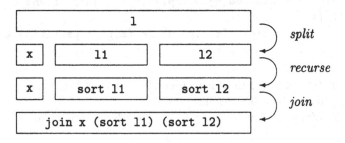

A list l is split into an element x and two other lists l1 and l2. These lists are sorted by recursion. Next x and the sorted sub-lists are joined. We are left with a two design decisions here.

- The choice of x. Sensible choices here are the head of the list, using the structure of the list, or the minimum or median of the list, exploiting the ordering relation. If we take the minimum, we obtain a variant of heap sort. A derivation of heap sort is given in Sect. 4.5. For quicksort, we choose to take the head of the list. Taking the median is left to the reader.
- The choice of the two sub-lists. An essential choice here is to make them dependent on the element x or not. If not, there seems to be no particular reason to separate x. If we do not use the head x at all, the algorithm obeys a different recursion pattern, which we treat in Sect. 3.

  The remaining option, making the sub-lists depend on x, still leaves some choices open. The most natural one seems to let them consists of the elements that are smaller than, respectively at least x, exploiting the ordering relation. This can be done for x being either the head or the median of the list, where the latter gives a better balanced algorithm with a superior worst case behavior. We will take the head for simplicity reasons here.

Given the decisions that we take x to be head of the list and split the tail into small and large elements w.r.t. to x, the only way in which we can combine the sorted sub-lists with x is to concatenate them in the proper order.

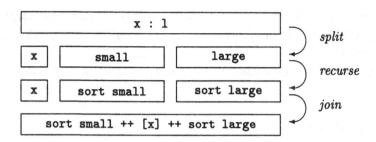

The final result is an implementation of *quicksort* as a hylomorphism from lists, via trees, onto lists.

```
> quick_sort l = bintree_hylo (split,([],join)) l where
>   split []    = Left ()
>   split (x:l) = Right (x,s,g) where (s,g) = partition (<x) l
>   join x l r  = l ++ x : r
```

The function `partition` which splits a list into two lists w.r.t. to some predicate p appears to be a list catamorphism.
Exercise 9: Write the function `partition` as a list catamorphism.

4.5 Heap Sort

In this section we analyze the recursion pattern of heap sort. This algorithm operates by first constructing a binary tree that has the so called *heap property*, which means that for such a tree Branch m l r, m is the minimum element in the tree. The two sub-trees l and r must also have the heap property, but are not related to each other.
After constructing such a heap, the heap is mapped onto a sorted list. Therefore, the definition of heap sort is simply:

```
> heap_sort l = (heap2list . list2heap) l
```

Such a tree is transformed into a sorted list in the following way, where combine l r combines two heaps into a new one. It is clearly a list anamorphism.

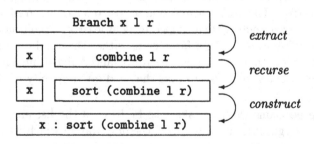

Thus, heapsort can be implemented as below, leaving `list2heap`, which transforms an unsorted list into a heap, to be specified. The `b@(Branch x l r)` construction in Hugs matches an argument to the pattern `Branch x l r` as usual, but also binds the argument as a whole to `b`.

```
> heap2list l = list_ana extract l where
>    extract Tip            = Left ()
>    extract (Branch x l r) = Right (x, combine l r)

> combine :: Ord a => BinTree a -> BinTree a -> BinTree a
> combine t Tip   = t
> combine Tip t   = t
> combine b@(Branch x l r) c@(Branch y s t)
>      | x < y       = Branch x l (combine r c)
>      | otherwise = Branch y (combine b s) t
```

Three recursion patterns that could be applicable to the function `list2heap` are a list catamorphism, a tree anamorphism, or a hylomorphism over some additional data type. Let us analyze the recursion pattern of such a function, where we assume that we use `list2heap` recursively in a binary tree pattern (note that this a design decision), more particularly, let us choose the tree anamorphism. The other options work just as well, but for simplicity, we do not persue them here.

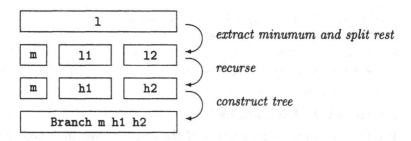

The decomposition is a variant of `bubble`: it should not only select the minimum but also split the remainder of the list into two sub-lists of (almost) equal length. This bubbling is once more a list catamorphism.

```
> list2heap l = bintree_ana decompose l where
>    decompose [] = Left ()
>    decompose l  = Right (bubble l)
>    bubble (x:l) = list_cata ((x,[],[]),bub) l
>    bub x (y,l,r) = if x < y then (x,y:r,l) else (y,x:r,l)
```

Thus, heap sort can be written as the composition of a binary tree anamorphism and a list anamorphism.

5 Paramorphisms

Several sub-functions, like **insert** and **remove** used above where almost cata-morphisms on lists. They deviate by the fact that in the construction of the result, they do not only use the recursive result of the tail, but also the tail itself. This recursion pattern is known as *paramorphism*, after the Greek word $\pi\alpha\rho\alpha$, which among other things means 'parallel with'.

Paramorphisms can be expressed as catamorphisms by letting the recursive call return its intended result, tupled with its argument. Here, we study them as a separate recursion pattern however.

5.1 The List Paramorphism

The list paramorphism follows the recursion patterns of the following diagram.

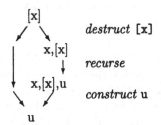

Its implementation is straight-forward, just supply the tail 1 as an additional argument to the constructor function f.

```
> type List_para x u = (u, x -> [x] -> u -> u)

> list_para :: List_para x u -> [x] -> u
> list_para (a,f) = para where
>    para []    = a
>    para (x:l) = f x l (para l)
```

5.2 Insert As Paramorphism

The insertion operation **insert** x of the insertion sort from Sect. 2.4 can be expressed as a paramorphism. First we analyze its recursive structure.

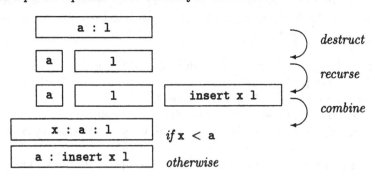

The list a:l is split into head a and tail l. Recursively, x is inserted into l. Depending on where x < a, we need to use the original tail, or the recursive result.

Although it may seem inefficient to construct the recursive result and then optionally throw it away again, laziness comes to help here. If the recursive result is not used, it is simply not computed.

```
> insertion_sort' l = list_cata ([],insert) l where
>    insert x = list_para ([x],combine) where
>       combine a l rec | x < a      = x : a : l
>                       | otherwise = a : rec
```

5.3   Remove As Paramorphism

The selection operation **remove** x of the straight selection sort from Sect. 2.5 can be expressed as a paramorphism as well. First we analyze its recursive structure.

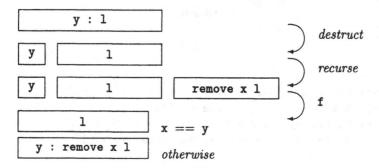

It destructs the list into the head y and tail l. It recursively removes x from l. Next, it chooses between using the non-recursive tail l (when x == y, it suffices to remove y), or, in the other case, to maintain y and use the recursive result.

Below, we give the paramorphic version of the straight selection sort algorithm. Observe that **minimum** has been written as a catamorphism.

```
> straight_selection_sort' l = selection_sort extract l where
>    extract l  = (m, remove m l) where m = minimum l
>    minimum (x:l) = list_cata (x,min) l
>    remove x = list_para ([],f) where
>       f y l rec | x == y    = l
>                 | otherwise = y : rec
```

6   Generalizing Data Structures

The previous sections have shown that the use of patterns of recursion gives rise to a classification of sorting algorithms. One can obtain a refined taxonomy of sorting algorithms by introducing yet another level of generalization. This extra level is the generalization of data types. We illustrate this by generalizing the binary tree data type to the rose tree data type. This type is equivalent to the so called B-trees in [8], where they are used for searching.

```
> data RoseTree a = RoseTree [a] [RoseTree a]
```

A binary tree has 1 element and 2 branches, a rose tree n elements and m branches. The empty rose tree is represented by the $m = n = 0$ case. Since quicksort is a hylomorphism on binary trees, a hylomorphism on rose trees is expected to be a generalization of quicksort. The rose tree hylomorphism is given by the following diagram and definition.

$$
\begin{array}{ll}
\text{u} & \\
\downarrow & \quad destruct \; \text{u} \\
[\text{x}], [\text{u}] & \\
\downarrow & \quad recurse \\
[\text{x}], [\text{v}] & \\
\downarrow & \quad construct \; \text{v} \\
\text{v} &
\end{array}
$$

```
> type Rosetree_alg x v = [x] -> [v] -> v
> type Rosetree_coalg u x = u -> ([x],[u])
> type Rosetree_hylo u x v
>       = (Rosetree_coalg u x, Rosetree_alg x v)

> rosetree_hylo :: Rosetree_hylo u x v -> u -> v
> rosetree_hylo (f,g) = hylo where
>    hylo t = g x (map hylo l) where (x,l) = f t
```

6.1   Generalizing Quicksort

The generalization of quicksort can be obtained by using n pivots, rather than 1. These n pivots are sorted, e.g. by insertion_sort for small n, and the remaining elements are grouped into $n + 1$ intervals w.r.t. the pivots. I.e. the first internal contains all elements less than the first pivot, the second internal contains all remaining elements less than the second pivot, etc., while the $n + 1$-th interval contains all elements not less than the n-th pivot. These intervals are sorted recursively, and the intervals and pivots are joined together. The following diagram illustrates this process.

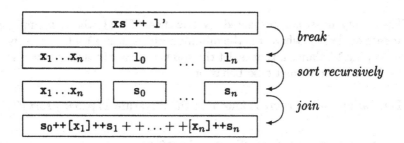

The implementation is relatively straight-forward after this design. The case where l==[] needs to be treated specially to ensure termination. First, l is split into its first (at most) n elements xs and the remainder l'. Next xs is sorted to obtain sx. Then l' is split w.r.t. to sx.

```
> rose_sort n l = rosetree_hylo (break,join) l where
>    break [] = ([],[])
>    break l  = (sx,split sx l') where
>      (xs,l') = take_drop n l
>      sx = insertion_sort xs
>    split sx l = list_cata ([l],f) sx where
>      f x (a:l) = s:g:l where (s,g) = partition (<x) a
>    join xs []    = xs
>    join xs (s:l) = s++concat (zipWith (:) xs l)

> take_drop 0 l = ([],l)
> take_drop n [] = ([],[])
> take_drop n (x:l) = (x:a,b) where (a,b) = take_drop (n-1) l
```

Experiments show that this algorithm behaves superior to the quick_sort function when applied to random list of various sizes. The optimal value of n appears to be independent of the length of the list (it equals 3 in this implementation). A decent analysis of the complexity of this algorithm should reveal why this is the case. The split size can be adapted to the length of the list L by replacing n by some function of L. It is an open problem which function will give the best behavior.

Since rose trees can be viewed as a generalization of linear lists, binary trees and leaf trees together, the other sorting algorithms generalize as well. E.g. the two-way merge sort becomes a k-way merge sort. We leave this generalization as an exercise to the reader.

6.2 Generalizing Heap Sort

Heap sort can be generalized by means of rose trees as well. The obvious way is to define a heap on rose trees, instead of binary trees, construct the tree from a list and map it onto a sorted list.

The empty heap is represented by `Rosetree [] []`, the non-empty heap by `Rosetree [x] l`, where x is the minimum element and l a list of heaps. We aim at keeping l balanced, that is, let the sub heaps vary in sizes as little as possible, to obtain a good worst-case behavior.

This variant of heap sort is known in the literature as *pairing sort* [5].

```
> pairingSort l = (rose2list . list2rose) l
```

The function `rose2list` is a variant of `heap2list`. Instead of combining two heaps into a new heap, it should combine (meld) a list of heaps into heap. we postpone the treatment of this function `roses_meld`.

```
> rose2list :: (Ord a) => RoseTree a -> [a]
> rose2list = list_ana destruct where
>    destruct (RoseTree []  ts) = Left ()
>    destruct (RoseTree [a] ts) = Right (a, roses_meld ts)
```

Mapping a list into a heap is simple if we use the postponed function `roses_meld`.

```
> list2rose  :: (Ord a) => [a] -> RoseTree a
> list2rose  = roses_meld . map single where
>    single a = RoseTree [a] []
```

The function `roses_meld` can be designed best by first defining a function that melds two heaps onto a new heap. This is the rose tree variant of the function `combine` from Sect. 4.5.

```
> rose_meld :: Ord a => RoseTree a -> RoseTree a -> RoseTree a
> rose_meld (RoseTree [] _) u = u
> rose_meld t (RoseTree [] _) = t
> rose_meld t@(RoseTree [a] ts) u@(RoseTree [b] us)
>     | a < b      = RoseTree [a] (u:ts)
>     | otherwise = RoseTree [b] (t:us)
```

The function `roses_meld` is now a simple list catamorphism over `rose_meld`. Implementing it that way has one draw-back however: it is not balanced. A list catamorphisms groups the elements together in a linear way. If the combining function is associative, the grouping can take place in a tree-shaped way as well, giving a balanced heap. We call this form of folding a list of values into a single value `treefold` and it is a leaf-tree hylomorphism.

```
> roses_meld :: Ord a => [RoseTree a] -> RoseTree a
> roses_meld = treefold rose_meld no_roses

> treefold :: (a -> a -> a) -> a -> [a] -> a
> treefold f e l = leaftree_hylo (select,(id,f)) l where
>    select []  = Left e
>    select [a] = Left a
>    select l   = Right (split l)

> no_roses = RoseTree [] []
```

7 Conclusions

We have shown that it is possible to express the most well-known sorting algorithms as functional programs, using fixed patterns of recursion. Given such a pattern of recursion there is little or no additional design freedom left. The approach shows that functional programming in general and the study of recursion patterns in particular form a powerful tool in both the characterization and derivation of algorithms. In this paper we studied the three data types linear lists, binary trees and binary leaf trees. Generalizing these data types to rose trees revealed a generalization of quick-sort, which is, as far as the author knows, a novel sorting algorithm. It may well be that other data types, and their corresponding recursion patterns, can be used to derive even more sorting algorithms.

By distinguishing a hierarchy of data structures on the one hand, and different patterns of recursions on the other hand, a taxonomy of algorithms can be constructed. It would be nice to compare this with other techniques for constructing algorithm taxonomies as e.g. presented in [10].

Of course, other algorithms than sorting can be classified by means of their pattern of recursion. See e.g. [1], where similar techniques were used to characterize parsing algorithms.

The question whether the presentation of the algorithms as such is clarified by their expression in terms of morphisms has not been raised yet. When we compare the catamorphic version of insertion sort to the following straight implementation, the latter should be appreciated over the first.

```
insertion_sort []    = []
insertion_sort (x:l) = insert x (insertion_sort l) where
  insert x [] = [x]
  insert x (a:l) | x < a    = x :a:l
                 | otherwise = a : insert x l
```

The value of this approach is not so much in obtaining a nice presentation or implementation of some algorithm, but in unraveling its structure. Especially in the case of heap sort, this approach gives a very good insight in the structure of the algorithm, compared for instance to [8] or [11].

We based the recursion patterns on the natural recursive functions over data types, the catamorphism, anamorphism, hylomorphism and paramorphism. This let to a very systematic derivation of recursion patterns. The category theory that underlies these morphisms was not needed in this presentation. There definition follows so trivially from the data type definition that any functional programmer should be able to define them. A generation of these recursion patterns by a compiler for a functional language is even more desirable: then there is not need at all for a programmer to write them.

Acknowledgements

Above all, I wish to thank Frans Kruseman Aretz for the patient and careful supervision during the writing of my thesis, of which this contribution is a natural continuation. I am also grateful to Doaitse Swierstra and Tanja Vos for stimulating discussions about the different morphisms, to Erik Meijer for his illuminating thesis and to Herman ter Horst for his refereeing.

References

1. Lex Augusteijn. *Functional Programming, Program Transformations and Compiler Construction.* PhD thesis, Eindhoven Technical University, October 1993.
2. R.S. Bird and O. de Moor. *Algebra of Programming.* Prentice-Hall, 1994.
3. K.L. Clark and J.Darlington. Algorithm classification through synthesis. *The Computer Journal*, 23(1):61–65, 1980.
4. Maarten M. Fokkinga. *Law and order in algorithmics.* PhD thesis, Twente University, 1992.
5. Michael L. Fredman, Robert Sedgewick, Daniel D. Sleator, and Robert E. Tarjan. The pairing heap: A new form of self-adjusting heap. *Algorithmica*, 1(1):111–129, 1986.
6. Paul Hudak, Philip Wadler, Arvind, Brian Boutel, Jon Fairbairn, Joseph Fasel, Kevin Hammond, John Hughes, Thomas Johnsson, Dick Kieburtz, Rishiyur Nikhil, Simon Peyton Jones, Mike Reeve, David Wise, and Jonathan Young. Report on the Programming Language Haskell, A Non-Strict, Purely Functional Language, Version 1.2. *ACM SIGPLAN Notices*, 27(5):Section R, 1992.
7. Mark P. Jones and John C. Peterson. *Hugs 1.4 User Manual*, November 1998. Included as part of the Hugs distribution, http://www.cs.nott.ac.uk/ mpj/hugs14/.

8. Donald E. Knuth. *The Art of Computer Programming*, volume 3. Addison-Wesley, 1973. Sorting and Searching.
9. Erik Meijer. *Calculating Compilers*. PhD thesis, Utrecht State University, Utrecht, the Netherlands, 1992.
10. Bruce W. Watson. *Taxonomies and Toolkits of Regular Language Algorithms*. PhD thesis, Eindhoven University of Technology, 1995.
11. Niklaus Wirth. *Algorithms + Data Structures = Programs*. Prentice Hall, 1976.

Solutions to Exercises

Solution to exercise 1: Write the list reversal function as a list catamorphism.
The empty list is reversed onto the empty list. The construct function takes the original head and the reversed tail. There only one way to combine these: append the head to the reversed tail.

```
> rev1 = list_cata ([],construct) where
>   construct x r = r++[x]
```

Solution to exercise 2: Write a prime number generator as a list anamorphism.
We will filter a list of prime candidates onto a list of primes. The head p of the candidate list is a prime, which will be the head of the result. The multiples of p are removed from the tail, which is recursively mapped onto a list of primes.

```
> primes = sieve [2..]
> sieve = list_ana destruct where
>   destruct (p:l) = Right (p, [ x | x <- l, x 'rem' p /= 0 ])
```

Solution to exercise 3: Write the function x^n as a list hylomorphism.
We destruct an integer n onto a list of n x's, which is than folded by the catamorphism part of the hylomorphism onto the product of the's n x's.

```
> power x = list_hylo (destruct, (1,(*))) where
>   destruct 0 = Left ()
>   destruct n = Right (x,n-1)
```

Solution to exercise 4: Write the factorial function as a leaf-tree hylomorphism.
A tree hylomorphism contains two recursive calls. We therefore choose to compute the product of the interval $(1, n)$ which can be recursively split into halves.

```
> tree_fac n = leaftree_hylo (destruct, (id,(*))) (1,n)  where
>   destruct (a,b)
>     | a > b      = Left 1
>     | a == b     = Left a
>     | otherwise = Right ((a,m), (m+1,b)) where m = (a+b)/2
```

Solution to exercise 5: Write the function x^n as a leaf-tree hylomorphism. What is its complexity? Can you write it as a hylomorphism with $\mathcal{O}(\log n)$ complexity?

The exponent n can be divided by 2 and the recursive results can be multiplied.

```
> pow2 x = leaftree_hylo (destruct,(id,(*))) where
>    destruct 0 = Left 1
>    destruct 1 = Left x
>    destruct n | even n    = Right (n/2,n/2)
>               | otherwise = Right (n/2,n/2+1)
```

The complexity is $\mathcal{O}(n)$, since the hylomorphism has no information about the two recursively being identical. This can be fixed by using a list hylomorphism, that uses only one recursively call and squaring the result of that call. We need an addi tional factor x in the case of n being odd.

```
> pow3 x = list_hylo (destruct, (1,construct)) where
>    destruct 0 = Left ()
>    destruct n | even n    = Right (1,n/2)
>               | otherwise = Right (x,n/2)
>    construct y p = y * p * p
```

Solution to exercise 6: Write the factorial function as a binary tree hylomorphism.
Again, we split the the interval $(1, n)$ recursively in halves. Since we not only need two sub-intervals, but also an additional value (as required by the binary tree structure), we use the middle value of the interval for that.

```
> btree_fac n =
>    bintree_hylo (destruct, (1,construct)) (1,n)  where
>      construct m x y = m*x*y
>      destruct (a,b)
>        | a > b     = Left ()
>        | otherwise = Right (m, (a,m-1), (m+1,b)) where
>                      m = (a+b)/2
```

Solution to exercise 7: Write the function x^n as a binary tree hylomorphism. What is its complexity?
This solution is close the leaf-tree solution. It split n into halves and use the remainder as the addtional binary tree value. The complexity is $\mathcal{O}(n)$, as the tree hylomorphism has no idea about its two recursive calls being equal. Observe that this solution is very close to the linear list hylomorphism of complexity $\mathcal{O}(\log n)$. In general, a binary-tree hylomorphism with equal recursive calls can be rewritten into a linear list hylomorphism with improved complexity.

```
> pow4 x = bintree_hylo (destruct,(1,construct)) where
>    destruct 0 = Left ()
>    destruct n | even n    = Right (1,n/2,n/2)
>               | otherwise = Right (x,n/2,n/2)
>    construct y p q = y * p * q
```

Solution to exercise 8: Write the towers of Hanoi as a binary tree hylomorphism.

The towers of Hanoi has a natural binary tree-shaped solution:

```
hanoi 0 a b c = []
hanoi n a b c = hanoi (n-1) a c b ++
               [a++"-"++c] ++
               hanoi (n-1) b a c
```

This is easily written as a hylomorphism:
```
> hanoi = bintree_hylo (destruct, ([],construct)) where
>    construct m l r = l ++ [m] ++ r
>    destruct (0,a,b,c) = Left ()
>    destruct (n,a,b,c) =
>      Right (a++"-"++c, (n-1,a,c,b), (n-1,b,a,c))

> h_test n = hanoi (n,"a","b","c")
```

Solution to exercise 9: Write the function partition *as a list catamorphism.*
The empty list is mapped onto the pair of empty lists, ([],[]). the tail of a non-empty list is recursively mapped onto a pair of lists, and the head is prepended to the left of these in case of p and to the right otherwise. Observe that the fuction definition below is much shorter than this description in English.

```
> partition p l = list_cata (([],[]),f) l where
>    f x (a,b) = if p x then (x:a,b) else (a,x:b)
```

Generic Programming
– An Introduction –

Roland Backhouse[1], Patrik Jansson[2], Johan Jeuring[3], and Lambert Meertens[4]

[1] Department of Mathematics and Computing Science
Eindhoven University of Technology
P.O. Box 513
5600 MB Eindhoven
The Netherlands
rolandb@win.tue.nl
http://www.win.tue.nl/~rolandb/

[2] Department of Computing Science
Chalmers University of Technology
S-412 96 Göteborg
Sweden
patrikj@cs.chalmers.se
http://www.cs.chalmers.se/~patrikj/

[3] Department of Computer Science
Utrecht University
P.O. Box 80.089
3508 TB Utrecht
The Netherlands
johanj@cs.uu.nl
http://www.cs.uu.nl/~johanj/

[4] CWI & Utrecht University
P.O. Box 80.089
3508 TB Utrecht
The Netherlands
lambert@cwi.nl
http://www.cwi.nl/~lambert/

1 Introduction

1.1 The Abstraction-Specialisation Cycle

The development of science proceeds in a cycle of activities, the so-called abstraction-specialisation cycle. *Abstraction* is the process of seeking patterns or commonalities, which are then classified, often in a formal mathematical framework. In the process of abstraction, we gain greater understanding by eliminating irrelevant detail in order to identify what is essential. The result is a collection of general laws which are then put to use in the second phase of the cycle, the *specialisation* phase. In the specialisation phase the general laws are instantiated to

S.D. Swierstra et al. (Eds.): Advanced Functional Programming, LNCS 1608, pp. 28–115, 1999.

specific cases which, if the abstraction is a good one, leads to novel applications, yet greater understanding, and input for another round of abstraction followed by specialisation.

The abstraction-specialisation cycle is particularly relevant to the development of the science of computing because the modern digital computer is, above all else, a *general-purpose* device that is used for a dazzling range of tasks. Harnessing this versatility is the core task of software design.

Good, commercially viable, software products evolve in a cycle of abstraction and *customisation*. Abstraction, in this context, is the process of identifying a single, general-purpose product out of a number of independently arising requirements. Customisation is the process of optimizing a general-purpose product to meet the special requirements of particular customers. Software manufacturers are involved in a continuous process of abstraction followed by customisation.

1.2   Genericity in Programming Languages

The abstraction-specialisation/customisation cycle occurs at all levels of software design. Programming languages play an important role in facilitating its implementation. Indeed, the desire to be able to name and reuse "programming patterns" —capturing them in the form of parametrisable abstractions— has been a driving force in the evolution of high-level programming languages to the extent that the level of "genericity" of a programming language has become a vital criterion for usability.

To determine the level of genericity there are three questions we can ask:

- Which entities can be named in a definition and then referred to by that given name?
- Which entities can be supplied as parameters?
- Which entities can be used "anonymously", in the form of an expression, as parameters? (For example, in $y = \sin(2 \times x)$, the number resulting from $2 \times x$ is not given a name. In a language allowing numeric parameters, but not anonymously, we would have to write something like $y = \sin(z)$ **where** $z = 2 \times x$.)

An entity for which all three are possible is called a *first-class citizen* of that language.

In one of the first high-level programming languages, FORTRAN (1957), procedures could be named, but not used as parameters. In ALGOL 60 procedures (including functions) were made almost first-class citizens: they were allowed as parameters, but only by name. In neither language could types be named, nor passed as parameters. In ALGOL 68 procedures were made true first-class citizens, making higher-order functions possible (but not practical, because of an awkward scope restriction[1]). Further, types could be named, but not used as parameters.

---

[1] Anything that —in implementation terms— would have required what is now known as a "closure", was forbidden.

Functional programming languages stand out in the evolution of programming languages because of the high-level of abstraction that is achieved by the combination of higher-order functions and parametric polymorphism. In, for example, Haskell higher-order functions are possible *and practical*. But the level of genericity still has its limitations. Types can be defined *and* used as parameters, but ... types can only be given as parameters in "type expressions". They cannot be passed to functions. The recent Haskell-like language Cayenne [2] which extends Haskell with dependent types does allow types as arguments and results of functions.

In these lecture notes we introduce another dimension to the level of abstraction in programming languages, namely parameterisation with respect to classes of algebras of variable signature. This first chapter is intended to introduce the key elements of the lectures in broad terms and to motivate what is to follow. We begin by giving a concrete example of a generic algorithm. (The genericity of this algorithm is at a level that can be implemented in conventional functional programming languages, since the parameter is a class of algebras with a fixed signature.) This is followed by a plan of the later chapters.

1.3   Path Problems

A good example of parameterising programs by a class of algebras is provided by the problem of finding "extremal" paths in a graph.

Extremal path problems have as input a finite, labelled graph such as the one shown below.

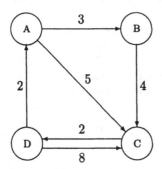

Formally, a *directed graph* consists of a finite set of *nodes*, V, a finite set of *edges*, E, and two functions source and target, each with domain E and range V. If source e is the node x and target e is the node y, we say that e is *from x to y*. (In the figure the nodes are circled and an edge e is depicted by an arrow that begins at source e and points to target e.) A *path* through the graph from node s to node t of *edge length n* is a finite list of edges $[e_1, e_2, \ldots, e_n]$ such that $s = $ source e_1 and $t = $ target e_n and, for each i, $0 < i < n$, target $e_i = $ source e_{i+1}. A graph is *labelled* if it is supplied with a function label whose domain is the set of edges, E.

In an extremal path problem the edge labels are used to weight paths, and the problem is to find the extreme (i.e. best or least, in some sense) weight of paths between given pairs of nodes. We discuss three examples: the reachability problem, the least-cost path problem and the bottleneck problem.

Reachability The reachability problem is the problem of determining for each pair of nodes x and y whether there is a path in the graph from x to y. It is solved by a very elegant (and now well-known) algorithm discovered by Roy [42] and Warshall [46]. The algorithm assumes that the nodes are numbered from 1 to N (say) and that the existence of edges in the graph is given by an $N \times N$ matrix a where a_{ij} is true if there is an edge from node numbered i to the node numbered j, and false otherwise. The matrix is updated by the following code. On termination a_{ij} is true if there is a path from node i to node j of edge length at least one; otherwise a_{ij} is false.

```
for  each k, 1 ≤ k ≤ N
do  for  each pair (i,j), 1 ≤ i,j ≤ N
      do  a_ij  :=  a_ij ∨ (a_ik ∧ a_kj)
      end_for
end_for
```

(The order in which the nodes are numbered, and the order in which pairs of nodes (i,j) are chosen in the inner loop, is immaterial.)

The reachability problem is an extremal path problem in which all edges have the same label and all paths have the same weight, namely true.

Least-Cost Paths About the same time as Warshall's discovery of the reachability algorithm, Floyd [17] discovered a very similar algorithm that computes the cost of a least cost path between each pair of nodes in the graph. The algorithm assumes that the matrix a is a matrix of numbers such that a_{ij} represents the least cost of traversing an edge from node i to node j. If there is no edge from i to j then a_{ij} is ∞. The cost of a path is the sum of the costs of the individual edges on the path. Floyd's algorithm for computing the cost of a least cost path from each node to each other node is identical to the Roy-Warshall algorithm above except for the assignment statement which instead is:

$$a_{ij} \quad := \quad a_{ij} \downarrow (a_{ik} + a_{kj})$$

where $x \downarrow y$ denotes the minimum of x and y.

Bottleneck Problem A third problem that can be solved with an algorithm of identical shape to the Roy-Warshall algorithm is called the *bottleneck* problem. It is most easily explained as determining the best route to negotiate a high load under a series of low bridges. Suppose an edge in a graph represents a road between two cities and the label is the height of the lowest underpass on the road. The *height* of a path between two nodes is defined to be the minimum of the heights of the individual edges that make up the path. The problem is to determine, for each pair of nodes i and j, the maximum of the heights of the paths from node i to node j (thus the maximum of the minimum height underpass on a path from i to j).

The bridge height problem is solved by an algorithm identical to the Roy-Warshall algorithm above except for the assignment statement which in this case is:

$$a_{ij} \quad := \quad a_{ij} \uparrow (a_{ik} \downarrow a_{kj})$$

where $x \downarrow y$ denotes the minimum of x and y and $x \uparrow y$ denotes their maximum. (In the case that there is no edge from i to j then the initial value of a_{ij} is 0.)

A Generic Path Algorithm If we abstract from the general shape of these three algorithms we obtain a single algorithm of the form

$$\begin{aligned}
&\text{for each } k, 1 \leq k \leq N \\
&\text{do for each pair } (i,j), 1 \leq i,j \leq N \\
&\quad \text{do } a_{ij} \quad := \quad a_{ij} \oplus (a_{ik} \otimes a_{kj}) \\
&\quad \text{end\_for} \\
&\text{end\_for}
\end{aligned}$$

where $\oplus$ and $\otimes$ are binary operators. The initial value of a_{ij} is the label of the edge from i to j if such an edge exists, and is a constant 0 otherwise. (For the purposes of exposition we assume that there is at most one edge from i to j for each pair of nodes i and j.) The algorithm is thus parameterised by an algebra. In the case of the Roy-Warshall algorithm the carrier of the algebra is the two-element set containing true and false, the constant 0 is false, the operator $\oplus$ is disjunction and the operator $\otimes$ is conjunction. In the case of the least-cost path problem the carrier is the set of positive real numbers, the constant 0 is ∞, the operator $\oplus$ is the binary minimum operator, and the operator $\otimes$ is addition. Finally, in the case of the bridge height problem the carrier is also the set of positive real numbers, the operator $\oplus$ is the binary maximum operator, and the operator $\otimes$ is minimum.

Correctness The above generic algorithm will compute "something" whatever actual parameters we supply for the formal parameters $\oplus$, $\otimes$ and 0, the only proviso being that the parameters have compatible types. But, that "something" is only guaranteed to be meaningful if the operators obey certain algebraic properties. The more general *transitive closure* algorithm shown below

$$\begin{aligned}
&\text{for each } k, 1 \leq k \leq N \\
&\text{do for each pair } (i,j), 1 \leq i,j \leq N \\
&\quad \text{do } a_{ij} \quad := \quad a_{ij} \oplus (a_{ik} \otimes (a_{kk})^* \otimes a_{kj}) \\
&\quad \text{end\_for} \\
&\text{end\_for}
\end{aligned}$$

is guaranteed to be correct if the algebra is *regular* [6,8][2]. By correctness is meant that if initially

$$a_{ij} \;=\; \Sigma\langle e\text{: } e \text{ is an edge from } i \text{ to } j\text{: label } e\rangle \;,$$

where Σ is the generalisation of the binary operator $\oplus$ to arbitrary bags, then on termination

$$a_{ij} \;=\; \Sigma\langle p\text{: } p \text{ is a path of positive edge length from } i \text{ to } j\text{: weight } p\rangle$$

where weight p is def ined recursively by

$$\text{weight } [\,] = 1$$

for the empty path $[\,]$, and for paths $e : p$ (the edge e followed by path p)

$$\text{weight } (e : p) = (\text{label } e) \otimes (\text{weight } p) \;.$$

Exercise 1.1   Suppose that the edges of a graph are coloured. (So there are blue edges, red edges, etc.) We say that a path has *colour* c if all the edges on the path have colour c. Suggest how to use the above algorithm to determine for each pair of nodes x and y the set of colours c such that there is a path of colour c from x to y in the graph.

□

1.4   The Plan

The difference between executability and correctness is an important one that shows up time and time again, and it is important to stress it once more. The transitive closure algorithm presented above can be *executed* provided only that instantiations are given for the two constants 0 and 1, the two binary operators $\oplus$ and $\otimes$, the unary operator *, the number N and the matrix a. An implementation of the algorithm thus requires just the specification of these seven parameters. Moreover, if we bundle the first five parameters together into an algebra, all that is required for the implementation is the *signature* of the algebra: the knowledge that there are two binary operators (with units) and one unary operator. For the *correctness* of the algorithm much, much more is needed. We have to supply a specification relative to which correctness is asserted, and establishing correctness demands that we require the algebra to be in a certain *class* of algebras (in this case the class of regular algebras).

---

[2] Without going into complete details, an algebra is regular if it has two constants 0 and 1, two binary operators $\oplus$ and $\otimes$, and one unary operator *. The constants 0 and 1 and operators $\oplus$ and $\otimes$ should behave like 0, 1, + and × in real arithmetic except that × is not required to be commutative, and + is required to be idempotent. The * operator is a least fixed point operator. The three algebras mentioned above are all regular, after suitably defining the constant 1 and defining a^* to be 1 for all a.

As for conventional programs, the specification is absent from a generic program's implementation. Nevertheless, it is the complete process of *program construction* —from program specification to a systematic derivation of the final implementation— that will dominate the discussion in the coming pages. Our aim is not to show how to derive functional programs but to show how to derive functional programs that are correct by construction. To this end we borrow a number of concepts from category theory, emphasising the calculational properties that these concepts entail.

Algebras, Functors and Datatypes The emphasis on calculational properties begins right at the outset in chapter 2 where we introduce the notion of a *functor* and an *initial algebra* and rela te these notions to *datatypes*.

An *algebra* (in its simplest form) is a set, called the *carrier* of the algebra, together with a number of operations on that set. A Boolean algebra, for example, has as carrier a set with two elements, commonly named true and false and binary operations ∧ (conjunction) and ∨ (disjunction) and unary operation ¬ (negation). The *signature* of the algebra specifies the types of the basic operations in the algebra.

In order to implement a generic algorithm we need to provide the compiler with information on the signature of the operators in the algebra on which the algorithm is parameterised. In order to calculate and reason about generic algorithms we also need a *compact* mechanism for defining signatures. The use of functors provides such a mechanism, compactness being achieved by avoiding naming the operators of the algebra. The use of functors entails much more however than just defining the signature of an algebra. As we shall see, a datatype is a functor and inductively defined datatypes are (the carriers of) *initial* algebras. The concepts of functor, datatype and algebra are thus inextricably intertwined.

PolyP Following the discussion of algebras and datatypes, we introduce *PolyP*, an extension of the Haskell programming language in which generic functions can be implemented.

The name of PolyP is derived from "polytypic programming", polytypic programs being generic programs defined on a particular class of datatypes, the so-called regular datatypes. Writing programs in PolyP means that one can get hands-on experience of generic programming thus reinforcing one's understanding and, hopefully, leading to further insights.

A Unification Algorithm Chapter 4 presents a more substantial example of generic programming — a generic unification algorithm. The basis for the algorithm is a generic construction of a type representing terms with variables, and substitution of terms for variables. The algorithm is implemented using type classes in a style similar to object-oriented programming.

Relations The discussion in chapters 2 and 3 is on *functional* programs. In chapter 5 we outline how the concepts introduced in chapter 2 are extended to *relations*, and we show how the extension is used in establishing one element of the correctness of the generic unification algorithm.

There are several reasons for wanting to take the step from functions to relations. The most pressing is that specifications are *relations* between the input and the output, and our concern is with both specifications and implementations. Related to this is that termination properties of programs are typically established by appeal to a well-founded *relation* on the state space. We will not go into termination properties in these lecture notes but the use of well-founded relations will play an integral part in our discussion of one element of the correctness of a generic unification algorithm in chapter 4.

Another reason for wanting to extend the discussion to relations lies in the theoretical basis of generic programming. In chapter 5 we demonstrate how every parametrically polymorphic function satisfies a so-called *logical relation*.

The final reason is *why not?* As we shall see, extending the theory to relations does not significantly increase the complexity whilst the benefits are substantial.

1.5   Why Generic Programming?

The form of genericity that we present in the coming pages is novel and has not yet proved its worth. Our goal is to stimulate your interest in exploring it further, and to provide evidence of its potential value.

Generic programming has indeed, potentially, major advantages over "one-shot" programming, since genericity makes it possible to write programs that solve a class of problems once and for all, instead of writing new code over and over again for each different instance. The two advantages that we stress here are the greater potential for reuse, since generic programs are natural candidates for incorporation in library form, and the increased reliability, due to the fact that generic programs are stripped of irrelevant detail which often makes them easier to construct. But what we want to stress most of all is that generic programming is fun. Finding the right generic formulation that captures a class of related problems can be a significant challenge, whose achievement is very satisfying.

Acknowledgements The work that is presented here emerged out of the Dutch STOP (Specification and Transformation of Programs) project which ran formally from 1988 to 1992. The project was particularly successful because of the real spirit of cooperation among those participating. Project members (both official and unofficial) included, in alphabetical order, Roland Backhouse, Richard Bird, Henk Doornbos, Maarten Fokkinga, Paul Hoogendijk, Johan Jeuring, Grant Malcolm, Lambert Meertens, Erik Meijer, Oege de Moor , Frans Rietman, Doaitse Swierstra, Jaap van der Woude, Nico Verwer, Ed Voermans. Our thanks go to all who made participation in the project such an enjoyable and stimulating experience.

Development of both practical applications of generic programming and the underlying theory is continuing: see the bibliography for a selection of recent (formally-published and web-published) papers.

2 Algebras, Functors and Datatypes

This chapter introduces the concepts fundamental to generic programming. The first section (section 2.1) introduces algebras and homomorphisms between algebras. In this section we see that datatypes (like the natural numbers) are also algebras, but of a special kind. The presentation in section 2.1 is informal. In section 2.4 we make precise in what way datatypes are special: we introduce the all-important notion of an "initial" algebra and the notion of a "catamorphism" (a special sort of homomorphism). The link between the two sections is provided by the intermediate sections on functors. The first of these (section 2.2) provides the formal definition of a functor, motivating it by examples from functional programming. Then section 5 introduces further examples of functors forming a class called the "polynomial functors". Section 2.4 augments the class of polynomial functors with so-called type functors; the resulting class is called the class of "regular functors", and generic programs defined over the regular functors are called "polytypic" programs. The final section (section 2.5) presents an elementary example of a polytypic program.

2.1 Algebras and Homomorphisms

In this section we review the notion of an algebra. The main purpose is to introduce several examples that we can refer to later. The examples central to the discussion are datatypes. At the end of the section we consider how we might formalise the notion of an algebra. We recall a formulation typical of ones in texts on Universal Algebra and remark why this is inadequate for our purposes. We then present the definition of an algebra in category theory based on the notion of a "functor" and outline how the latter expresses the content of the traditional definitions much more succinctly and in a much more structured way.

Algebras An algebra is a set, together with a number of operations (functions) that return values in that set. The set is called the *carrier* of the algebra. Here are some concrete examples of algebras:

$$
\begin{array}{lll}
(\mathbf{N},\ 0\ ,(+)), & \text{with}\quad 0\ ::1\to\mathbf{N}, & (+)::\mathbf{N}\times\mathbf{N}\to\mathbf{N} \\
(\mathbf{N},\ 0\ ,(\uparrow)\ ), & \text{with}\quad 0\ ::1\to\mathbf{N}, & (\uparrow)::\mathbf{N}\times\mathbf{N}\to\mathbf{N} \\
(\mathbf{R},\ 1\ ,(\times)), & \text{with}\quad 1\ ::1\to\mathbf{R}, & (\times)::\mathbf{R}\times\mathbf{R}\to\mathbf{R} \\
(\mathbf{B},\text{true},(\equiv)), & \text{with}\quad \text{true}::1\to\mathbf{B}, & (\equiv)::\mathbf{B}\times\mathbf{B}\to\mathbf{B} \\
(\mathbf{B},\text{false},(\vee)), & \text{with}\quad \text{false}::1\to\mathbf{B}, & (\vee)::\mathbf{B}\times\mathbf{B}\to\mathbf{B} \\
(\mathbf{B},\text{true},(\wedge)), & \text{with}\quad \text{true}::1\to\mathbf{B}, & (\wedge)::\mathbf{B}\times\mathbf{B}\to\mathbf{B} \\
(A^{\star},\ \varepsilon\ ,(+\!\!+)), & \text{with}\quad \varepsilon\ ::1\to A^{\star}, & (+\!\!+)::A^{\star}\times A^{\star}\to A^{\star}
\end{array}
$$

In the last line $A^{\star}$ stands for the words over some alphabet A, with "$+\!\!+$" denoting word concatenation, and "ε" the empty word. This is, of course, basically the same algebra as $(List\,A, [\,], (+\!\!+))$, the (finite) lists of A-elements with list concatenation. Note that in the typing of the operations we use the notation "source-type $\to$ target-type". In an algebra all operations have the same target type[3]: its carrier. Note further that we use the "uncurried" view in which a binary operation takes a pair (2-tuple) of arguments and so has some type like $A \times B \to C$. To make fixed elements, like $0 \in \mathbf{N}$, fit in, they are treated here as nullary operations: operations with a 0-tuple of arguments. This is indicated by the source type 1, which in Haskell would be denoted as "()". Sometimes we will instantiate a generic program to a specific Haskell program, and in doing so we will switch back to the curried view for binary operations, having some type $A \to (B \to C)$, and to the view of nullary operations as plain elements, having type A rather than $1 \to A$. Conversely, going from a Haskell program to an algebraic view, we will uncurry n-ary functions, $n \geq 2$, and treat constants as nullary functions.

The concrete algebras above were chosen in such a way that they all have the same number of operations with the same typing pattern. They can be unified generically into the following abstract algebra:

$$(A, e, \oplus), \quad \text{with} \quad e :: 1 \to A, \quad \oplus :: A \times A \to A$$

So they all belong to the same *class* of algebras. An example of another class of algebras is:

$$(\mathbf{N}, (+), (+1)), \quad \text{with} \quad (+) :: \mathbf{N} \times \mathbf{N} \to \mathbf{N}, \quad (+1) :: \mathbf{N} \to \mathbf{N}$$
$$(\mathbf{R}, (\times), (\times 2)), \quad \text{with} \quad (\times) :: \mathbf{R} \times \mathbf{R} \to \mathbf{R}, \quad (\times 2) :: \mathbf{R} \to \mathbf{R}$$
$$(A, \oplus, f\,), \quad \text{with} \quad \oplus :: A \times A \to A, \quad f :: A \to A$$

Here, the first two are concrete, while the last is the generic algebra.

By just looking at an algebra, it is not possible (in general) to tell what class of algebras it belongs to: a given algebra can belong to several different classes. So the class information has to be supplied additionally. Take for example the following class:

$$(\quad \mathbf{N} \quad, 0, (+)), \quad \text{with} \quad 0 :: 1 \to \quad \mathbf{N} \quad, \quad (+) :: \mathbf{N} \times \quad \mathbf{N} \quad \to \quad \mathbf{N}$$
$$(\quad \mathbf{N} \quad, 0, (\uparrow)), \quad \text{with} \quad 0 :: 1 \to \quad \mathbf{N} \quad, \quad (\uparrow) :: \mathbf{N} \times \quad \mathbf{N} \quad \to \quad \mathbf{N}$$
$$(List\,\mathbf{N}, [\,], (:)), \quad \text{with} \quad [\,] :: 1 \to List\,\mathbf{N}, \quad (:) :: \mathbf{N} \times List\,\mathbf{N} \to List\,\mathbf{N}$$
$$(\quad A \quad, e, \oplus), \quad \text{with} \quad e :: 1 \to \quad A \quad, \quad \oplus :: \mathbf{N} \times \quad A \quad \to \quad A$$

The first two concrete algebras also occur in the first class treated above, but the generic algebra reveals that this is a different class.

To give a concluding example of an algebra class:

$$(\mathbf{N}, \quad 0 \quad, (+1)), \quad \text{with} \quad 0 \quad :: 1 \to \mathbf{N}, \quad (+1) :: \mathbf{N} \to \mathbf{N}$$
$$(\mathbf{R}, \quad 1 \quad, (\times 2)), \quad \text{with} \quad 1 \quad :: 1 \to \mathbf{R}, \quad (\times 2) :: \mathbf{R} \to \mathbf{R}$$
$$(\mathbf{B}, \text{true}, (\neg)\,), \quad \text{with} \quad \text{true} :: 1 \to \mathbf{B}, \quad (\neg) :: \mathbf{B} \to \mathbf{B}$$
$$(\mathbf{B}, \text{false}, (\neg)\,), \quad \text{with} \quad \text{false} :: 1 \to \mathbf{B}, \quad (\neg) :: \mathbf{B} \to \mathbf{B}$$
$$(A, \quad e \quad, f\,), \quad \text{with} \quad e \quad :: 1 \to A, \quad f :: A \to A$$

---

[3] We freely identify types and sets whenever convenient.

A recursively defined datatype determines, in a natural way, an algebra. A simple example is the datatype *Nat* defined by[4]:

data *Nat* = zero | succ *Nat*

The corresponding algebra is:

$$(Nat, \text{zero}, \text{succ}), \quad \text{with} \quad \text{zero} :: 1 \to Nat, \quad \text{succ} :: Nat \to Nat$$

This belongs to the last class mentioned; in fact, if we ignore the possibility of infinite data structures —made possible by lazy evaluation— this is essentially the same algebra as $(\mathbb{N}, 0, (+1))$. Another example is:

data *Natlist* = nil | cons $\mathbb{N}$ *Natlist*

The corresponding algebra is:

$$(Natlist, \text{nil}, \text{cons}), \quad \text{with} \quad \text{nil} :: 1 \to Natlist, \quad \text{cons} :: \mathbb{N} \times Natlist \to Natlist$$

This is basically the same as $(List\ \mathbb{N}, [], (:))$. Both of these examples illustrate the general phenomenon that a recursively defined datatype determines an algebra in which the carrier of the algebra is the datatype itself, and the constructors of the datatype are the operations of the algebra.

Homomorphisms A homomorphism between two algebras, which must be *from the same class*, is a function between their carrier sets that "respects the structure" of the class. For example, the function exp $:: \mathbb{N} \to \mathbb{R}$ is a homomorphism with as *source algebra* $(\mathbb{N}, 0, (+))$ and as *target algebra* $(\mathbb{R}, 1, (\times))$. In this case, respecting the structure of this algebra class means that it satisfies the following two properties:

$$\begin{aligned} \exp 0 \quad &= 1 \\ \exp(x + y) &= (\exp x) \times (\exp y) \end{aligned}$$

Another example in the same class is length $:: (A^\star, \varepsilon, (+\!\!+)) \to (\mathbb{N}, 0, (+))$. (This notation is shorthand for the statement that the function length $:: A^\star \to \mathbb{N}$ is a homomorphism from source algebra $(A^\star, \varepsilon, (+\!\!+))$ to target algebra $(\mathbb{N}, 0, (+))$. In this case, respecting the structure means:

$$\begin{aligned} \text{length } \varepsilon \quad &= 0 \\ \text{length}(x +\!\!+ y) &= (\text{length } x) + (\text{length } y) \end{aligned}$$

In general (for this class of algebras), $h :: (A, u, \otimes) \to (B, e, \oplus)$ means:

$$\begin{aligned} h &:: A \to B \\ h\, u \quad &= e \\ h(x \otimes y) &= (h\, x) \oplus (h\, y) \end{aligned}$$

---

[4] We use Haskell syntax for defining datatypes, except that we write constructors using a sans serif font where Haskell would capitalize the first letter. The Haskell definition of *Nat* would be **data Nat = Zero | Succ Nat**.

So to apply h to a value in A that resulted from a u-operation (and there is only one such value), we may equally apply h to the operands (of which there are none) and apply e to the resulting 0-tuple. Similarly, to apply h to a value in A that resulted from a $\otimes$-operation, we may equally well apply h to the operands (which gives two B-values) and combine these with the operation $\oplus$. Here are some more examples of homomorphisms in this class:

$$
\begin{aligned}
(\downarrow 1) &:: (\mathbf{N},\ 0\ ,(+)) \rightarrow (\mathbf{N},\ 0\ ,(\uparrow)) \\
\text{even} &:: (\mathbf{N},\ 0\ ,(+)) \rightarrow (\mathbf{B}, \text{true}, (\equiv)) \\
(> 0) &:: (\mathbf{N},\ 0\ ,(\uparrow)) \rightarrow (\mathbf{B}, \text{false}, (\vee)) \\
(\neg) &:: (\mathbf{B}, \text{false}, (\vee)) \rightarrow (\mathbf{B}, \text{true}, (\wedge)) \\
(\neg) &:: (\mathbf{B}, \text{true}, (\wedge)) \rightarrow (\mathbf{B}, \text{false}, (\vee))
\end{aligned}
$$

If we have two homomorphisms in which the target algebra of the first homomorphism $h :: (A, e, \oplus) \rightarrow (B, u, \otimes)$ is the source algebra of the second homomorphism $k :: (B, u, \otimes) \rightarrow (C, z, \odot)$, then their composition is also a homomorphism $k \bullet h :: (A, e, \oplus) \rightarrow (C, z, \odot)$. For example,

$$
\begin{aligned}
(> 0) \bullet (\downarrow 1) &:: (\mathbf{N},\ 0\ ,(+)) \rightarrow (\mathbf{B}, \text{false}, (\vee)) \\
(\neg) \bullet (\neg) &:: (\mathbf{B}, \text{false}, (\vee)) \rightarrow (\mathbf{B}, \text{false}, (\vee))
\end{aligned}
$$

Now $(> 0) \bullet (\downarrow 1) = (> 0)$ on $\mathbf{N}$, and $(\neg) \bullet (\neg) = \text{id}_\mathbf{B}$ (the identity function on $\mathbf{B}$), so we have

$$
\begin{aligned}
(> 0) &:: (\mathbf{N},\ 0\ ,(+)) \rightarrow (\mathbf{B}, \text{false}, (\vee)) \\
\text{id} &:: (\mathbf{B}, \text{false}, (\vee)) \rightarrow (\mathbf{B}, \text{false}, (\vee))
\end{aligned}
$$

The identity function id_A is of course a homomorphism between any algebra with carrier A and itself.

For the class of algebras whose generic algebra is

$$
(A, e, \oplus), \quad \text{with} \quad e :: 1 \rightarrow A, \quad \oplus :: \mathbf{N} \times A \rightarrow A
$$

we have that $h :: (A, e, \oplus) \rightarrow (B, u, \otimes)$ means:

$$
\begin{aligned}
h &:: A \rightarrow B \\
h\, e &\quad = u \\
h(x \oplus y) &= x \otimes (h\, y)
\end{aligned}
$$

So why is h for this class not applied to the occurrence of x in the righthand side of the second equality? The answer is that that would not make sense, since h has source type A, but x is of type $\mathbf{N}$. (Later, after we have introduced functors, we shall see how to define the notion of homomorphism generically, independent of the specific algebra class.) We have:

$$
\begin{aligned}
\text{sum} &:: (List\ \mathbf{N}, [\,], (:)) \rightarrow (\mathbf{N}, 0, (+)) \\
\text{foldr} \oplus e &:: (List\ \mathbf{N}, [\,], (:)) \rightarrow (A, e,\ \oplus\ )
\end{aligned}
$$

In fact, $\text{sum} = \text{foldr}\ (+)\ 0$.

Uniqueness We have given several examples of algebra classes and their homomorphisms. The first class had generic algebra

$$(A, e, \oplus) \quad \text{with} \quad e :: 1 \rightarrow A, \quad \oplus :: A \times A \rightarrow A \ .$$

Note that the fact that a function is a homomorphism of algebras in this class does not uniquely define the function. For example, we observed above that length is a homomorphism with source $(A^*, \varepsilon, (\text{+}\!\text{+}))$ and target $(\mathbb{N}, 0, (+))$. But the function that is constantly 0 for all lists is also a homomorphism with exactly the same source and target algebras. Indeed, in the case of all the examples we gave of homomorphisms between algebras in this class the constant function returning the value e of the target algebra has the same homomorphism type as the given function.

Contrast this with the third class of algebras. The generic algebra has the form

$$(A, e, \oplus) \quad \text{with} \quad e :: 1 \rightarrow A, \quad \oplus :: \mathbb{N} \times A \rightarrow A$$

Again, the fact that a function is a homomorphism of algebras in this class does not uniquely define the function. But there is something rather special about the algebra $(List \ \mathbb{N}, [\,], (:))$ in this class of algebras. Specifically, foldr $\oplus \ e$ is the *unique* homomorphism with source algebra $(List \ \mathbb{N}, [\,], (:))$ and target algebra $(A, e, \oplus)$. For example, sum is the unique homomomorphism with source $(List \ \mathbb{N}, [\,], (:))$ and target $(\mathbb{N}, 0, (+))$. That is, function h satisfies the equations

$$\begin{aligned} h &:: \ List \ \mathbb{N} \rightarrow \mathbb{N} \\ h \ [\,] &= 0 \\ h(x{:}xs) &= x + (h \ xs) \end{aligned}$$

if and only if $h = \mathsf{sum}$.

This uniqueness is an important property that will be a focus of later discussion.

Isomorphisms Above, we said several times that two algebras were "basically" or "essentially" the same. We want to make this notion precise. The technical term for this is that these algebras are *isomorphic*. In set theory, two sets A and B are called isomorphic whenever there exists a bijection between A and B. Equivalently, A and B are isomorphic whenever there exist functions $f :: A \rightarrow B$ and $g :: B \rightarrow A$ that cancel each other, that is:

$$\begin{aligned} f{\cdot}g &= \mathsf{id}_B \\ g{\cdot}f &= \mathsf{id}_A \end{aligned}$$

The generalisation for algebras is now that we require these functions to be *homomorphisms* between the algebras involved. A homomorphism that has a cancelling homomorphism is called an *isomorphism*. From the examples above we see that the algebras $(\mathbf{B}, \mathsf{true}, (\wedge))$ and $(\mathbf{B}, \mathsf{false}, (\vee))$ are isomorphic.

Algebras with laws Although we will hardly use this, no account of the notion of algebra is complete without mentioning the following. A class of algebras can be further determined by a set of laws. In a "lawful" class of algebras, all algebras satisfy the same set of (possibly conditional) equational laws. Monoids form the best-known example of a lawful algebra class. The generic monoid is $(A, e, \oplus)$, with $e :: 1 \to A$, $\oplus :: A \times A \to A$, and the monoid laws are the following two:

$\oplus$ is *associative*: $(x \oplus y) \oplus z = x \oplus (y \oplus z)$
e is *neutral* for $\oplus$: $e \oplus x = x = x \oplus e$

If an operation $\oplus$ has a neutral element, it is unique, and we denote it as $\nu_\oplus$. For example, $\nu_+ = 0$ and $\nu_\times = 1$. The examples of concrete algebras from the first class treated in this chapter are actually all monoids. For lawful algebras the definition of homomorphism is the same as before.

Graphs The notion of homomorphism is more general than that of a "structure-respecting" function between algebras. Homomorphisms can generally be defined for anything having structure. As an example, we consider homomorphisms between directed graphs. Recall that a directed graph is a structure

$(V, E, \text{source}, \text{target})$, with $\text{source} :: E \to V$, $\text{target} :: E \to V$

in which the elements of V are called "vertices" or "nodes", and the elements of E are called "edges" or "arcs". If edge e is an edge from node m to node n, we have: $\text{source}\, e = m$ and $\text{target}\, e = n$. Directed graphs are just like an algebra class, except that we have *two* "carrier sets": V and E. (There is a term for algebras with more carrier sets: *heterogeneous* or *multi-sorted* algebras.) A homomorphism from graph $(V_0, E_0, \text{source}_0, \text{target}_0)$ to graph $(V_1, E_1, \text{source}_1, \text{target}_1)$ is a *pair* of functions, one with the typing $V_0 \to V_1$ and one with the typing $E_0 \to E_1$, and if we overload the identifier h to denote both functions, they satisfy:

$h(\text{source}\, a) = \text{source}(h\, a)$
$h(\text{target}\, a) = \text{target}(h\, a)$

As before for algebras, two graphs are isomorphic whenever there are cancelling homomorphisms between them. Informally, this means that one graph can be obtained from the other by systematic renaming. In standard Graph Theory, for unlabelled graphs like the ones we are considering here, two isomorphic graphs are usually considered *identical*. Still, there can be non-trivial *automorphisms*, that is, isomorphisms between a graph and itself that are not the identity isomorphism.

Summarising and looking ahead In this section we have introduced the notion of a class of algebras and homomorphisms between algebras in the same class. We have observed that datatype definitions in a functional programming language define an algebra, the carrier of the algebra being the datatype itself and the operations being the constructors of the datatype. We have also made the important observation that in some cases a function is uniquely characterised by its homomorphism type (the fact that it is a homomorphism combined with knowledge about its source and target algebras).

In the remaining sections of this chapter our goal is to formalise all these ideas in a way that facilitates the calculational construction of programs. Let us give an outline of what is in store.

The notion of an algebra is formalised in many textbooks on Universal Algebra. Here is an example of such a definition. This is *not* the definition we intend to use so you don't need to understand it in detail.

Σ-*algebra* A Σ-algebra with respect to a signature with operators $\Sigma = (S, \Gamma)$ is a pair (V, F) such that

  − V is an S-sorted set, and
  − $F = \{\gamma : \gamma \in \cup \Gamma : f_\gamma\}$ is a set of functions such that

$$\gamma \in \Gamma_{\langle\langle s_0, \ldots, s_{n-1}\rangle, r\rangle} \quad \Rightarrow \quad f_\gamma \in V_{s_0} \times \ldots \times V_{s_{n-1}} \to V_r$$

$$\gamma \in \Gamma_{\langle s, r\rangle} \quad \Rightarrow \quad f_\gamma \in V_s \to V_r$$

V is called the *carrier set* of the Σ-algebra and set F is its *operator set*.

Contrast this with the definition we are going to explain in the coming sections.

F-*algebra* Suppose F is a functor. Then an F-algebra is a pair(A, α) such that $\alpha \in FA \to A$.

Neither definition is complete since in the first definition the notion of a signature has not been defined, and in the second the notion of a functor hasn't been defined. In the first definition, however, it's possible to guess what the definition of a signature is and, after struggling some time with the subscripts of subscripts, it is possible to conclude that the definition corresponds to the "intuitive" notion of an algebra. The disadvantage is that the definition is grossly unwieldy. If the definitions of one's basic concepts are as complicated as this then one should give up altogether any hope that one can calculate with them.

The second definition is very compact and, as we shall see, gives an excellent basis for program construction. Its disadvantage, however, is that it is impossible to guess what the definition of a functor might be, and it is difficult to see how it corresponds to the familiar notion of an algebra. How is it possible to express the idea that an algebra consists of a set of operations? On the face of it, it would appear that an F-algebra has just one operation α. Also, how does one express the fact that the operations in an algebra have various arities?

The answer to these questions is hidden in the definition of a "functor". And, of course, if its definition is long and complicated then all the advantages of the compactness of the definition of an algebra are lost. We shall see, however, that the definition of a functor is also very compact. We shall also see that functors can be constructed from primitive functors in a systematic way. The "disjoint sum" of two functors enables one to express the idea that an algebra has a set of operations; the "cartesian product" of functors allows one to express the arity of the various operations; "constant functors" enable the expression of the existence of designated constants in an algebra. An additional major bonus is that the categorical notion of an "initial algebra" leads to a very compact and workable definition of inductively defined datatypes in a programming language. The remaining sections of this chapter thus provide a veritable arsenal of fundamental concepts whose mastery is tremendously worthwhile.

Exercise 2.1 Check the claim that even $:: (\mathbf{N}, 0, (+)) \to (\mathbf{B}, \text{true}, (\equiv))$ is a homomorphism.

□

Exercise 2.2 Give the composition of the following two homomorphisms:

$$(\neg) \ :: (\mathbf{B}, \text{false}, (\vee)) \to (\mathbf{B}, \text{true}, (\wedge))$$
$$(> 0) :: (\mathbf{N}, \quad 0 \ , (+)) \to (\mathbf{B}, \text{false}, (\vee))$$

□

Exercise 2.3 An automorphism is an isomorphism with the same source and target algebra. Show that the only automorphism on the algebra $(\mathbf{B}, \text{true}, (\equiv))$ is the trivial automorphism id.

□

Exercise 2.4 Give an example of a non-trivial automorphism on the algebra $(\mathbf{R}, 0, (\times))$.

□

2.2   Functors

To a first approximation, datatypes are just sets. A second approximation, which we have just seen, is that a datatype is the carrier of an algebra. In this section we identify *parameterised* datatypes with the categorical notion of functor, giving us a third approximation to what it is to be a datatype. It is in this section that we take the first steps towards a generic theory of datatypes.

Examples The best way to introduce the notion of a functor is by abstraction from a number of examples. Here are a few datatype definitions:

data *List a* = nil | cons *a* (*List a*)

data *Maybe a* = none | one *a*

$$\textbf{data } Bin\ a\ =\ \textsf{tip }a\ |\ \textsf{join }(Bin\ a)\ (Bin\ a)$$

$$\textbf{data } Rose\ a\ =\ \textsf{fork }a\ (List(Rose\ a))$$

Each of these types can be viewed as a structured repository of information, the type of information being specified by the parameter a in the definition. Each of these types has its own map combinator. "Mapping" a function over an instance of one of these datatypes means applying the function to all the values stored in the structure without changing the structure itself. The typings of the individual map combinators are thus as follows.

$$
\begin{aligned}
\textsf{map}_{List} &\ ::\ (a \to b) \to (List\ a \to List\ b) \\
\textsf{map}_{Maybe} &\ ::\ (a \to b) \to (Maybe\ a \to Maybe\ b) \\
\textsf{map}_{Bin} &\ ::\ (a \to b) \to (Bin\ a \to Bin\ b) \\
\textsf{map}_{Rose} &\ ::\ (a \to b) \to (Rose\ a \to Rose\ b)
\end{aligned}
$$

A datatype that has more than one type parameter also has a map combinator, but with more arguments. For instance, defining the type of trees with leaves of type a and interior nodes of type b by

$$\textbf{data } Tree\ a\ b\ =\ \textsf{leaf }a\ |\ \textsf{node }(Tree\ a\ b)\ b\ (Tree\ a\ b)$$

the corresponding map combinator has type

$$\textsf{map}_{Tree}\ ::\ (a \to c) \to (b \to d) \to (Tree\ a\ b \to Tree\ c\ d)$$

Given a tree of type $Tree\ a\ b$, the combinator applies a function of type $a \to c$ to all the leaves of the tree, and a function of type $b \to d$ to all the nodes, thus creating a tree of type $Tree\ c\ d$.

In general, the map combinator for an n-ary datatype maps n functions over the values stored in the datatype. (This also holds for the case that n is zero. Datatypes having *no* type parameter also have a map combinator, but with *no* functional arguments! The map in this case is the identity function on the elements of the datatype.)

Functors Defined The idea that parameterised datatypes are structured repositories of information over which arbitrary functions can be mapped is captured by the concept of a *functor*. We first explain the concept informally for unary functors. Consider the world of typed functions. Functors are the structure-respecting functions for that world. So what is the structure involved? First, that world can be viewed as a directed graph, in which the nodes are types and the arcs are functions. So, as for graphs, we require that a functor is a *pair of mappings*, one acting on types and one acting on functions, and if we overload the identifier F to denote both functions, they satisfy the typing rule:

$$\frac{f :: a \to b}{Ff :: Fa \to Fb}$$

Further, functions can be composed with the operation "$\bullet$", which is associative and has neutral element the identity function, id, so this world forms a monoid algebra. Functors also respect the monoid structure:

$$F\,(f \bullet g) = (F\,f) \bullet (F\,g)$$
$$F\ \ \mathrm{id}_a\ \ = \mathrm{id}_{Fa}$$

The first of these laws says that there is no difference between mapping the composition of two functions over an F structure in one go and mapping the functions over the structure one by one. The second law says that mapping the identity function over an F structure of a's has no effect on the structure.

To be completely precise, the world of functions is not quite a monoid, since the algebra is *partial*: the meaning of $f \bullet g$ is only defined when this composition is well-typed, that is, when the source type of f is the target type of g. The first equality above should therefore only be applied to cases for which $f \bullet g$ is defined, and from now on we assume this as a tacit condition on such equations. It follows from the typing rule that then also the composition $(F\,f) \bullet (F\,g)$ is well-typed, so that is not needed as a condition.

Now, in general, an n-ary *functor* F is a pair of mappings that maps an n-tuple of types $a_0, \ldots, a_{n-1}$ to a type $F\,a_0 \cdots a_{n-1}$ and an n-tuple of functions $f_0, \ldots, f_{n-1}$ to a function $F\,f_0 \cdots f_{n-1}$ in such a way that typing, composition and identity are respected:

$$\frac{f_i\quad ::\quad a_i\quad \to\quad b_i\quad \text{for } i = 0, \ldots, n-1}{F f_0 \cdots f_{n-1} :: F a_0 \cdots a_{n-1} \to F b_0 \cdots b_{n-1}}$$

$$F\,(f_0 \bullet g_0) \cdots (f_{n-1} \bullet g_{n-1}) = (F\,f_0 \cdots f_{n-1}) \bullet (F\,g_0 \cdots g_{n-1})$$
$$F\ \ \mathrm{id}\ \ \cdots\ \ \mathrm{id}\ \ = \mathrm{id}$$

Examples Revisited As anticipated in the introduction to this section, the pairs of mappings F (on types) and map_F (on functions) for $F = List, Maybe$, etcetera, are all unary functors since they satisfy the typing rule

$$\frac{f :: a \to b}{\mathrm{map}_F\,f :: Fa \to Fb}$$

and the functional equalities

$$\mathrm{map}_F\,(f \bullet g) = (\mathrm{map}_F\,f) \bullet (\mathrm{map}_F\,g)$$
$$\mathrm{map}_F\ \ \mathrm{id}\ \ = \mathrm{id}\ \ .$$

An example of a binary functor is the pair of mappings *Tree* and map_{Tree} since the pair satisfies the typing rule

$$\frac{\begin{array}{ccc} f &::& a \to c \\ g &::& b \to d \end{array}}{\mathrm{map}_{Tree}\,f\,g :: Tree\,a\,b \to Tree\,c\,d}$$

and the functional equalities

$$\mathrm{map}_{Tree}\,(f \bullet g)\,(h \bullet k) = (\mathrm{map}_{Tree}\,f\,h) \bullet (\mathrm{map}_{Tree}\,g\,k)$$
$$\mathrm{map}_{Tree}\ \ \mathrm{id}\ \ \mathrm{id}\ \ = \mathrm{id}\ \ .$$

Notational convention Conventionally, the same notation is used for the type mapping and the function mapping of a functor, and we follow that convention here. Moreover, when applicable, we use the name of the type mapping. So, from here on, for function f, we write *List* f rather than $\mathsf{map}_{List}\ f$.

Exercise 2.5   Consider the following datatype declarations. Each defines a mapping from types to types. For example, *Error* maps the type a to the type *Error* a. Extend the definition of each so that it becomes a functor.

> **data** *Error* a $=$ error *String* $\mid$ ok a
>
> **data** *Drawing* a $=$ above (*Drawing* a) (*Drawing* a)
> $\qquad\qquad\qquad$ $\mid$ beside (*Drawing* a) (*Drawing* a)
> $\qquad\qquad\qquad$ $\mid$ atom a

□

2.3   Polynomial Functors

Now that we have defined the notion of a functor and have seen some non-trivial examples it is time to consider more basic examples. Vital to the usefulness of the notion is that non-trivial functors can be constructed by composing more basic functors. In this section we consider the *polynomial* functors. As the name suggests, these are the functors that can be obtained by "addition" and "multiplication" possibly combined with the use of a number of "constants".

The technical terms for addition and multiplication are "disjoint sum" and "cartesian product". The use of disjoint sum enables one to capture in a *single* functor the fact that an algebra has a *set* of operations. The use of cartesian product enables one to express the fact that an operator in an algebra has an arity greater than one. We also introduce constant functors and the identity functor; these are used to express the designated constants (functions of arity zero) and unary functions in an algebra, respectively. For technical reasons, we also introduce a couple of auxiliary functors in order to complete the class of polynomial functors. We begin with the simpler cases.

The identity functor The simplest example of a functor is the *identity functor* which is the trivial combination of two identity functions, the function that maps every type to itself and the function that maps every function to itself. Although trivial, this example is important and shouldn't be forgotten. We denote the identity functor by Id.

Constant functors For the constant mapping that maps any n-tuple of arguments to the same result x we use the notation x^{K}. As is easily verified, the pair of mappings a^{K} and $\mathsf{id}_a{}^{\mathsf{K}}$, where a is some type, is also a functor. It is n-ary for all n.

Following the naming convention introduced above, we write a^{K} to denote both the mapping on types and the mapping on functions. That is, we write

a^κ where strictly we should write $\text{id}_a{}^\kappa$. So, for functions $f_0 \ldots f_{n-1}$, we have $a^\kappa f_0 \ldots f_{n-1} = \text{id}_a$.

A constant functor that we will use frequently is the constant functor associated with the *unit type*, 1. The unit type is the type that is denoted () in Haskell. It is a type having exactly one element (which element is also denoted () in Haskell). This functor will be denoted by 1 rather than 1^κ.

Extraction Each extraction combinator

$$\text{Ex}_i^n \; z_0 \; \cdots \; z_{n-1} \;\; = \;\; z_i, \quad \text{for } i \; = \; 0, \ldots, n-1$$

is an n-ary functor. The extractions that we have particular use for are the identity functor Id, which is the same as Ex_0^1, and the binary functors Ex_0^2 and Ex_1^2, for which we use the more convenient notations Par and Rec. (The reason for this choice of identifiers will become evident in chapter 3. When defining recursive datatypes like *List*, we identify a binary "pattern functor". The first parameter of the pattern functor is the parameter of the recursive datatype — and is thus called the Par parameter— and the second parameter is used as the argument for recursion —and is thus called the Rec parameter.)

The sum functor The binary sum functor + gives the "disjoint union" of two types. We write it as an infix operator. It is defined by:

$$\textbf{data } a + b \; = \; \text{inl } a \; | \; \text{inr } b$$

$$
\begin{aligned}
f + g \; = \;\; & h \;\; \textbf{where} \\
& h(\text{inl } u) \; = \; \text{inl}(f \; u) \\
& h(\text{inr } v) \; = \; \text{inr}(g \; v)
\end{aligned}
$$

$$
\begin{aligned}
f \triangledown g \; = \;\; & h \;\; \textbf{where} \\
& h(\text{inl } u) \; = \; f \; u \\
& h(\text{inr } v) \; = \; g \; v
\end{aligned}
$$

The datatype definition introduces both the type $a+b$, called the *disjoint sum* of a and b, and the two constructor functions $\text{inl} :: a \to a + b$ and $\text{inr} :: b \to a + b$. The name "disjoint sum" is used because $a+b$ is like the set union of a and b except that each element of the sets a and b is, in effect, tagged with either the label inl, to indicate that it originated in set a, or inr, to indicate that it originated in set b. In this way $a+a$ is different from a since it effectively contains two copies of every element in a, one with label inl and one with label inr. In particular $1+1$ has two elements. The constructors inl and inr are called *injections* and are sa id to *inject* elements of a and b into the respective components of $a+b$.

In order to extend the sum mapping on types to a functor we have to define the sum of two functions. This is done in the definition of $f+g$ above. Its definition is obtained by type considerations — if + is to be a functor, we require that if $f :: a \to b$ and $g :: c \to d$ then $f+g \;\; :: \;\; a+c \to b+d$. It is easily checked that the above definition of $f+g$ meets this requirement; indeed, there is no other way to do so.

In addition to defining $f+g$ we have defined another way of combining f and g, namely $f \triangledown g$, which we pronounce f "junc" g. ("Junc" is short for "junction".) As we'll see shortly, $f \triangledown g$ is more basic than $f+g$. The meaning of $f \triangledown g$ is only defined when f and g have the same target type; its source type is a disjoint sum of two types. Operationally, it inspects the label on its argument to see whether the argument originates from the left or right component of the disjoint sum. Depending on which component it is, either the function f or the function g is applied to the argument after first stripping off the label. In other words, $f \triangledown g$ acts like a case statement, applying f or g depending on which component of the disjoint sum the argument comes from.

The *typing rule* for $\triangledown$ is a good way of memorising its functionality:

$$\frac{\begin{array}{l} f \quad :: a \quad \to c \\ g :: \quad b \to c \end{array}}{f \triangledown g :: a+b \to c}$$

(Haskell's prelude contains a definition of disjoint sum:

data *Either a b* $=$ Left a | Right b

with *either* playing the role of $\triangledown$.)

Now that we have defined $+$ on types and on functions in such a way as to fulfill the typing requirements on a (binary) functor it remains to verify that it respects identities and composition. We do this now. In doing so, we establish a number of calculational properties that will prove to be very useful for other purposes.

Note first that the definitions of $+$ (on functions) and of $\triangledown$ can be rewritten in point-free style as the following *characterisations*:

$$\boxed{\begin{array}{lll} h = f+g & \equiv & h \bullet \mathsf{inl} = \mathsf{inl} \bullet f \ \wedge \ h \bullet \mathsf{inr} = \mathsf{inr} \bullet g \\ h = f \triangledown g & \equiv & h \bullet \mathsf{inl} = \quad f \ \wedge \ h \bullet \mathsf{inr} = \quad g \end{array}}$$

This style is convenient for reasoning. For example, we can prove the *identity rule*:

$$\boxed{\mathsf{inl} \triangledown \mathsf{inr} = \mathsf{id}}$$

by calculating as follows:

$$\begin{array}{ll} & \mathsf{id} \ = \ \alpha \triangledown \beta \\ \equiv & \{ \qquad \text{characterisation of } \triangledown \quad \} \\ & \mathsf{id} \bullet \mathsf{inl} = \alpha \ \wedge \ \mathsf{id} \bullet \mathsf{inr} = \beta \\ \equiv & \{ \qquad \text{id is the identity of composition} \quad \} \\ & \mathsf{inl} = \alpha \wedge \mathsf{inr} = \beta \ . \end{array}$$

This last calculation is a simple illustration of the way we often *derive* programs. In this case the goal is to express id in terms of $\triangledown$. We therefore introduce the unknowns α and β, and calculate expressions for α and β that satisfy the goal.

If we substitute $f + g$ or $f\triangledown g$ for h in the corresponding characterisation, the left-hand sides of the equivalences become trivially true. The right-hand sides are then also true, giving the *computation rules*:

$$
\begin{array}{ll}
(f{+}g) \bullet \mathsf{inl} = \mathsf{inl} \bullet f & (f{+}g) \bullet \mathsf{inr} = \mathsf{inr} \bullet g \\
(f\triangledown g) \bullet \mathsf{inl} = \quad f & (f\triangledown g) \bullet \mathsf{inr} = \quad g
\end{array}
$$

The validity of the so-called $\triangledown$-*fusion* rule:

$$
h \bullet (f\triangledown g) = (h\bullet f) \triangledown (h\bullet g)
$$

is shown by the following calculation[5]:

$$
\begin{array}{rl}
& h \bullet f\triangledown g \quad = \quad \alpha\triangledown\beta \\
\equiv & \quad \{ \qquad \text{characterisation of } \triangledown \quad \} \\
& h \bullet f\triangledown g \bullet \mathsf{inl} \;=\; \alpha \;\wedge\; h \bullet f\triangledown g \bullet \mathsf{inr} \;=\; \beta \\
\equiv & \quad \{ \qquad \text{computation rules for } \triangledown \quad \} \\
& h \bullet f \;=\; \alpha \;\wedge\; h \bullet g \;=\; \beta \;.
\end{array}
$$

Note once again the style of calculation in which the right side of the law is constructed rather than verified.

It is also possible to express $+$ in terms of $\triangledown$, namely by:

$$
f + g = (\mathsf{inl}\bullet f) \triangledown (\mathsf{inr}\bullet g)
$$

We derive the rhs of this rule as follows:

$$
\begin{array}{rl}
& f{+}g \quad = \quad \alpha\triangledown\beta \\
\equiv & \quad \{ \qquad \text{characterisation of } \triangledown \quad \} \\
& f{+}g \bullet \mathsf{inl} \;=\; \alpha \;\wedge\; f{+}g \bullet \mathsf{inr} \;=\; \beta \\
\equiv & \quad \{ \qquad \text{computation rules for } + \quad \} \\
& \mathsf{inl}\bullet f \;=\; \alpha \;\wedge\; \mathsf{inr}\bullet g \;=\; \beta \;.
\end{array}
$$

Another fusion rule is the $\triangledown$-$+$ *fusion* rule:

$$
(f\triangledown g) \bullet (h + k) = (f\bullet h) \triangledown (g\bullet k)
$$

We leave its derivation as an exercise.

---

[5] We adopt the convention that composition has lower precedence than all other operators. Thus $h \bullet f\triangledown g$ should be read as $h \bullet (f\triangledown g)$. In the statement of the basic rules, however, we always parenthesise fully.

These rules are useful by themselves, but they were proved to lead to the result that $+$ respects function composition:

$$\boxed{(f + g) \bullet (h + k) = (f \bullet h) + (g \bullet k)}$$

The proof is simple:

$$
\begin{aligned}
& f{+}g \ \bullet \ h{+}k \\
= \quad & \{ \qquad \text{definition of } + \ \} \\
& (\mathsf{inl} \bullet f) \ \triangledown \ (\mathsf{inr} \bullet g) \ \bullet \ h{+}k \\
= \quad & \{ \qquad \triangledown\text{-}{+} \ \text{fusion} \ \} \\
& (\mathsf{inl} \bullet f \bullet h) \ \triangledown \ (\mathsf{inr} \bullet g \bullet k) \\
= \quad & \{ \qquad \text{definition of } + \ \} \\
& (f \bullet h) + (g \bullet k) \ .
\end{aligned}
$$

The proof that $+$ also respects id, that is,

$$\boxed{\mathsf{id} + \mathsf{id} = \mathsf{id}}$$

is also left as an exercise.

An important property that we shall use is that the mapping $\triangledown$ is injective, that is:

$$f \triangledown g = h \triangledown k \ \equiv \ f = h \wedge g = k \ .$$

Just two simple steps are needed for the proof. Note, in particular, that there is no need for separate "if" and "only if" arguments.

$$
\begin{aligned}
& f \triangledown g = h \triangledown k \\
\equiv \quad & \{ \qquad \text{characterisation} \ \} \\
& f \triangledown g \bullet \mathsf{inl} = h \ \wedge \ f \triangledown g \bullet \mathsf{inr} = k \\
\equiv \quad & \{ \qquad \text{computation rules} \ \} \\
& f = h \wedge g = k \ .
\end{aligned}
$$

Further, the mapping is surjective (within the typing constraints): if $h :: a + b \to c$, then there exist functions $f :: a \to c$ and $g :: b \to c$ such that $h = f \triangledown g$. In fact, they can be given explicitly by $f = h \bullet \mathsf{inl}$ and $g = h \bullet \mathsf{inr}$.

The product functor While sums give a choice between values of two types, products combine two values. In Haskell the product type former and the pair constructor are syntactically equal. However, we want to distinguish between the type former $\times$ and the value constructor $(\_, \_)$. The binary product functor $\times$ is given by:

data $a \times b = (a, b)$

$\mathsf{exl}(u, v) = u$
$\mathsf{exr}(u, v) = v$

$f \times g = h$ **where**
$\qquad h(u, v) = (f\ u,\ g\ v)$

$f \vartriangle g = h$ **where**
$\qquad h\ u = (f\ u,\ g\ u)$

The functions $\mathsf{exl} :: a \times b \to a$ and $\mathsf{exr} :: a \times b \to b$ are called *projections* and are said to *project* a pair onto its components.

Just as for disjoint sum, we have defined $f \times g$ in such a way that it meet the type requirements on a functor. Specifically, if $f :: a \to b$ and $g :: c \to d$ then $f \times g :: a \times c \to b \times d$, as is easily checked. Also, we have defined a second combination of f and g, namely $f \vartriangle g$, which we pronounce f "split" g.

The operational meaning of $f \times g$ is easy to see. Given a pair of values, it produces a pair by applying f to the first component and g to the second component. The operational meaning of $f \vartriangle g$ is that it constructs a pair of values from a single value by applying both f and g to the given value. (In particular, $\mathsf{id} \vartriangle \mathsf{id}$ constructs a pair by "splitting" a given value into two copies of itself.)

A curious fact is the following. *All* the rules for sums are *also* valid for products under the following systematic replacements: replace $+$ by $\times$, $\triangledown$ by $\vartriangle$, inl and inr by exl and exr, and switch the components f and g of each composition $f \cdot g$. (In category theory this is called *dualisation*.) This gives us the *characterisations*:

$$
\begin{array}{lll}
h = f \times g & \equiv & \mathsf{exl} \cdot h = f \cdot \mathsf{exl} \ \wedge \ \mathsf{exr} \cdot h = g \cdot \mathsf{exr} \\
h = f \vartriangle g & \equiv & \mathsf{exl} \cdot h = f \qquad \wedge \ \mathsf{exr} \cdot h = g
\end{array}
$$

the *identity rule*:

$$\mathsf{exl} \vartriangle \mathsf{exr} = \mathsf{id}$$

the *computation rules*:

$$
\begin{array}{ll}
\mathsf{exl} \cdot (f \times g) = f \cdot \mathsf{exl} & \mathsf{exr} \cdot (f \times g) = g \cdot \mathsf{exr} \\
\mathsf{exl} \cdot (f \vartriangle g) = f & \mathsf{exr} \cdot (f \vartriangle g) = g
\end{array}
$$

the $\vartriangle$-*fusion rule*:

$$(f \vartriangle g) \cdot h = (f \cdot h) \vartriangle (g \cdot h)$$

$\times$ expressed in terms of $\vartriangle$:

$$\boxed{f \times g = (f \bullet \mathsf{exl}) \vartriangle (g \bullet \mathsf{exr})}$$

the $\times$-$\vartriangle$-*fusion rule*:

$$\boxed{(f \times g) \bullet (h \vartriangle k) = (f \bullet h) \vartriangle (g \bullet k)}$$

and finally the fact that $\times$ *is a binary functor*:

$$\boxed{\begin{array}{rcl} (f \times g) \bullet (h \times k) &=& (f \bullet h) \times (g \bullet k) \\ \mathsf{id} \times \mathsf{id} &=& \mathsf{id} \end{array}}$$

Functional Composition of Functors It is easily verified that the composition of two unary functors F and G is also a functor. By their composition we mean the pair of mappings, the first of which maps type a to $F(Ga)$ and the second maps function f to $F(Gf)$. We use juxtaposition —thus FG— to denote the composition of unary functors F and G. For example, *Maybe Rose* denotes the composition of the functors *Maybe* and *Rose*. The order of composition is important, of course. The functor *Maybe Rose* is quite different from the functor *Rose Maybe*.

It is also possible to compose functors of different arities. For instance we may want to compose a binary functor like disjoint sum with a unary functor like *List*. A simple notational device to help define such a functor is to overload the meaning of the symbol "+" and write *List+List*, whereby we mean the functor that maps x to $(List\ x) + (List\ x)$. Similarly we can compose disjoint sum with two unary functors F and G: we use the notation $F+G$ and mean the functor that maps x to $(F\ x) + (G\ x)$.

Two ways of reducing the arity of a functor are *specialisation* and *duplication*. An example of specialisation is when we turn the binary disjoint sum functor into a unary functor by specialising its first argument to the unit type. We write $1+\mathsf{Id}$ and mean the functor that maps type a to the type $1+a$, and function f to the function id_1+f. Duplication means that we duplicate the argument as many times as necessary. For example, the mapping $x \mapsto x+x$ is a unary functor.

Both duplication and specialisation are forms of functional composition of functors. To formulate them precisely we need to extend the notion of functor so that the arity of the target of a functor may be more than one. (Up till now we have always said that a functor maps an n-tuple of types/functions to a single type/function.) Then a tuple of functors is also a functor, and, for each n, there is a duplication functor of arity n. In this way duplication and specialisation can be expressed as the composition of a functor with a tuple of functors. (In the case of specialisation, one of the functors is a constant functor.)

For our current purposes, a complete formalisation is an unnecessary complication and the ad hoc notation introduced above will suffice. Formalisations can be found in [18,19,37,22].

Polynomial functors A functor built only from constants, extractions, sums, products and composition is called a *polynomial* functor.

An example of a polynomial functor is *Maybe* introduced in section 2.2. Recalling its definition:

data *Maybe a* = none | one *a*

we see that, expressed in the notation introduced above, *Maybe* = 1+Id

The remaining examples introduced in section 2.2 are not polynomial because they are defined recursively. We need one more mechanism for constructing functors. That is the topic of the next section.

Exercise 2.6 ($\triangledown$-$\triangle$ abide)   Prove that, for all f, g, h and k,

$$(f \triangledown g) \triangle (h \triangledown k) = (f \triangle h) \triangledown (g \triangle k) \ .$$

☐

Exercise 2.7 (Abide laws)   The law proved in exercise 2.6 is called the $\triangledown$-$\triangle$ *abide* law because of the following two-dimensional way of writing the law in which the two operators are written either *above* or *beside* each other. (The two-dimensional way of writing is originally due to C.A.R.Hoare, the catchy name is due to Richard Bird.)

$$\begin{array}{ccc} f \triangledown g & f & g \\ \triangle & = \triangle & \triangledown \ \triangle \\ h \triangledown k & h & k \end{array}$$

What other operators abide with each other in this way? (You have already seen examples in this text, but there are also other examples from simple arithmetic.)

☐

Exercise 2.8 Consider the mapping *Square* that takes a type a to $a \times a$ and a function f to $f \times f$. Check that *Square* is a functor.

☐

Exercise 2.9 In checking that something is a functor, we must check that it respects composition *and* identity. The last part may not be omitted, as is shown by the existence of "almost-functors". Call F an almost-functor when F is a pair of mappings on types and functions (just like true functors) that respects typing and composition, but fails to respect identity: $F\mathsf{id} \neq \mathsf{id}$. Can you find a simple example of such an almost-functor? (Hint: Look at constant mappings.)

☐

Exercise 2.10 If $\mathsf{inl} :: a \to a + b$ and $\mathsf{inr} :: b \to a + b$, what is the typing of id in the identity rule $\mathsf{inl} \triangledown \mathsf{inr} = \mathsf{id}$?

☐

Exercise 2.11 Complete the verification that $+$ is a functor by proving the $\triangledown$-$+$ fusion rule and the identity rule ($\mathsf{id} + \mathsf{id} = \mathsf{id}$). In the calculation you may use all the other rules stated before these two rules.

☐

2.4 Datatypes Generically

By now the notion of a functor should be becoming familiar to you. Also, it should be clear how to extend the definition of non-inductive datatypes not involving function spaces to a polynomial functor. In this section we take the step to inductively defined datatypes.

The basic idea is that an inductively defined datatype is a fixed point of a functor, which functor we call the *pattern* functor of the datatype. For the simplest examples (such as the natural numbers) the pattern functor is polynomial but for more complicated examples (like the *Rose* datatype) it is not. We therefore need to extend the class of functors we can define beyond the polynomial functors to the so-called *regular* functors by adding the *type* functors. The basic technical device to achieve this is the *catamorphism*, which is a generalisation of the fold function on lists.

We begin by discussing pattern functors following which we can, at long last, define the notion of an F-algebra. Catamorphisms form the next —substantial— topic, following which we introduce type functors and the class of regular functors.

Pattern functors and recursion We first look at a simple inductively (= recursively) defined datatype, that of the Peano naturals, which we also saw in section 2.1:

> **data** Nat = zero | succ Nat

There is only one number zero, which we can make explicit by:

> **data** Nat = zero 1 | succ Nat

Instead of fancy constructor function names like succ and zero we now employ boring standard ones:

> **data** Nat = inl 1 | inr Nat

The choice here is that afforded by sum, so we replace this by

> **data** Nat = in(1 + Nat)

in which there is one explicit constructor function left, called "in".

Now note that *Nat* occurs both on the left and the right of the datatype definition (which is why it is called an inductively defined or recursive datatype). In order to view this as a fixed point definition, let us abstract from *Nat* on the right side replacing it by the variable z. In this way we are led to consider the unary functor N defined by

$$N\ z\ =\ 1 + z$$

(Note that, although we have only defined N explicitly on types, we understand its extension to a functor. Using the notations introduced earlier, this functor is expressed as $N\ =\ 1^\kappa + \mathsf{Id}$.) The functor N captures the pattern of the inductive formation of the Peano naturals. The point is that we can use this to rewrite the definition of *Nat* to

data $Nat\ =\ \mathsf{in}(N\ Nat)$

Apparently, the *pattern functor* N uniquely determines the datatype *Nat*. Whenever F is a unary polynomial functor, as is the case here, a definition of the form **data** $Z\ =\ \mathsf{in}(F\ Z)$ uniquely determines Z.

We need a notation to denote the datatype Z that is obtained, and write $Z\ =\ \mu F$. So $Nat\ =\ \mu N$. Replacing Z by μF in the datatype definition, and adding a subscript to the single constructor function in in order to disambiguate it, we obtain:

$$\boxed{\textbf{data } \mu F\ =\ \mathsf{in}_F(F\ \mu F)}$$

Now in_F is a generic function, with typing

$$\mathsf{in}_F :: F\ \mu F \to \mu F$$

We can "reconstruct" the original functions zero and succ by defining:

$$\begin{aligned}
\mathsf{zero} &= \mathsf{in}_N \bullet \mathsf{inl} \ ::\ \ 1\ \to Nat \\
\mathsf{succ} &= \mathsf{in}_N \bullet \mathsf{inr} \ ::\ Nat \to Nat
\end{aligned}$$

Conversely, $\mathsf{in}_N :: N\ Nat \to Nat$ is then of course

$$\mathsf{in}_N = \mathsf{zero} \triangledown \mathsf{succ}$$

Playing the same game on the definition of *List* gives us:

data $List\ a\ =\ \mathsf{in}(1\ +\ (a \times List\ a))$

Replacing the datatype being defined, *List a*, systematically by z, we obtain the "equation"

data $z\ =\ \mathsf{in}(1\ +\ (a \times z))$

Thus, we see that the pattern functor here is $(z \mapsto 1\ +\ (a \times z))$. It has a parameter a, which we make explicit by putting

$$L\, a \;=\; (z \mapsto 1 + (a \times z))$$

Now $List\, a \;=\; \mu(L\, a)$, or, abstracting from a:

$$List \;=\; (a \mapsto \mu(L\, a))$$

Exercise 2.12 What is the pattern functor for Bin? Is it polynomial? What is the pattern functor for Rose? Is it polynomial?

□

F-algebras Before we traded in the names of the constructor functions for the uniform 'in', we saw that the algebra naturally corresponding to the datatype *Nat*, together with the generic algebra of its class, were:

$$(Nat, \text{zero}, \text{succ}), \quad \text{with} \;\; \text{zero} :: 1 \rightarrow Nat, \;\; \text{succ} :: Nat \rightarrow Nat$$
$$(\;A\;,\; e\;,\; f\;), \quad \text{with} \quad e \;:: 1 \rightarrow A\;, \quad f\;:: A \;\rightarrow A$$

Using 'in', this should be replaced by:

$$(Nat, \text{in}_N), \quad \text{with} \;\; \text{in}_N :: 1 + Nat \rightarrow Nat$$
$$(\;A\;,\; \varphi\;), \quad \text{with} \quad \varphi \;:: 1 + A \;\rightarrow A$$

in which the relation between φ and the pair (e, f) is, of course,

$$\varphi = e \triangledown f$$
$$e = \varphi \bullet \text{inl}$$
$$f = \varphi \bullet \text{inr}$$

Using the pattern functor N, we can also write:

$$(Nat, \text{in}_N), \quad \text{with} \;\; \text{in}_N :: N\, Nat \rightarrow Nat$$
$$(\;A\;,\; \varphi\;), \quad \text{with} \quad \varphi \;:: N\, A \;\rightarrow A$$

In general, for a functor F, an algebra (A, φ) with $\varphi :: FA \rightarrow A$ is called an *F-algebra* and A is called the *carrier* of the algebra. So *Nat* is the carrier of an N-algebra, and likewise *List a* is the carrier of an $(L\, a)$-algebra.

Catamorphisms In the class of F-algebras, a homomorphism $h :: (A, \varphi) \rightarrow (B, \psi)$ is a function $h :: A \rightarrow B$ that satisfies:

$$h \bullet \varphi = \psi \bullet Fh$$

This can be expressed in a diagram:

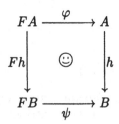

The smiley face signifies that the diagram *commutes*: the two paths from FA to B are equivalent.

A specific example of such a diagram is given by the homomorphism even from the natural numbers to the booleans:

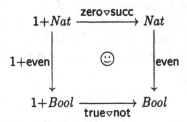

which expresses the equation

$$\text{even} \bullet (\text{zero} \triangledown \text{succ}) \;=\; (\text{true} \triangledown \text{not}) \bullet (1 + \text{even}) \;.$$

Rather than use such a diagram, the standard way of defining a function on an inductive datatype is by "pattern matching" on the argument, giving a clause for each constructor function. For the naturals, the typical definition has this form:

data Nat = zero | succ Nat

$$
\begin{aligned}
h\ \text{zero} \quad &= \; e \\
h\ (\text{succ } n) &= \; f\ (h\ n)
\end{aligned}
$$

For example, the function even is defined by the equations:

$$
\begin{aligned}
\text{even zero} \quad &= \; \text{true} \\
\text{even } (\text{succ } n) &= \; \text{not } (\text{even } n)
\end{aligned}
$$

(Exercise 2.13 asks you to show that these two equations are equivalent to the commuting diagram above.) For lists, the typical pattern-matching has the form:

data $List\ a$ = nil | cons a $(List\ a)$

$$
\begin{aligned}
h\ \text{nil} \quad\quad\ &= \; e \\
h\ (\text{cons } x\ xs) &= \; x \oplus h\ xs
\end{aligned}
$$

In these definitions, the function being defined, h, is "pushed down" recursively to the components to which the constructor functions are applied. The effect is to replace the constructor functions by the corresponding arguments in the definition of h — in the case of the natural numbers, zero is replaced by e and succ is replaced by f, and in the case of lists nil is replaced by e and cons is replaced by $\oplus$.

For the naturals, the function h defined above is determined *uniquely* by e and f. Likewise, for lists, h is *uniquely* determined by e and $\oplus$, and there is a standard notation for the function thus defined, namely foldr $\oplus$ e. Generalizing this, we get the following:

$$\mathbf{data}\ \mu F\ =\ \mathrm{in}_F(F\ \mu F)$$

$$h\,(\mathrm{in}_F x)\ =\ \varphi\,((F\,h)\,x)$$

in which simple typing considerations show that φ has to have a typing of the form $FA \to A$, and then h has the typing $\mu F \to A$; in other words, φ is the operation of some F-algebra whose carrier is the target type of h. The function h thus defined is uniquely determined by φ. We call such functions *catamorphisms* and use the following notation: $h = (\![\varphi]\!)$. So $(\![\_]\!)$ is defined by:

$$(\![\varphi]\!)\ =\ h\ \mathbf{where}$$
$$h\,(\mathrm{in}_F x)\ =\ \varphi\,((F\,h)\,x)$$

In words, when catamorphism $(\![\varphi]\!)$ is applied to a structure of type μF, this means it is applied recursively to the components of the structure, and the results are combined by applying its "body" φ. Specialised to lists, the $(\![\_]\!)$-combinator becomes foldr restricted to finite lists. The importance of having generic catamorphisms is that they embody a closed expression for a familiar inductive definition technique and thereby allow the generic expression of important programming rules.

Exercise 2.13   Show that the single equation

$$\mathsf{even} \bullet \mathsf{zero}\triangledown\mathsf{succ}\ =\ \mathsf{true}\triangledown\mathsf{not} \bullet 1{+}\mathsf{even}$$

is equivalent to the two equations

$$\mathsf{even\ zero}\qquad =\ \mathsf{true}$$
$$\mathsf{even\,(succ}\ n)\ =\ \mathsf{not\,(even}\ n)\quad .$$

□

Initial Algebras Catamorphisms enjoy a number of attractive calculational properties which we now discuss.

We start with giving the *typing rule* for $(\![\_]\!)$:

$$\frac{\varphi\ ::\ Fa \to a}{(\![\varphi]\!)\ ::\ \mu F \to a}$$

Taking the definition

$$h\,(\mathrm{in}_F x)\ =\ \varphi\,((F\,h)\,x)$$

we can rewrite this equivalently as:

$$(h{\bullet}\mathrm{in}_F)\,x\ =\ (\varphi \bullet F\,h)\,x$$

or, abstracting from x:

$$h \bullet \mathrm{in}_F\ =\ \varphi \bullet F\,h$$

This functional equation in h has a unique solution, so we conclude that $(\![\varphi]\!)$ is *characterised* by

$$\boxed{h = (\![\varphi]\!) \;\equiv\; h \cdot \mathrm{in}_F \;=\; \varphi \cdot Fh}$$

The right-hand side of this equivalence states that h is a homomorphism, and if A is the carrier of φ, we can also express this characterisation as:

$$h = (\![\varphi]\!) \;\equiv\; h :: (\mu F, \mathrm{in}_F) \to (A, \varphi)$$

In words, every F-algebra is the target algebra of a unique homomorphism with $(\mu F, \mathrm{in}_F)$ as its source algebra, and the catamorphisms consist of these unique homomorphisms. Source algebras that have the property that there is a unique homomorphism to any target algebra are known as *initial algebras*. So $(\mu F, \mathrm{in}_F)$ is an initial algebra. It is easy to prove that all initial algebras in a given algebra class are isomorphic.

The following diagram expresses the fact that $(\![\varphi]\!) :: (\mu F, \mathrm{in}) \to (A, \varphi)$ (but not the uniqueness):

$$
\begin{array}{ccc}
F\,\mu F & \xrightarrow{\ \ \mathrm{in}\ \ } & \mu F \\[2pt]
\Big\downarrow{\scriptstyle F(\![\varphi]\!)} & \ \ \ \smiley & \Big\downarrow{\scriptstyle (\![\varphi]\!)} \\[2pt]
F A & \xrightarrow[\ \varphi\ ]{} & A
\end{array}
$$

In formula form we get the *computation rule* for catamorphisms:

$$\boxed{(\![\varphi]\!) \cdot \mathrm{in} \;=\; \varphi \cdot F(\![\varphi]\!)}$$

The function in is itself an F-algebra, so $(\![\mathrm{in}]\!)$ is defined. What is it? By substituting $(A, \varphi) := (\mu F, \mathrm{in})$ in the last equivalence above, we obtain:

$$h = (\![\mathrm{in}]\!) \;\equiv\; h :: (\mu F, \mathrm{in}) \to (\mu F, \mathrm{in})$$

But we know that $\mathrm{id} :: (\mu F, \mathrm{in}) \to (\mu F, \mathrm{in})$! The conclusion is the *identity rule* for catamorphisms:

$$\boxed{(\![\mathrm{in}]\!) = \mathrm{id}_{\mu F}}$$

This generalises the equality for lists: foldr cons nil $=$ id.

Further properties of catamorphisms The identity rule is easy to remember if one thinks of a catamorphism as a function that replaces the constructor functions of the datatype by the supplied arguments. Thus foldr cons nil is the identity function on lists because cons is replaced by cons and nil is replaced by nil. In general, $([in])$ replaces all occurrences of in by itself in an element of the datatype μF.

The identity rule is surprisingly important. As an illustration of its importance, we prove that in is a bijection between μF and $F\mu F$. That is, we use the rule to construct a function out of type $\mu F \to F\mu F$ such that in•out $= \mathrm{id}_{\mu F}$ and out•in $= \mathrm{id}_{F\mu F}$. Our calculation starts with the first requirement and derives a candidate for out in a systematic way:

$$in\bullet out = \mathrm{id}_{\mu F}$$
$$\equiv \qquad \{ \qquad \text{identity rule} \quad \}$$
$$in\bullet out = ([in])$$
$$\equiv \qquad \{ \qquad \text{catamorphism characterisation} \quad \}$$
$$in\bullet out\bullet in = in\bullet F(in\bullet out)$$
$$\Leftarrow \qquad \{ \qquad \text{cancel in• from both sides} \quad \}$$
$$out\bullet in = F(in\bullet out)$$
$$\equiv \qquad \{ \qquad F \text{ respects composition} \quad \}$$
$$out\bullet in = F in \bullet F out$$
$$\equiv \qquad \{ \qquad \text{catamorphism characterisation} \quad \}$$
$$out = ([F in]) \ .$$

This completes the first step in the calculation: we have derived the candidate $([F in])$ for out.

Note that the identity rule is not used to *simplify* $([in])$ to $\mathrm{id}_{\mu F}$ in this calculation; rather, it is used in quite the opposite way to *complicate* $\mathrm{id}_{\mu F}$ to $([in])$. There is a tendency to view algebraic properties as left-to-right rewrite rules, where the left side is the complicated side and the right side is its simplified form. Calculations that use the rules in this way are straightforward and do not require insight. On the other hand, calculations (such as the one above) which include at least one complication step are relatively difficult and do require insight. The importance of the identity rule for catamorphisms is its use in introducing a catamorphism into a calculation (see also the MAG system [38], in which identity catamorphisms are introduced in calculations in order to be able to apply fusion). It can require ingenuity to use because it involves replacing an identity function which is not visible. That is, a step in a calculation may involve replacing some composition $f\bullet g$ by $f\bullet([in])\bullet g$, the invisible intermediate step being to replace $f\bullet g$ by $f\bullet \mathrm{id}_{\mu F}\bullet g$. This is valid if f has source μF (equivalently, g has target μF) so it is important to be aware of the types of the quantities involved.

To complete the calculation we have to check that the candidate $([F in])$ we have derived for out satisfies the second requirement on out. That is, we have to verify that $([Fin])\bullet\text{in} = \text{id}_{F_\mu F}$. This is an exercise in the use of the computation rule which we leave to the reader (specifically, exercise 2.14).

As another illustration of the use of the properties of catamorphisms we derive a condition under which it is possible to fuse a post-composed function with a catamorphism. The goal of the calculation is to eliminate the catamorphism brackets from the equation.

$$h\bullet([\varphi]) = ([\psi])$$
$$\equiv \qquad \{ \qquad \text{characterisation of } ([\psi]) \quad \}$$
$$h\bullet([\varphi])\bullet\text{in} = \psi\bullet F(h\bullet([\varphi]))$$
$$\equiv \qquad \{ \qquad \text{computation rule for } ([\varphi]) \quad \}$$
$$h\bullet\varphi\bullet F([\varphi]) = \psi\bullet F(h\bullet([\varphi]))$$
$$\equiv \qquad \{ \qquad F \text{ respects composition} \quad \}$$
$$h\bullet\varphi\bullet F([\varphi]) = \psi\bullet Fh\bullet F([\varphi])$$
$$\Leftarrow \qquad \{ \qquad \text{cancel } \bullet F([\varphi]) \text{ from both sides} \quad \}$$
$$h\bullet\varphi = \psi\bullet Fh \ .$$

So we have derived the $([\_])$-*fusion rule*:

$$\boxed{h\bullet([\varphi]) \ = \ ([\psi]) \quad \Leftarrow \quad h\bullet\varphi \ = \ \psi\bullet Fh}$$

Note that the condition states that h is a homomorphism. So the rule states that composing a homomorphism after a catamorphism is a catamorphism.

The way this rule is typically used is that we want to fuse a given function h into a given catamorphism $([\varphi])$, for example to improve efficiency. In order to do so, we try to solve the equation $h\bullet\varphi = \psi\bullet Fh$ for the unknown ψ. If we find a solution, we know that the answer is $([\psi])$.

An example We show this in action on a simple example: sum•concat on lists of lists of numbers. Recall that the pattern functor of *List Nat* is

$$L \ Nat \ = \ (z \mapsto 1 + (Nat \times z)) \quad .$$

By definition, concat = $([\text{nil} \triangledown (+\!\!\!+)])$, so we try to fuse sum and concat into a catamorphism. Applying the fusion rule we have:

$$\text{sum•concat} = ([\psi])$$
$$\Leftarrow \qquad \{ \qquad \text{concat} = ([\text{nil} \triangledown (+\!\!\!+)]), \text{ fusion} \quad \}$$
$$\text{sum} \bullet \text{nil} \triangledown (+\!\!\!+) \ = \ \psi \bullet (L \ Nat) \ \text{sum} \ .$$

Now, the pattern functor $(L \ Nat)$ is a disjoint sum of two functors. Also, the composition on the left side can be fused together:

$$\text{sum} \bullet \text{nil} \triangledown (+\!\!\!+)$$
$$= \qquad \{ \qquad \triangledown \text{ fusion} \quad \}$$
$$(\text{sum} \bullet \text{nil}) \triangledown (\text{sum} \bullet (+\!\!\!+)) \quad .$$

This suggests that we should try instantiating ψ to $\alpha\triangledown\beta$ for some α and β. In this way, we get:

$$\mathsf{sum}\bullet\mathsf{concat} = (\!|\psi|\!)$$

$\Leftarrow$ { two steps above, definition of $(L\ Nat)$ }

$$(\mathsf{sum}\bullet\mathsf{nil})\triangledown(\mathsf{sum}\bullet(\text{++})) = \psi\bullet(\mathsf{id}+(\mathsf{id}\times\mathsf{sum}))$$

$\equiv$ { postulate $\psi=\alpha\triangledown\beta$, fusion }

$$(\mathsf{sum}\bullet\mathsf{nil})\triangledown(\mathsf{sum}\bullet(\text{++})) = (\alpha\bullet\mathsf{id})\triangledown(\beta\bullet\mathsf{id}\times\mathsf{sum})$$

$\equiv$ { $\triangledown$ is injective, simplification }

$$\mathsf{sum}\bullet\mathsf{nil} = \alpha \wedge \mathsf{sum}\bullet(\text{++}) = \beta\bullet\mathsf{id}\times\mathsf{sum}\ .$$

We now continue with each conjunct in turn. The first conjunct is easy, we have: $\mathsf{sum}\bullet\mathsf{nil} = \mathsf{zero}$. For the second conjunct, we have:

$$\mathsf{sum}\bullet(\text{++})$$

$=$ { property of summation }

$$(+)\bullet\mathsf{sum}\times\mathsf{sum}$$

$=$ { $\times$ is a binary functor }

$$(+)\bullet\mathsf{sum}\times\mathsf{id}\bullet\mathsf{id}\times\mathsf{sum}\ .$$

And thus we have found that the function $\beta = (+)\bullet\mathsf{sum}\times\mathsf{id}$ satisfies the equality $\mathsf{sum}\bullet(\text{++}) = \beta\bullet\mathsf{id}\times\mathsf{sum}$.

Combining everything, we have found that

$$\mathsf{sum}\bullet\mathsf{concat} = (\!|\mathsf{zero}\triangledown((+)\bullet\mathsf{sum}\times\mathsf{id})|\!)$$

or, expressed in a more familiar sty le:

$$\mathsf{sum}\bullet\mathsf{concat} = \mathbf{foldr}\odot\mathbf{0}\ \mathbf{where}$$
$$xs\odot y = \mathsf{sum}\ xs + y$$

This derivation was not generic but specific for lists of lists. Meertens [37] shows how to do this generically, and also that the generic solution is no more complicated to obtain than this specific one, whilst being much more general.

Exercise 2.14 We calculated above that $\mathsf{out} = (\!|F\ \mathsf{in}|\!)$ satisfies $\mathsf{in}\bullet\mathsf{out} = \mathsf{id}_{\mu F}$. Verify that $\mathsf{out}\bullet\mathsf{in} = \mathsf{id}_{F\mu F}$.

□

Exercise 2.15 Suppose that (A,φ) is an initial F-algebra. Prove that (A,φ) is isomorphic to $(\mu F,\mathsf{in}_F)$. *Hint.* Consider the unique homomorphism h of type $h::(A,\varphi)\to(\mu F,\mathsf{in}_F)$.

□

Exercise 2.16   Consider the datatype *Bin a* for some arbitrary type *a*. The pattern functor for this type is *F* where $Ff = id_a + (f \times f)$. Catamorphisms over this type take the form $([f \triangledown \odot])$ where *f* is a function and $\odot$ is a binary operator.

Define a catamorphism that counts the number of tips in a *Bin*. Define, in addition, a catamorphism that counts the number of joins in a *Bin*. Use the fusion rule for catamorphisms to determine a relation between the number of tips and the number of joins in a *Bin*. That is, derive the definition of a function *f* such that

$$f \cdot NoOfTips = NoOfJoins .$$

□

Banana split   In this subsection we demonstrate the beauty of generic programming. We solve the following problem. Suppose we have two catamorphisms $([f])$ :: $\mu F \to a$ and $([g])$ :: $\mu F \to b$, and we want to have a function that returns the combined result of both. One solution is the program $([f]) \vartriangle ([g])$, but this can be inefficient since, computationally, the source data value is traversed twice, once for each of the two catamorphisms. So the question we want to solve is: can we combine these two into a single catamorphism $([\chi])$?

This generic problem is motivated by our knowledge of specific cases. Take, for example, the problem of finding both the sum and the product of a list of numbers. The sum can of course be expressed as a catamorphism —it is the catamorphism $([0 \triangledown add])$, where add is ordinary addition of real numbers—. Similarly the product function is a catamorphism, namely $([1 \triangledown mul])$, where mul is the ordinary multiplication of real numbers. Equally obvious is that it should be possible to combine the sum and product of a list of numbers into one catamorphism. After all, the function $sp = sum \vartriangle product$ is straightforward to express as a fold in Haskell:

$$
\begin{aligned}
sp \;=\; & \textbf{foldr } \odot \; e \textbf{ where} \\
& x \odot (u, v) = (x + u, \; x \times v) \\
& e \qquad\quad = (0, 1)
\end{aligned}
$$

We can try to derive this special case in our calculus but more effective is to derive the solution to the generic problem. The benefit is not only that we then have a very general result that can be instantiated in lots of ways (one of which is the sum△product problem), but also that the derivation is much simpler because it omits irrelevant detail.

We begin the calculation of χ as follows:

$$([f]) \vartriangle ([g]) \;=\; ([\chi])$$

$\equiv$ {   There is a choice here. We can either use the

     characterisation of $([\chi])$ or the characterisation

     of $f \vartriangle g$. For no good reason, we choose the latter. }

$$([f]) \;=\; exl \cdot ([\chi]) \quad \wedge \quad ([g]) \;=\; exr \cdot ([\chi]) .$$

This first step involves a difficult choice. At this point in time there is no reason why the use of one characterisation is preferable to the other (since both are equivalences). In fact, choosing to use the characterisation of $(\![\chi]\!)$ first does lead to a successful calculation of χ of a similar length. We leave it as an exercise.

We now have to satisfy two conjuncts. Since the two conjuncts are symmetrical we proceed with just the first.

$$
\begin{aligned}
& (\![f]\!) \;=\; \text{exl} \bullet (\![\chi]\!) \\
\Leftarrow \quad & \{ \quad \text{Fusion} \quad \} \\
& f \bullet F\text{exl} \;=\; \text{exl} \bullet \chi \\
\equiv \quad & \{ \quad \bullet \quad \chi := \alpha \triangle \beta . \quad \} \\
& f \bullet F\text{exl} \;=\; \text{exl} \bullet \alpha \triangle \beta \\
\equiv \quad & \{ \quad \triangle \text{ computation} \quad \} \\
& f \bullet F\text{exl} \;=\; \alpha \; .
\end{aligned}
$$

The crucial step here (indicated by the bullet) is where we postulate the form of the solution, the motivation being the step that immediately follows.

In summary we have calculated that

$$(\![f]\!) \;=\; \text{exl} \bullet (\![\chi]\!) \quad \Leftarrow \quad \chi = \alpha \triangle \beta \;\wedge\; \alpha = f \bullet F\text{exl} \; .$$

Similarly,

$$(\![g]\!) \;=\; \text{exr} \bullet (\![\chi]\!) \quad \Leftarrow \quad \chi = \alpha \triangle \beta \;\wedge\; \beta = g \bullet F\text{exr} \; .$$

Putting everything together, we conclude that

$$(\![f]\!) \triangle (\![g]\!) \;=\; (\![(f \bullet F\text{exl}) \triangle (g \bullet F\text{exr})]\!) \; .$$

This is affectionately called the *banana-split* theorem (because the brackets denoting a catamorphism look like bananas, and the $\triangle$ operator is pronounced "split").

Exercise 2.17   Calculate χ but start by using the characterisation of $(\![f]\!)$. In other words, calculate χ as a solution of the equation

$$(\![f]\!) \triangle (\![g]\!) \bullet \text{in} \;=\; \chi \bullet F((\![f]\!) \triangle (\![g]\!)) \; .$$

(You may find that you get a solution that is equivalent to the one above but not syntactically identical.)

□

Type functors In general, a binary functor gives rise to a new functor by a combination of parameterisation and constructing an initial algebra. For example, the binary pattern functor L that maps x and y to $1+(x{\times}y)$ gives rise to the functor *List*. Such functors are called *type functors*. Here we show how this is done.

For greater clarity we will use an infix notation for binary functors. Suppose that $\oslash$ is a binary functor, which we write as an infix operator. That is, for types a and b, $a\oslash b$ is a type and, for functions $f :: a{\to}b$ and $g :: c{\to}d$, $f\oslash g$ is a function of type $a\oslash c \to b\oslash d$. Suppose a is an arbitrary type. Then the pair of mappings $b \mapsto a\oslash b$ and $f \mapsto \mathrm{id}_a\oslash f$ is a functor (the functor formed by specialising the first operand of $\oslash$ to the type a). We denote this functor by $(a\oslash)$ and call it a *parameterised* functor.

Now, since $(a\oslash)$ is a unary functor, we can consider an initial $(a\oslash)$-algebra with carrier $\mu(a\oslash)$. Abstracting from a we have constructed a mapping from types to types. Let us introduce a special notation for this mapping:

$$\boxed{\tau(\oslash) \;=\; (a \mapsto \mu(a\oslash))}$$

So *List* $= \tau(L)$, with L the binary functor defined above.

For $\tau(\oslash)$ to be a functor, we need, in addition to the action on types, an action on functions, which has to satisfy, for a function $f :: a \to b$,

$$\tau(\oslash)\, f \;::\; \tau(\oslash)\, a \to \tau(\oslash)\, b \;.$$

We derive a candidate for $\tau(\oslash)\, f$ from type considerations. In the calculation, catamorphisms are $(a\oslash)$ catamorphisms and $\mathrm{in}_{b\oslash}$ is an initial $(b\oslash)$-algebra.

$$
\begin{array}{lll}
& \tau(\oslash)\, f \;::\; \tau(\oslash)\, a \to \tau(\oslash)\, b & \\
\equiv & \{ \qquad \text{definition of } \tau(\oslash) \text{ on types } \} & \\
& \tau(\oslash)\, f \;::\; \mu(a\oslash) \to \mu(b\oslash) & \\
\Leftarrow & \{ \quad \bullet \quad \tau(\oslash)\, f \;:=\; (\!|\varphi|\!) \,, \text{ typing rule for } (\!|\_|\!) \;\} & \\
& \varphi \;::\; a \oslash \mu(b\oslash) \to \mu(b\oslash) & \\
\Leftarrow & \{ \quad \bullet \quad \varphi := \mathrm{in}_{b\oslash} \bullet \psi \,, \text{ type of in } \} & \\
& \psi \;::\; a \oslash \mu(b\oslash) \to b \oslash \mu(b\oslash) & \\
\Leftarrow & \{ \quad f :: a{\to}b, \quad \mathrm{id}_{\mu(b\oslash)} \;::\; \mu(b\oslash) \to \mu(b\oslash), & \\
& \qquad \oslash \text{ respects typing } \} & \\
& \psi \;=\; f \oslash \mathrm{id}_{\mu(b\oslash)} \;. &
\end{array}
$$

Performing the collected substitutions gives us this candidate definition

$$\boxed{\tau(\oslash)\, f \;=\; (\!|\,\mathrm{in}_{b\oslash} \bullet (f \oslash \mathrm{id}_{\mu(b\oslash)})\,|\!)}$$

Exercise 2.20 is to show that $\tau(\oslash)$ respects composition and identities. According to the notational convention introduced earlier the action of $\tau(\oslash)$ on functions can also be written $\mathsf{map}_{\tau(\oslash)}$.

A final comment: The parameter a in a parameterised functor may actually be an n-tuple if functor $\oslash$ is $(n+1)$-ary, and then $\tau(\oslash)$ is an n-ary functor. However, we only consider unary type functors, derived with $\tau(\oslash)$ from binary functors in these lectures.

Exercise 2.18 Consider the datatype $Bool = \mu((1+1)^\kappa)$. Define $false = \mathsf{in}_{Bool}\bullet\mathsf{inl}$, $true = \mathsf{in}_{Bool}\bullet\mathsf{inr}$. Examine and explain the meaning of the catamorphism $(\!|u\triangledown v|\!)$ for $Bool$.

□

Exercise 2.19 (cata-map fusion)   Derive a fusion rule of the form

$$(\!|f|\!) \bullet (\tau(\oslash)\, g) = (\!|h|\!) \ .$$

Hint: instantiate the fusion rule for catamorphisms with $F := (b\oslash)$. Note also that $\tau(\oslash)g$ is a catamorphism.

□

Exercise 2.20   Complete the verification of the fact that $\tau(\oslash)$ is a functor by showing that $\tau(\oslash)\ \mathsf{id}_a = \mathsf{id}_{\tau(\oslash)a}$ and $\tau(\oslash)\ (f\bullet g) = (\tau(\oslash)\ f) \bullet (\tau(\oslash)\ g)$. (Hint: make use of exercise 2.19.)

□

Exercise 2.21 Specialise the definition of $\tau(\oslash)f$ for $\oslash = L$, the bifunctor giving the type functor $List = \tau(L)$, using $\mathsf{in} = \mathsf{nil}\triangledown\mathsf{cons}$, and verify that this is the familiar map function for lists. Also, instantiate your solution to exercise 2.19 and use it to express the sum of the squares of a list of numbers as a catamorphism. (That is, express the sum of a list of numbers as a catamorphism, and the list of squares of a list on numbers as a map. Then fuse the two functions together.)

□

Regular Functors and Datatypes We are now in a position to complete our discussion of the datatypes introduced in section 2.2 by giving a complete analysis of the definition of the Rose datatype. As we saw in exercise 2.12, its pattern functor is $a\oslash z = a\times(List\ z)$, or, in terms of the extraction functors Par and Rec, $(\oslash) = \mathsf{Par}\times(List\ \mathsf{Rec})$, which is not a polynomial functor, because of the appearance of the type functor $List$. Yet $\tau(\oslash)$ is well defined. Incorporating type functors into the ways of constructing functors extends the class of polynomial functors to the class of *regular* functors.

A functor built only from constants, extractions, sums, products, composition and $\tau()$ is called a *regular* functor. All the datatypes we have seen, including $List$ and $Rose$ are regular functors, and their constructor functions (combined together using the $\triangledown$ combinator) are initial algebras with respect to the pattern functors of the datatype.

This concludes the theory development. We have shown precisely what it means to say that a datatype is both an algebra and a functor.

2.5 A Simple Polytypic Program

We began section 2.2 with four representative examples of datatypes: *List*, *Maybe*, *Bin* and *Rose*. For each of these datatypes we can define a summation function that sums all the values stored in an instance of the datatype — assuming the values are numbers. Here is how one would do that in a non-generic programming style.

$$
\begin{aligned}
\text{sum}_{List} \quad &\text{nil} &=\;& 0 \\
\text{sum}_{List} \quad &(\text{cons } u \; us) &=\;& u \; + \; \text{sum}_{List} \; us \\[6pt]
\text{sum}_{Maybe} \; &\text{none} &=\;& 0 \\
\text{sum}_{Maybe} \; &(\text{one } u) &=\;& u \\[6pt]
\text{sum}_{Bin} \quad &(\text{tip } u) &=\;& u \\
\text{sum}_{Bin} \quad &(\text{join } x \; y) &=\;& \text{sum}_{Bin} \; x \; + \; \text{sum}_{Bin} \; y \\[6pt]
\text{sum}_{Rose} \; &(\text{fork } u \; rs) &=\;& u \; + \; \text{sum}_{List} \; (\text{map}_{List} \; \text{sum}_{Rose} \; rs)
\end{aligned}
$$

We now want to replace all these definitions by a single generic definition sum_F for arbitrary unary functor F, which can be specialised to any of the above datatype constructors and many more by taking F to be *List*, *Maybe*, *Bin*, and so on. We do this by induction on the structure of the regular functors. That is, we define summation for a constant functor, for the extraction functors, for the composition of functors, for disjoint sum and cartesian product, and finally for a type functor. Let us begin with the type functors since this is where we see how to formulate the induction hypothesis.

For the type functor $\tau(\oslash)$, the requirement is to construct a function $\text{sum}_{\tau(\oslash)}$ of type $\mu(\mathbf{N}\oslash) \to \mathbf{N}$. The obvious thing to do here is to define sum as a catamorphism, $(\!(f)\!)$ say. In that case, the type requirement on f is that $f \;::\; \mathbf{N}\oslash\mathbf{N} \to \mathbf{N}$. Note that the two arguments to the binary functor $\oslash$ are both $\mathbf{N}$. This suggests the inductive hypothesis that there is a sum function of type $F \, \mathbf{N} \to \mathbf{N}$ for all unary regular functors F obtained from an arbitrary non-constant n-ary regular functor by copying the (single) argument n times. We also need to define sum for the constant functor 1. With this preparation, we can begin the analysis.

For the constant functor 1, we define

$$\text{sum}_1 \;=\; 0 \; .$$

This is because the sum of zero numbers is zero.

For the extraction functors, it is clear that

$$\text{sum}_{\text{Ex}} \;=\; \text{id}_{\mathbf{N}}$$

since the sum of a single number is that number itself.

For disjoint sum and cartesian product, we have:

$$\mathsf{sum}_{F+G} \quad = \quad \mathsf{sum}_F \triangledown \mathsf{sum}_G$$
$$\mathsf{sum}_{F\times G}\ (x,y) \quad = \quad \mathsf{sum}_F\ x + \mathsf{sum}_G\ y \ .$$

In the case of disjoint sum, either the sum_F function has to be applied, or the sum_G function, depending on the type of the argument. In the case of cartesian product, an element of an $F \times G$ structure is a pair consisting of an element of an F structure and an element of a G structure, and the two sums have to be added together.

For the composition of two functors, we have:

$$\mathsf{sum}_{FG} \quad = \quad \mathsf{sum}_F \bullet F\mathsf{sum}_G \ .$$

Here the argument is that an FG structure is an F structure of G structures.

The function $F\mathsf{sum}_G$ applies sum_G to all the individual G structures, and then sum_F adds their values.

The final case is a type functor, which we have already discussed.

$$\mathsf{sum}_{\tau(\oslash)} \quad = \quad (\!|\mathsf{sum}_\oslash|\!) \ .$$

We leave it to the reader to check that application of the above rules results in the particular instances of sum given above.

3   PolyP

The previous chapter introduces datatypes and functions on datatypes such as the catamorphism. The formal language used to introduce datatypes and functions is the language of category theory. The language of category theory is not a programming language, and although the accompanying text mentions programming, it is impossible to 'run' catamorphisms. This chapter introduces PolyP, a programming language with which generic functions such as the catamorphism can be implemented. The name of PolyP is derived from 'polytypic programming', an alternative name for generic programming.

PolyP is an extension of (a subset of) the functional programming language Haskell. The extension consists of a new kind of top level definition: the `polytypic` construct, which is used to define functions by induction over pattern functors, which describe the structure of (a subset of) regular datatypes. PolyP is based on the initial algebra approach to datatypes and work in the Squiggol community on datatypes. It is a tool that supports polytypic programming, and as such it has spurred the development of new polytypic programs.

In Haskell, datatypes are defined by means of the `data` construct, examples of which have been given in chapter 2. PolyP extracts the pattern functor from a datatype definition, and uses this structure information to instantiate generic programs on particular datatypes. We will use the name *polytypic function* for a generic program in PolyP.

PolyP has a number of limitations. The datatypes PolyP can handle are a subset of the datatypes induced by the regular functors defined in the previous chapter: PolyP's pattern functors are binary and the type functors are unary which means that it can only handle datatypes with one type argument. Furthermore, datatypes cannot be mutually recursive.

Information about PolyP and polytypic programming in general can be found on

http://www.cs.chalmers.se/~patrikj/poly/

The names of pattern functors in PolyP differ slightly from the names in the previous chapter. Section 3.1 introduces PolyP's functor names. Section 3.2 gives an implementation of the polytypic function sum from section 2.5. Section 3.3 defines most of the basic polytypic concepts. Type checking of polytypic functions is explained in section 3.4. Since we will use a number of polytypic functions in the rest of these notes, section 3.5 gives more examples of polytypic functions, and section 3.6 introduces PolyLib: a library of polytypic functions.

3.1   Regular Functors in PolyP

The previous chapter explains how datatypes are defined by means of pattern functors. A pattern functor is a regular functor, i.e., a polynomial functor possibly extended with a type functor. PolyP defines polytypic functions by induction over the pattern functor of a datatype. The names for the pattern functors constructors used in PolyP differs slightly from the names in the previous chapter. This section defines the syntax for pattern functors used in PolyP.

PolyP's functors are specified by the following context-free grammar:

```
f,g  ::=  f + g | f * g | Empty | Par | Rec | d @ g | Const t
```

The following table relates this syntax to the functors introduced in the previous chapter.

+	*	Empty	Par	Rec	d @ g	Const t
+	×	1^K	exl	exr	$a \mapsto b \mapsto d(g\ a\ b)$	t^K

+ and * are the standard sum and product functors lifted to act on functors. Empty is the constant binary version of functor 1^K. Par and Rec are mentioned in chapter 2, and are exl and exr, respectively. Composition of functors d and g is denoted by d @ g and is only defined for a unary functor d and a binary functor g. Finally, Const t is the binary variant of t^K. The t stands for a monotype such as Bool, Char or (Int,[Float]).

In PolyP, as in Haskell, type functors (recursive datatypes) are introduced by the **data** construct. Every Haskell datatype constructor d is equal to $\tau(f)$ for some pattern functor f. In PolyP this f is denoted by FunctorOf d. A datatype d a is regular (satisfies `Regular d`) if it contains no function spaces, and if the argument of the type constructor d is the same on the left- and right-hand side of its definition. For each one parameter regular datatype d a, PolyP automatically generates `FunctorOf d` using roughly the same steps as those used manually in section 2.4. For example, for

```
data Error a  =  Error String | Ok a
data List a   =  Nil | Cons a (List a)
data Bin a    =  Tip a | Join (Bin a) (Bin a)
data Rose a   =  Fork a (List (Rose a))
```

PolyP generates the following functors:

```
FunctorOf Error  =  Const String + Par
FunctorOf List   =  Empty + Par * Rec
FunctorOf Bin    =  Par + Rec * Rec
FunctorOf Rose   =  Par * (List @ Rec)
```

Pattern functors are *only* constructed for datatypes defined by means of the data construct. If somewhere in a program a polytypic function is applied to a value of type Error (List a), PolyP will generate an instance of the polytypic function on the datatype Error b, not on the type (Error @ List) a. This also implies that the functor d in the functor composition d @ g is always a type functor.

3.2   An Example: psum

PolyP introduces a new construct `polytypic` for defining polytypic functions by induction on the structure of a binary pattern functor:

$$\texttt{polytypic p :: t = case f of \{fi -> ei\}}$$

where p is the name of the value being defined, t is its type, f is a functor variable, fi are functor patterns and ei are PolyP expressions. The explicit type in the `polytypic` construct is needed since we cannot in general infer the type from the cases.

The informal meaning is that we define a function that takes (a representation of) a pattern functor as its first argument. This function selects the expression in the first branch of the case matching the functor, and the expression may in turn use the polytypic function (on subfunctors). Thus the polytypic construct is a (recursive) template for constructing instances of polytypic functions given the pattern functor of a datatype. The functor argument of the polytypic function need not (and cannot) be supplied explicitly but is inserted by the compiler during type inference.

As an example we take the function psum defined in figure 1. (The subscripts indicating the type are included for readability and are not part of the defin-ition.) Function psum sums the integers in a structure with integers. It is the

```
        psum_d :: Regular d => d Int -> Int
        psum_d = cata_d fsum_FunctorOf d

        polytypic fsum_f :: f Int Int -> Int
            = case f of
                g + h    -> fsum_g 'either' fsum_h
                g * h    -> \(x,y) -> fsum_g x + fsum_h y
                Empty    -> \x -> 0
                Par      -> id
                Rec      -> id
                d @ g    -> psum_d . (pmap_d fsum_g)
                Const t -> \x -> 0
```

Fig. 1. The definition of psum

PolyP implementation of the function sum defined in section 2.5. The function either :: (a -> c) -> (b -> c) -> Either a b -> c (corresponding to $\triangledown$) and datatype Either a b (corresponding to a+b) are defined in Haskell's prelude. The definition of functions cata and pmap (the implementations in PolyP of the catamorphism and the map, see chapter 2) will be given later. When psum is used on an element of type Bin Int, the compiler performs roughly the following rewrite steps to construct the actual instance of psum for Bin:

$$\text{psum}_{\text{Bin}} \rightarrow \text{cata}_{\text{Bin}} \text{ fsum}_{\text{FunctorOf Bin}}$$

It follows that we need an instance of cata for the type functor Bin, and an instance of function fsum for the pattern functor FunctorOf Bin = Par + Rec * Rec. For the latter instance, we use the definition of fsum to transform as follows:

$$\text{fsum}_{\text{FunctorOf Bin}} \rightarrow \text{fsum}_{\text{Par+Rec*Rec}} \rightarrow \text{fsum}_{\text{Par}} \text{ 'either' fsum}_{\text{Rec*Rec}}$$

We transform the functions fsum_{Par} and $\text{fsum}_{\text{Rec*Rec}}$ separately. For fsum_{Par} we have

$$\text{fsum}_{\text{Par}} \rightarrow \text{id}$$

and for $\text{fsum}_{\text{Rec*Rec}}$ we have

$$\text{fsum}_{\text{Rec*Rec}}$$
$$\rightarrow \backslash(x,y) \rightarrow \text{fsum}_{\text{Rec}} \ x + \text{fsum}_{\text{Rec}} \ y$$
$$\rightarrow \backslash(x,y) \rightarrow \text{id} \ x + \text{id} \ y$$

The last function can be rewritten into uncurry (+), and thus we obtain the following function for summing a tree:

$$\text{cata}_{\text{Bin}} \ (\text{id 'either' (uncurry (+)))}$$

By expanding cata_{Bin} in a similar way we obtain a Haskell function for the instance of psum on Bin. The function we obtain is the same as the function sum_{Bin} defined in section 2.5.

3.3   Basic Polytypic Functions

In the definition of function psum we used functions like cata and pmap. This subsection defines these and other basic polytypic functions.

Since polytypic functions cannot refer to constructor names of specific datatypes, we introduce the predefined functions out and inn. Function out is used in polytypic functions instead of pattern matching on the constructors of a datatype. For example out on Bin is defined as follows:

```
out_Bin :: Bin a    -> Either a (Bin a,Bin a)
out_Bin (Tip x)   = Left x
out_Bin (Join l r) = Right (l,r)
```

Function inn is the inverse of function out. It collects the constructors of a datatype into a single constructor function.

```
out :: Regular d => FunctorOf d a (d a) <- d a
inn :: Regular d => FunctorOf d a (d a) -> d a
```

Function inn is an implementation of in from chapter 2. The following calculation shows that the type of inn really corresponds to the type of in:

$$
\begin{aligned}
&\texttt{FunctorOf d a (d a) -> d a}\\
&= \{ \qquad d = \tau(f) \text{ for some regular functor } f. \}\\
&\texttt{FunctorOf } \tau(f)\texttt{ a } (\tau(f)\texttt{ a}) \texttt{ -> } \tau(f)\texttt{ a}\\
&= \{ \qquad \text{Definition of FunctorOf } \}\\
&\texttt{f a } (\tau(f)\texttt{ a}) \texttt{ -> } \tau(f)\texttt{ a}\\
&= \{ \qquad \text{Definition of } \tau() \}\\
&\texttt{f a } \mu(\texttt{f a}) \texttt{ -> } \mu(\texttt{f a})
\end{aligned}
$$

PolyP generates definitions of inn and out for all datatypes.

As explained in chapter 2, a functor is a mapping between categories that preserves the algebraic structure of the category. Since a category consists of objects (types) and arrows (functions), a functor consists of two parts: a definition on types, and a definition on functions. A pattern functor f in PolyP is a function that take two types and return a type. The part of the functor that takes two functions and returns a function is called fmap_f, see figure 2.

Using fmap we can define the polytypic version of function map, pmap, as follows:

```
pmap    :: Regular d => (a -> b) -> d a -> d b
pmap f  = inn . fmap f (pmap f) . out
```

where out takes the argument apart, fmap applies f to parameters and (pmap f) recursively to substructures and inn puts the parts back together again. Function pmap_d is the function action of the type functor d.

```
        polytypic fmap_f :: (a -> c) -> (b -> d) -> f a b -> f c d
          = \p r -> case f of
                        g + h    -> (fmap_g p r) -+- (fmap_h p r)
                        g * h    -> (fmap_g p r) -*- (fmap_h p r)
                        Empty    -> id
                        Par      -> p
                        Rec      -> r
                        d @ g    -> pmap_d (fmap_g p r)
                        Const t  -> id

    (-*-) :: (a -> c) -> (b -> d) -> (a,b) -> (c,d)
    (f -*- g) (x,y) = (f x , g y)

    (-+-) :: (a -> c) -> (b -> d) -> Either a b -> Either c d
    (f -+- g) = either (Left . f) (Right . g)
```

Fig. 2. The definition of `fmap`.

Function `cata` is also defined in terms of function `fmap`:

```
cata :: Regular d =>  (FunctorOf d a b -> b) -> (d a -> b)
cata f  =  f . fmap id (cata f) . out
```

Note that this definition is a copy of the computation rule for the catamorphism in section 2.4, with in on the left-hand side replaced by out on the right-hand side.

3.4   Type Checking Polytypic Functions

We want to be sure that functions generated by polytypic functions are type correct, so that no run-time type errors occur. For that purpose PolyP type checks definitions of polytypic functions. This subsection briefly discusses how to type check polytypic functions, the details of the type checking algorithm can be found in [25].

Functor expressions contain +, *, etc., and such expressions have to be translated to real types. For this translation we interpret functor constructors as type synonyms:

```
type (f + g) a b  =  Either (f a b) (g a b)
type (f * g) a b  =  (f a b , g a b)
type Empty a b    =  ()
type Par a b      =  a
type Rec a b      =  b
type (d @ g) a b  =  d (g a b)
type Const t a b  =  t
```

So, for example, interpreting the functors in the pattern functor for `List` as type synonyms, we have:

```
FunctorOf List a b
= {        FunctorOf List = Empty + Par * Rec }
  (Empty + Par * Rec) a b
= {        Type synonym for + }
  Either (Empty a b) ((Par * Rec) a b)
= {        Type synonyms for Empty and * }
  Either () (Par a b,Rec a b)
= {        Type synonyms for Par and Rec }
  Either () (a,b)
```

To infer the type of a polytypic definition from the types of the expressions in the `case` branches, higher-order unification would be needed. As general higher-order unification is undecidable we require inductive definitions of polytypic functions to be explicitly typed, and we only check that this type is valid. Given an inductive definition of a polytypic function

```
polytypic foo :: ... f ...
  = case f of
      g + h -> bar
      ...
```

where `f` is a functor variable, the rule for type checking these definitions checks among other things that the declared type of function `foo`, with `g + h` substituted for `f`, is an instance of the type of expression `bar`. For all of the expressions in the branches of the `case` it is required that the declared type is an instance of the type of the expression in the branch with the left-hand side of the branch substituted for `f` in the declared type. The expression `g + h` is an abstraction of a type, so by substituting `g + h` (or any of the other abstract type expressions) for `f` in the type of `foo` we mean the following: substitute `g + h` for `f`, and rewrite the expression obtained thus by interpreting the functor constructors as type synonyms. As an example we take the case `g * h` in the definition of `fsum`:

```
polytypic fsum :: f Int Int -> Int
  = case f of
      ...
      g * h  ->  \(x,y) -> fsum x + fsum y
      ...
```

The type of the expression `\(x,y) -> fsum x + fsum y` is `(r Int Int, s Int Int) -> Int`. Substituting the functor to the left of the arrow in the case branch, `g * h`, for `f` in the declared type `f Int Int -> Int` gives `(g * h) Int Int -> Int`, and rewriting this type using the type rewrite rules, gives `(g Int Int, h Int Int) -> Int`. This type is α-convertible to (and hence certainly an instance of) the type of the expression to the right of the arrow in the case branch, so this part of the polytypic function definition is type correct.

3.5   More Examples of Polytypic Functions

This section describes some polytypic functions that will be used in the sequel. These functions can be found in PolyLib, the library of PolyP. The next section gives an overview of PolyLib.

Function `flatten` takes a value of type `d a` and flattens it into a list of values of type `[a]`. It is defined using function `fflatten :: f a [a] -> [a]`, which takes a value v of type `f a [a]`, and returns the concatenation of all the values (of type `a`) and lists (of type `[a]`) occurring at the top level in v. The definition of `flatten` and `fflatten` is given in figure 3. As an example, we unfold the

```
flatten_d :: Regular d => d a -> [a]
flatten_d = cata_d fflatten_FunctorOf d

polytypic fflatten_f :: f a [a] -> [a]
    = case f of
        g + h   -> either fflatten_g fflatten_h
        g * h   -> \(x,y) -> fflatten_g x ++ fflatten_h y
        Empty   -> nil
        Par     -> singleton
        Rec     -> id
        d @ g   -> concat . flatten_d . pmap_d fflatten_g
        Const t -> nil

nil x = []
singleton x = [x]
```

Fig. 3. The definition of `flatten` and `fflatten`.

definition of `fflatten` when used on the type `List a` (remember that `FunctorOf List = Empty+Par*Rec`):

```
fflatten_Empty+Par*Rec
    -> either fflatten_Empty fflatten_Par*Rec
    -> either nil (\(x,y) -> fflatten_Par x ++ fflatten_Rec y)
    -> either nil (\(x,y) -> id x ++ id y)
    -> either nil (uncurry (++))
```

The expression `pequal eq x y` checks whether or not the values x and y are equivalent using the equivalence operator `eq` to compare the elements pairwise. It is defined in terms of function `fequal eq (pequal eq)`, where the first argument, `eq`, compares parameters for equality and the second argument, `(pequal eq)`, compares the subterms recursively. The third and fourth arguments are the two (unfolded) terms to be compared. These functions are defined in figure 4.

```
polytypic fequal_f :: (a -> b -> Bool) -> (c -> d -> Bool) ->
                      f a c -> f b d -> Bool
  = \p r -> case f of
            g + h    -> sumequal  (fequal_g p r) (fequal_h p r)
            g * h    -> prodequal (fequal_g p r) (fequal_h p r)
            Empty    -> \_ _ -> True
            Par      -> p
            Rec      -> r
            d @ g    -> pequal_d (fequal_g p r)
            Const t  -> (==)

pequal :: (a -> b -> Bool) -> d a -> d b -> Bool
pequal eq x y = fequal eq (pequal eq) (out x) (out y)

sumequal :: (a -> b -> Bool) -> (c -> d -> Bool) ->
            Either a c -> Either b d -> Bool
sumequal f g (Left  x) (Left  v) = f x v
sumequal f g (Right y) (Right w) = g y w
sumequal f g _          _        = False

prodequal :: (a -> b -> Bool) -> (c -> d -> Bool) ->
             (a,c) -> (b,d) -> Bool
prodequal f g (x,y) (v,w) = f x v && g y w
```

Fig. 4. The definition of pequal and fequal.

3.6   PolyLib: A Library of Polytypic Functions

Using different versions of PolyP (and its predecessors) we have implemented a number of polytypic programs. For example, we have implemented a polytypic equality function, a polytypic show function, and a polytypic parser. Furthermore, we have implemented some more involved polytypic programs for pattern matching, unification and rewriting. These polytypic programs use several basic polytypic functions, such as the relatively well-known cata and pmap, but also less well-known functions such as propagate and thread. We have collected these basic polytypic functions in the library of PolyP: PolyLib [27, app. B]. This paper describes the polytypic functions in PolyLib, motivates their presence in the library, and gives a rationale for their design. This section first introduces the format used for describing polytypic library functions, then it gives an overview of the contents of the library, followed by a description of each of the submodules in the library.

Describing Polytypic Functions   The description of a polytypic function consists of (some of) the following components: its name and type; an (in)formal description of the function; other names the function is known by; known uses of the function; and its background and relationship to other polytypic functions. For example:

```
pmap :: (a -> b) -> d a -> d b
```

Function pmap takes a function f and a value x of datatype d a, and applies f ... **Also known as**: map [31], map$_n$ [29]. **Known uses**: Everywhere! **Background**: This was one of the first ...

A problem with describing a library of polytypic functions is that it is not completely clear how to *specify* polytypic functions. The most basic combinators have immediate category theoretic interpretations that can be used as a specification, but for more complicated combinators the matter is not all that obvious. Thus, we will normally not provide formal specifications of the library functions, though we try to give references to more in-depth treatments.

The polytypic functions in the library are only defined for regular datatypes d a. In the type this is indicated by adding a context `Regular d =>` ..., but we will omit this for brevity.

Library Overview We have divided the library into six parts, see figure 5. The first part of the library contains powerful recursion combinators such as **map**, **cata** and **ana**. This part is the core of the library in the sense that it is used in the definitions of all the functions in the other parts. The second part deals with zips and some derivates, such as the equality function. The third part consists of functions that manipulate monads (see section 4.1). The fourth and fifth parts consist of simpler (but still very useful) functions, like flattening and summing. The sixth part consists of functions that manipulate constructors and constructor names. The following sections describe each of these parts in more detail.

Recursion Operators

```
pmap :: (a -> b) -> d a -> d b
fmap :: (a -> c) -> (b -> d) -> f a b -> f c d
```

Function pmap takes a function f and a value x of datatype d a, and applies f recursively to all occurrences of elements of type a in x. With d as a functor acting on types, pmap$_d$ is the corresponding functor action on functions. Function fmap$_f$ is the corresponding functor action for a pattern functor f. **Also known as**: map [31], map$_n$ [29]. In **charity** [13] map$_d$ f x is written d{f}(x). **Known uses**: Everywhere! Function fmap is used in the definition of pmap, cata, ana, hylo, para and in many other PolyLib functions. **Background**: The map function was one of the first combinators distinguished in the work of Bird and Meertens,

| pmap, fmap, cata
ana, hylo, para
crush, fcrush

(a) Recursion op's | pzip, fzip
punzip, funzip
pzipWith, pzipWith'
pequal, fequal
(b) Zips etc. | pmapM, fmapM, cataM
anaM, hyloM, paraM
propagate, cross
thread, fthread
(c) Monad op's |

| flatten, fflatten
fl_par, fl_rec, conc

(d) Flatten functions | psum, size, prod
pand, pall
por, pany, pelem
(e) Miscellaneous |

constructorName, fconstructorName
constructors, fconstructors
constructor2Int, fconstructor2Int
int2constructor, int2fconstructor
(f) Constructor functions

Fig. 5. Overview of PolyLib

[12,35]. The traditional map in functional languages maps a function over a list of elements. The current Haskell version of map is overloaded:

```
map :: Functor f => (a->b) -> f a -> f b
```

and can be used as the polytypic pmap if instance declarations for all regular type constructors are given. Function pmap can be used to give default instances for the Haskell map.

```
cata :: (FunctorOf d a b -> b) -> (d a -> b)
ana  :: (FunctorOf d a b <- b) -> (d a <- b)
hylo :: (f a b -> b) -> (c -> f a c) -> (c -> b)
para :: (d a -> FunctorOf d a b -> b) -> (d a -> b)
```

Four powerful recursion operators on the type d a: The catamorphism, cata, "evaluates" a data structure by recursively replacing the constructors with functions. The typing of cata may seem unfamiliar but with the explanation of FunctorOf above it can be seen as equivalent to:

$$\texttt{cata} :: (\texttt{f a -> b}) \to (\tau(\texttt{f}) \texttt{ a -> b})$$

The anamorphism, ana, works in the opposite direction and builds a data structure. The hylomorphism, hylo, is the generalisation of these two functions that simultaneously builds and evaluates a structure. Finally, the paramorphism, para, is a generalised form of cata that gives its parameter function access not only to the results of evaluating the substructures, but also the structure itself. **Also known as:**

PolyLib	Functorial ML [9]	Squiggol	charity [13]
cata i	fold$_1$ i	$(\!(i)\!)$	{| i |}
ana o	-	$[\![o]\!]$	(| o |)

Functions **cata** and **para** are instances of the Visitor pattern in [21]. **Known uses**: Very many polytypic functions are defined using **cata**: **pmap**, **crush**, **thread**, **flatten**, **propagate**, and all our applications use it. Function **para** is used in **rewrite**. **Background**: The catamorphism, **cata**, is the generalisation of the Haskell function **foldr** and the anamorphism, **ana**, is the (category theoretic) dual. Catamorphisms were introduced by Malcolm [33,34]. A hylomorphism is the fused composition of a catamorphism and an anamorphism specified by: **hylo i o = cata i . ana o**. The paramorphism [36], **para**, is the elimination construct for the type **d a** from Martin–Löf type theory. It captures the recursion pattern of primitive recursive functions on the datatype **d a**.

```
crush  :: (a->a->a) -> a -> d a -> a
fcrush :: (a->a->a) -> a -> f a a -> a
```

The function **crush op e** takes a structure **x** and inserts the operator **op** from left to right between every pair of values of type **a** at every level in **x**. (The value **e** is used in empty leaves.) **Known uses**: within the library see section 6. Many of the functions in that section are then used in the different applications. **Background**: The definition of **crush** is found in [37]. For an associative operator **op** with unit **e**, **crush op e** can be defined as **foldr op e . flatten**. As **crush** has the same arguments as **fold** on lists it can be seen as an alternative to **cata** as the generalisation of **fold** to regular datatypes.

Zips

```
pzip   :: (d a,d b) -> Maybe ( d (a,b) )
punzip :: d (a,b) -> (d a,d b)
fzip   :: (f a b,f c d) -> Maybe ( f (a,c) (b,d) )
funzip :: f (a,c) (b,d) -> (f a b,f c d)
```

Function **punzip** takes a structure containing pairs and splits it up into a pair of structures containing the first and the second components respectively. Function **pzip** is a partial inverse of **punzip**: it takes a pair of structures and zips them together to **Just** a structure of pairs if the two structures have the same shape, and to **Nothing** otherwise. **Also known as**: zip$_m$ [29], zip.×.d [23], **Known uses**: Function **fzip** is used in the definition of **pzipWith**. **Background**: The traditional function **zip**

```
zip :: [a] -> [b] -> [(a,b)]
```

combines two lists and does not need the **Maybe** type in the result as the longer list can always be truncated. (In general such truncation is possible for all types that have a nullary constructor, but not for all regular types.) A more general ("doubly polytypic") variant of `pzip`: **transpose** (called **zip.d.e** in [23])

```
transpose :: d (e a) -> e (d a)
```

was first described by Fritz Ruehr [43]. For a formal and relational definition, see Hoogendijk & Backhouse [23].

```
pzipWith  :: ((a,b) -> Maybe c) -> (d a,d b) -> Maybe (d c)
pzipWith' :: (FunctorOf d c e -> e) -> ((d a,d b) -> e) ->
             ((a,b) -> c) -> (d a,d b) -> e
```

Function `pzipWith` op works like `pzip` but uses the operator op to combine the values from the two structures instead of just pairing them. As the zip might fail, we also give the operator a chance to signal failure by giving it a **Maybe**-type as a result.[6]

Function `pzipWith'` is a generalisation of `pzipWith` that can handle two structures of different shape. In the call `pzipWith' ins fail op`, op is used as long as the structures have the same shape, `fail` is used to handle the case when the two structures mismatch, and `ins` combines the results from the substructures. (The type of `ins` is the same as the type of the first argument to `cata`.) **Also known as:** $zipop_m$ [29]. **Known uses:** Function `pzipWith'` is used in the definition of equality, matching and even unification. **Background:** Function `pzipWith` is the polytypic variant of the Haskell function `zipWith`

```
zipWith :: (a->b->c) -> [a] -> [b] -> [(a,b)]
```

but `pzipWith'` is new. Function `pzip` is just `pzipWith Just`.

```
pequal :: (a->b->Bool) -> d a -> d b -> Bool
fequal :: (a->b->Bool) -> (c->d->Bool) -> f a c -> f b d -> Bool
```

The expression `pequal eq x y` checks whether or not the structures x and y are equivalent using the equivalence operator eq to compare the elements pairwise. **Known uses:** fequal is used in the unification algorithm to determine when two terms are top level equal. **Background:** An early version of a polytypic equality function appeared in [44]. Function `pequal` can be instantiated to give a default for the Haskell Eq-class for regular datatypes:

---

[6] The type constructor **Maybe** can be replaced by any monad with a zero, but we didn't want to clutter up the already complicated type with contexts.

```
(==) :: Eq a => d a -> d a -> Bool
(==) =  pequal (==)
```

In Haskell the equality function can be automatically derived by the compiler, and our polytypic equality is an attempt at moving that derivation out of the compiler into the prelude.

Monad Operations

```
pmapM  :: Monad m => (a -> m b) -> d a -> m (d b)
pmapMr :: Monad m => (a -> m b) -> d a -> m (d b)
fmapM  :: Monad m => (a->m c) -> (b->m d) -> f a b -> m (f c d)
cataM  :: Monad m => (FunctorOf d a b->m b) -> (d a -> m b)
anaM   :: Monad m => (b->m (FunctorOf d a b)) -> (b -> m (d a))
hyloM  :: Monad m => (f a b->m b) -> (c->m (f a c)) -> c -> m b
paraM  :: Monad m => (d a->FunctorOf d a b->m b) -> d a -> m b
```

Function pmapM is a variant of pmap that threads a monad m from left to right through a structure after applying its function argument to all elements in the structure. Function pmapMr is the same but for threading a monad m from right to left through a structure. For symmetry's sake, the library also contains a function pmapMl, which is equal to pmapM. Furthermore, the library also contains the left and right variants of functions like cataM etc. A monadic map can, for example, use a state monad to record information about the elements in the structure during the traversal. The other recursion operators are generalised in the same way to form even more general combinators. **Also known as:** traversals [29]. **Known uses:** in unify and in the parser. **Background:** Monadic maps and catamorphisms are described in [20]. Monadic anamorphisms and hylomorphisms are defined in [39]. The monadic map (also called active traversal) is closely related to thread (also called passive traversal):

```
pmapM f = thread . pmap f
thread  = pmapM id
```

```
propagate :: d (Maybe a) -> Maybe (d a)
cross     :: d [a] -> [d a]
```

Function propagate propagates Nothing to the top level. Function cross is the cross (or tensor) product that given a structure x containing lists, generates a list of structures of the same shape. This list has one element for every combination of values drawn from the lists in x. These two functions can be generalised to thread any monad through a value. **Known uses:** propagate is used in the definition of pzip. **Background:** Function propagate is an instance of transpose [43], and both propagate and cross are instances of thread below.

```
thread  :: Monad m => d (m a) -> m (d a)
fthread :: Monad m => f (m a) (m b) -> m (f a b)
```

Function thread is used to tie together the monad computations in the elements from left to right. **Also known as**: dist$_d$ [20]. **Known uses**: Function thread can be used to define the monadic map: pmapM f = thread . pmap f. Function fthread is also used in the parser to thread the parsing monad through different structures. Function thread can be instantiated (with d = []) to the Haskell prelude function

```
        accumulate :: Monad m => [m a] -> m [a]
```

but also orthogonally (with m = Maybe) to propagate and (with m = []) to cross.

Flatten Functions

```
flatten  :: d a -> [a]
fflatten :: f a [a] -> [a]
fl_par   :: f a b -> [a]
fl_rec   :: f a b -> [b]
```

Function flatten x traverses the structure x and collects all elements from left to right in a list. The other three function are variants of this for a pattern functor f. **Also known as**: extract$_{m,i}$ [29], listify [23]. **Known uses**: fl_rec is used in the unification algorithm to find the list of immediate subterms of a term. Function fflatten is used to define flatten

```
        flatten = cata fflatten
```

Background: In the relational theory of polytypism [23] there is a membership relation **mem.d** for every relator (type constructor) **d**. Function flatten can be seen as a functional implementation of this relation:

$$\textbf{a mem.d x} \equiv \textbf{a 'elem' (flatten}_d \textbf{ x)}$$

Miscellaneous A number of simple polytypic functions can be defined in terms of crush and pmap. For brevity we present this part of PolyLib below by providing only the name, the type and the definition of each function.

```
psum :: d Int -> Int            psum = crush (+) 0
prod :: d Int -> Int            prod = crush (*) 1
conc :: d [a] -> [a]            conc = crush (++) []
pand :: d Bool -> Bool          pand = crush (&&) True
por  :: d Bool -> Bool          por  = crush (||) False

size    :: d a -> Int           size    = psum . pmap (\_->1)
flatten :: d a -> [a]           flatten = conc . pmap (:[])
pall    :: (a->Bool) -> d a -> Bool  pall p = pand . pmap p
pany    :: (a->Bool) -> d a -> Bool  pany p = por  . pmap p
pelem   :: Eq a => a -> d a -> Bool  pelem x = pany (\y->x==y)
```

Constructors

```
constructorName  :: d a -> String
fconstructorName :: f a b -> String
constructors     :: [d a]
fconstructors    :: [f a b]
constructor2Int  :: d a -> Int
fconstructor2Int :: f a b -> Int
int2constructor  :: Int -> d a
int2fconstructor :: Int -> f a b
```

Function constructorName takes a value of type d a and returns its outermost constructor name. Function constructors returns a list with all the constructors of a datatype d a. For example, for the datatype Bin it returns [Tip undefined, Join undefined undefined]. The functions constructor2Int and int2constructor take constructors to integers and vice versa. **Known uses**: constructorName is used in pshow, the polytypic version of the derived show function in Haskell, constructors is used in showing, parsing and compressing values, and both int2constructor and constructor2Int in compressing values.

4   Generic Unification

This chapter presents a substantial application of the techniques that have been developed thus far. The topic is a generic unification algorithm.

Briefly, unification is the process of making two terms (such as arithmetic expressions or type expressions) equal by suitably instantiating the variables in the terms. It is very widely used in, for example, pattern matching, type checking and theorem proving. For those who haven't already encountered it, let us first give an informal explanation before giving a summary of the development of the generic algorithm.

We explain the process in terms of a specific case before considering the generic version. Consider the datatype definition

> **data** *Expr* = var *V*
> | number *Nat*
> | plus *Expr Expr*
> | times *Expr Expr*

This can be read as the datatype of abstract syntax trees for a context-free grammar

$$E \ ::= \ V \mid N \mid (E + E) \mid (E * E)$$

for *terms* like "((1+x)*3)" when *V* produces variables and *N* produces numbers.

Another view is that a *term* of the datatype *Expr* is a tree with the constructors var, number, plus and times at the nodes, and numbers and variables at the leaves. In this view, the constructors are *uninterpreted*, which means that trees corresponding to equal but non-identical arithmetic expressions are considered different. For example, the trees corresponding to ((1+x)*3) and (3+(x*3)) are different. It is this view of terms as tree structures that is used in unification. Nevertheless, for ease of writing we shall use the concrete syntax of arithmetic expressions to write terms.

Now consider two terms, say ((1+x)*3) and ((y+z)*3). "Unifying" these terms means substituting terms for the variables x, y and z so that the terms become identical. One possibility, in this case, is to substitute z for x and 1 for y. After this substitution both terms become equal to ((1+z)*3). There are many other possibilities. For example, we could substitute 1 for all of x, y and z, thus unifying the two terms in the term ((1+1)*3). This latter substitution is however less general than the former. Unification involves seeking a "most general" unifier for two given terms. Of course, some pairs of terms are not unifiable: a trivial example is the pair of terms 0 and 1. These are not unifiable because they contain no variables. The pair of terms x and (1+x) is also not unifiable, but for a different reason: namely, the first term will always have fewer constructors than the second whatever substitution we make for x.

We have described unification for arithmetic expressions but unification is also used for other term algebras. A major application is in polymorphic type inference, as in most modern functional languages. In this application it is type expressions that are unified. Suppose that a program contains the function application f x, and at that stage the term representing the type inferred for f is (p->q), and for x it is r. Then first p and r are unified. If that fails, there is a type error. Otherwise, let (p'->q') be the result of applying the most general unifier to $(p\text{-}{>}q)$. That is the new type inferred for f, while we get p' for x, and q' for the application f x.

In a *generic* unification algorithm we make the term structure a parameter of the algorithm. So, one instance of the algorithm unifies arithmetic expressions, another type expressions. In order to formalise this we use F to denote a functor (the pattern functor of the constant terms we want to unify) and show how to extend F to a functor F^* such that F^*V, for type V of variables, is the set of all terms. We also define substitution of variables, and most general unifiers.

The functor F^* is (the functor part of) a *monad*. In the last ten years, monads have been recognised to be an important concept in many applications of functional programming. We therefore begin in section 4.1 by introducing the concept at first without reference to unification. There is much that can be said about monads but our discussion is brief and restricted to just what we need to present the unification algorithm. The monad F^* defined by an arbitrary functor F is then discussed along with the definition of a substitution.

The discussion of the unification algorithm proper begins in section 4.2. Here the discussion is also brief since we assume that the non-generic algorithm is known from the literature. In order to compare the calculational method of proof with traditional proofs, chapter 5 presents a generic proof of one aspect of the algorithm's correctness, namely that a non-trivial expression is not unifiable with any variable that occurs properly in it.

4.1   Monads and Terms

Monads and Kleisli composition A monad is a concept introduced in category theory that has since proved its worth in functional programming. It is a general concept which we introduce via a particular instance, the *Maybe* monad.

Suppose we have two functions

$$f :: a \to Maybe\ b$$
$$g :: b \to Maybe\ c$$

Think of these total functions as modelling partial functions: f computes a b-value from an a-value, or fails, and likewise, g computes a c-value from a b-value, or fails. Can we combine these functions into a single function

$$g \diamond f :: a \to Maybe\ c$$

that combines the computations of f and g when both succeed, and fails when either of them fails? The types don't fit for normal composition, but here is how to do it:

$$(g \diamond f)\,x\ =\ h\,(f\,x)\ \textbf{where}$$
$$h\ \text{none}\quad =\ \text{none}$$
$$h\,(\text{one}\ y)\ =\ g\,y$$

This form of composition is called *Kleisli composition*. Kleisli composition shares some pleasant properties with normal composition. First, the operation is associative:

$$f \diamond (g \diamond h) = (f \diamond g) \diamond h$$

for f, g and h such that the expressions involved are well-typed. We may therefore drop the parentheses in chains of Kleisli compositions and write $f \diamond g \diamond h$. Moreover, $\diamond$ has neutral element one, which we call the *Kleisli identity*:

$$\mathsf{one} \diamond f = f = f \diamond \mathsf{one} \quad .$$

Kleisli composition gives a convenient way to fit functions together that would not fit together with normal composition. Kleisli composition is not just possible for *Maybe*, but for many other functors as well. A functor with a Kleisli composition and Kleisli identity —that satisfy a number of laws to be discussed shortly— is called a *monad*. A trivial example is the functor Id: take normal function composition as its Kleisli composition. A less trivial example is the functor *Set*. For this functor, Kleisli composition takes the form

$$(f \diamond g)x = \{z \mid \exists(y:: y \in gx \wedge z \in fy)\} \quad .$$

Its Kleisli identity is the singleton former $\{\_\}$. We shall encounter more monads later.

Formally, the triple $(M, \diamond, \eta)$ is a monad, where M is a functor, $\diamond$ and η are its Kleisli composition and Kleisli identity, if the following properties hold. First, $\diamond$ is a function of polymorphic type

$$(b \rightarrow Mc) \times (a \rightarrow Mb) \rightarrow (a \rightarrow Mc)$$

and η is a function of polymorphic type

$$a \rightarrow Ma \quad .$$

Second, $\diamond$ is associative with η as neutral element. Finally, the following rules are satisfied:

$$
\begin{aligned}
Mf \bullet (g \diamond h) &= (Mf \bullet g) \diamond h \\
(f \diamond g) \bullet h &= f \diamond (g \bullet h) \\
(f \bullet g) \diamond h &= f \diamond (Mg \bullet h)
\end{aligned}
$$

In fact, these equalities are automatically satisfied in all the monads that we consider here. They are consequences of the so-called *free theorem* for $\diamond$. Their validity depends on a property called *(polymorphic) parametricity* that is satisfied by Haskell restricted to total functions which we discuss in section 5.2.

Exercise 4.1   Let $(M, \diamond, \eta)$ be a monad. Express Mf in terms of Kleisli composition and identity. Define

$$\mathsf{mul} = \mathsf{id} \diamond \mathsf{id} :: MMa \rightarrow Ma$$

(The function mul is called the *multiplier* of the monad.) What is the function mul for the case $M = Set$?

Prove that $f \diamond g = \text{mul} \cdot M f \cdot g$. Also prove the following three equalities:

$$\text{mul} \cdot \text{mul} \;=\; \text{mul} \cdot M\text{mul}$$

$$\text{mul} \cdot \eta \;=\; \text{id} \;=\; \text{mul} \cdot M\eta \;.$$

□

Terms with variables Recall the datatype *Expr* introduced at the beginning of this section. We can regard it as a datatype for terms involving numbers, addition and multiplication to which has been added an extra alternative for variables.

Let F be the pattern functor corresponding to the definition of *Expr* without variables. Then $Expr = \mu G$, where $G\,a = V + F a$. This can be done generically. Consider, for unary functor F, the unary functor $V^\kappa + F$. This, we recall, is defined by

$$(V^\kappa + F)a \;=\; V + F a$$

where a ranges over types, and

$$(V^\kappa + F)f \;=\; \text{id}_V + F f$$

where f ranges over functions. For fixed F, the mapping $a \mapsto \mu(a^\kappa + F)$ is a functor, namely the type functor $\tau(\oslash)$ of the bifunctor $a \oslash b = a + F b$. Denote this type functor by $F^\star$ (so $F^\star V = \mu(V^\kappa + F))$[7]. Its action on functions is as follows. For $f :: a \to b$:

$$F^\star f \;=\; (\!| a^\kappa + F ; \; \text{in}_{b^\kappa + F} \cdot f + \text{id} |\!)$$

Note that we have specified the pattern functor "$a^\kappa + F$" inside the catamorphism brackets here since there is a possibility of confusion between different algebras. Note also that

$$(V^\kappa + F)F^\star V \;=\; V + F F^\star V$$

so that

$$\text{in}_{V^\kappa + F} \;::\; V + F F^\star V \;\to\; F^\star V \;.$$

Given a datatype μF, we can then extend it with variables by switching to $F^\star V$. We define two embeddings by:

$$\text{embl}_V \;::\; V \to F^\star V \qquad\qquad \text{embr}_V \;::\; F F^\star V \to F^\star V$$

$$\text{embl}_V \;=\; \text{in}_{V^\kappa + F} \cdot \text{inl} \qquad\qquad \text{embr}_V \;=\; \text{in}_{V^\kappa + F} \cdot \text{inr}$$

---

[7] The star notation is used here to suggest a link with the Kleene star, denoting iteration in a regular algebra. $F^\star$ can be seen as iterating functor F an arbitrary number of times. More significantly, the notation highlights a formal link between monads and closure operators. See, for example, [3] for more details.

The functor F^* forms the *substitution monad* $(F^*, \diamond, \eta)$ with, for some functions $f :: a \to F^*b$ and $g :: b \to F^*c$,

$$g \diamond f = (\![b^\kappa + F; g \triangledown \text{embr}_c]\!) \cdot f$$

$$\eta = \text{embl} .$$

Note that the catamorphism in the definition of $g \diamond f$ has pattern functor $b^\kappa + F$, as indicated by the parameter before the semicolon. We omit explicit mention of this information later, but it is vital to the correct use of the computation and other laws. In addition we omit type information on the initial algebra, although again it is vitally important.

Exercise 4.2   Take F to be $a\times$ for some type a. What is the type $(a\times)^*1$? What is the multiplier, what is Kleisli identity and what is Kleisli composition? (Hint: use exercise 4.1 for the last part of this exercise.)

$\square$

Exercise 4.3   Consider the case $F = (1+)$. Show that $(1+)^*V \cong \mathbb{N}\times(V+1)$. Specifically, construct an initial algebra.

$$\text{in}   ::   V + (1 + (\mathbb{N}\times(V+1))) \to \mathbb{N}\times(V+1)$$

and express catamorphisms on elements of type $\mathbb{N}\times(V+1)$ in terms of catamorphisms on $\mathbb{N}$.

$\square$

Exercise 4.4   Verify that Kleisli composition as defined above is indeed associative and that embl is its neutral element.

$\square$

Assignments and Substitutions An *assignment* is a mapping of variables to terms, for example $\{\, x := (y+x) , y := 0 \,\}$. An assignment can be *performed* on a term. This means a *simultaneous* and *systematic* replacement of the variables in the term by the terms to which they are mapped. For example, performed on the term $(x+y)$ our example assignment gives $((y+x)+0)$. We model assignments as functions with the typing $V \to F^*V$. Because we want functions to be total, this means we also have to define the assignment for all variables in V. If $V = \{\, x , y , z \,\}$, we can make the above assignment total by writing it as $\{\, x := (y+x) , y := 0 , z := z \,\}$. Note that to the left of ":=" in an assignment we have an element of V, and to the right an element of F^*V. So to be precise, if assignment f has "$z := z$", this means that $f\, z = \eta\, z$. In particular, the (empty) *identity assignment* is η.

Given an assignment $f :: V \to F^*V$, we want to define the *substitution* subst f as a function performing f on a term. The result is again a term. The term consisting of the single variable x is $\eta\, x$. Applying subst f to it, the result should be $f\, x$. So

$$(\text{subst } f) \cdot \eta$$

$=\qquad\{\qquad \text{desired result}\quad\}$

$$f$$

$=\qquad\{\qquad \text{Kleisli identity}\quad\}$

$$f \diamond \eta$$

$=\qquad\{\qquad \text{monad equality}\quad\}$

$$(f\diamond\text{id}) \cdot \eta\ .$$

Since subst f is clearly a catamorphism that distributes through constructors —
for example, $(\text{subst } f)\,(x{+}y)\ =\ ((\text{subst } f\,x){+}(\text{subst } f\,y))$ — it is fully determined
by its action on variables. We have found:

$$\text{subst} :: (V{\rightarrow}F^{*}V) \rightarrow (F^{*}V{\rightarrow}F^{*}V)$$
$$\text{subst } f = f\diamond\text{id}$$

Two substitutions can always be merged into a single one:

$$(\text{subst } f) \cdot (\text{subst } g)$$

$=\qquad\{\qquad \text{definition of subst}\quad\}$

$$(f \diamond \text{id}) \cdot (g \diamond \text{id})$$

$=\qquad\{\qquad \text{monad equalities}\quad\}$

$$f \diamond (\text{id} \cdot (g \diamond \text{id}))$$

$=\qquad\{\qquad \text{id is identity of } \cdot\ \}$

$$f \diamond (g \diamond \text{id})$$

$=\qquad\{\qquad \diamond \text{ is associative}\quad\}$

$$(f \diamond g) \diamond \text{id}$$

$=\qquad\{\qquad \text{definition of subst}\quad\}$

$$\text{subst } (f \diamond g)\ .$$

4.2   Generic Unification

Unifiers Two terms x and y containing variables can be *unified* if there is some
assignment f such that performing f on x gives the same result as performing
f on y. For example, the two terms

$$\texttt{(u+((1*v)*2))} \quad \text{and} \quad \texttt{((w*v)+(u*2))}$$

can be unified by the assignment

$$\{\texttt{u} := \texttt{(1*(z+3))}, \texttt{v} := \texttt{(z+3)}, \texttt{w} := \texttt{1}\}$$

into the unification

$$\texttt{((1*(z+3))+((1*(z+3))*2))}$$

Such a unifying assignment is called a *unifier* of the terms. Unifiers are not unique. Another unifier of the same two terms of the example is

$\{u := (1*z), v := z, w := 1\}$

which results in the unification

$((1*z)+((1*z)*2))$

This last unification is more general. If f is a unifier, then, for any assignment h, the combined substitution $h \diamond f$ is also a unifier, since

$$h \diamond f \quad \text{is a unifier of } (x,y)$$
$$\equiv \qquad \{ \qquad \text{definition of unifier} \quad \}$$
$$\text{subst } (h \diamond f) \; x \; = \; \text{subst } (h \diamond f) \; y$$
$$\equiv \qquad \{ \qquad \text{combined substitutions} \quad \}$$
$$(\text{subst } h) \; (\text{subst } f \; x) \; = \; (\text{subst } h) \; (\text{subst } f \; y)$$
$$\Leftarrow \qquad \{ \qquad \text{cancel } (\text{subst } h) \quad \}$$
$$\text{subst } f \; x \; = \; \text{subst } f \; y$$
$$\equiv \qquad \{ \qquad \text{definition of unifier} \quad \}$$
$$f \quad \text{is a unifier of } (x,y) \quad .$$

In the example, the first, less general unifier, can be formed from the more general one by taking $h = \{v := (z+3)\}$. This notion of generality gives a pre-ordering on unifiers (and actually on all assignments): define

$$f \sqsubseteq g \quad \equiv \quad \exists (h \, \text{such that} \, f = h \diamond g)$$

The relation $\sqsubseteq$ is obviously transitive and reflexive, but in general not anti-symmetric. If two unifiers are equally general: $f \sqsubseteq g \wedge g \sqsubseteq f$, then f and g can be different. But they are to all intents and purposes equivalent: they differ at most in the choice of names for the variables in the result.

If two terms are unifiable at all, then among all unifiers there is a *most general unifier*. That term is commonly abbreviated to *mgu*. Clearly, any two mgu's are equivalent. In the example, the second unifier is an mgu.

A generic shell for unification We develop the unification algorithm in two stages. In this stage we give a generic "shell" in terms of type classes. In the second stage, we show how to make any regular functor into an instance of the classes involved.

Terms may have children, they may happen to be variables, and we should be able to see if superficially —at the top level of the term trees— the constructors are equal. As before, we assume a fixed type V for variables. Here are the corresponding class declarations:

$$\textbf{class } \textit{Children } t \quad \textbf{where } \textit{children} \qquad :: t \rightarrow \textit{List } t$$
$$\textit{mapChildren} :: (t \rightarrow t) \rightarrow (t \rightarrow t)$$
$$\textbf{class } \textit{VarCheck } t \textbf{ where } \textit{varcheck} \qquad :: t \rightarrow \textit{Maybe } V$$
$$\textbf{class } \textit{TopEq } t \qquad \textbf{where } \textit{topEq} \qquad :: t \times t \rightarrow \textit{Bool}$$

$$\textbf{class } (\textit{Children } t, \textit{VarCheck } t, \textit{TopEq } t) \quad \Rightarrow \quad \textit{Term } t$$

We give a concrete instantiation as an example — illustrating some fine points at the same time. Let C be some type for representing constructors. Here is the datatype we will use to instantiate the classes:

data $T = Var\ V\ |\ Con\ C\ (List\ T)$

First we make T into an instance of $Children$:

instance $Children\ T$ **where**
$$children \qquad (Var\ v) \quad = \ \text{nil}$$
$$children \qquad (Con\ c\ ts) = \ ts$$
$$mapChildren\ f\ (Var\ v) \quad = \ Var\ v$$
$$mapChildren\ f\ (Con\ c\ ts) = \ Con\ c\ (List\ f\ ts)$$

Note here that $mapChildren\ f$ only maps function f over the *immediate* children of its argument. No recursion is involved.

Here is how T fits in the $VarCheck$ class:

instance $VarCheck\ T$ **where**
$$varcheck\ (Var\ v) \quad = \ \text{one}\ v$$
$$varcheck\ (Con\ c\ ts) \ = \ \text{none}$$

For $TopEq$ we assume that eq is an equality test on C and on V:

instance $TopEq\ T$ **where**
$$topEq\ (Var\ v_0, Var\ v_1) \qquad\qquad = \ \text{eq}\ v_0\ v_1$$
$$topEq\ (Con\ c_0\ ts_0, Con\ c_1\ ts_1) = \ \text{eq}\ c_0\ c_1\ \wedge$$
$$\qquad\qquad\qquad\qquad\qquad\qquad \text{length}\ ts_0 = \text{length}\ ts_1$$
$$topEq\ (\_,\_) \qquad\qquad\qquad\qquad = \ \text{false}$$

Note that for this test the children of the terms are irrelevant. This is why we give it the name $topEq$.

Having made T an instance of the three superclasses of $Term$, we can now proudly announce:

instance $Term\ T$

So much for this concrete instantiation. We continue with the generic problem. Here is a function to collect all subterms of a term in the $Term$ class (or actually the $Children$ class):

$$subTerms :: Children\ t \ \Rightarrow\ t \to List\ t$$
$$subTerms\ x = \ \text{cons}\ x\ (\text{concat}\ (List\ subTerms\ (children\ x)))$$

and here is a function that uses a list comprehension to collect all variables occurring in a term:

$$vars :: Term\ t \ \Rightarrow\ t \to List\ V$$
$$vars\ x = \ [\,v\ |\ \text{one}\ v\ \leftarrow\ List\ varCheck\ (subTerms\ x)\,]$$

Earlier we saw a treatment of assignments as functions. Here we introduce a class for assignments, so that it is also possible to make other concrete representations into instances. The parameter t stands for terms.

$$
\begin{aligned}
\textbf{class } Assig \ t \ \textbf{where } idAssig \ &::\ V \to t \\
modBind \ &::\ V \times t \to ((V \to t) \to (V \to t)) \\
lookupIn \ &::\ (V \to t) \times V \ \to \ Maybe \ t
\end{aligned}
$$

The type F^*V can be made into a generic instance by:

$$
\begin{aligned}
&\textbf{instance } Assig \ (F^* V) \ \textbf{where} \\
&\quad idAssig \qquad = \ \mathsf{embl} \\
&\quad modBind \ (v, x) \ = \ (f \mapsto (v' \mapsto \textbf{if } \mathsf{eq} \ v' \ v \ \textbf{then } x \ \textbf{else } f \ v')) \\
&\quad lookupIn \ (f, v) \ = \ \textbf{if } \mathsf{eq} \ (f \ v) \ (idAssig \ v) \ \textbf{then } \mathsf{none} \ \textbf{else } \mathsf{one} \ (f \ v)
\end{aligned}
$$

in which we see both the Kleisli identity embl of the substitution monad, and one of the *Maybe* monad. The result none signifies that v is mapped to itself (embedded in the term world).

We have chosen a particular implementation for assignments: assignments are functions. If Haskell would allow multiple parameter type classes we could abstract from the particular implementation, and replace the occurrences of $V \to t$ in the types of the functions of the class *Assig* by a type variable a. Thus we could obtain a more concrete instance of *Assig* by taking list of pairs (v, x), with v a variable and x a term, instead of functions. Then *idAssig* is the empty list, *modBind* can simply cons the pair onto the list, and *lookupIn* looks for the first pair with the given variable and returns the corresponding term. If the given variable is not found, it fails. An efficient implementation of *Assig* would use balanced trees, or even better hash tables. With the class mechanism the implementation can be *encapsulated*, that is, hidden to the rest of the program, so that the program can first be developed and tested with a simple implementation. It can later be replaced by a more efficient sophisticated implementation without affecting the rest of the program. It should be clear that this is an important advantage.

The unification algorithm proper We give the algorithm — which is basically the algorithm found in the literature — without much explanation. As to notation, we use the monad $(Maybe, \diamond, \eta)$.

$$
\begin{aligned}
unify \ &::\ (Term \ t, Assig \ t) \ \Rightarrow \ t \times t \to Maybe \ (V \to t) \\
unify' \ &::\ (Term \ t, Assig \ t) \ \Rightarrow \ t \times t \to ((V \to t) \to Maybe \ (V \to t))
\end{aligned}
$$

The definition of *unify* is now simply to start up *unify'* with the empty assignment. The function *unify'* is defined as a higher order function, threading "assignment transformations" together with $\diamond$.

$$
\begin{aligned}
&unify\ (x, y) = unify'\ (x, y)\ idAssig \\
&unify'\ (x, y) = uni\ (varCheck\ x,\ varCheck\ y)\ \textbf{where} \\
&\quad uni\ (\textsf{none}\ ,\ \textsf{none}\ ) \mid topEq\ (x, y) \quad = \quad uniTerms\ (x, y) \\
&\qquad\qquad\qquad\qquad\quad\ \mid \text{otherwise} \quad = \quad \textsf{const none} \\
&\quad uni\ (\textsf{one}\ u,\ \textsf{one}\ v) \mid \textsf{eq}\ u\ v \quad\ \ = \quad \eta \\
&\quad uni\ (\textsf{one}\ u,\ \ \_\ \ ) \qquad\qquad\quad = \quad u \mapsto y \\
&\quad uni\ (\ \ \_\ \ ,\ \textsf{one}\ v) \qquad\qquad\quad\ = \quad v \mapsto x \\[4pt]
&\quad uniTerms\ (x, y)\ = \\
&\qquad\qquad threadList(List\ unify'\ (\textsf{zip}\ (children\ x)\ (children\ y)))
\end{aligned}
$$

All the right-hand sides here are functions that return maybe an assignment, given an assignment. The function *threadList* is simply the list catamorphism with Kleisli composition:

$$
\begin{aligned}
&threadList\ ::\ Monad\ m \Rightarrow List\ (a \to m\ a) \to (a \to m\ a) \\
&threadList\ =\ \textsf{foldr}\ (\diamond)\ \eta
\end{aligned}
$$

The auxiliary operator $(\mapsto)$ should "*modBind*" its arguments into the unifier being collected, but there are two things to be taken care of. No binding may be introduced that would mean an infinite assignment. This is commonly called the *occurs check*. And if the variable is already bound to a term, that term must be unified with the new term, and the unifier obtained must be threaded into the assignment being collected.

$$
\begin{aligned}
&(\mapsto)\ ::\ (Term\ t, Assig\ t)\ \Rightarrow\ V \times t \to ((V \to t) \to Maybe\ (V \to t)) \\
&(v \mapsto x)\ s\ =\ \textbf{if}\ occursCheck\ (v, s, x) \\
&\qquad\qquad\qquad \textbf{then none} \\
&\qquad\qquad\qquad \textbf{else case}\ lookupIn\ (s, v)\ \textbf{of} \\
&\qquad\qquad\qquad\quad \textsf{none}\ \ \to\ \ (\eta \bullet modBind\ (v, x))\ s \\
&\qquad\qquad\qquad\quad \textsf{one}\ y\ \to\ ((\eta \bullet modBind\ (v, x)) \diamond unify'\ (x, y))\ s
\end{aligned}
$$

The following is a hack to implement the occurs check. This is basically a reachability problem in a graph — is there a cycle from v to itself?, or rather: are we about to create a cycle? We must take account both of the unifier collected already, and the new term. Because we know no cycles were created yet, the graph is more like a tree, so any search strategy terminates. The approach here is not optimally efficient, but in practice quite good with lazy evaluation (and horrible with eager evaluation). There exist linear-time solutions, but they require much more bookkeeping.

$$
\begin{aligned}
&occursCheck\ ::\ (Term\ t, Assig\ t)\ \Rightarrow\ V \times (V \to t) \times t \to Bool \\
&occursCheck\ (v, s, x)\ =\ v \in reachlist\ (vars\ x)\ \textbf{where} \\
&\quad reachlist\ \ vs\ =\ vs + \!\!+\ \textsf{concat}\ (List\ reachable\ vs) \\
&\quad reachable\ v\ =\ reachlist\ (mayvars\ (lookupIn\ (s, v))) \\
&\quad mayvars\ \textsf{none}\quad\ =\ [\,] \\
&\quad mayvars\ (\textsf{one}\ y)\ =\ vars\ y
\end{aligned}
$$

Here, *reachlist* collects the variables reachable from a *list* of variables, while *reachable* collects the variables reachable from a *single* variable.

The generic Term instance All we have to do now is make F^*V an instance of the *Term* class. That is surprisingly easy. For the *Children* class:

> **instance** *Children* (F^*V) **where**
>   *children* $=$ $((\text{nil} \bullet !) \triangledown \text{fl\_rec}) \bullet \text{out}$
>   *mapChildren* f $=$ $\text{in} \bullet (\text{id}_V + Ff) \bullet \text{out}$

where fl_rec is defined in PolyLib, see Section 6. For the *VarCheck* class:

> **instance** *VarCheck* $(F^* V)$ **where**
>   *varcheck* $=$ $(\text{one} \triangledown (\text{none} \bullet !)) \bullet \text{out}$

For *TopEq* we use the fact that fequal tests on equality of functor structures. fequal is defined in PolyLib, see Section 6.

> **instance** *TopEq* $(F^* V)$ **where**
>   *topEq* (t, t') $=$ $\text{fequal} \; (==) \; (x \mapsto y \mapsto \text{True}) \; (\text{out } t) \; (\text{out } t')$

For a complete implementation of the generic unification program, see [26].

5   From Functions to Relations

In the preceding chapter we have done what we ourselves have decried: we have presented an algorithm without even a verification of its correctness, let alone a construction of the algorithm from its specification. An excuse is that a full discussion of correctness would have distracted from the main goal of that chapter, which was to show how the generic form of the —known to be correct— algorithm is implemented. That is, however, only an excuse since, so far as we know, no proof of correctness of the generic algorithm has ever been constructed. In section 5.4 we remedy this lacuna partially by presenting one lemma in such a proof of correctness. To that end, however, we need to extend the programming calculus from total functions to relations.

5.1   Why Relations?

In a summer school on advanced *functional* programming, it may seem odd to want to introduce relations but there are several good reasons for making it an imperative. In the first place, specifications are typically relations, not total functions. The specification of the unification algorithm is a case in point since it embodies both nondeterminism and partiality. Nondeterminism is embodied in the requirement to compute a most general unifier, not *the* most general unifier. It would be infeasible to require the latter since, in general, there is no single most general unifier of two terms. Partiality is also present in the fact that a most general unifier may not exist. Partiality can be got around in the implementation by using the *Maybe* monad as we did here, but avoiding nondeterminism in the specification is undesirable.

A second reason for introducing relations is that termination arguments are typically based on well-founded relations. Our discussion of the correctness of the unification algorithm in section 5.4 is based on the construction of a well-founded relation, although in this case termination is not the issue at stake.

A third, compelling reason for introducing relations is that the "free theorem" for polymorphic functions alluded to above and discussed in detail below is based on *relations* on functions and necessitates an extension of the concept of functor to relations. Also, the most promising work we know of that aims to be precise about what is really meant by "generic" is that due to Hoogendijk [22] which is based on a relational semantics of higher-order polymorphism .

5.2   Parametric Polymorphism

Space does not allow us to consider the extension to relations in full depth and so we will have to make do with a brief account of the issues involved. For more detail see [11,1]. We believe, nevertheless, that a discussion of generic programming would be incomplete without a summary of Reynolds' [40] *abstraction theorem* which has since been popularised under the name "theorems for free" by Wadler [45]. (This summary is taken from [23] which may be consulted for additional references.)

Reynolds' goal in establishing the abstraction theorem was to give a precise meaning to the statement that a function is "parametrically polymorphic". Suppose we have a polymorphic function f of type $T\alpha$ for all types α. That is, for each type A there is an instance f_A of type TA. The action of T is extended —in a way to be made precise shortly— to binary relations, where if relation R has type $A \sim B$, relation TR has type $TA \sim TB$. Then *parametricity* of the polymorphism of f means that for any binary relation R of type $A \sim B$ we have $(f_A , f_B) \in TR$. Reynolds' abstraction theorem is the theorem that any polymorphic function expressible in the language defined in his paper is parametric. Wadler called this a "theorem for free" because, as we show shortly, the parametricity of a polymorphic function predicts algebraic properties of that function just from knowing the type of the function! Another way of viewing the theorem is as a healthiness property of functions expressible in a programming language — a programming language that guarantees that all polymorphic functions are parametric is preferable to one that cannot do so.

In order to make the notion of parametricity completely precise, we have to be able to extend each type constructor T in our chosen programming language to a function $R \mapsto TR$ from relations to relations. Reynolds did so for function spaces and product. For product he extended the (binary) type constructor $\times$ to relations by defining $R \times S$ for arbitrary relations R of type $A \sim B$ and S of type $C \sim D$ to be the relation of type $A \times C \sim B \times D$ satisfying

$$((u,v) , (x,y)) \in R \times S \;\equiv\; (u,x) \in R \land (v,y) \in S \; .$$

For function spaces, Reynolds extended the $\rightarrow$ operator to relations as follows. For all relations R of type $A \sim B$ and S of type $C \sim D$ the relation $R \rightarrow S$ is the relation of type $(A \rightarrow C) \sim (B \rightarrow D)$ satisfying

$$(f,g) \in R \rightarrow S \quad \equiv \quad \forall(x,y:: (x,y) \in R \Rightarrow (fx, gy) \in S) \ .$$

Note that if we equate a function f of type $A \rightarrow B$ with the relation f of type $B \sim A$ satisfying

$$b = fa \quad \equiv \quad (b,a) \in f$$

then the definition of $f \times g$, for functions f and g, coincides with the definition of the cartesian product of f and g given in section 5. Thus, not only does Reynolds' definition extend the definition of product beyond types, it also extends the definition of the product functor. Note also that the relational composition $f \cdot g$ of two functions is the same as their functional composition. That is, $a = f(gc) \equiv (a,c) \in f \cdot g$. So relational composition also extends functional composition. Note finally that $h \rightarrow k$ is a *relation* even for *functions* h and k. It is the relation defined by

$$(f,g) \in h \rightarrow k \quad \equiv \quad \forall(x,y:: \ x = hy \ \Rightarrow \ fx = k(gy)) \ .$$

Simplified and expressed in point-free form this becomes:

$$(f,g) \in h \rightarrow k \quad \equiv \quad f \cdot h = k \cdot g \ .$$

Writing the relation $h \rightarrow k$ as an infix operator makes the rule easy to remember:

$$f \ (h \rightarrow k) \ g \quad \equiv \quad f \cdot h = k \cdot g \ .$$

An example of Reynolds' parametricity property is given by function application. The type of function application is $(\alpha \rightarrow \beta) \times \alpha \rightarrow \beta$. The type constructor T is thus the function mapping types A and B to $(A \rightarrow B) \times A \rightarrow B$. The extension of T to relations maps relations R and S to the relation $(R \rightarrow S) \times R \rightarrow S$. Now suppose @ is any parametrically polymorphic function with the same type as function application. Then Reynolds' claim is that @ satisfies

$$(@_{A,C} \ , \ @_{B,D}) \ \in \ (R \rightarrow S) \times R \rightarrow S$$

for all relations R and S of types $A \sim B$ and $C \sim D$, respectively. Unfolding the definitions, this is the property that, for all functions f and g, and all c and d,

$$\forall(x,y:: (x,y) \in R \Rightarrow (fx, gy) \in S) \wedge (c,d) \in R \ \Rightarrow \ (f@c, g@d) \in S \ .$$

The fact that function application itself satisfies this property is in fact the basis of Reynolds' inductive proof of the abstraction theorem (for a particular language of typed lambda expressions). But the theorem is stronger because function application is *uniquely* defined by its parametricity property. To see this, instantiate R to the singleton set $\{(c,c)\}$ and S to the singleton set $\{(fc \ , \ fc)\}$. Then, assuming @ satisfies the parametricity property, $(f@c \ , \ f@c) \in S$. That is, $f@c = fc$. Similarly, the identity function is the unique function f satisfying the parametricity property $(f_A , f_B) \in R{\to}R$ for all types A and B and all relations R of type $A \sim B$ —the parametricity property corresponding to the polymorphic type, $\alpha{\to}\alpha$ for all α, of the identity function—, and the projection function exl is the unique function f satisfying the parametricity property $(f_{A,B} , f_{C,D}) \in R{\times}S \to R$ for all types A, B, C and D and all relations R and S of types $A \sim B$ and $C \sim D$, respectively —the parametricity property corresponding to the polymorphic type, $\alpha{\times}\beta \to \alpha$ for all α and β, of the exl function.

The import of all this is that certain functions can be *specified* by a parametricity property. That is, certain parametricity properties have unique solutions. Most parametricity properties do not have unique solutions however. For example, both the identity function on lists and the reverse function satisfy the parametricity property of function f, for all $R :: A \sim B$,

$$(f_A , f_B) \in List\ R \to List\ R \ .$$

Here *List R* is the relation holding between two lists whenever the lists have the same length and corresponding elements of the two lists are related by R.

Free Theorem for Monads Let us show the abstraction theorem at work on Kleisli composition. Kleisli composition is a polymorphic function of type

$$(b{\to}Mc) \times (a{\to}Mb) \to (a{\to}Mc)$$

for all types a, b and c. If it is parametrically polymorphic then it satisfies the property that, for all relations R, S and T and all functions f_0, f_1, g_0 and g_1, if

$$((f_0 , g_0) , (f_1 , g_1)) \in (S{\to}MT) \times (R{\to}MS)$$

then

$$(f_0{\diamond}g_0 , f_1{\diamond}g_1) \in R{\to}MT \ .$$

This assumes that we have shown how to extend the functor M to relations. For our purposes here, we will only need to instantiate R, S and T to functions, and it simplifies matters greatly if we use the point-free definition of $h{\to}k$ given above. Specifically, we have, for all functions h, k and l,

$$((f_0 , g_0) , (f_1 , g_1)) \in (k{\to}Ml) \times (h{\to}Mk)$$
$$\equiv \quad \{ \quad \text{definition of } \times \quad \}$$
$$f_0\ (k{\to}Ml)\ f_1 \ \wedge \ g_0\ (h{\to}Mk)\ g_1$$
$$\equiv \quad \{ \quad \text{point-free definition of } \to \text{ for functions} \quad \}$$
$$f_0 \bullet k \ = \ Ml \bullet f_1 \ \wedge \ g_0 \bullet h \ = \ Mk \bullet g_1 \ .$$

In this way, we obtain the property that for all functions f_0, f_1, g_0, g_1, h, k and l, if

$$(1) \qquad f_0 \bullet k \ = \ Ml \bullet f_1 \ \wedge \ g_0 \bullet h \ = \ Mk \bullet g_1$$

then

(2) $(f_0 \diamond g_0) \bullet h \ = \ Ml \bullet (f_1 \diamond g_1)$.

With its seven free variables, this is quite a complicated property. More manageable properties can be obtained by instantiating the functions in such a way that the premise becomes true. An easy way to do this is to reduce the premise to statements of the form

$$f_i \ = \ \ldots \ \wedge \ g_j \ = \ \ldots \ ,$$

where i and j are either 0 or 1, by instantiating suitable combinations of h, k and l to the identity function. For instance, by instantiating h and k to the identity function the premise (1) reduces to

$$f_0 \ = \ Ml \bullet f_1 \ \wedge \ g_0 = g_1 \ .$$

Substituting the right sides for f_0 and g_0 in the conclusion (2) together with the identity function for h and k, we thus obtain

$$(Ml \bullet f_1) \diamond g_1 \ = \ Ml \bullet (f_1 \diamond g_1) \ .$$

for all functions l, f_1 and g_1. This is the first of the "free theorems" for Kleisli composition listed in section 4.1.

Exercise 5.1   Derive the other two "free theorems" stated in section 4.1 from the above parametricity property. Investigate other properties obtained by setting combinations of f_0, f_1, g_0, g_1 to the identity function.

□

Exercise 5.2   Instantiating M to the identity functor we see that the free theorem for Kleisli composition predicts that any parametrically polymorphic function with the same type as (ordinary) function composition is associative. Can you show that function composition is uniquely defined by its parametricity property?

□

Exercise 5.3   Derive the free theorem for catamorphisms from the polymorphic type of $f \mapsto (\!(f)\!)$. Show that the fusion law is an instance of the free theorem.

□

5.3   Relators

As we have argued, an extension of the calculus of datatypes to relations is desirable from a practical viewpoint. In view of Reynolds' abstraction theorem, it is also highly desirable from a theoretical viewpoint, at least if one's goal is to develop generic programming. We have also shown how the product functor is extended to relations. In a relational theory of datatypes, all functors are extended to relations in such a way that when restricted to functions all their algebraic properties remain unchanged. Functors extended in this way are called *relators*.

The formal framework for this extension is known as an *allegory*. An allegory is a category with additional structure, the additional structure capturing the most essential characteristics of relations. The additional axioms are as follows. First of all, relations of the same type are ordered by the *partial order* $\subseteq$ and composition is monotonic with respect to this order. That is,

$$S_1 {\cdot} T_1 \subseteq S_2 {\cdot} T_2 \quad \Leftarrow \quad S_1 \subseteq S_2 \ \wedge \ T_1 \subseteq T_2 \ .$$

Secondly, for every pair of relations $R\,,\,S \,::\, A \sim B$, their *intersection* (*meet*) $R \cap S$ exists and is defined by the following universal property, for each $X \,::\, A \sim B$,

$$X \subseteq R \ \wedge \ X \subseteq S \quad \equiv \quad X \subseteq R \cap S \ .$$

Finally, for each relation $R \,::\, A \sim B$ its *converse* $R^{\cup} \,::\, B \sim A$ exists. The converse operator satisfies the requirements that it is its own Galois adjoint, that is,

$$R^{\cup} \subseteq S \quad \equiv \quad R \subseteq S^{\cup} \ ,$$

and is contravariant with respect to composition,

$$(R {\cdot} S)^{\cup} \ = \ S^{\cup} \bullet R^{\cup} \ .$$

All three operators of an allegory are connected by the *modular law*, also known as Dedekind's law [41]:

$$R {\cdot} S \ \cap \ T \ \subseteq \ (R \ cap \ T {\cdot} S^{\cup}) \bullet S \ .$$

Now, a *relator* is a monotonic functor that commutes with converse. That is, the functor F is a relator iff,

(3) $FR \bullet FS \ = \ F(R {\cdot} S)$ for each $R \,::\, A \sim B$ and $S \,::\, B \sim C$,

(4) $F \mathrm{id}_A \ = \ \mathrm{id}_{FA}$ for each A,

(5) $FR \subseteq FS \quad \Leftarrow \quad R \subseteq S$ for each $R \,::\, A \sim B$ and $S \,::\, A \sim B$,

(6) $(FR)^{\cup} \ = \ F(R^{\cup})$ for each $R \,::\, A \sim B$.

Relators extend functors A design requirement which led to the above definition of a relator [4,5] is that a relator should extend the notion of a functor but in such a way that it coincides with the latter notion when restricted to functions. Formally, relation $R :: A \sim B$ is everywhere defined or *total* iff

$$\mathsf{id}_B \subseteq R^\cup \cdot R \; ,$$

and relation R is single-valued or *simple* iff

$$R \cdot R^\cup \subseteq \mathsf{id}_A \; .$$

A *function* is a relation that is both total and simple. It is easy to verify that total and simple relations are closed under composition. Hence, functions are closed under composition too. In other words, the functions form a sub-category. For an allegory $\mathcal{A}$, we denote the sub-category of functions by $Map(\mathcal{A})$. Moreover, it is easily shown that our definition guarantees that relators preserve simplicity and totality, and thus functionality of relations.

Having made the shift from categories to allegories, the extension of the functional theory of datatypes in chapter 2 is surprisingly straightforward (which is another reason why not doing it is short-sighted). The extension of the disjoint sum functor to a disjoint sum relator can be done in such a way that all the properties of $+$ and $\triangledown$ remain valid, as is the case for the extension of the theory of initial algebras, catamorphisms and type functors. For example, catamorphisms with relations as arguments are well-defined and satisfy the fusion property, the map-fusion property etc. There is, however, one catch — the process of dualising properties of disjoint sum to properties of cartesian product is not valid. Indeed, almost all of the properties of cartesian product that we presented are not valid, in the form presented here, when the variables range over arbitrary relations. (The banana split theorem is a notable exception.)

An example of what goes wrong is the fusion law. Consider $\mathsf{id} \triangle \mathsf{id} \bullet R$ and $R \triangle R$, where R is a relation. If R is functional —that is, if for each y there is at most one x such that $(x, y) \in R$ then these two are equal. This is an instance of the fusion law presented earlier. However, if R is not functional then they may not be equal. Take R to be, for example, the relation $\{(0,0), (1,0)\}$ in which both 0 and 1 are related to 0. Then,

$$\mathsf{id} \triangle \mathsf{id} \bullet R \;=\; \{((0,0), 0), ((1,1), 0)\}$$

whereas

$$R \triangle R \;=\; \{((0,0), 0), ((1,1), 0), ((0,1), 0), ((1,0), 0)\} \; .$$

The relation $\mathsf{id} \triangle \mathsf{id}$ is the *doubling* relation: it relates a pair of values to a single value whereby all the values are equal. Thus, $\mathsf{id} \triangle \mathsf{id} \bullet R$ relates a pair of *equal* values to 0. On the other hand, $R \triangle R$ relates a pair of values to a single value, whereby each component of the pair is related by R to the single value. The difference thus arises from the nondeterminism in R.

In conclusion, extending the functional theory of datatypes to relations is desirable but not without pitfalls. The pitfalls are confined, however, to the properties of cartesian product. We give no formal justification for this. The reader will just have to trust us that in the ensuing calculations, where one or more argument is a relation, that the algebraic properties that we exploit are indeed valid.

Membership We have argued that a datatype is not just a mapping from types to types but also a functor. We have now argued that a datatype is a relator. For the correctness of the generic unification algorithm we also need to know that a membership relation can be defined on a datatype.

The full theory of membership and its consequences has been developed by Hoogendijk and De Moor [24,22]. Here we give only a very brief account.

Let F be a relator. A *membership relation* on F is a parametrically polymorphic relation mem of type $a \sim Fa$ for all a. Parametricity means that for all relations R,

$$\text{mem} \cdot FR \supseteq R \cdot \text{mem} .$$

In fact, mem is required to be the largest parametrically polymorphic relation of this type.

The existence of a membership relation captures the idea that a datatype is a structured repository of information. The relation mem_a holds between a value x of type a and an F-structure of a's if x is stored somewhere in the F-structure. The parametericity property expresses the fact that determining membership is independent of the type a, and the fact that mem is the largest relation of its type expresses the idea that determining membership is independent of the position in the data structure at which a value is stored.

The parametricity property has the following consequence which we shall have occasion to use. For all (total) functions f of type $a \rightarrow b$,

$$f \cdot \text{mem}_a = \text{mem}_b \cdot Ff .$$

5.4   Occurs-In

This section contains a proof of the generic statement that two expressions are not unifiable if one occurs in the other. We define a (generic) relation occurs_properly_in and we then show that occurs_properly_in is indeed a proper ordering on expressions (that is, if expression x occurs_properly_in expression y then x and y are different). We also show that the occurs_properly_in relation is invariant under substitution. Thus, if expression x occurs_properly_in expression y no substitution can unify them. To show that occurs_properly_in is proper we define a (generic) function size of type $F^*V \rightarrow \mathbb{N}$ and we show that size is preserved by the relation occurs_properly_in. The definition of size involves a restriction on the relator F which is used to guarantee correctness of the algorithm[8].

---

[8] A more general proof [7] using the generic theory of F-reductivity [15,14,16] avoids this assumption and, indeed, avoids the introduction of the size function altogether.

Definition 7   The relation occurs_properly_in of type $F^*V \sim F^*V$ is defined by

$$\text{occurs\_properly\_in} \;=\; (\text{mem} \bullet \text{embr}_V{}^{\cup})^+ \;.$$

(Recall that mem is the membership relation of F and that $\text{embr}_V = \text{in}_{V^{\kappa}+F} \bullet \text{inr}$ where $(F^*V, \text{in}_{V^{\kappa}+F})$ is an initial algebra.) Informally, the relation $\text{embr}_V{}^{\cup}$ (which has type $FF^*V \sim F^*V$) destructs an element of F^*V into an F structure and then mem identifies the data stored in that F structure. Thus $\text{mem} \bullet \text{embr}_V{}^{\cup}$ destructs an element of F^*V into a number of immediate subcomponents. Application of the transitive closure operation repeats this process thus breaking the structure down into all its subcomponents.

□

In our first lemma we show that the occurs_properly_in relation is closed under substitutions. That is, for all substitutions f,

$$x \text{ occurs\_properly\_in } y \;\Rightarrow\; (fx) \text{ occurs\_properly\_in } (fy) \;.$$

The property is formulated without mention of the points x and y and proved using point-free relation algebra.

Lemma 8   For all substitutions f,

$$\text{occurs\_properly\_in} \;\subseteq\; f^{\cup} \bullet \text{occurs\_properly\_in} \bullet f \;.$$

Proof   Suppose f is a substitution. That is, $f = g \diamond \text{id}$ for some g. Since the relation occurs_properly_in is the transitive closure of the relation $\text{mem} \bullet \text{embr}_V{}^{\cup}$ it suffices to establish two properties: first, that $f^{\cup} \bullet \text{occurs\_properly\_in} \bullet f$ is transitive and, second,

$$\text{mem} \bullet \text{embr}_V{}^{\cup} \;\subseteq\; f^{\cup} \bullet \text{occurs\_properly\_in} \bullet f \;.$$

The first of these is true for all functions f (i.e. relations f such that $f \bullet f^{\cup} \subseteq \text{id}$). (To be precise, if R is a transitive relation and f is a function then $f^{\cup} \bullet R \bullet f$ is transitive.) We leave its simple proof to the reader. The second is proved as follows:

$$f^{\cup} \bullet \text{occurs\_properly\_in} \bullet f$$
$$\supseteq \qquad \{ \qquad R^+ \supseteq R \quad \}$$
$$f^{\cup} \bullet \text{mem} \bullet \text{embr}_V{}^{\cup} \bullet f$$
$$\supseteq \qquad \{ \qquad \text{embr}_V \text{ is a function, definition of embr}_V \quad \}$$
$$f^{\cup} \bullet \text{mem} \bullet \text{embr}_V{}^{\cup} \bullet f \bullet \text{in} \bullet \text{inr} \bullet \text{embr}_V{}^{\cup}$$
$$= \qquad \{ \qquad f = g \diamond \text{id} = (\!|g \triangledown \text{embr}_V|\!), \text{ computation} \quad \}$$
$$f^{\cup} \bullet \text{mem} \bullet \text{embr}_V{}^{\cup} \bullet g \triangledown \text{embr}_V \bullet \text{id} + Ff \bullet \text{inr} \bullet \text{embr}_V{}^{\cup}$$
$$= \qquad \{ \qquad \text{computation} \quad \}$$
$$f^{\cup} \bullet \text{mem} \bullet \text{embr}_V{}^{\cup} \bullet \text{embr}_V \bullet Ff \bullet \text{embr}_V{}^{\cup}$$
$$= \qquad \{ \qquad \text{embr}_V{}^{\cup} \bullet \text{embr}_V = \text{id} \quad \}$$

$$f^{\cup} \bullet \text{mem} \bullet Ff \bullet \text{embr}_V{}^{\cup}$$

$\sqsupseteq$ {   parametricity of mem   }

$$\text{mem} \bullet Ff^{\cup} \bullet Ff \bullet \text{embr}_V{}^{\cup}$$

$\sqsupseteq$ { F is a relator and f is a total function.

Thus, $Ff^{\cup} \bullet Ff \sqsupseteq \text{id}$ }

$$\text{mem} \bullet \text{embr}_V{}^{\cup} \quad .$$

$\square$

We now define a function size of type $F^*V \rightarrow \mathbb{N}$ by

$$\text{size} \;=\; (\!|\text{zero} \triangledown (\text{succ} \bullet \varSigma\text{mem})|\!) \quad .$$

Here, $\varSigma$ is the *summation quantifier*. That is, for an arbitrary relation R with target $\mathbb{N}$,

$$(\varSigma R)x \;\;=\;\; \varSigma(m\colon\, m\,R\,x\colon\, m) \quad .$$

The assumption in the definition of size is that F is finitely branching: that is, for each F structure x, the number of m such that m mem x is finite.

Expressed in terms of points, the next lemma says that if a term x occurs properly in a term y then the size of x is strictly less than the size of y.

Lemma 9

$$\text{occurs\_properly\_in} \quad \subseteq \quad \text{size}^{\cup} \bullet < \bullet \text{size} \quad .$$

Proof   Note that occurs_properly_in and $<$ are both transitive relations. This suggests that we use the leapfrog rule:

$$a \bullet b^* \subseteq c^* \bullet a \;\;\Leftarrow\;\; a{\bullet}b \subseteq c{\bullet}a$$

which is easily shown to extend to transitive closure:

$$a \bullet b^+ \subseteq c^+ \bullet a \;\;\Leftarrow\;\; a{\bullet}b \subseteq c{\bullet}a \quad .$$

We have:

$$\text{occurs\_properly\_in} \quad \subseteq \quad \text{size}^{\cup} \bullet < \bullet \text{size}$$

$\equiv$ {   size is a total function,

definition of occurs_properly_in   }

$$\text{size} \bullet (\text{mem} \bullet \text{embr}_V{}^{\cup})^+ \quad \subseteq \quad < \bullet \text{size}$$

$\Leftarrow$ { $<$ is transitive. Thus, $< \,=\, <^+$.

Leapfrog rule   }

$$\text{size} \bullet \text{mem} \bullet \text{embr}_V{}^{\cup} \quad \subseteq \quad < \bullet \text{size}$$

$\equiv$ { embr_V is a total function   }

$$\text{size} \bullet \text{mem} \quad \subseteq \quad < \bullet \text{succ} \bullet \text{embr}_V$$

$\equiv$ {   definition of size, embr_V and computation   }

$$\text{size} \bullet \text{mem} \quad \subseteq \quad < \bullet \text{succ} \bullet \Sigma\text{mem} \bullet F\text{size}$$
$$\equiv \quad \{ \quad < \bullet \text{succ} = \leq \quad \}$$
$$\text{size} \bullet \text{mem} \quad \subseteq \quad \leq \bullet \Sigma\text{mem} \bullet F\text{size}$$
$$\Leftarrow \quad \{ \quad \text{property of natural numbers: for all } R, R \subseteq \leq \bullet \Sigma R$$
$$\text{That is, } m \; R \; x \; \Rightarrow \; m \leq \Sigma(m: m \; R \; x: m). \quad \}$$
$$\text{size} \bullet \text{mem} \quad \subseteq \quad \text{mem} \bullet F\text{size}$$
$$\equiv \quad \{ \quad \text{size is a total function,}$$
$$\text{parametricity of mem for functions} \quad \}$$
$$\text{true} \; .$$

□

Corollary 10   Suppose F is a finitely branching relator. Then

$$x \text{ occurs\_properly\_in } y \; \Rightarrow \; x \neq y \; .$$

Proof   By the above lemma,

$$x \text{ occurs\_properly\_in } y \; \Rightarrow \; \text{size } x < \text{size } y \; .$$

Thus, since $m < n \Rightarrow m \neq n$,

$$x \text{ occurs\_properly\_in } y \; \Rightarrow \; x \neq y \; .$$

□

Corollary 11   If x occurs_properly_in y then x and y are not unifiable.

Proof   By lemma 8, if x occurs_properly_in y then, fx occurs_properly_in fy, for every substitution f. Thus, for every substitution f, $fx \neq fy$.
□

Exercise 5.4   Take F to be $(1+)$. What is occurs_properly_in? Show that the relation is proper. (Note that the membership relation for $(1+)$ is $\text{inr}^\cup$.)
   Take F to be $a\times$ for some fixed a. What is occurs_properly_in?

□

6   Solutions to Exercises

1.1 Take $\otimes$ to be set intersection, $\oplus$ to be set union, **0** to be the empty set and **1** to be the universe of all colours. The initial value of $a[i, j]$ is the singleton set containing the edge colour as its element
□

2.5

$\text{map}_{Error}\ f\ (\text{error } s) = \text{error } s$

$\text{map}_{Error}\ f\ (\text{ok } x)\ \ \ = \text{ok } (fx)$

$\text{map}_{Drawing}\ f\ (\text{above } x\ y) = \text{above } (\text{map}_{Drawing}\ f\ x)\ (\text{map}_{Drawing}\ f\ y)$

$\text{map}_{Drawing}\ f\ (\text{beside } x\ y) = \text{beside } (\text{map}_{Drawing}\ f\ x)\ (\text{map}_{Drawing}\ f\ y)$

$\text{map}_{Drawing}\ f\ (\text{atom } x)\ \ \ = \text{atom } (f\ x)$

□

2.6

$$(f \triangledown g) \triangle (h \triangledown k) = (f \triangle h) \triangledown (g \triangle k)$$

$\equiv$ $\qquad\{\qquad \triangle\text{-characterisation}\quad\}$

$$f \triangledown g = \text{exl} \bullet (f \triangle h) \triangledown (g \triangle k)\ \wedge\ h \triangledown k = \text{exr} \bullet (f \triangle h) \triangledown (g \triangle k)$$

$\equiv$ $\qquad\{\qquad \triangledown\text{-fusion}\quad\}$

$$f \triangledown g = (\text{exl} \bullet (f \triangle h)) \triangledown (\text{exl} \bullet (g \triangle k))$$

$$\wedge\ h \triangledown k = (\text{exr} \bullet (f \triangle h)) \triangledown (\text{exr} \bullet (g \triangle k))$$

$\equiv$ $\qquad\{\qquad \text{injectivity of } \triangledown\quad\}$

$$f = \text{exl} \bullet (f \triangle h)\ \wedge\ g = \text{exl} \bullet (g \triangle k)$$

$$\wedge\ h = \text{exr} \bullet (f \triangle h)\ \wedge\ k = \text{exr} \bullet (g \triangle k)$$

$\equiv$ $\qquad\{\qquad \triangle\text{- computation}\quad\}$

true .

□

2.7 The most obvious example is multiplication and division in ordinary arithmetic. (Indeed this is where the two-dimensional notation is commonly used.) Addition and subtraction also abide with each other.

Examples in the text are: disjoint sum and composition, and cartesian product and composition. (Indeed all binary functors abide with composition.)

The example used by Hoare was conditionals. The binary operator **if** p, where p is a proposition, (which has two statements as arguments) abides with **if** q, where q is also a proposition.

□

2.11 First, the $\triangledown$-+ fusion rule:

$$f \triangledown g\ \bullet\ h+k\ =\ (f \bullet h) \triangledown (g \bullet k)$$

$\equiv\ \{\quad \triangledown \text{ characterisation}\quad\}$

$$f \triangledown g\ \bullet\ h+k\ \bullet\ \text{inl}\ =\ f \bullet h \bullet \text{inl}\ \wedge\ f \triangledown g\ \bullet\ h+k\ \bullet\ \text{inr}\ =\ g \bullet k \bullet \text{inr}$$

$\equiv\ \{\quad \text{computation rules (applied four times)}\quad\}$

true .

Second, the identity rule:

$$\text{id}+\text{id}$$

$$= \quad \{ \quad \text{definition of } + \quad \}$$
$$\text{inl}\triangledown\text{inr}$$
$$= \quad \{ \quad \text{above} \quad \}$$
$$\text{id} \ .$$

□

2.12 The pattern functor for Bin is $\text{Exl} + (\text{Exr}\times\text{Exr})$ and the pattern functor for Rose is $(\text{Exl} \times (\textit{List } \text{Exr}))$. That is, for Bin it is the binary functor mapping a and z to $a + (z\times z)$, which is polynomial, and for Rose it is the binary functor mapping a and z to $a \times (\textit{List } z)$, which is not polynomial.
□

2.13

$$\text{even} \bullet \text{zero}\triangledown\text{succ} \ = \ \text{true}\triangledown\text{not} \bullet 1+\text{even}$$
$$\equiv \quad \{ \quad \triangledown \text{ fusion and } \triangledown\text{-}+ \text{ fusion,}$$
$$\text{definition of functor } +1 \quad \}$$
$$(\text{even}\bullet\text{zero}) \triangledown (\text{even}\bullet\text{succ}) \ = \ (\text{true}\bullet\text{id}_1) \triangledown (\text{not}\bullet\text{even})$$
$$\equiv \quad \{ \quad \text{true}\bullet\text{id}_1 = \text{true}, \triangledown \text{ is injective} \quad \}$$
$$\text{even}\bullet\text{zero} \ = \ \text{true} \ \wedge \ \text{even}\bullet\text{succ} \ = \ \text{not}\bullet\text{even}$$
$$\equiv \quad \{ \quad \text{extensionality, identifying values zero and true}$$
$$\text{with functions zero and true with domain 1} \quad \}$$
$$\text{even}(\text{zero}) \ = \ \text{true} \ \wedge \ \forall(n:: \text{even}(\text{succ } n) \ = \ \text{not}(\text{even } n)) \ .$$

□

2.14

$$\text{out}\bullet\text{in}$$
$$= \quad \{ \quad \text{definition of out} \quad \}$$
$$(\!(F\text{in})\!)\bullet\text{in}$$
$$= \quad \{ \quad \text{computation rule} \quad \}$$
$$F\text{in}\bullet F(\!(F\text{in})\!)$$
$$= \quad \{ \quad F \text{ is a functor} \quad \}$$
$$F(\text{in}\bullet(\!(F\text{in})\!))$$
$$= \quad \{ \quad \text{definition of out} \quad \}$$
$$F(\text{in}\bullet\text{out})$$
$$= \quad \{ \quad \text{in}\bullet\text{out} = \text{id}_{\mu F} \quad \}$$
$$F\text{id}_{\mu F}$$
$$= \quad \{ \quad F \text{ is a functor} \quad \}$$
$$\text{id}_{F\mu F} \ .$$

□

2.16   We have

$$NoOfTips \ = \ (\!|1^{\kappa} \triangledown add0|\!)$$

where $add0(m, n) = m+n$, and

$$NoOfJoins \ = \ (\!|0^{\kappa} \triangledown add1|\!)$$

where $add1(m, n) = m+n+1$. Now,

$$f \bullet NoOfTips \ = \ NoOfJoins$$
$\Leftarrow$ { definitions and fusion }
$$f \bullet 1^{\kappa} \triangledown add0 \ = \ 0^{\kappa} \triangledown add1 \bullet \mathsf{id} + (f \times f)$$
$\equiv$ { fusion }
$$(f \bullet 1^{\kappa}) \triangledown (f \bullet add0) \ = \ 0^{\kappa} \triangledown (add1 \bullet f \times f)$$
$\equiv$ { injectivity }
$$f \bullet 1^{\kappa} = 0^{\kappa} \ \wedge \ f \bullet add0 \ = \ add1 \bullet f \times f$$
$\equiv$ { pointwise definitions, for all m and n }
$$f1 = 0 \ \wedge \ f(m+n) \ = \ fm+1+fn$$
$\Leftarrow$ { arithmetic, for all m }
$$fm = m-1 \ .$$

We conclude that there is always one less join in a *Bin* than there are tips.
□

2.17

$$(\!|f|\!) \vartriangle (\!|g|\!) \bullet \mathsf{in} \ = \ \chi \bullet F((\!|f|\!) \vartriangle (\!|g|\!))$$
$\equiv$ { $\vartriangle$ fusion }
$$((\!|f|\!) \bullet \mathsf{in}) \vartriangle ((\!|g|\!) \bullet \mathsf{in}) \ = \ \chi \bullet F((\!|f|\!) \vartriangle (\!|g|\!))$$
$\equiv$ { catamorphism computation }
$$(f \bullet F(\!|f|\!)) \vartriangle (g \bullet F(\!|g|\!)) \ = \ \chi \bullet F((\!|f|\!) \vartriangle (\!|g|\!))$$
$\equiv$ { $\vartriangle$ characterisation }
$$f \bullet F(\!|f|\!) \ = \ \mathsf{exl} \bullet \chi \bullet F((\!|f|\!) \vartriangle (\!|g|\!))$$
$$\wedge \ g \bullet F(\!|g|\!) \ = \ \mathsf{exr} \bullet \chi \bullet F((\!|f|\!) \vartriangle (\!|g|\!)) \ .$$

Once again, we continue with just one of the conjuncts, the other being solved by symmetry.

$$f \bullet F(\!|f|\!) \ = \ \mathsf{exl} \bullet \chi \bullet F((\!|f|\!) \vartriangle (\!|g|\!))$$
$\equiv$ { postulate $\chi = \alpha \vartriangle \beta$ }
$$f \bullet F(\!|f|\!) \ = \ \mathsf{exl} \bullet \alpha \vartriangle \beta \bullet F((\!|f|\!) \vartriangle (\!|g|\!))$$
$\equiv$ { $\vartriangle$ computation }
$$f \bullet F(\!|f|\!) \ = \ \alpha \bullet F((\!|f|\!) \vartriangle (\!|g|\!))$$

$$\equiv \qquad \{ \qquad \text{postulate } \alpha = f{\cdot}\gamma \quad \}$$
$$f \cdot F(\!(f)\!) \;\; = \;\; f \cdot \gamma \cdot F((\!(f)\!) \vartriangle (\!(g)\!))$$
$$\Leftarrow \qquad \{ \qquad F \text{ respects composition, } \vartriangle \text{ computation} \quad \}$$
$$\gamma \;\; = \;\; F\mathsf{exl} \; .$$

Combining the two postulates with the final statement, we get

$$(\!(\chi)\!) \;\; = \;\; (\!(f)\!) \vartriangle (\!(g)\!) \;\; \Leftarrow \;\; \chi \;\; = \;\; (f{\cdot}F\mathsf{exl}) \vartriangle (g{\cdot}F\mathsf{exr}) \; .$$

$\square$

2.19 Substituting $(a\oslash)$ for F in the catamorphism rule we get the rule:

$$h{\cdot}(\!(\varphi)\!) \;\; = \;\; (\!(\psi)\!) \;\; \Leftarrow \;\; h{\cdot}\varphi \;\; = \;\; \psi \cdot ms\mathsf{1}\mathsf{id}\oslash h \; .$$

This is the fusion rule used below.

$$(\!(f)\!) \cdot (\tau(\oslash)\, g) \;\; = \;\; (\!(h)\!)$$
$$\equiv \qquad \{ \qquad \tau(\oslash)\, g = (\!(\mathsf{in} \cdot g\oslash\mathsf{id})\!) \quad \}$$
$$(\!(f)\!) \cdot (\!(\mathsf{in} \cdot g\oslash\mathsf{id})\!) \;\; = \;\; (\!(h)\!)$$
$$\Leftarrow \qquad \{ \qquad \text{fusion rule} \quad \}$$
$$(\!(f)\!) \cdot \mathsf{in} \cdot g\oslash\mathsf{id} \;\; = \;\; h \cdot \mathsf{id}\oslash(\!(f)\!)$$
$$\equiv \qquad \{ \qquad \text{catamorphism computation} \quad \}$$
$$f \cdot \mathsf{id}\oslash(\!(f)\!) \cdot g\oslash\mathsf{id} \;\; = \;\; h \cdot \mathsf{id}\oslash(\!(f)\!)$$
$$\equiv \qquad \{ \qquad \oslash \text{ is a binary functor. Thus,}$$
$$\mathsf{id}\oslash(\!(f)\!) \cdot g\oslash\mathsf{id} = g\oslash(\!(f)\!) = g\oslash\mathsf{id} \cdot \mathsf{id}\oslash(\!(f)\!) \quad \}$$
$$f \cdot g\oslash\mathsf{id} \cdot \mathsf{id}\oslash(\!(f)\!) \;\; = \;\; h \cdot \mathsf{id}\oslash(\!(f)\!)$$
$$\Leftarrow \qquad \{ \qquad \text{cancellation} \quad \}$$
$$f \cdot g\oslash\mathsf{id} \;\; = \;\; h \; .$$

We have thus established the rule:

$$(\!(f)\!) \cdot (\tau(\oslash)\, g) \;\; = \;\; (\!(f \cdot g\oslash\mathsf{id})\!) \; .$$

$\square$

2.20 First,

$$\tau(\oslash)\, \mathsf{id}_a$$
$$= \qquad \{ \qquad \text{definition} \quad \}$$
$$(\!(\mathsf{in} \cdot \mathsf{id}\oslash\mathsf{id})\!)$$
$$= \qquad \{ \qquad \oslash \text{ respects identities,}$$
$$\text{identity is the unit of composition} \quad \}$$
$$(\!(\mathsf{in})\!)$$
$$= \qquad \{ \qquad \text{identity rule} \quad \}$$
$$\mathsf{id}_{\tau(\oslash)\, a} \; .$$

Second,

$$\tau(\oslash) \, (f \bullet g)$$
$$= \qquad \{ \qquad \text{definition} \quad \}$$
$$(\!| \text{in} \bullet (f \bullet g) \oslash \text{id} |\!)$$
$$= \qquad \{ \qquad \text{id} = \text{id} \bullet \text{id}, \, \oslash \text{ respects composition} \quad \}$$
$$(\!| \text{in} \bullet f \oslash \text{id} \bullet g \oslash \text{id} |\!)$$
$$= \qquad \{ \qquad \text{exercise 2.19} \quad \}$$
$$(\!| \text{in} \bullet f \oslash \text{id} |\!) \bullet (\tau(\oslash) \, g)$$
$$= \qquad \{ \qquad \text{definition} \quad \}$$
$$(\tau(\oslash) \, f) \bullet (\tau(\oslash) \, g) \ .$$

□

4.1 To express $M f$ we use the last of the three monad equalities:

$$M f$$
$$= \qquad \{ \qquad \text{identities} \quad \}$$
$$\eta \diamond (M f \bullet \text{id})$$
$$= \qquad \{ \qquad \text{monad equality} \quad \}$$
$$(\eta \bullet f) \diamond \text{id} \ .$$

Using $\text{mul} = \text{id} \diamond \text{id}$, we obtain that, for the functor *Set*,

$$\text{mul} \ x \ = \ \{ z \mid \exists(y :: \ z \in y \wedge y \in x) \} \ .$$

The equalities are proven as follows: First,

$$\text{mul} \bullet M \text{mul}$$
$$= \quad \{ \quad \text{mul} = \text{id} \diamond \text{id} \quad \}$$
$$(\text{id} \diamond \text{id}) \bullet M \text{mul}$$
$$= \quad \{ \quad \text{2nd monad equality, id is identity of composition} \qquad \}$$
$$\text{id} \diamond M \text{mul}$$
$$= \quad \{ \quad \text{id is identity of composition,}$$
$$\qquad \text{3rd monad equality, id is identity of composition} \qquad \}$$
$$\text{mul} \diamond \text{id}$$
$$= \quad \{ \quad \text{mul} = \text{id} \diamond \text{id}, \text{ Kleisli composition is associative,}$$
$$\qquad \text{mul} = \text{id} \diamond \text{id} \quad \}$$
$$\text{id} \diamond \text{mul}$$
$$= \quad \{ \quad \text{id is identity of composition, 2nd monad equality} \qquad \}$$
$$(\text{id} \diamond \text{id}) \bullet \text{mul}$$
$$= \quad \{ \quad \text{mul} = \text{id} \diamond \text{id} \quad \}$$
$$\text{mul} \bullet \text{mul} \ .$$

Second,

$$\text{mul} \bullet \eta$$

$$= \qquad \{ \qquad \text{mul} = \text{id} \diamond \text{id, 2nd monad equality} \quad \}$$

$$\text{id} \diamond \eta$$

$$= \qquad \{ \qquad \eta \text{ is unit of Kleisli composition} \quad \}$$

$$\text{id} \ .$$

Third,

$$\text{mul} \bullet M\eta$$

$$= \qquad \{ \qquad \text{mul} = \text{id} \diamond \text{id, 2nd monad equality} \quad \}$$

$$\text{id} \diamond M\eta$$

$$= \qquad \{ \qquad \text{id is identity of composition, 3rd monad equality,}$$
$$\text{id is identity of composition} \quad \}$$

$$\eta \diamond \text{id}$$

$$= \qquad \{ \qquad \eta \text{ is unit of Kleisli composition} \quad \}$$

$$\text{id} \ .$$

□

4.2 $(a \times)^* 1$ is *List a*. The Kleisli identity is the function mapping x to $[x]$. The multiplier is the function concat that concatenates a list of lists to a list, preserving the order of the elements. The Kleisli composition $g \diamond f$ first applies f to a value x of type a, which results in a list of b's. Then g is mapped to all the elements of this list, and the resulting list of lists of c's is flattened to a list of c's.

□

4.3 Since $(1+)^* \emptyset = \mathbb{N}$ we obtain from the fusion theorem that

$$(1+)^* V \ = \ \mathbb{N} \times (V+1).$$

Specifically,

$$\mathbb{N} \times (V+1) \text{ is an initial } X :: V+(1+X) \text{ algebra}$$

$$\Leftarrow \qquad \{ \qquad \text{fusion, } \mathbb{N} \text{ is an initial } 1+ \text{ algebra} \quad \}$$

$$\forall (X :: (1+X) \times (V+1) \cong V+(1+(X \times (V+1))))$$

$$\Leftarrow \qquad \{ \qquad \text{rig} \quad \}$$

$$\text{true} \ .$$

The witness to the last step, rig, is the inverse of a natural isomorphism rig of type

$$Y+(1+(X \times (Y+1))) \rightarrow (1+X) \times (Y+1) \ .$$

It is easily constructed:

$$\mathsf{rig} \;=\; ((\mathsf{inl}\bullet!)\vartriangle\mathsf{inl}) \;\triangledown\; ((\mathsf{inl}\vartriangle\mathsf{inr}) \;\triangledown\; (\mathsf{inr}\times\mathsf{id})) \;\;.$$

The initial algebra is $\mathsf{in}_{(1+)^*} \;=\; (\mathsf{zero}\triangledown\mathsf{succ}) \times \mathsf{id} \bullet \mathsf{rig}.$

$\square$

4.4

$$f\diamond(g\diamond h) \;=\; (f\diamond g)\diamond h$$

$\equiv \{$ definition $\}$

$(\![f \triangledown \mathsf{embr}]\!) \bullet (g\diamond h) = (\![(f\diamond g) \triangledown \mathsf{embr}]\!) \bullet h$

$\Leftarrow \{$ definition of $f\diamond g$, cancel $\bullet h$ $\}$

$(\![f \triangledown \mathsf{embr}]\!) \bullet (\![g \triangledown \mathsf{embr}]\!) \;=\; (\![(f\diamond g) \triangledown \mathsf{embr}]\!)$

$\Leftarrow \{$ fusion, definition of embr $\}$

$(\![f \triangledown \mathsf{embr}]\!) \bullet g \triangledown (\mathsf{in} \bullet \mathsf{inr}) \;=\; (f\diamond g) \triangledown (\mathsf{in} \bullet \mathsf{inr}) \bullet \mathsf{id} + F(\![f \triangledown \mathsf{embr}]\!)$

$\equiv \{$ fusion properties of disjoint sum,

$\qquad \triangledown$ is injective $\}$

$(\![f \triangledown \mathsf{embr}]\!) \bullet g \;=\; f\diamond g$

$\wedge \; (\![f \triangledown \mathsf{embr}]\!) \bullet \mathsf{in} \bullet \mathsf{inr} \;=\; \mathsf{in} \bullet \mathsf{inr} \bullet F(\![f \triangledown \mathsf{embr}]\!)$

$\equiv \{$ definition of $f\diamond g$, computation laws $\}$

true .

The verification that embl is its neutral element is a straightforward use of the computation rules.

$\square$

5.1 Substituting the identity function for h and l, we get

$$f_0 \diamond (Mk \bullet g_1) \;=\; (f_0 \bullet k) \diamond g_1 \;\;.$$

Substituting the identity function for k and h, we get

$$(f_0 \diamond g_0) \bullet l \;=\; f_1 \diamond (g_0 \bullet l) \;\;.$$

$\square$

5.2 Suppose $\circ$ is a function that has the same polymorphic type as function composition. Then, if it satisfies the parametricity property of composition, it is the case that, for all relations R, S and T and all functions f_0, f_1, g_0 and g_1, if

$$(f_0 \,,\, f_1) \in S{\to}R \;\wedge\; (g_0 \,,\, g_1) \in T{\to}S$$

then

$$(f_0{\circ}f_1 \,,\, g_0{\circ}g_1) \in T{\to}R \;\;.$$

Take R to be the singleton set $\{(f(gc) \,,\, f(gc))\}$, S to be the singleton set $\{(gc \,,\, gc)\}$ and T to be the singleton set $\{(c, c)\}$, where f and g are two functions, and c is some value such that $f(gc)$ is defined. Then $(f \,,\, f) \in S{\to}R$

and $(g\,,\,g)\in T{\to}S$. So $(f{\circ}g\,,\,f{\circ}g)\in T{\to}R$. That is, $(f{\circ}g)(c)=f(gc)$. Thus, by extensionality, $f{\circ}g=f{\bullet}g$. The parametricity property does indeed uniquely characterise function composition!

□

5.3 The type of an F-catamorphism is

$$(Fa{\to}a)\to(\mu F\to a)\ .$$

The free theorem is thus that, for all relations R and all functions f and g, if

$$(f\,,\,g)\ \in\ FR{\to}R$$

then

$$(([f])\,,\,([g]))\ \in\ \mathrm{id}_{\mu F}{\to}R\ .$$

Taking R to be a function h and use the point-free definition of $\to$, this is the statement that

$$f\bullet Fh\ =\ h\bullet g\quad\Rightarrow\quad ([f])\ =\ h\bullet([g])\ .$$

□

5.4 Instantiating F to $(1+)$ we get

$\mathsf{occurs\_properly\_in}_{1+}$

$=\quad\{\quad$ definition $\quad\}$

$(\mathsf{mem}_{1+}\bullet(\mathsf{in}_{(1+)_{\ast}}\bullet\mathsf{inl})^{\cup})^{+}$

$=\quad\{\quad\mathsf{mem}_{1+}=\mathsf{inr}^{\cup},\quad\mathsf{in}_{(1+)_{\ast}}\ =\ (\mathsf{zero}{\triangledown}\mathsf{succ})\times\mathsf{id}\bullet\mathsf{rig}\quad\}$

$((\mathsf{zero}{\triangledown}\mathsf{succ})\times\mathsf{id}\bullet\mathsf{rig}\bullet\mathsf{inl}\bullet\mathsf{inr})^{\cup+}$

$=\quad\{\quad$ definition of rig, computation $\quad\}$

$(\mathsf{succ}\times\mathsf{id})^{\cup+}\ .$

A pair (m,x) "occurs properly in" a pair (n,y) if $m<n$ and $x=y$. This particular instance of occurs_properly_in is thus proper in the sense that if u "occurs properly in" v then u and v are not equal.

$F^{\ast}1$ is *List a*, membership is the projection exr and occurs_properly_in is the relation "is a (proper) tail of".

□

References

1. C.J. Aarts, R.C. Backhouse, P. Hoogendijk, T.S. Voermans, and J. van der Woude. A relational theory of datatypes. Available via World-Wide Web at http://www.win.tue.nl/cs/wp/papers, September 1992.
2. Lennart Augustsson Cayenne, a language with dependent types. This volume, 1999.

3. R. C. Backhouse, M. Bijsterveld, R. van Geldrop, and J.C.S.P. van der Woude. Category theory as coherently constructive lattice theory. Department of Mathematics and Computing Science, Eindhoven University of Technology. Working document. Available via World-Wide Web at http://www.win.tue.nl/cs/wp/papers, Last revision: March 1997, 146 pages, 1995.

4. R.C. Backhouse, P. de Bruin, P. Hoogendijk, G. Malcolm, T.S. Voermans, and J. van der Woude. Polynomial relators. In M. Nivat, C.S. Rattray, T. Rus, and G. Scollo, editors, *Proceedings of the 2nd Conference on Algebraic Methodology and Software Technology, AMAST'91*, pages 303–326. Springer-Verlag, Workshops in Computing, 1992.

5. R.C. Backhouse, P. de Bruin, G. Malcolm, T.S. Voermans, and J. van der Woude. Relational catamorphisms. In Möller B., editor, *Proceedings of the IFIP TC2/WG2.1 Working Conference on Constructing Programs from Specifications*, pages 287–318. Elsevier Science Publishers B.V., 1991.

6. R.C. Backhouse and B.A. Carré. Regular algebra applied to path-finding problems. *Journal of the Institute of Mathematics and its Applications*, 15:161–186, 1975.

7. Roland Backhouse. Fixed point calculus applied to generic programming: Part 1. In Zoltan Esik, editor, *Proceedings, Workshop on Fixed Points in Computer Science*, August 1998.

8. Roland C. Backhouse, J.P.H.W. van den Eijnde, and A.J.M. van Gasteren. Calculating path algorithms. *Science of Computer Programming*, 22(1–2):3–19, 1994.

9. G. Bellè, C.B. Jay, and E. Moggi. Functorial ML. In *PLILP96*, volume 1140 of *LNCS* . Springer-Verlag, 1996.

10. Richard Bird, Oege de Moor, and Paul Hoogendijk. Generic functional programming with types and relations. *J. of Functional Programming*, 6(1):1–28, January 1996.

11. Richard S. Bird and Oege de Moor. *Algebra of Programming*. Prentice-Hall International, 1996.

12. R.S. Bird. An introduction to the theory of lists. In M. Broy, editor, *Logic of Programming and Calculi of Discrete Design*. Springer-Verlag, 1987. NATO ASI Series, vol. F36.

13. Robin Cockett and Tom Fukushima. About Charity. Yellow Series Report No. 92/480/18, Dep. of Computer Science, Univ. of Calgary, 1992.

14. H. Doornbos. *Reductivity arguments and program construction*. PhD thesis, Eindhoven University of Technology, Department of Mathematics and Computing Science, June 1996.

15. Henk Doornbos and Roland Backhouse. Induction and recursion on datatypes. In B. Möller, editor, *Mathematics of Program Construction, 3rd International Conference*, volume 947 of *LNCS*, pages 242–256. Springer-Verlag, July 1995.

16. Henk Doornbos and Roland Backhouse. Reductivity. *Science of Computer Programming*, 26(1–3):217–236, 1996.

17. R.W. Floyd. Algorithm 97. Shortest Path. *Comm. ACM*, 5(6):345, June 1962.

18. Maarten M. Fokkinga. *Law and Order in Algorithmics*. PhD thesis, Universiteit Twente, The Netherlands, 1992.

19. Maarten M. Fokkinga. Datatype laws without signatures. *Mathematical Structures in Computer Science*, 6:1–32, 1996.

20. M.M. Fokkinga. Monadic maps and folds for arbitrary datatypes. Memoranda Informatica 94-28, University of Twente, June 1994.

21. E. Gamma, R. Helm, R. Johnson, and J. Vlissides. *Design Patterns – Elements of Reusable Object-Oriented Software*. Addison-Wesley, 1995.

22. Paul Hoogendijk. *A Generic Theory of Datatypes*. PhD thesis, Department of Mathematics and Computing Science, Eindhoven University of Technology, 1997.

23. Paul Hoogendijk and Roland Backhouse. When do datatypes commute? In Eugenio Moggi and Giuseppe Rosolini, editors, *Category Theory and Computer Science, 7th International Conference*, volume 1290 of *LNCS*, pages 242–260. Springer-Verlag, September 1997.

24. Paul Hoogendijk and Oege de Moor. What is a datatype? Technical Report 96/16, Department of Mathematics and Computing Science, Eindhoven University of Technology, 1996. Submitted to Science of Computer Programming. Available via World-Wide Web at http://www.win.tue.nl/cs/wp/papers.

25. P. Jansson and J. Jeuring. PolyP - a polytypic programming language extension. In *POPL '97: The 24th ACM SIGPLAN-SIGACT Symposium on Principles of Programming Languages*, pages 470–482. ACM Press, 1997.

26. P. Jansson and J. Jeuring. Functional pearl: Polytypic unification. *Journal of Functional Programming*, 1998. In press.

27. Patrik Jansson. Functional polytypic programming — use and implementation. Technical report, Chalmers Univ. of Tech., Sweden, 1997. Lic. thesis. Available from http://www.cs.chalmers.se/~patrikj/lic/.

28. C.B. Jay. A semantics for shape. *Science of Computer Programming*, 25(251–283), 1995.

29. C.B. Jay, G. Bellè, and E. Moggi. Functorial ML. Extended version of [9] in press for Journal of Functional Programming '98, 1998.

30. C.B. Jay and J.R.B. Cockett. Shapely types and shape polymorphism. In D. Sannella, editor, *ESOP '94: 5th European Symposium on Programming*, pages 302–316. Springer Verlag Lecture Notes in Computer Science, April 1994.

31. J. Jeuring. Polytypic pattern matching. In *Conference Record of FPCA '95, SIGPLAN-SIGARCH-WG2.8 Conference on Functional Programming Languages and Computer Architecture*, pages 238–248, 1995.

32. J. Jeuring and P. Jansson. Polytypic programming. In J. Launchbury, E. Meijer, and T. Sheard, editors, *Proceedings of the Second International Summer School on Advanced Functional Programming Techniques*, pages 68–114. Springer-Verlag, 1996. LNCS 1129.

33. G. Malcolm. *Algebraic data types and program transformation*. PhD thesis, Groningen University, 1990.

34. G. Malcolm. Data structures and program transformation. *Science of Computer Programming*, 14(2–3):255–280, October 1990.

35. L. Meertens. Algorithmics – towards programming as a mathematical activity. In *Proceedings of the CWI Symposium on Mathematics and Computer Science*, pages 289–334. North-Holland, 1986.

36. L. Meertens. Paramorphisms. *Formal Aspects of Computing*, 4(5):413–424, 1992.

37. Lambert Meertens. Calculate polytypically! In Herbert Kuchen and S. Doaitse Swierstra, editors, *Proceedings of the Eighth International Symposium PLILP '96 Programming Languages: Implementations, Logics and Programs*, volume 1140 of *Lecture Notes in Computer Science*, pages 1–16. Springer Verlag, 1996.

38. Oege de Moor and Ganesh Sittampalam Generic program transformation. This volume, 1999.

39. A. Pardo. Monadic corecursion —definition, fusion laws, and applications—. *Electronic Notes in Theoretical Computer Science*, 11, 1998.

40. J.C. Reynolds. Types, abstraction and parametric polymorphism. In R.E. Mason, editor, *IFIP '83*, pages 513–523. Elsevier Science Publishers, 1983.

41. J. Riguet. Relations binaires, fermetures, correspondances de Galois. *Bulletin de la Société Mathématique de France*, 76:114–155, 1948.

42. B. Roy. Transitivité et connexité. *C.R. Acad. Sci.*, 249:216, 1959.

43. Fritz Ruehr. *Analytical and Structural Polymorphism Expressed Using Patterns Over Types*. PhD thesis, University of Michigan, 1992.

44. Tim Sheard. Automatic generation and use of abstract structure operators. *ACM TOPLAS*, 13(4):531–557, 1991.

45. P. Wadler. Theorems for free! In *4'th Symposium on Functional Programming Languages and Computer Architecture, ACM, London*, September 1989.

46. S. Warshall. A theorem on boolean matrices. *J. ACM*, 9:11–12, 1962.

Generic Program Transformation

Oege de Moor and Ganesh Sittampalam

Programming Research Group, Oxford University Computing Laboratory, Wolfson
Building, Parks Road, OX1 3QD, United Kingdom

1 Introduction

When writing a program, especially in a high level language such as Haskell,
the programmer is faced with a tension between abstraction and efficiency. A
program that is easy to understand often fails to be efficient, while a more
efficient solution often compromises clarity.

Fortunately Haskell permits us to reason about programs, so that we can start
out with a program that is clear but inefficient, and transform it into a program
that is efficient, but perhaps less readable. Indeed, such a *transformational* style
of programming is as old as the subject of functional programming itself.

Programs developed in this style continue to suffer from a lack of readability,
however: typically a functional programmer will develop his program on the
back of an envelope, and only record the final result in his code. Of course he
could document his ideas in comments, but as we all know, this is rarely done.
Furthermore, when the programmer finds himself in a similar situation, using
the same technique to develop a new piece of code, there is no way he can reuse
the development recorded as a comment.

We claim that there is a handful of techniques that functional programmers
routinely use to transform their programs, and that these techniques can themselves be coded as *meta programs*, allowing one to reuse the same optimisation
technique on different pieces of code. In these lectures we shall explore this claim,
and ways in which such meta programs might be implemented.

The structure of these notes is as follows. We first discuss three motivating examples, to clarify what type of optimisation we have in mind, and how
an inefficient program might be annotated with transformations that effect the
optimisation. Next, we discuss how the application of transformations can be
mechanised. Our main design decision at this point is that transformations are
never applied backwards. These ideas are then put to practice in a series of
practical assignments, with a toy transformation system especially developed to
accompany these notes. Finally, we discuss the matching problem in some detail, and explain how we have chosen to circumvent the undecidability inherent
in matching of λ-terms.

Throughout, we shall take a cavalier attitude towards semantics. In particular, we have chosen to ignore all issues of strictness: some of our transformation
rules ought to state side conditions about strictness. While it is admittedly incorrect to ignore such side conditions, they would clutter the presentation and
detract from the main thesis of these lectures.

S.D. Swierstra et al. (Eds.): Advanced Functional Programming, LNCS 1608, pp. 116–149, 1999.
© Springer-Verlag Berlin Heidelberg 1999

2   Abstraction Versus Efficiency

For concreteness, let us first examine a number of examples of the type of optimi-sation that we wish to capture, and the kind of programs on which they operate. This will give us a specific aim when developing the machinery for automating the process, and a yardstick for evaluating our results.

2.1   Minimum Depth of a Tree

Consider the data type of leaf labelled binary trees:

$$\text{data } Btree\, a = Leaf\, a \mid Bin\,(Btree\, a)\,(Btree\, a)$$

The minimum depth of such a tree is returned by the function $mindepth$ :: $Btree\, a \to Int$:

$$mindepth\,(Leaf\, a) = 0$$
$$mindepth\,(Bin\, s\, t) = min\,(mindepth\, s)\,(mindepth\, t) + 1$$

This program is clear, but rather inefficient. It traverses the whole tree, regardless of leaves that may occur at a small depth. A better program would keep track of the 'minimum depth so far', and never explore subtrees beyond that current best solution. One possible implementation of that idea is

$$mindepth\, t = md\, t\, 0\, \infty$$
$$md\,(Leaf\, a)\, d\, m = min\, d\, m$$
$$md\,(Bin\, s\, t)\, d\, m = \text{if } d' \geq m$$
$$\qquad\qquad\qquad\quad \text{then } m$$
$$\qquad\qquad\qquad\quad \text{else } md\, s\, d'\,(md\, t\, d'\, m)$$
$$\qquad\qquad\qquad\quad \text{where } d' = 1 + d$$

The second parameter of md is called d, and it represents the current depth. The third parameter, called m, is the 'minimum depth so far'. When computing the minimum depth of a leaf, we simply take the minimum of m and d. To compute the minimum depth of a composite tree, we first see whether there is any point in exploring beyond this node: if the new depth $d' = 1 + d$ is greater or equal to m, we can cut the search. Otherwise, we first compute the minimum depth of the right subtree t, and using that as the new 'minimum depth so far' we explore the left subtree as well.

Our purpose in these lectures is to explore whether we could annotate the original, clear program for $mindepth$ with the optimisations needed to obtain the second, efficient program. We could then leave the generation of the efficient code to a computer. Here, to obtain the efficient program, we need to know the definition of md in terms of the original function $mindepth$:

$$md\, t\, d\, m = min\,(mindepth\, t + d)\, m$$

as well as some facts about minimum and addition: (a, b and c are assumed to be natural numbers)

$$0 + a = a$$
$$(a + b) + c = a + (b + c)$$
$$min(min\,a\,b)\,c = min\,a\,(min\,b\,c)$$
$$min\,a\,b + c = min(a + c)(b + c)$$
$$min(a + b)\,c = \text{if } b \geq c \text{ then } c \text{ else } min(a + b)\,c$$

The full annotated program, as presented to a transformation system, might thus read as follows (the syntax is ad hoc, and won't be used in the practical exercises):

$$mindepth\,(Leaf\,a) = 0$$
$$mindepth\,(Bin\,s\,t) = min\,(mindepth\,s)(mindepth\,t) + 1$$

transform	$mindepth\,t = md\,t\,0\,\infty$
where	$md\,t\,d\,m = min(mindepth\,t + d)\,m$
with	$0 + a = a$
	$(a + b) + c = a + (b + c)$
	$min(min\,a\,b)\,c = min\,a\,(min\,b\,c)$
	$min\,a\,b + c = min(a + c)(b + c)$
	$min(a + b)\,c = \text{if } b \geq c \text{ then } c \text{ else } min(a + b)\,c$

Would it not be much preferable to write the program in this form, and have the efficient program automatically generated? Obviously a system that allows one to do so would have to offer an inspection of the generated code, so that the programmer can be sure that he has indeed specified the efficient program he wished to write in the first place.

Some readers may object that we have left out an important transformation rule necessary to obtain the efficient program, namely some form of induction. As shown in the lectures by Backhouse and Jeuring at this summer school, such induction principles (and their associated program structures, known as *folds* or *catamorphisms*) can be deduced from the type definition of trees. For this reason, we do not need to state them in annotating a program for optimisation. Some practical restrictions apply, however, and we shall return to this point below.

2.2   Decorating a Tree

We stay with leaf labelled binary trees, and consider their decoration with a list. That is, we wish to implement the function $decorate :: Btree\,a \rightarrow [b] \rightarrow Btree\,(a, b)$ defined by

$$decorate\,(Leaf\,a)\,bs = Leaf\,(a, head\,bs)$$
$$decorate\,(Bin\,s\,t)\,bs = Bin\,(decorate\,s\,bs)\,(decorate\,t\,(drop\,(size\,s)\,bs))$$

Here the function *size s* returns the number of leaves in *s*, and *drop n bs* leaves off the first *n* elements of *bs*. Clearly the definition of *decorate t bs* makes sense only if *size t* ≤ *length bs*, but we shall not need that assumption below.

Consider a left skewed tree *t* of size *n*, where every right hand child of *Bin* is a leaf. To evaluate *decorate t bs*, we will have to compute each of *drop (n − 1) bs*, *drop (n − 2) bs*, and so on, until *drop 1 bs*. Because *drop i bs* takes about *i* steps to evaluate, it follows that the decoration takes $\theta(n^2)$ time: the above program is clear, but of unacceptable inefficiency.

Here is the program that a skilled Haskell programmer would write:

$$decorate\,t\,bs = fst\,(dec\,t\,bs)$$
$$dec\,(Leaf\,a)\,bs = (Leaf\,(a, head\,bs),\ drop\,1\,bs)$$
$$dec\,(Bin\,s\,t)\,bs = (Bin\,s'\,t',\,bs'')$$
$$where\,(s',\,bs') = dec\,s\,bs$$
$$(t',\,bs'') = dec\,t\,bs'$$

The function *dec t bs* decorates *t*, and also returns what is left over of *bs* after the decoration. When we decorate a leaf, we have to drop one element from the supply *bs* of decorations. To decorate a composite tree, we first decorate the left subtree, and then, with what is left over of the decorations (here called *bs'*) we decorate the right subtree. What is left over after decorating the right subtree (in the above program *bs''*), is the net result of the whole decoration. It is immediate from the above program that at each node of the tree, we spend only constant time, and therefore its time complexity is linear in the size of the tree.

How is the efficient program obtained from the first definition of *decorate*? What is the reasoning that the skilled Haskell programmer implicitly applied in writing *dec*? First of all, the original function *decorate* is related to *dec* by:

$$dec\,t\,bs = (decorate\,t\,bs,\ drop\,(size\,t)\,bs)$$

Furthermore, the function *drop* satisfies the identity

$$drop\,(n + m)\,x = drop\,m\,(drop\,n\,x)$$

No further facts are needed. It does of course take a bit of a specialist to know that only these rules are needed to make the program efficient: but it is such knowledge that turns programming from a craft (where the rules are acquired by each programmer through experience) into a science (where the rules are made explicit, and communicated between programmers).

2.3   Partitioning a List

Finally, we consider a rather mundane example, which is representative of a large class of functions that occur frequently. In the standard *List* library of Haskell, there exists a function called *partition* :: $(a \to Bool) \to [a] \to ([a], [a])$. It takes a predicate *p* and a list *x*, and it splits the list *x* into two subsequences: one that contains those elements of x that do satisfy the predicate p, and the other containing those elements of x that fail to satisfy p. A neat program for *partition* might read

$$partition\,p\,x = (filter\,p\,x, filter\,(not \cdot p)\,x)$$

The function *filter* $q\,x$ retains those elements of x that satisfy the predicate q. Using *filter* to code *partition* is pretty, but it requires two passes over the list x, and for each element of x, the predicate p will be evaluated twice.

A more efficient program (and indeed the definition found in the library) is

$$partition\,p\,[\,] = ([\,],[\,])$$
$$partition\,p\,(a:x) = \text{if}\,p\,a\,\text{then}\,(a:y,z)\,\text{else}\,(y,a:z)$$
$$\text{where}\,(y,z) = partition\,p\,x$$

The only way to split the empty list is into two copies of itself. Furthermore, if we have partitioned x into (y,z), and a satisfies the predicate p, we append it to y. If a fails to satisfy p we append it to z.

To develop the more efficient program, we need to know the following facts about *if-then-else*:

$$\text{if}\,not\,c\,\text{then}\,e_1\,\text{else}\,e_2 = \text{if}\,c\,\text{then}\,e_2\,\text{else}\,e_1$$
$$\text{if}\,c\,\text{then}\,(\text{if}\,c\,\text{then}\,e_1\,\text{else}\,e_2)\,\text{else}\,e_3 = \text{if}\,c\,\text{then}\,e_1\,\text{else}\,e_3$$
$$\text{if}\,c\,\text{then}\,e_1\,\text{else}\,(\text{if}\,c\,\text{then}\,e_2\,\text{else}\,e_3) = \text{if}\,c\,\text{then}\,e_1\,\text{else}\,e_3$$
$$f\,(\text{if}\,c\,\text{then}\,e_1\,\text{else}\,e_2) = \text{if}\,c\,\text{then}\,f\,e_1\,\text{else}\,f\,e_2$$

Of course these rules are not particular to the problem in hand. In fact, they are themselves instances of more general transformations involving *case* expressions [19].

Exercises

2.1 Can the computation of the *maximum* depth of a tree be made more efficient in the same way as the computation of the minimum depth? If not, which property of *min* fails for *max*?

2.2 A leaf labelled binary tree is said to be *perfectly balanced* if for every subtree t, the size of the left hand child is precisely $size\,t\,`div`\,2$. Given a list x, the function *build* x produces a perfectly balanced tree whose inorder traversal is x. First give a naive program for computing *build*, and then show how it can be made efficient.

2.3 Are there circumstances where the original definition of *partition* is as efficient as the 'improved' version?

3   Automating the Transition: Fusion and Higher Order Rewriting

The time has come to be more precise about the mechanical application of transformation rules. The main principle in designing a transformation system is that its operation should be transparent: the programmer must be able to predict its results without running experiments. For that reason, we reject any form of artificial intelligence, and also sophisticated procedures from automated theorem proving. Approaches based on such sophisticated techniques have been tried, and shown to fail. Few transformation systems have been used outside the laboratory of their creators, and we believe this is due to the lack of transparency in their operation.

The most obvious strategy is therefore a simple process of rewriting, where the rules are applied from left to right. That still leaves some freedom in specifying the order in which rules are tried, and on which subexpressions. It does seem rather restrictive, however, for it does not allow for the application of rules in reverse direction. In particular, program development by means of the well known unfold/fold strategy [7] is not applicable: we can use a function definition in its evaluating direction, but never backwards, matching the right hand side and producing an instance of the left hand side.

Instead, all inductive arguments must be carried out through so-called *fusion* rules, which encapsulate the induction in a higher order function called a *fold* (or, by residents of the Netherlands, a *catamorphism*). There is precisely one *fold* and an accompanying fusion rule for each data type.

To illustrate, consider the data type of lists. Its *fold* operator *foldr* has type $(a \to b \to b) \to b \to [a] \to b$, and is defined by

$$foldr\, step\, e\, [\,] = e$$
$$foldr\, step\, e\, (a : x) = step\, a\, (foldr\, step\, e\, x)$$

If we write $a \oplus y$ for $step\, a\, y$, we can visualise the computation of *foldr* by

$$foldr\, (\oplus)\, e\, (a_0 : (a_1 : (a_2 : \ldots (a_n : [\,])))) = a_0 \oplus (a_1 \oplus (a_2 \oplus \ldots (a_n \oplus e)))$$

From this equation, it is apparent that *foldr step e* replaces the cons operator (:) by *step*, and the empty list by e. This is the general pattern of a *fold*: it replaces the constructor functions of a given type by new functions.

Many functions on lists can be expressed as instances of *foldr*. For example, $concat = foldr\, (+\!\!+)\, [\,]$ is the function that concatenates the components of a list whose elements are lists themselves, and

$$filter\, p = foldr\, step\, [\,]$$
$$\text{where } step\, a\, y\, = \text{if}\, p\, a\, \text{then}\, a : y\, \text{else}\, y$$

The advantage of expressing a function through *foldr* is that the definition becomes nonrecursive, and therefore much easier to manipulate. In particular, we get a simple way of doing induction that only requires us to apply rewrite rules in one direction.

Suppose that we apply a function f to the result of *foldr*:

$$f(a_0 \oplus (a_1 \oplus (a_2 \oplus \ldots (a_n \oplus e))))$$

In a sense this is a two pass computation: first we compute the sum of the a_i, and then we apply f to that sum. If we know that $f(a \oplus z) = a \otimes f\, z$, (for all a

and z) we can distribute f through the sum, to get a single pass computation:

$$f(a_0 \oplus (a_1 \oplus (a_2 \oplus \ldots (a_n \oplus e)))) =$$
$$a_0 \otimes f(a_1 \oplus (a_2 \oplus \ldots (a_n \oplus e))) =$$
$$a_0 \otimes (a_1 \otimes f(a_2 \oplus \ldots (a_n \oplus e))) =$$

$$\ldots$$

$$a_0 \otimes (a_1 \otimes (a_2 \otimes \ldots (a_n \otimes f e))))$$

That last line is of course nothing but an application of $foldr(\otimes)(f\,e)$. This principle can be formally stated as the *fusion* rule:

$$f(foldr(\oplus)\,e\,x) = foldr(\otimes)\,c\,x, \text{ if } f\,e = c \quad \text{and}$$
$$\lambda a z \to f(a \oplus z) = \lambda a z \to a \otimes f z$$

As remarked above, the distributivity condition should hold for *all* a and x: here we have encoded that by abstracting over these variables, and requiring the two functions to be equal.

As a simple example of the fusion rule, consider $sum(foldr(+\!\!+)[\,]\,x)$. Because $sum[\,] = 0$ and $sum(a +\!\!+ z) = sum\,a + sum\,z$, we have

$$sum(foldr(+\!\!+)[\,]\,x) = foldr(\lambda a\,y \to sum\,a + y)\,0\,x$$

In the mechanical application of the fusion rule, we first match the pattern $f(foldr(\oplus)\,e\,x)$ with $sum(foldr(+\!\!+)[\,]\,x)$. That match succeeds, with $f = sum$, $(\oplus) = (+\!\!+)$, and $e = [\,]$. Next, we attempt to prove the provisos, starting with the second equation. We rewrite its left hand side until no more rules apply:

$$\lambda a z \to sum(a +\!\!+ z) = \lambda a z \to sum\,a + sum\,z$$

The result of the rewriting process (here $\lambda a z \to sum\,a + sum\,z$) is then matched with the pattern $\lambda a z \to a \otimes sum\,z$ in the right hand side of the condition. That match yields a definition for the operator $(\otimes)$, namely $a \otimes y = sum\,a + y$. This completes the verification of the distributivity condition, and next we prove $sum[\,] = 0$: this only involves rewriting.

It is worthwhile to reflect on the mechanical application of fusion before proceeding further. Most of the work goes into the matching process: in particular, the definition of $(\otimes)$ is 'invented' by matching the right hand side of the distributivity condition against a fully rewritten version of the left hand side. A matching algorithm that performs the synthesis of function definitions is said to be a *higher order* matching algorithm. The observation that higher order matching should be a key ingredient of any program transformation tool was first made by Huet and Lang [13].

While fusion is elegant and amenable to mechanisation, it may appear that it only applies to programs that were written in terms of *foldr* to start with. What if we wish to improve a program that uses explicit recursion? The answer is that the identity function is itself an instance of *foldr*:

$$id = foldr(:)[\,]$$

Therefore, if we wish to write a function f in terms of *foldr*, we just apply fusion to the expression

$$\lambda x \rightarrow f(\mathit{foldr}\,(:)\,[\,]\,x)$$

The reader may care to work out for herself how this can be used to write *sum* (the function that returns the sum of a list) as an instance of *foldr*.

Our insistence on the principle that rules are never applied backwards, combined with a matching procedure that is unable to synthesise function definitions that involve pattern matching, sometimes forces us to use multiple variants of the fusion rule. When doing program derivation by hand, a single rule suffices, but in mechanised program synthesis, multiple variants are required. Fortunately, these variants are again dictated by type considerations, just as the fusion rule itself can be deduced from the type to which it applies.

To appreciate why multiple variants of fusion are needed, recall the function *partition*, defined by

$$\mathit{partition}\,p\,x = (\mathit{filter}\,p\,x, \mathit{filter}\,(\mathit{not}\cdot p)\,x)$$

Now let us try and write *partition p* as an instance of *foldr*, by applying fusion to

$$\mathit{partition}\,p\,(\mathit{foldr}\,(:)\,[\,]\,x)$$

We start by rewriting

$$\mathit{partition}\,p\,(a:x)$$
$$=\quad \{\text{definition of } \mathit{partition}\}$$
$$(\mathit{filter}\,p\,(a:x), \mathit{filter}\,(\mathit{not}\cdot p)\,(a:x))$$
$$=\quad \{\text{definition of } \mathit{filter}\ (\text{twice})\}$$
$$(\ \text{if}\,p\,a\,\text{then}\,a:\mathit{filter}\,p\,x\,\text{else}\,\mathit{filter}\,p\,x,$$
$$\quad \text{if}\,\mathit{not}(p\,a)\,\text{then}\,a:\mathit{filter}\,(\mathit{not}\cdot p)\,x\,\text{else}\,\mathit{filter}\,(\mathit{not}\cdot p)\,x\ )$$
$$=\quad \{\text{various facts about } \mathit{if}\}$$
$$\text{if}\,p\,a\,\text{then}\,(a:\mathit{filter}\,p\,x, \mathit{filter}\,(\mathit{not}\cdot p)\,x)$$
$$\quad \text{else}\,(\mathit{filter}\,p\,x, a:\mathit{filter}\,(\mathit{not}\cdot p)\,x)$$

Our procedure for the mechanical application of fusion requires that we match the expression derived above,

$$\lambda\,a\,x \rightarrow \text{if}\,p\,a\,\text{then}\,(a:\mathit{filter}\,p\,x, \mathit{filter}\,(\mathit{not}\cdot p)\,x)$$
$$\quad \text{else}\,(\mathit{filter}\,p\,x, a:\mathit{filter}\,(\mathit{not}\cdot p)\,x)$$

against the pattern

$$\lambda\,a\,x \rightarrow a \otimes \mathit{partition}\,p\,x$$

This clearly fails, because we do not rewrite the right hand side of the pattern before matching, as that would go against our design principle that no rule is applied backwards. Nevertheless, let us assume for the moment that the pattern is rewritten, which results in the definition of *partition* to be expanded. We then have to find $(\otimes)$ so that

$$
\begin{aligned}
\lambda\, a\, x \to\ &\text{if}\, p\, a\, \text{then}\, (a : \textit{filter}\, p\, x, \textit{filter}\, (\textit{not} \cdot p)\, x) \\
&\text{else}\, (\textit{filter}\, p\, x, a : \textit{filter}\, (\textit{not} \cdot p)\, x) \\
=\quad \lambda\, a\, x \to\ &a \otimes (\textit{filter}\, p\, x, \textit{filter}\, (\textit{not} \cdot p)\, x)
\end{aligned}
$$

The only solution is

$$
a \otimes (y, z) = \text{if}\, p\, a\, \text{then}\, (a : y, z)\, \text{else}\, (y, a : z)
$$

Now observe that this requires $(\otimes)$ to perform pattern matching on its right hand argument. To make the matching algorithm synthesise such definitions that involve pattern bindings is rather complicated: to be consistent, it would have to cope not only with tuples, but also with types that have multiple constructor functions.

The conclusion is that to make the above example work with standard fusion, we would have to compromise our guiding design principle (no backward steps), as well as the matching algorithm. Clearly it is preferable to have a specialised fusion rule for dealing with examples such as *partition*. Define the function $split :: (a \to b) \to (a \to c) \to a \to (b, c)$ by

$$
split\, f\, g\, a = (f\, a, g\, a)
$$

This higher order operator captures the idea of two separate functions applied to the same argument. For example, we have

$$
partition\, p = split\, (\textit{filter}\, p)\, (\textit{filter}\, (\textit{not} \cdot p))
$$

We can now formulate a specialised fusion rule that applies to instances of *split*:

$$
split\, f\, g\, (\textit{foldr}\, step\, e\, x) = \textit{foldr}\, (\lambda\, a \to \textit{uncurry}\, (h\, a))\, c\, x
$$

provided

$$
\begin{aligned}
&split\, f\, g\, e = c, \quad \text{and} \\
\lambda\, a\, y \to\ &split\, f\, g\, (step\, a\, y) = \lambda\, a\, y \to h\, a\, (f\, y)\, (g\, y)
\end{aligned}
$$

The function *uncurry* is defined by

$$
uncurry\, k\, (a, b) = k\, a\, b
$$

It explicitly introduces the pattern binding that our matching algorithm cannot synthesise.

Cognoscenti will recognise the above variant of fusion as the *tupling* principle, a well studied technique in transformational program development You will have a chance to explore its applications in the next section, which consists entirely of practical assignments.

Exercises

3.1 Define the *fold* operator on natural numbers. Its type is

$$foldn :: (a \rightarrow a) \rightarrow a \rightarrow Int \rightarrow a$$

You could think of the first argument as replacing the successor function (+1) and the second argument as replacing 0. If there were a data type *Nat* of natural numbers in Haskell, the type of the third argument would be *Nat* and not *Int*. What is the fusion rule for *foldn*?

3.2 Define the *fold* operator on leaf labelled binary trees. Its type is

$$foldbtree :: (a \rightarrow a \rightarrow a) \rightarrow (b \rightarrow a) \rightarrow Btree\, b \rightarrow a$$

What is its fusion rule?

4   The MAG System

Before we proceed to explore the intricacies of pattern matching with function variables, it is important to gain some experience with the concepts introduced so far. We have produced a little system for this purpose, called MAG, after the place where it was written, Magdalen College, Oxford. The name also reminds us of its overriding design principle, famously coined by a former British prime minister, Margaret Thatcher: *the lady is not for turning!* In MAG, transformation rules are applied in one direction only.

MAG is not a serious research tool, it is just a little program rather hastily written for these lectures. It is also an experiment in the use of the pretty printing, parsing and attribute grammar libraries provided by Swierstra and his colleagues at Utrecht University [20]: by using their libraries, we aimed to produce a system that is truly light weight and easy to modify. Finally, we took inspiration from an unpublished term rewriting system by Mike Spivey. An elegant exposition of Spivey's program, with a number of important improvements, can be found in [5]. Bird also shows how Spivey's program can be used as a tool in program verification. A much more advanced tool for transforming Haskell programs is the HYLO system [16]. Other systems that perform the type of transformation considered here are described in [2,14].

4.1   Getting Acquainted

MAG takes two kinds of input file: programs and theories. A *program* is just a program in a functional programming language that is a small subset of Haskell. A *theory* is a set of conditional equations that are applied in the rewriting process. The program file merely exists to infer the types of all the constants in a theory. If you wish the definitions to be used as rewrite rules, they have to be repeated in the theory.

Getting started If you use MAG as a precompiled binary, simply invoke mag. If you use MAG from Hugs (this may be slow!) start up Hugs with a heap of at least 1M, load the file `Main.hs`, and evaluate the function `main`. The system will respond with the message:

```
MAG calculator
Type program name <filename>.p:
```

Respond by typing `program`, followed by a carriage return. This loads a program from the file `program.p`. The system will now ask you to specify a theory:

```
Type theory name <filename>.eq:
```

Respond by typing `sumsq`, followed by a carriage return. This loads a set of equations from the file `sumsq.eq`. The system is ready to transform an expression, and it prompts:

```
Type expression:
```

Type `sumsq`, followed by a carriage return. In response, the system applies rewrite rules from `sumsq.eq` to `sumsq`, until no more apply. It will show the result of each rewrite step, as follows:

```
    sumsq
= { sumsq }
    sum . map sq
= { compose }
    \a -> sum (map sq a)
= { sum }
    \a -> foldr (+) 0 (map sq a)
= { map }
    \a -> foldr (+) 0 (foldr ((:) . sq) [] a)
= { compose }
    \a -> foldr (+) 0 (foldr (\d -> (:) (sq d)) [] a)
= { fusion

        foldr (+) 0 []
    = { foldr0 }
        0

        \b c -> foldr (+) 0 (sq b : c)
    = { foldr1 }
        \b c -> sq b + foldr (+) 0 c
    }
    foldr (\b -> (+) (sq b)) 0
```

There are a couple of things worth noting here. First of all, in order to apply the definition of function composition, the system introduces a new argument called a. Furthermore, when fusion is applied, it does two nested calculations, one for each of the applicability conditions of fusion. In the resulting expression, the argument a is no longer needed, and therefore it is not displayed.

After the calculation is completed, MAG asks you again for a theory file, and then an expression. When you enter an empty name for the theory file (just a carriage return) it stops executing. It will also halt when certain errors occur; we discuss error reporting in more detail below.

Program files Have a look at the contents of program.p. It contains definitions of all functions that you need to carry out the exercises below: it follows that in principle, all can be done in a single session with MAG, only giving program.p as the program file. It should not be necessary to modify program.p. A typical fragment of program.p is

```
{
map f [] = [];
map f (a : x) = f a : map f x
}

{
foldr f e [] = e;
foldr f e (x : xs) = f x (foldr f e xs)
}

{
data Tree a = Node a [Tree a]
}

{
foldtree f step e (Node a ts) = f a (foldr (step . r) e ts)
                                where r = foldtree f step e
}
```

As you can see, it looks a lot like Haskell, but each definition or family of mutually recursive definitions have to be grouped together in curly braces. Also, there is no offside rule, so all definitions within such a group have to be separated by semicolons. Finally, you can only use functions that have been defined earlier in the file: it would be incorrect to define foldr after foldtree, for example. These restrictions are necessary because MAG does not perform dependency analysis on program files.

Theory files A theory file contains a set of conditional rewrite rules. If you wish to use definitions from a program file as rewrite rules, you have to repeat them in the theory file. The syntax for rewrite rules is fairly obvious, except that local definitions (*let* and *where*) are not allowed: the matching algorithm does not know how to cope with them.

As an example, here are the contents of `sumsq.eq`:

```
sumsq: sumsq = sum . map sq;

compose: (f . g) x = f (g x);

sum: sum = foldr (+) 0;

map: map f = foldr ((:).f) [];

foldr0: foldr step e [] = e;
foldr1: foldr step e (a:x) = step a (foldr step e x);

fusion: f (foldr step e x) = foldr g c x,
        if {f e = c;
            \ a y -> f (step a y) = \ a y -> g a (f y)}
```

Each rule starts with an identifier that is the name of the rule, followed by a colon, followed by an equation. Equations are separated by semicolons. When an equation has side conditions (in the above example, only `fusion` has side conditions), they are introduced by a comma, followed by `if`, followed by the conditions in braces, separated by semicolons. For reasons of efficiency, it is advisable to put the conditions in order of increasing complexity, so that the most stringent condition (the last in the list) is tried first. Equations should never introduce variables on the right hand side of equations that do not occur on the left.

Expressions for transformation Expressions to be transformed should not contain any local definitions, and no free variables at all. If you want to transform an expression with variables, bind them with λ. There is no way of transforming local definitions, except by writing them as λ-abstractions.

Error reporting Error reporting from Swierstra's parsing combinators is excellent, so you should get fairly comprehensible messages about syntax errors: these occur when the files are read in. Due to lazy evaluation, there is no telling when a type inference error might occur, and the messages do not give any indication which input line is at fault. Should this occur, eyeball your code, and if there is no obvious mistake, call one of the authors for help.

4.2   Accumulation Parameters

The first set of practical exercises is about *accumulation parameters*. This is a technique for improving functional programs where the original, inefficient definition is generalised by introducing an extra parameter. The parameter is used to *accumulate* additional information during a computation — hence the name. The technique was studied in [4]; see also [11].

Fast reverse A naive definition of the function *reverse* is

$$reverse\,[\,] = [\,]$$
$$reverse\,(a : x) = reverse\,x \mathbin{+\mkern-8mu+} [a]$$

Write down the recursive definition of $(\mathbin{+\mkern-8mu+})$, and estimate how much time it takes to evaluate *reverse* x when x has length n.

The time complexity of *reverse* can be improved by defining:

$$fastrev\,x\,y = reverse\,x \mathbin{+\mkern-8mu+} y$$

Why is this a generalisation of *reverse*? Using the fact that $(\mathbin{+\mkern-8mu+})$ is associative

$$(x \mathbin{+\mkern-8mu+} y) \mathbin{+\mkern-8mu+} z = x \mathbin{+\mkern-8mu+} (y \mathbin{+\mkern-8mu+} z)$$

one can synthesise an efficient program for *fastrev*.

The above definitions, and the associativity of $(\mathbin{+\mkern-8mu+})$, have been recorded in the theory file `reverse.eq`. There is one peculiarity, however: the definition of *fastrev* reads

$$fastrev\,x\,y = reverse\,(foldr\,(:)\,[\,]\,x) \mathbin{+\mkern-8mu+} y$$

Why is the instance of *foldr* there? Confirm your answer by loading the theory file `reverse.eq` in MAG, and transforming *fastrev*. Estimate the time complexity of the resulting program.

Postorder traversal The example of fast reverse is in fact representative of a much larger class of programs, where the concatenation operator is eliminated by introducing an extra parameter, and exploiting the fact that concatenation $(\mathbin{+\mkern-8mu+})$ is associative.

Consider the data type of rose trees, defined by

$$\text{data } Tree\,a = Node\,a\,[Tree\,a]$$

The fold operator on this type of tree is

$$foldtree\,f\,step\,e\,(Node\,a\,ts) = f\,a\,(foldr\,(step \cdot r)\,e\,ts)$$
$$\text{where } r = foldtree\,f\,step\,e$$

In particular, the identity function on rose trees is given by $foldtree\,Node\,(:)\,[\,]$.

The *postorder* *traversal* of a rose tree lists all the elements in the descendants of a node, followed by the label of that node itself:

$$postorder\,(Node\,a\,ts) = concat\,(map\,postorder\,ts) \mathbin{+\mkern-8mu+} [a]$$

This definition is inefficient, because of the concatenation operator. It is your task to produce an efficient definition through the use of MAG.

The theory file `postorder.eq` contains the relevant fusion law, and the definitions of the functions involved. In analogy with the preceding exercise, add the definition of *fastpost* $:: Tree\,a \to [a] \to [a]$ (that is *postorder* with an extra parameter), and also the associativity of concatenation. Load the theory file, and if there are no error messages, transform *fastpost*.

Now consult Section 7.3 of Bird's text *Introduction to functional programming in Haskell*. (If you do not have a copy of this book, we warmly recommend you get one. It teaches you functional programming with *taste*.) In particular, read section 7.3.2. Congratulations! With the help of MAG, you have beaten an Oxford professor at his own game! Your program solves a slightly more complicated problem (postorder instead of preorder), is much simpler than his, and obtained in exactly the same way as fast reverse.

Breadth first traversal It would be wrong to suggest that the technique of accumulating parameters only applies to examples that involve simple concatenation. One can exploit accumulation parameters in almost every program where a tree is traversed using an associative operator.

Consider, for example, the problem of listing the elements of a rose tree in breadth first order. This can be achieved by listing the elements level by level, and then concatenating the result:

$$breadthfirst = concat \cdot levels$$

The function *levels* :: *Tree a* → [[a]] first gives the elements that occur at depth 0, then the elements at depth 1, depth 2 and so on. It is defined by

$$levels\,(Node\,a\,ts) = [a] : glues\,(map\,levels\,ts)$$

$$glues\,[\,] = [\,]$$
$$glues\,(x\,:\,xs) = lzc\,x\,(glues\,xs)$$

$$lzc\,[\,]\,x = x$$
$$lzc\,(a\,:\,x)\,y = \mathbf{if}\,null\,y$$
$$\qquad\qquad\qquad \mathbf{then}\,a : lzc\,x\,[\,]$$
$$\qquad\qquad\qquad \mathbf{else}\,(a \,+\!\!+\, head\,y) : lzc\,x\,(tail\,y)$$

Here *lzc* stands for *long zip with concatenation*. What is the difference between *lzc* and *zipWith*(++)? Is *lzc* associative? What is the time complexity of *levels*?

You know what has to be done: all the definitions can be found in the theory file **levels.eq**. Produce an efficient program with MAG. This program and its derivation were first discovered and presented by [10], and Jeremy Gibbons suggested it as an exercise in the use of MAG. His paper also presents another, arguably more elegant, method of computing the breadth first traversal.

Minimum depth Let us now return to the problem discussed at the beginning of these lectures, namely computing the minimum depth of a leaf labelled binary tree. It was claimed there that apart from the definitions, all we need to produce an efficient program is the following set of rules:

$$0 + a = a$$
$$(a + b) + c = a + (b + c)$$
$$min(min\,a\,b)\,c = min\,a\,(min\,b\,c)$$
$$min\,a\,b + c = min(a + c)(b + c)$$
$$min(a + b)\,c = \text{if } b \geq c \text{ then } c \text{ else } min(a + b)\,c$$

Unfortunately, there is a problem when this set of equations is implemented by rewriting. Why?

In this particular example, the most elegant solution might be to single out rules that should be applied at most once. However, we wish to avoid any ad hoc features in the code of MAG itself, so instead we modify the rules. One can take the last two rules together in a single, composite rule:

$$min\,(min\,a\,b + c)\,d = \text{if } c \geq d$$
$$\text{then } d$$
$$\text{else } min\,(min\,(a + c)(b + c))\,d$$

Even with this fix, however, we cannot directly generate an efficient program. The *mindepth* example is different from those that went before in that there are *two* accumulation parameters. Due to certain limitations in our matching algorithm (which will be discussed in depth later), we have to slightly adapt the fusion rule to cope with the two parameters at once.

These modifications have been installed for you in the file `mindepth.eq`, and transforming the expression `md` will produce the efficient program we discussed above. Because of the large number of free variables in the fusion rule, its generation can take a while: on a Pentium 90 running Linux and Hugs 1.4, it took almost 28 minutes. Which variables in the fusion rule could be bound to improve efficiency of the transformation process? Make that change in `mindepth.eq`, and generate an efficient program for *mindepth*.

4.3 Tupling

The next set of exercises is about tupling: improving the efficiency of a program by computing several values at once. Tupling is in a sense the dual of accumulation parameters: in the first case, we generalise the *range* of a function, and in the second case the *domain*. There is quite a large body of literature on tupling, e.g. [3,6,8,12,17]. In the exercises below, you will have the opportunity to explore its versatility: many programs can be improved through tupling. One could even say that the attribute grammar system presented by Swierstra at this summer school is a specialised tool for tupling.

Fibonacci The standard example of tupling, found in any introductory text on programming, is the Fibonacci function. This function, which is amazingly ubiquitous in computer science, is defined by

$$fib\,0 = 0$$
$$fib\,1 = 1$$
$$fib\,(n + 2) = fib\,(n + 1) + fib\,n$$

This program is inefficient because there are many duplicated calls to *fib*.

To improve the efficiency, we compute *fib n* simultaneously with *fib*(n + 1). That is, we aim to apply the tupling transformation to

$$fastfib = split\,fib\,(\lambda n \to fib\,(n + 1))$$

Of course one also needs some arithmetic to do that transformation. Which two facts about addition are needed? Install these equations in the file fib.eq, and generate the efficient program.

As an aside, we remark that there exists a much better program still, which exploits the identity

$$\begin{pmatrix} 1 & 1 \\ 1 & 0 \end{pmatrix}^{n} \begin{pmatrix} 1 \\ 0 \end{pmatrix} = \begin{pmatrix} fib\,(n + 1) \\ fib\,n \end{pmatrix}$$

together with the fact that exponentiation can be performed in logarithmic time.

Steep sequences A list of numbers is said to be *steep* if each element is greater than the sum of the elements that follow it. We might define the predicate *steep* :: [Int] → *Bool* by

$$steep\,[\,] = True$$
$$steep\,(a : x) = a > sum\,x \wedge steep\,x$$

Estimate the time complexity of *steep*.

How would you improve the efficiency of *steep*? The file steep.eq contains the rules you need to apply tupling. Add a definition of

$$faststeep :: [Int] \to (Bool, Int)$$

note the type carefully!) and generate an efficient program for *faststeep*. In this case you need no rules besides the definitions.

Partition Need we say more? Just do it, and imagine how tedious and error prone it would be to do a derivation by hand! All you need is in partition.eq. In this example, the ordering of the rules in the theory file is rather important: in the rewriting process, they are tried in the order they occur. Why does the rule about distributing a function over a conditional come last?

Decorate Finally, recall the problem of decorating a leaf labelled binary tree. The original, inefficient program is

$$decorate\,(Leaf\,a)\,bs = Leaf\,(a,\,head\,bs)$$
$$decorate\,(Bin\,s\,t)\,bs = Bin\,(decorate\,s\,bs)\,(decorate\,t\,(drop\,(size\,s)\,bs))$$

We aim to improve *decorate* by defining a new function

$$dec\,t\,bs = (decorate\,t\,bs,\,drop\,(size\,t)\,bs)$$

This does not conform exactly to the pattern in our previous examples of tupling, because *dec* is not an instance of *split*. We do have

$$dec\,t = split\,(decorate\,t)\,(drop\cdot size\,t)$$

but this does not make the repeated use of t explicit — and that use must be explicit to obtain a single pass algorithm. Instead, what we need here is

$$split2\,f\,g\,a\,b = (f\,a\,b,\,g\,a\,b)$$

We then have

$$dec = split2\,decorate\,(\lambda t\,bs \to drop\,(size\,t)\,bs)$$

Furthermore, associated with *split2*, one obtains the *double tupling* rule

$$split2\,f\,g\,(foldbtree\,join\,start\,x)$$
$$=$$
$$foldbtree\,(uncurry2\,h)\,k\,x,$$
$$\text{if}\quad \lambda a \to split2\,f\,g\,(start\,a) = \lambda a \to k\,a$$
$$\lambda x\,y \to split2\,f\,g\,(join\,x\,y) = \lambda x\,y \to h\,(f\,x)\,(g\,x)\,(f\,y)\,(g\,y)$$

The function *uncurry2* in the conclusion of this rule is defined by

$$uncurry2\,e\,fg\,hk = e\,(fst\cdot fg)\,(snd\cdot fg)\,(fst\cdot hk)\,(snd\cdot hk)$$

While this may all seem a bit complicated, once *split2* is defined, the rest follows purely from type considerations.

Returning to the problem of optimising *decorate*, the above machinery can be found in the file **decorate.eq**. Run MAG on *dec*. Is the result identical to the program discussed earlier in the lectures? What further transformation needs to be performed?

4.4   Carrying On

In the above examples, we have illustrated the use of MAG in only two kinds of optimisation, namely accumulation parameters and tupling. There is no reason why MAG could not apply more sophisticated transformations. Indeed, one exercise that any transformation tool must tackle is the derivation of the so-called *maximum segment sum* problem. The file **mss.eq** shows how that is done. You now have sufficient knowledge to attempt such exercises yourself. The authors would be pleased to hear of your experience.

5 Matching Typed λ-Expressions

The choice of matching algorithm (for matching the left hand side of rewrite rules to expressions) determines the scope of applicability of transformation rules such as fusion. If we had been able to implement an 'ideal' matching algorithm, all programming exercises in these notes would have been applications of a single formulation of fusion. Put another way, it is the matching algorithm which determines how *generic* our program transformations are.

In the light of this observation, it is perhaps unsurprising that no such ideal algorithm exists: in its full generality, the matching problem is not computable. To cope with that incomputability, we have to somehow restrict the matching problem.

In the context of program transformation, the most popular restriction is to *second-order* matching: roughly speaking, this restricts pattern variables to be of base type (such as *Int*, *Bool* or [*Int*]), or functions between base types. For example, the KORSO transformation system, developed at Bremen, uses second-order matching [9].

Unfortunately the restriction to second-order variables is not a natural one when transforming Haskell programs. Consider, for example, our synthesis of a fast program for *reverse*: this would be beyond the scope of a second-order matching algorithm. We therefore investigate a different restriction of the matching problem, which seems better suited to the applications we have in mind.

We start by reviewing matching of types, both because this will refresh the elementary definitions in the reader's mind, and because we shall need these operations on types later on. We then turn to the definitions on expressions that include λ-bound variables. After these elementary definitions, we introduce substitutions and some related operations. Finally, we discuss a number of variants of the matching problem. We conclude with a rigorous specification of our restricted matching problem, which pins down the algorithm that is implemented in MAG.

This section admittedly requires a little bit more background knowledge than the preceding material: a good introduction to the concepts used here can be found in [18].

5.1 Types

Expressions are typed in the Hindley-Milner discipline, without any modern extensions such as type classes [15]. More precisely, we shall be working with *type schemes*, as defined by the declaration

data *Type* = *Tid Tname* | *Tcon Cname* [*Type*]   deriving *Eq*

That is, a type scheme is a variable (a type identifier), or a constructor applied to a list of argument types. Equality on types is straightforward structural equality.

Substitution. A *type substitution* is a mapping from type variables to types:

    type $Tsub = Tname \rightarrow Type$

The function $tapply :: Tsub \rightarrow Type \rightarrow Type$ applies a substitution to a type in the obvious way.

Generality. We say that τ is *less general* than σ if there exists another substitution ϕ so that

$$tapply\,\tau = tapply\,\phi \cdot tapply\,\sigma$$

Matching. Consider the problem of matching one type against another. Given types p and t a *match* is a substitution τ such that

$$tapply\,\tau\,p = t$$

If there exists a match at all, there exists a most general match. The function $tmatch\,p\,t$ returns a singleton list $[\sigma]$ of that most general match σ, or (if no matches exist) it returns the empty list. Here, *most general* means that σ leaves any variable not occurring in p unchanged.

5.2 Expressions

An expression is a constant, a variable, an application, or a λ-abstraction. Furthermore, each expression is decorated with its type:

    data $Exp = $ $Con\,Constant\,Type$ |
                   $Var\,Name\,Type$ |
                   $Ap\,Exp\,Exp\,Type$ |
                   $Lam\,Name\,Exp\,Type$

This representation is highly redundant, because much of the type information is duplicated. In our experience, however, this redundancy is worth the overhead when programming a system such as MAG: in any form of meta programming, it is very easy to produce terms that are ill-typed. Carrying around the types everywhere makes it easier to track such errors down. In the examples below, we shall often leave the type information implicit to improve readability.

α-*conversion* In λ-expressions, the names of bound variables do not matter. We have, for example, the identity

$$\lambda x \rightarrow x + z = \lambda y \rightarrow y + z$$

Note, however, that

$$\lambda x \rightarrow x + z \neq \lambda z \rightarrow z + z$$

because z is a free variable on the left hand side. This principle, that bound variables can be renamed to any identifier that is not free in the body of a λ-abstraction, is called α-*conversion*. The function

    $alphaconvertible :: Exp \rightarrow Exp \rightarrow Bool$

tests whether two expressions are equal up to renaming of bound variables.

η-conversion If you do not use a bound variable in an abstraction body, there is no need to mention it. We have, for instance,

$$map = \lambda f \to map\, f$$

Again we have to be careful with free variables, however:

$$e = \lambda x \to e\, x$$

only if x does not occur free in e. This principle is called *η-conversion*. One can write a function

$$etacontract :: Exp \to Exp$$

that systematically applies η-conversion to eliminate all redundant abstractions. Conversely, it is also possible to expand a term so that every expression of function type is an abstraction, or applied to an argument. Expansion is a bit trickier to code in Haskell than contraction, however, because of the need to generate fresh identifiers — a notorious difficulty in a purely functional setting [1].

Equality. We define two expressions to be *equal* if one can be obtained from the other through repeated application of α- and η-conversion. That test could be coded in Haskell as follows:

$$\text{instance } Eq\ Exp \text{ where}$$
$$e_1 == e_2 = alphaconvertible\,(etacontract\ e_1)\,(etacontract\ e_2)$$

β-reduction. It is important to realise that $e_1 == e_2$ is *not* the same as saying that e_1 and e_2 represent the same value. That is because our notion of equality does not entail any notion of evaluation. For example

$$(\lambda x \to x + 1)2 \ /= 2 + 1$$

The fundamental evaluation rule for expressions is

$$(\lambda x \to e_1)\, e_2 = subst\ x\ e_2\ e_1$$

That is, all free occurrences of x in e_1 are replaced by e_2. The substitution function *subst* is defined in the usual way (we assume that all naming conflicts are resolved by appropriate renaming). This evaluation rule is called *β-reduction*.

The function *betareduce* :: $Exp \to Exp$ exhaustively applies the β-reduction rule to all subexpressions of its argument. It is a fact that *betareduce* will always terminate, thanks to the type system that we employ (provided we ignore user-defined types). Furthermore, it does not matter in what order the reductions are carried out: the result is always the same.

If we ignore the semantics of constants, two expressions e_1 and e_2 represent the same value iff *betareduce* $e_1 ==$ *betareduce* e_2. Because *betareduce* is terminating, we could have taken this as our definition of equality, but we want to vary the notion of β-reduction in our discussion of matching below.

One step reduction. In particular, we shall consider the function *betastep*, which carries out one pass over an expression, applying β-reduction where possible:

$$betastep(Var\,x\,t) = Var\,x\,t$$
$$betastep(Con\,c\,t) = Con\,c\,t$$
$$betastep(Lam\,x\,e\,t) = Lam\,x\,(betastep\,e)\,t$$
$$betastep(Ap\,e_1\,e_2\,t) = \text{case}\,e_1'\,\text{of}$$
$$Lam\,x\,b_- \rightarrow subst\,x\,e_2'\,b$$
$$_- \qquad \rightarrow Ap\,e_1'\,e_2'\,t$$
$$\text{where } e_1' = betastep\,e_1$$
$$e_2' = betastep\,e_2$$

Its name derives from the fact that it captures the notion of one *parallel* reduction step. To appreciate the difference between *betareduce* and *betastep*, consider the expression

$$e = (\lambda f\,a \rightarrow 1 + f\,a)(\lambda b \rightarrow b + 2)$$

We have

$$betareduce\,e = \lambda a \rightarrow 1 + (a + 2)$$

However, application of *betastep* yields

$$betastep\,e = \lambda a \rightarrow 1 + (\lambda b \rightarrow b + 2)\,a$$

because the result of applying a substitution is not reduced again. It is not the case, therefore, that *betareduce* e == *betastep* e. Note that (for the particular e defined above) we do have

$$betastep(betastep\,e) == betareduce\,e$$

More generally, for any expression e, there exists a natural number n so that

$$betastep^n\,e == betareduce\,e$$

In this sense *betastep* is an approximation of *betareduce*. The importance of *betastep* is that it can be undone in the process of matching against a pattern.

Exercises

5.1 Write a program for *alphaconvertible*.

5.2 Write a program for *etacontract*.

5.3 Write a program for *subst*, assuming that there are no name conflicts.

5.4 Write a program for *betareduce*.

5.3   Substitutions

An *expression substitution* is a mapping from variables to expressions:

$$\text{type } Esub = Name \rightarrow Type$$

Note that an expression substitution applies only to variables in the expression, not to type identifiers that might occur in the type attributes of an expression.

A *substitution* is a pair of an expression substitution and a type substitution

$$\text{type } Sub = (Esub, Tsub)$$

The application of such a substitution (ϵ, τ) applies ϵ to the variables in an expression, and τ to all the type attributes (ϵ and τ should be consistent with each other so that the result of applying a substitution is well-typed):

$$apply\,(\epsilon, \tau)\,(Var\,x\,t) = \epsilon\,x$$
$$apply\,(\epsilon, \tau)\,(Con\,c\,t) = Con\,c\,(tapply\,\tau\,t)$$
$$apply\,(\epsilon, \tau)\,(Ap\,e_1\,e_2\,t) = Ap\,(apply\,(\epsilon, \tau)\,e_1)\,(apply\,(\epsilon, \tau)\,e_2)\,(tapply\,\tau\,t)$$
$$apply\,(\epsilon, \tau)\,(Lam\,x\,e\,t) = Lam\,x\,(apply\,(\epsilon, \tau)\,e)\,(tapply\,\tau\,t)$$

In the last clause of this definition, we tacitly assumed that there are no name clashes: ϵ does not substitute for x, and x does not occur in the range of ϵ. If this cannot be guaranteed, the variable x has to be removed from the domain of ϵ before processing the body of $Lam\,x\,e\,t$, and the bound occurrence of x has to be renamed.

A substitution (ϵ, τ) is *closed* if all variables substituted for by ϵ are mapped to closed λ-terms (since closed λ-terms can contain free type variables, we cannot impose this restriction on the type substitution τ too).

Generality of substitutions is defined the same as for type substitutions. A substitution Ψ is said to be *less general* than Φ if there exists another substitution Δ so that

$$apply\,\Psi\,e == apply\,\Delta\,(apply\,\Phi\,e)\ , \text{ for all } e.$$

We write $\Psi \leq \Phi$ when Ψ is less general than Φ. Two substitutions are *incomparable* if neither is more general than the other.

5.4   Matching

Simple matching We are now in a position to define what we mean exactly by *simple matching* of λ-expressions. Given a pattern p and a closed λ-term e, a *simple match* is a closed substitution Φ which satisfies the additional restriction that variables are only mapped to beta-normal forms (i.e. fully beta-reduced expressions), such that

$$apply\,\Phi\,p == e$$

As in the case of types, if there exists a simple match, there exists a most general simple match.

It is fairly easy to extend standard matching algorithms to cope with bound variables and η-conversion. Let

$$simplematch :: Exp \rightarrow Exp \rightarrow [Sub]$$

be the function so that $simplematch\,p\,e$ returns a singleton containing the most general match if a match exists at all, and the empty list otherwise.

Ideal matching Now suppose that we modify the condition in the above definition of simple matching to read

$$betareduce(apply\,\Phi\,p) == betareduce\,e$$

A substitution Φ that satisfies this equation is said to be an *ideal match*. Ideal matches may be incomparable in the generality order, and not have a common generalisation. To see this, let

$$p = f\,x \text{ and } e = 0$$

then both

$$\left\{ \begin{array}{l} f := \lambda a \rightarrow a \\ x := 0 \end{array} \right\} \text{ and } \{ f := \lambda a \rightarrow 0 \}$$

are ideal matches, the two are incomparable, and there exists no ideal match that generalises both.

It follows that we need to modify the concept of a 'most general match'. Given p and e, the *ideal match set* is a set X of ideal matches for p and e such that

- for each ideal match Φ there exists Ψ in X so that $\Phi \leq \Psi$
- the elements of X are pairwise incomparable.

The first clause is a completeness condition: it says that every ideal match is represented in X. The second clause says that there are no redundant elements in X.

Unfortunately, it is not even decidable whether an ideal match set is empty or not [13]. It follows that we cannot hope to solve the matching problem in its full generality. Intuitively, this is unsurprising because the inverse image of *betareduce* is potentially infinite. This is also true of *betastep*, but because it is an approximation of *betareduce*, it is easier to invert it in the process of matching against a pattern.

One-step matching We are thus led to the following definition. Given a pattern p and an expression e, a *one-step match* is a substitution Φ such that

$$betastep(apply\,\Phi\,p) == betareduce\,e$$

The definition of a *one-step match set* is analogous to that of an ideal match set. The matching algorithm in MAG computes this one-step match set.

To understand the behaviour of MAG, it is important that the reader develops an intuition for one-step matching, so that she can adapt the transformation rules (as we have done in the *mindepth* exercise). As a simple but typical example, consider the pattern and term

$$\lambda\, a\, x \to f\, a((\!+\!)x) \text{ and } \lambda\, a\, x\, y \to x +\!\!\!+ (a : y)$$

The one-step match set of this pair is a singleton, namely

$$\{ f := \lambda\, a\, b\, c \to b(a : c) \}$$

To illustrate the difference between one-step matching and ideal matching, consider $f\, x$ and $\lambda\, a \to 1 + (a + 2)$. The match

$$\begin{cases} f := \lambda\, g\, a \to 1 + g\, a \\ x := \lambda\, b \to b + 2 \end{cases}$$

is in the ideal match set, but since

$$betastep((\lambda\, g\, a \to 1 + g\, a)(\lambda\, b \to b + 2)) == \lambda\, a \to 1 + (\lambda\, b \to b + 2)\, a$$

which is not the same as $\lambda\, a \to 1 + (a + 2)$, it is not in the one-step match set.

It is beyond the scope of these notes to go into the details of an algorithm for computing one-step match sets. Essentially it proceeds by repeatedly extracting subexpressions. Such an algorithm, its proof of correctness and a performance comparison with similar algorithms are the subject of a forthcoming paper.

6   Concluding Remarks

In these lectures, we have attempted to demonstrate that the fusion transformation is itself a generic program, whose parameters are the distributivity conditions needed in its application. The scope of its applicability is marred only by the limitations of the matching algorithm used to implement rewriting.

We have proposed the *one-step matching* algorithm for typed λ-expressions, which appears not to be commonly known. Compared to more traditional matching algorithms (which restrict the order of variables), this algorithm greatly enhances the applicability of transformations such as fusion. It is however still necessary to state special cases of fusion as separate rules, most notably for tupling.

These ideas were illustrated by a cheap-and-cheerful Haskell program, the MAG system. We found the libraries for pretty printing and parsing from Utrecht University an invaluable tool. The attribute grammar system from Utrecht made it easy to experiment with different versions of the type checker.

Acknowledgements

Mike Spivey's rewriting system was the starting point of these investigations. He also commented on a draft of these notes, suggesting several corrections and improvements. Richard Bird generously shared insights gained while implementing his own Functional Calculator, and also commented on a draft. We are grateful for his advice and friendship. Jeremy Gibbons suggested many examples — unfortunately, time and space did not allow us to include them all. Doaitse Swierstra provided all three tools used in building MAG: the pretty-printing and parsing libraries, as well as his attribute grammar system. He furthermore provided encouragement and many suggestions during a visit to Oxford at the beginning of August. Ivan Sanabria pointed out a number of mistakes in an early draft.

References

1. L. Augustsson, M. Rittri, and D. Synek. Functional pearl: On generating unique names. *Journal of Functional Programming*, 4:117–123, 1994.
2. F. Bellegarde. A transformation system combining partial evaluation with term rewriting. In *Higher-Order Algebra, Logic and Term Rewriting*, volume 816 of *Lecture Notes in Computer Science*, pages 40–55. Springer-Verlag, 1994.
3. R. S. Bird. Tabulation techniques for recursive programs. *Computing Surveys*, 12(4):403–417, December 1980.
4. R. S Bird. The promotion and accumulation strategies in functional programming. *ACM Transactions on Programming Languages and Systems*, 6(4):487–504, 1984.
5. R. S Bird. *Introduction to Functional Programming in Haskell*. International Series in Computer Science. Prentice Hall, 1998.
6. E. A. Boiten. Improving recursive functions by inverting the order of evaluation. *Science of Computer Programming*, 18(2):139–179, 1992.
7. R. M. Burstall and J. Darlington. A transformation system for developing recursive programs. *Journal of the ACM*, 24(1):44–67, 1977.
8. W. N. Chin. Fusion and tupling transformations: Synergies and conflicts (invited paper). In *Fuji International Workshop on Functional and Logic Programming*, pages 176–195. World Scientific, 1995.
9. R. Curien, Z. Qian, and H. Shi. Efficient second-order matching. In *7th International Conference on Rewriting Techniques and Applications*, volume 1103 of *Lecture Notes in Computer Science*, pages 317–331. Springer Verlag, 1996.
10. J. Gibbons and G. Jones. The under-appreciated unfold. In *3rd ACM SIGPLAN International Conference on Functional Programming 1998*, 1998.
11. Z. Hu, H. Iwasaki, and M. Takeichi. Calculating accumulations. Technical Report METR 96-0-3, Department of Mathematical Engineering, University of Tokyo, Japan, 1996. Available from URL:
    `http://www.ipl.t.u-tokyo.ac.jp/ hu/pub/tech.html`.
12. Z. Hu, H. Iwasaki, M. Takeichi, and A. Takano. Tupling calculation eliminates multiple data traversals. In *2nd ACM SIGPLAN International Conference on Functional Programming (ICFP '97)*, pages 164–175, 1997.
13. G. Huet and B. Lang. Proving and applying program transformations expressed with second-order patterns. *Acta Informatica*, 11:31–55, 1978.
14. J. Launchbury and T. Sheard. Warm fusion: Deriving build-catas from recursive definitions. In *Functional Programming Languages and Computer Architecture*, pages 314–323. Association for Computing Machinery, 1995.
15. R. Milner. A theory of type polymorphism in programming. *Journal of Computer and System Sciences*, 17:348–375, 1978.

16. Y. Onoue, Z. Hu, H. Iwasaki, and M. Takeichi. A calculational fusion system hylo. In R. S. Bird and L. Meertens, editors, *IFIP TC2 Working Conference on Algorithmic Languages and Calculi*, pages 76–106. Chapman and Hall, 1997.
17. A. Pettorossi. Methodologies for transformations and memoing in applicative languages. Ph.D. thesis CST-29-84, University of Edinburgh, Scotland, 1984.
18. S. L. Peyton-Jones. *The Implementation of Functional Programming Languages*. Foundations of Computing Series. Prentice-Hall International, 1994.
19. S. L. Peyton-Jones and A. L. M. Santos. A transformation-based optimiser for haskell. *Science of Computer Programming*, 32(1–3):3–48, 1998.
20. S. D. Swierstra and L. Duponcheel. Deterministic, error-correcting combinator parsers. In J. Launchbury, E. Meijer, and T. Sheard, editors, *Second International Summer School on Advanced Functional Programming*, volume 1126 of *Lecture Notes in Computer Science*, pages 184–207. Springer-Verlag, 1996.

Generic Program Transformation
Answers to exercises

1   Introduction

No exercises.

2   Abstraction versus Efficiency

Exercises

2.1 Can the computation of the *maximum* depth of a tree be made more efficient in the same way as the computation of the minimum depth? If not, which
property of *min* fails for *max*?
Answer: The property $max(a + b)c = $ if $b \leq c$ then c else $max(a + b)c$ fails to
hold. It is thus not possible to cut the search for a maximum depth leaf in the
same way as we cut the search for a minimum depth leaf.

2.2 A leaf labelled binary tree is said to be *perfectly balanced* if for every subtree
t, the size of the left hand child is precisely $size\,t\,$div2. Given a list x, the function
build x produces a perfectly balanced tree whose inorder traversal is x. First give
a naive program for computing *build*, and then show how it can be made efficient.
Answer: The obvious algorithm follows the divide-and-conquer strategy, splitting the input into half at each step, and recursing on each half. That may be
coded as follows

$$build\,[a] = Leaf\,a$$
$$build\,x = Bin\,(build\,y)\,(build\,z)$$
$$\text{where}\,(y, z) = splitAt\,n\,x$$
$$n = length\,x\,\text{div}\,2$$

This is not efficient, because $splitAt\,n\,x$ takes n steps to evaluate; the cost adds
up to $\Omega(n \log n)$ for the evaluation of $build\,x$ where n is the length of x. To make
this more efficient, we compute

$$build'\,n\,x = (build\,(take\,n\,x), drop\,n\,x)$$

Note that this is very similar to the way we optimised *decorate*. The efficient
program for *build'* reads

$$build'\,1\,(a : x) = (Leaf\,a, x)$$
$$build'\,n\,x = (Bin\,s\,t, z)$$
$$\text{where}\,(s, y) = build'\,(n\,\text{div}\,2)\,x$$
$$(t, z) = build'\,(n - n\,\text{div}\,2)\,y$$

2.3 Are there circumstances where the original definition of *partition* is as efficient as the 'improved' version?
Answer: Yes, for instance when we select only one of the two components of its
result.

3   Automating the Transition: Fusion and Higher Order Rewriting

Exercises

3.1 Define the *fold* operator on natural numbers. Its type is

$$foldn :: (a \to a) \to a \to Int \to a$$

You could think of the first argument as replacing the successor function $(+1)$ and the second argument as replacing 0. If there were a data type *Nat* of natural numbers in Haskell, the type of the third argument would be *Nat* and not *Int*. What is the fusion rule for *foldn*?

Answer: The definition of *foldn* is

$$foldn\,step\,start\,0 = start$$
$$foldn\,step\,start\,(n+1) = step\,(foldn\,step\,start\,n)$$

The fusion rule is what allows you to push you another operator through this computation, in the following intuitive fashion:

$$f\,(step(step(step\ldots(step\,start)))) =$$
$$g(f\,(step(step\ldots(step\,start)))) =$$
$$g(g(f\,(step\ldots(step\,start)))) =$$
$$g(g(g(f\ldots(step\,start)))) =$$
$$\ldots$$
$$g(g(g\ldots f(step\,start))) =$$
$$g(g(g\ldots g(f\,start))) =$$
$$g(g(g\ldots g\,e))$$

Formally, we have

$$f\,(foldn\,step\,start\,x) = foldn\,g\,e\,x,$$

provided we have

$$f\,(step\,n) = g(f\,n)\ \text{ all } n,\text{ and}$$
$$f\,start = e$$

3.2 Define the *fold* operator on leaf labelled binary trees. Its type is

$$foldbtree :: (a \to a \to a) \to (b \to a) \to Btree\,b \to a$$

What is its fusion rule?
Answer: The fold operator is

$$foldbtree\,bin\,leaf\,(Leaf\,a) = leaf\,a$$
$$foldbtree\,bin\,leaf\,(Bin\,s\,t) = bin\,(foldbtree\,bin\,leaf\,s)\,(foldbtree\,bin\,leaf\,t)$$

The fusion rule says that

$$f(foldbtree\ bin\ leaf\ x) = foldbtree\ g\ h\ x$$

provided we have

$$f(bin\ s\ t) = g\ (f\ s)(f\ t), \quad \text{all } s \text{ and } t$$
$$f(leaf\ a) = h\ a, \quad \text{all } a$$

4   The MAG System

Model solutions to the practical assignments of this section are distributed with the MAG system. The MAG system is available from URL:

`http://www.comlab.ox.ac.uk/oucl/groups/progtools/mag.htm`

Below we answer the in-lined questions only.

4.1   Getting Acquainted

No exercises.

4.2   Accumulation Parameters

Fast reverse A naive definition of the function *reverse* is

$$reverse\ [\ ] = [\ ]$$
$$reverse\ (a : x) = reverse\ x \mathbin{+\!\!+} [a]$$

Write down the recursive definition of $(\mathbin{+\!\!+})$, and estimate how much time it takes to evaluate *reverse* x when x has length n.
Answer: The recursive definition of $(\mathbin{+\!\!+})$ is:

$$[\ ] \mathbin{+\!\!+} ys = ys$$
$$(x : xs) \mathbin{+\!\!+} ys = x : (xs \mathbin{+\!\!+} ys)$$

The time to evaluate a concatenation is thus proportional to the length of the left-hand argument. It follows that *reverse* takes quadratic time. **End of answer.** The time complexity of *reverse* can be improved by defining:

$$fastrev\ x\ y = reverse\ x \mathbin{+\!\!+} y$$

Why is this a generalisation of *reverse*?
Answer: Because

$$fastrev\ x\ [\ ] = reverse\ x \mathbin{+\!\!+} [\ ] = reverse\ x$$

End of answer.

Using the fact that $(+\!\!+)$ is associative

$$(x +\!\!+ y) +\!\!+ z = x +\!\!+ (y +\!\!+ z)$$

one can synthesise an efficient program for *fastrev*.

The above definitions, and the associativity of $(+\!\!+)$, have been recorded in the theory file `reverse.eq`. There is one peculiarity, however: the definition of *fastrev* reads

$$fastrev\, x\, y = reverse\, (foldr\, (:)\, [\,]\, x) +\!\!+ y$$

Why is the instance of *foldr* there?
Answer: It acts as a seed for the the use of fusion: if there is no *foldr* in the program, fusion cannot be applied. **End of answer.**

Confirm your answer by loading the theory file `reverse.eq` in MAG, and transforming *fastrev*. Estimate the time complexity of the resulting program.
Answer: The result is an instance of *foldr* where each of the operators takes constant time to evaluate, so the total time complexity is linear. **End of answer.**

Postorder traversal No in-lined exercises.

Breadth first traversal ...

The function *levels* :: *Tree a* $\rightarrow$ $[[a]]$ first gives the elements that occur at depth 0, then the elements at depth 1, depth 2 and so on. It is defined by

$$levels\, (Node\, a\, ts) = [a] : glues\, (map\, levels\, ts)$$

$$glues\, [\,] = [\,]$$
$$glues\, (x : xs) = lzc\, x\, (glues\, xs)$$

$$lzc\, [\,]\, x = x$$
$$lzc\, (a : x)\, y = \text{if } null\, y$$
$$\qquad\qquad\qquad \text{then } a : lzc\, x\, [\,]$$
$$\qquad\qquad\qquad \text{else } (a +\!\!+ head\, y) : lzc\, x\, (tail\, y)$$

Here *lzc* stands for *long zip with concatenation*. What is the difference between *lzc* and *zipWith* $(+\!\!+)$? Is *lzc* associative? What is the time complexity of *levels*?
Answer: *zipWith* truncates its result to the length of the shortest argument. By contrast, the length of the result of *lzc* is the maximum of the lengths of its arguments. Yes, *lzc* is associative. The time complexity of levels is at least quadratic. **End of answer.**

Minimum depth Let us now return to the problem discussed at the beginning of these lectures, namely computing the minimum depth of a leaf labelled binary tree. It was claimed there that apart from the definitions, all we need to produce an efficient program is the following set of rules:

$$0 + a = a$$
$$(a + b) + c = a + (b + c)$$
$$min(min\,a\,b)\,c = min\,a\,(min\,b\,c)$$
$$min\,a\,b + c = min\,(a + c)\,(b + c)$$
$$min\,(a + b)\,c = \text{if}\,b \geq c\,\text{then}\,c\,\text{else}\,min\,(a + b)\,c$$

Unfortunately, there is a problem when this set of equations is implemented by rewriting. Why?
Answer: The last rule can be applied to its own result, so application of this set of rules does not terminate. **End of Answer.**

4.3   Tupling

Fibonacci No in-lined exercises.

Steep sequences A list of numbers is said to be *steep* if each element is greater than the sum of the elements that follow it. We might define the predicate $steep :: [Int] \rightarrow Bool$ by

$$steep\,[\,] = True$$
$$steep\,(a : x) = a > sum\,x \wedge steep\,x$$

Estimate the time complexity of *steep*.
Answer: The time complexity of *sum* is linear. We call *sum* on each suffix of the argument of *steep*, so that makes for a quadratic program. **End of answer.**

Partition In this example, the ordering of the rules in the theory file is rather important: in the rewriting process, they are tried in the order they occur. Why does the rule about distributing a function over a conditional come last?
Answer: When applied in favour of *if* contraction (to a nested *if* statement) this rule is applicable to its own result. So it should come after *if* contraction. **End of answer.**

Decorate ...
Returning to the problem of optimising *decorate*, the above machinery can be found in the file `decorate.eq`. Run MAG on *dec*. Is the result identical to the program discussed earlier in the lectures? What further transformation needs to be performed?
Answer: We need to perform common sub-expression elimination. That is not easily expressed as a rewrite rule, and it is typical of the kind of transformation that MAG cannot do. **End of answer.**

4.4 Carrying On

No exercises.

5   Matching Typed λ-Expressions

Exercises

5.1 Write a program for *alphaconvertible*.
Answer:

$$\mathbf{data}\, Binding = Free\, Name \mid Bound\, Int$$
$$deriving\, Eq$$

$alphaconvertible\, e_1\, e_2 = ac[\,][\,]\, e_1\, e_2$
$\quad \mathbf{where}\, ac\, xs\, ys\,(Var\, x\, s)\,(Var\, y\, t) = (s == t)\, \wedge$
$\qquad\qquad getbinding\, xs\, x\, == getbinding\, ys\, y$
$\qquad\qquad\quad \mathbf{where}\, getbinding\, as\, a \mid a\,'elem'\, as = Bound\,(getpos\, a\, as)$
$\qquad\qquad\qquad\qquad\qquad\qquad\quad\mid otherwise = Free\, a$
$\qquad\qquad\qquad getpos\, a\,(b:bs) = \mathbf{if}\,(a == b)\,\mathbf{then}\, 0\, \mathbf{else}\, 1 + getpos\, a\, bs$
$\qquad\quad ac\, xs\, ys\,(Con\, x\, s)\,(Con\, y\, t) = (s == t)\, \wedge\, (x == y)$
$\qquad\quad ac\, xs\, ys\,(Ap\, f_1\, a_1\, s)\,(Ap\, f_2\, a_2\, t) = (s == t)\, \wedge\, ac\, xs\, ys\, f_1\, f_2\, \wedge\, ac\, xs\, ys\, a_1\, a_2$
$\qquad\quad ac\, xs\, ys\,(Lam\, p_1\, e_1\, s)\,(Lam\, p_2\, e_2\, t) = (s == t)\, \wedge\, ac\, xs'\, ys'\, e_1\, e_2$
$\qquad\qquad\qquad\qquad\qquad\qquad\qquad\qquad\qquad \mathbf{where}\, xs' = p_1 : xs$
$\qquad\qquad\qquad\qquad\qquad\qquad\qquad\qquad\qquad\qquad ys' = p_2 : ys$
$\qquad\quad ac\, \_\, \_\, \_\, \_ = False$

5.2 Write a program for *etacontract*.
Answer:

$etacontract\, exp@(Lam\, v_1\,(Ap\, e\,(Var\, v_2\, \_)\, \_)\, \_) =$
$\mathbf{if}\,(v_1 == v_2\, \wedge\, and\,(map\,(v_1/=)\,(freevars\, e)))$
$\mathbf{then}\,(etacontract\, e)$
$\mathbf{else}\, exp$
$etacontract\,(Lam\, pat\, bod\, t) = Lam\, pat\,(etacontract\, bod)\, t$
$etacontract\,(Ap\, f\, a\, t) = Ap\,(etacontract\, f)\,(etacontract\, a)\, t$
$etacontract\,(Var\, x\, t) = Var\, x\, t$
$etacontract\,(Con\, c\, t) = Con\, c\, t$

5.3 Write a program for *subst*, assuming that there are no name conflicts.
Answer:

$$subst\,x\,e\,(Var\,y\,t) = \text{if}\,x == y\,\text{then}\,e\,\text{else}\,Var\,y\,t$$
$$subst\,x\,e\,(Con\,c\,t) = Con\,c\,t$$
$$subst\,x\,e\,(Ap\,e_1\,e_2\,t) = Ap\,(subst\,x\,e\,e_1)\,(subst\,x\,e\,e_2)\,t$$
$$subst\,x\,e\,(Lam\,y\,b\,t) = \text{if}\,x == y\,\text{then}\,(Lam\,y\,b\,t)$$
$$\text{else}\,Lam\,y\,(subst\,x\,e\,b)\,t$$

5.4 Write a program for *betareduce*.
Answer:

$$betareduce\,(Var\,x\,t) = Var\,x\,t$$
$$betareduce\,(Con\,c\,t) = Con\,c\,t$$
$$betareduce\,(Lam\,x\,e\,t) = Lam\,x\,(betareduce\,e)\,t$$
$$betareduce\,(Ap\,e_1\,e_2\,t) = \text{case}\,e_1'\,\text{of}$$
$$Lam\,x\,b\_ \rightarrow betareduce(subst\,x\,e_2'\,b)$$
$$\_\quad \rightarrow Ap\,e_1'\,e_2'\,t$$
$$\text{where}\,e_1' = betareduce\,e_1$$
$$e_2' = betareduce\,e_2$$

Designing and Implementing Combinator Languages

S. Doaitse Swierstra[1], Pablo R. Azero Alcocer[1], and João Saraiva[2,1]

[1] Department of Computer Science, Utrecht University, P.O.Box 80.089, 3508 TB
Utrecht,The Netherlands,
{doaitse,pablo,saraiva}@cs.uu.nl
[2] University of Minho, Braga, Portugal

1 Introduction

1.1 Defining Languages

Ever since the Computer Science community has discovered the concept of a programming language there has been a continuous quest for the ideal, all-encompassing programming language; despite this we have been overwhelmed by an everlasting flow of all kinds of special purpose programming languages. Attempts to bridge this gap between a single language and infinitely many caused research into so-called extensible programming languages.

In a certain sense every programming language with a binding construct is extensible. In these lectures we will show that it is the unique combination of *higher order functions*, an *advanced type system* (polymorphism and type classes) and the availability of *lazy evaluation* that makes Haskell one of the most promising candidates for the "ideal extensible language".

Before we start with giving many examples and guidelines of how to use the features just mentioned, we want to spend some time on explaining what actually constitutes a programming language. A proper programming language description contains at least:

- a *concrete context-free grammar*, describing the appearance of the language
- an *abstract context-free grammar*, describing the structure of the language
- *context sensitive conditions* that capture the constraints that are not easily expressed at the context-free level, like correct name introduction and use and type checking; usually such context conditions can either be directly expressed in a compositional way, or in terms of a fixed-point of a function that itself may be computed in a compositional way; with *compositional* we mean here that a property of a construct can be expressed in terms of properties of its constituents.
- a mechanism of assigning a "meaning" to a program; one of the most common ways of doing so is by giving a *denotational semantics*, which boils down to describing how a function representing the meaning of that program can be derived from the abstract program structure.

Of course one can design a new language by defining all the above components from scratch. Languages, however, do have a lot in common like definitions, type

S.D. Swierstra et al. (Eds.): Advanced Functional Programming, LNCS 1608, pp. 150–206, 1999.

systems, abstraction mechanism, IO-systems etc. It would be a lot of work to implement this anew for every new language and it would be nice if we could borrow this from some existing language.

1.2   Extending Languages

There are many ways in which one can extend an existing language:

- By far the most common way to extend a language is by including some form of macro preprocessor. Such extensions are almost all syntactic and do not use any form of global analysis to steer their behavior. An exception to this is the C++ template mechanism, in which the programmer also gets access to the types of the manipulated expressions.
- By incorporating a term-rewriting system, which makes it in principle possible to acquire information about parts of the program and to move this information to other places where it may be used. The disadvantage of this approach is that on the one hand the method is very elaborate, and on the other hand it is hard to keep track of what happens if two independently designed term rewriting systems are used to transform the same program text: composition of two confluent term-rewriting systems is usually not confluent.
- By giving access to an underlying interpreter, providing reflection. In this way an almost endless world of possibilities appears. Unfortunately there is a price to be paid: as a consequence of constructs being analyzed dynamically one can in general not guarantee that the program will not terminate erroneously, and especially strong typing is easily lost.

Besides these approaches there is a fourth one, that we call *embedding*, described in the next subsection.

1.3   Embedding Languages

When we embed a language in another language we are not so much extending that other language, but we make it look as if this were the case. It is here that the concept of a combinator language shows up: we use the already available mechanisms in the language for describing the components mentioned in subsection 1.1:

- for describing the concrete representation (or syntax if you prefer that term) of our extension we introduce new operators and functions. It would be nice if we had an underlying language with distfix operators (like **if..then..else..fi**) available, but in practice we can do quite well with a sufficient number of operator priorities and the possibility to define new infix operators.
- for the representation of the abstract syntax we may use Haskell data types, that nicely correspond to abstract syntax trees.
- for describing context sensitive restrictions we will use catamorphisms (see the chapter on Generic Programming of these lecture notes and [15]), since they capture the notion of exploiting the compositional nature of our restrictions.

- for describing the semantic domains we will again use Haskell types. The way they are composed is again by using catamorphisms. It is here that the fact that we can use higher order functions plays a crucial role. For the domains and co-domains of the functions denoting the semantics we may use Haskell types again.

We want to emphasize that this approach has been very fruitful and has already led to several nice combinator libraries[2,3,5,13]. The main advantage of this approach is that when extending a language through the definition of a set of combinators, we get the naming, abstraction and typing mechanism for free, since this was already part of the underlying language.

There are two important aspects of the Haskell tping system that makes this approach even more attractive:

- *polymorphism* allows the language extension to be conservative. I.e. it may be possible to manipulate values of the original programs and at the same time we may guarantee that this is done in a safe way. We will see an example of this when we introduce the parser combinators.
- type classes allow us to link the new constructs to existing types, and to manipulate existing kind of values in a type-safe way without limiting ourselves to a fixed set of predefined types.

As we will see, it is not always attractive to explicitly code the catamorphisms needed, and thus we introduce a special notation for them based on attribute grammars: they can be seen as a way of defining catamorphisms in a more "programmer friendly" way.

Attribute grammars have traditionally been used for describing implementations of programming languages, and their use in describing programming language extensions should thus not come as a surprise. Using attribute grammars has always been limited by the need to choose a specific language for describing the semantic functions and a specific target language. Fortunately, as we will show, it is quite straightforward to use the attribute grammar based way of thinking when programming in the setting of a modern, lazily evaluated functional language: it is the declarative way of thinking in both formalisms that bridges the gap, and when using Haskell you get an attribute grammar evaluator almost for free [11,16].

Thinking in terms of attribute grammars is useful when writing complicated functions and their associated calls. By explicitly naming argument and result positions (by the introduction of attribute names), we are no longer restricted to the implicit positional argument passing enforced by conventional function definitions.

1.4 Overview

In section 2 we will describe a number of so-called circular programs. This introduction serves to make you more familiar with lazy evaluation, what can be done with it, and how to exploit it in a systematic way. It also serves to make you once more familiar with the algebraic approach to programming [7,4], and with how to design programs by way of defining algebras and combining them. Although this all works nicely when done in a systematic way, we will also show why this approach is extremely cumbersome if things are getting more complicated: soon one needs to be a book-keeping genius to keep track of what you are writing, calculating and combining. In the course of this discussion it will become clear that an approach that solely relies on monads in attacking these problems will not work out as expected.

In section 3 we will solve the same example problems again, but now by taking an attribute grammar based approach.

Section 4 forms a large case study in which we attack the pretty printing problem as described in [5]. Hughes defines a set of operators that may be used to describe the two-dimensional layout of documents, and especially documents that contain structured text that is to be formatted according to that structure. Designing this language has been a long standing testbed for program design techniques and we hope to show that when such problems are attacked in a step-wise fashion and with proper administrative support one may easily generate quite complicated programs, which many would not dare to write by hand.

Next we will show some of the consequences of our techniques when it is taken in its simplest form, and describe some program transformations, that finally may result in a large set of relatively small strict, pure functions. So even ML-programmers should be happy in the end. Finally we will summarise the approach taken.

2   Compositional Programs

We start by developing a somewhat unconventional way of looking at functional programs, and especially those programs that make heavy use of functions that recursively descend over data structures. In our case one may think about such data structures as abstract syntax trees. When computing a property of such a recursive object (i.e. the representation of a program in a new language) we define two kinds of functions: those for describing how to recursively visit the nodes of a tree (the catamorphisms), and those used in forming algebras that describes what to compute at each visited node.

One of the most important steps in this process is deciding what the carrier type of such algebras is to be. Once this step has been taken, these types will be a guideline for further design steps. We will see that such carrier types may be functions themselves, and that deciding on the type of such functions may not always be simple. In this section we will present a view on recursive computations that will enable us to "design" the carrier type in an incremental way. We will do so by constructing algebras out of other algebras. In this way we define the meaning of a language in a *semantically compositional* way. We will give three examples of the techniques involved, followed by a conclusion about the strengths and weaknesses of this approach.

2.1   The Rep_Min Problem

One of the famous examples in which the power of lazy evaluation is demon-strated is the so-called *Rep_Min* problem ([12]). Many have wondered how this

```
    data Tree = Leaf Int
              | Bin   Tree Tree

    type Tree_Algebra a = (Int -> a, a -> a -> a)
5
    cata_Tree :: Tree_Algebra a -> Tree -> a

    cata_Tree alg@(leaf, _  ) (Leaf i) = leaf i
    cata_Tree alg@(_   , bin) (Bin l r) = bin (cata_Tree alg l)
10                                            (cata_Tree alg r)
```

Listing 1: rm.start

program achieves its goal, since at first sight it seems that it is impossible to compute anything with this program. We will use this problem, and a sequence of different solutions, to build up understanding of a whole class of such programs.

In listing 1 we present the data type of interest, i.e. a Tree, which in this case stands for simple binary trees, together with their associated signature. The *carrier type* of an algebra is that type describing the objects of the algebra. We represent it by a type parameter to the signature type Tree_Algebra:

    type Tree_Algebra a = (Int -> a, a -> a -> a)

The associated evaluation function cata_Tree systematically replaces the constructors Leaf and Bin by their corresponding operations from the algebra alg that is passed as an argument.[1]

We now want to construct a function rep_min :: Tree -> Tree that returns a Tree with the same "shape" as its argument Tree, but with the values in its leaves replaced by the minimal value occurring in the original tree. In figure 1 an example of an argument with its result is given.

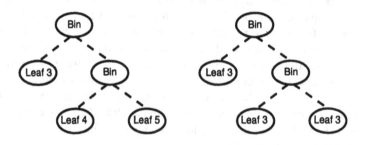

Fig. 1. The function rep_min

---

[1] Note that this function could have been defined using the language PolyP from the second lecture of this volume.

```
min_alg = (id, min::(Int->Int->Int))
replace_min :: Tree -> Tree
replace_min t = cata_Tree rep_alg t
                where m = cata_Tree min_alg t
                      rep_alg = (const (Leaf m), Bin)
```

Listing 2: rm.sol1

Straightforward Solution The straightforward solution to the Rep_Min problem consists of a function in which cata_Tree is called twice: once for computing the minimal leaf value, and once for constructing the resulting Tree. The function replace_min that solves the problem in this way is given in listing 2. Notice that the variable m is used as a global variable in the rep_algebra, that in its turn is an argument to the tree constructing call of cata_Tree. In figure 2 we have shown the flow of the data in a recursive call of cata_Tree, when computing the minimal value. One of the disadvantages of this solution is that, since

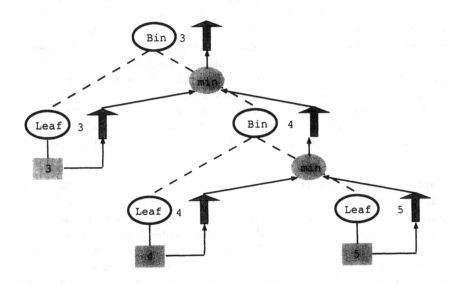

Fig. 2. Computing the minimum value

we call cata_Tree twice, in the course of the computation the pattern matching associated with the inspection of the tree nodes is performed twice for each node in the tree. Although this is not a real problem in this solution we will try to construct a solution that calls cata_Tree only once. We will do so by transforming the current program in a number of steps.

```
    rep_alg = (\ _               -> \m -> Leaf m
              ,\lfun rfun -> \m -> let lt = lfun m
                                       rt = rfun m
                                   in  Bin lt rt
  5            )
    replace_min' t = (cata_Tree rep_alg t) (cata_Tree min_alg t)
```

Listing 3: rm.sol2

Lambda Lifting Our first step results in listing 3. In this program the global variable m has been removed. The second call of cata_Tree now does not construct a Tree anymore, but instead *a tree constructing function* of type Int -> Tree, that takes the computed minimal value as an argument. Notice how we have emphasized the fact that a function is returned through some superfluous notation: the first lambda in the lambda expressions constituting the algebra rep_alg is there because of the signature of the algebra requires so, the second lambda is there because the carrier set of the algebra contains functions of type Int -> Tree. This process is done routinely by functional compilers and is known as *lambda-lifting*. In figure 3 we have shown the flow of information when this function is called. The down-arrows to the left of the non-terminals correspond to the parameters of the constructed function, and the up-arrows to the right correspond to the results of the constructed functions. When we look at the top level node we see that the final value is a function that takes one argument (down-arrow), in our case the minimum value, and that returns a Tree (up-arrow). The call of cata_Tree constructs this final function by using the small functions from the rep_alg algebra as building blocks. These small functions can be identified with the small data flow graphs in figure 4.

Tupling Computations In the next formulation of our solution cata_Tree is called only once. Note that in the last solution the two calls of cata_Tree don't interfere with each other. As a consequence we may perform both computation of the tree constructing function and the minimal value in one traversal, by tupling the results of the computations. The solution is given in listing 4. First a function tuple_tree is defined. This function takes two Tree_Algebras as arguments and constructs a third Tree_Algebra, that has as its carrier tuples of the carriers of the original algebra's. The resulting computation is shown in figure 5.

Merging Tupled Functions In the next step we transform the type of the carrier set in the previous example, i.e. (Int, Int -> Tree), into a, for this purpose equivalent, type Int -> (Int, Tree). This transformation is not essential here, but we use it to demonstrate that if we compute a cartesian product of functions, we may transform that type into a new type in which we compute a single function, that takes as its arguments the cartesian product of all the

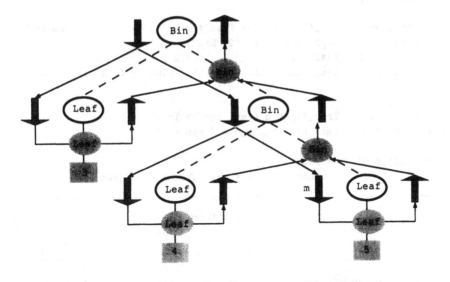

Fig. 3. The flow of information when building the result

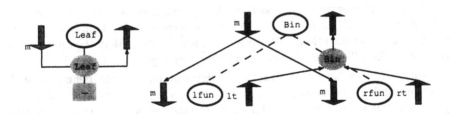

Fig. 4. The building blocks

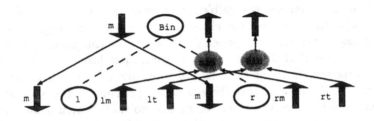

Fig. 5. Tupling the computations

```
infix 9 'tuple_tree'

  tuple_tree :: Tree_Algebra a -> Tree_Algebra b -> Tree_Algebra (a,b)
  (leaf1, bin1) 'tuple_tree' (leaf2, bin2)
5 = (\i   -> ( leaf1 i           , leaf2 i            )
    ,\l r -> ( bin1 (fst l) (fst r), bin2 (snd l) (snd r) )
    )

  min_tup_rep :: Tree_Algebra (Int, Int -> Tree)
10 min_tup_rep = (min_alg 'tuple_tree' rep_alg)

  replace_min'' t = r m
                  where (m, r) = cata_Tree min_tup_rep t
```

Listing 4: rm.sol3

arguments of the functions in the tuple, and returns as its result the cartesian product of the result types. In our example the computation of the minimal value may be seen as a function of type () -> Int. As a consequence the argument of the new type is ((), Int), that is isomorphic to just Int, and the result type becomes (Int, Tree), so as the carrier we get the type Int -> (Int, Tree).[2]

We want to mention here too that the reverse is in general not true; given a function of type (a, b) -> (c, d), it is in general not possible to split this function into two functions of type a -> c and b -> d, that together achieve the same effect. The new version of our program is given in listing 5.

Notice how we have again introduced extra lambdas in the definition of the functions making up the algebra, in an attempt to make the different rôles of the parameters explicit. The parameters after the second lambda are there because we construct values in a higher order carrier set. The parameters after the first lambda are there because we deal with a Tree_Algebra. A curious step taken here is that part of the result, in our case the value m, is passed back as an argument to the result of (cata_Tree merged_alg t). Lazy evaluation makes this work!

That such programs were possible came originally as a great surprise to many functional programmers, and especially to those who used to program in LISP or ML, languages that require arguments to be evaluated completely before the call is evaluated (so-called *strict evaluation* in contrast to lazy evaluation). Because of this surprising behavior this class of programs became known as *circular programs*. Notice however that there is nothing circular in this program. Each value is defined in terms of other values, and no value is even defined in terms of itself (as in ones=1:ones), although this would not have been a problem.

---

[2] Notice that the first component of the result does not depend on the Int-argument; it is just computed "at the same time" as the Tree that does depend on the argument.

```
merged_alg :: Tree_Algebra (Int -> (Int,Tree))
merged_alg = (\i          -> \m ->    ( i          , Leaf m    )
             ,\lfun rfun -> \m -> let  (lm,lt) = lfun m
                                       (rm,rt) = rfun m
                                  in  ( lm 'min' rm, Bin lt rt )
             )


replace_min''' t = r
                where (m, r) = (cata_Tree merged_alg t) m
```

Listing 5: rm.sol4

```
replace_min'''' t  = r
      where (m, r) = tree t m
            tree (Leaf i)  = \m -> (i, Leaf m)
            tree (Bin l r) = \m -> let (lm, lt) = tree l m
                                       (rm, rt) = tree r m
                                   in (lm 'min' rm, Bin lt rt)
```

Listing 6: rm.sol5

Finally we give in listing 6 the version of this program in which the function `cata_Tree` has been unfolded, thus obtaining the original solution given in Bird[12].

Recapulating we have systematically transformed a program that inspects each node twice into an equivalent program that inspects each node only once. In doing so we were forced to pass part of the result of a call as an argument to that very same call. Lazy evaluation made this possible.

2.2   Table_Formatting

In this section we will treat a more complicated example, in which we show how to systematically design the algebra's involved. Our goal is to develop a program that recognizes and formats (possibly nested) HTML style tables, as described by the following grammar:

$$
\begin{array}{rll}
table & \rightarrow \texttt{<TABLE>} \ rows & \texttt{</TABLE>} \\
rows & \rightarrow & row^* \\
row & \rightarrow \texttt{<TR>} \ elems & \texttt{</TR>} \\
elems & \rightarrow & elem^* \\
elem & \rightarrow \texttt{<TD>} \ string \mid table \ \texttt{</TD>}
\end{array}
$$

An example of accepted input and the associated output is given in figure 6.

```
<TABLE>
  <TR><TD>the</TD>
      <TD>table</TD>
  </TR>
  <TR><TD><TABLE>
        <TR><TD>formatter</TD>
            <TD>in        </TD>
        </TR>
        <TR> <TD>functional</TD>
             <TD>polytypic </TD>
        </TR>
          </TABLE>
      </TD>
      <TD>style</TD>
  </TR>
</TABLE>
```

```
|---------------------------|
|the                  |table|
|---------------------------|
||-------------------||style|
||formatter |in      ||     |
||-------------------||     |
||functional|polytypic||    |
||-------------------||     |
|---------------------------|
```

(a) HTML input   (b) Output

Fig. 6. Table formatting

A Parser for Tables We start defining the parser for the input language. As we will see the parser actually is a combination of the parsing process and the computation of a catamorphism over the abstract syntax tree constructed by the parsing process.

The parser is written with so-called parser combinators [13] – here mostly defined as infix operators: functions that construct parsers out of more elementary parsers, completely analogous to the well-known recursive descent parsing technique. An example of the advantages of embedding a formalism (in our case context-free grammars) in a language that provides powerful abstraction techniques is that this automatically gives us an abstraction mechanism for the embedded language (in our case the context-free grammars). Although it is not the main purpose of this paper to treat combinator parsers we have incorporated this part for the sake of completeness, and to show how to link the semantics of a language to recognized program structures.

Parsing with combinators: discovering structure In the first section we have mentioned that, when defining a programming language, we may want to distinguish the concrete syntax from the abstract syntax. In this paper we will assume the availability of a set of parsing combinators, that enables us to construct such a mapping without almost any effort.

Before we describe the structure of the combinator `taggedwith` that will be used to construct a parser for recognizing HTML-tagged structures, we will briefly discuss the basic combinators used in its construction.

The types of the basic combinators used in this example are:

```
<*>   :: Eq s => Parser s (a -> b) -> Parser s a -> Parser s b
<|>   :: Eq s => Parser s a         -> Parser s a -> Parser s a
succeed :: a -> Parser s a
sym   :: Eq s => s                               -> Parser s s
--
<$>   :: Eq s => (a -> b)        -> Parser s a -> Parser s b
<*-> :: Eq s => Parser s a      -> Parser s b -> Parser s a
<-*> :: Eq s => Parser s b      -> Parser s a -> Praser s a
<$-> :: Eq s => (a -> b)        -> Parser s c -> Parser s (a -> b)
```

The type `Parser` is rather complicated and has been taken from [13]. Here it suffices to know that a `Parser s a` will recognize a sequence of tokens (`[s]`) and return a value of type `a` as the result of the parsing process. The *sequence* combinator `<*>`, composes two parsers sequentially. The meaning of the combined result is computed by applying the result of the first component to the result of the second. The *choice* combinator `<|>` constructs a new parser that may perform the role of either argument parser. The parser combinator `succeed` creates a parser that always succeeds (recognizes the empty string) and returns the argument of `succeed` as its semantic value. The parser combinator `sym` returns a parser that recognizes the terminal symbol represented by its argument. Sequence, choice, succeed and sym form the basic constructors for parsers for context-free languages. In our example we will assume that we have a scanner that maps the input onto a sequence of `Tokens`, and that such tokens may be recognized by elementary parsers for keywords (constructed with `pKey`), and for lower case identifiers (`pVarid`).

One of the things to notice here is that the type of the parsers is completely polymorphic in the result of the parsers, and that the definitions of the parser combinators only allow us to combine partial results to the results of complete trees in a type safe manner. Furthermore we have introduced a context `Eq s` to precisely contrain the kind of token sequences we are able to parse.

A fifth combinator is defined for describing further processing of the semantic values returned by the parsers. It is the *application* defined as:

```
f <$> p = succeed f <*> p
```

Thus, it applies the function `f`, the so called *semantic function*, to the result of parser p. We will see how, by a careful combination of such semantic functions and parser combinators, we can prevent a parse tree from coming into existence at all [8,10].

Now let us take a look at the program in listing 7, and take the combinator `taggedwith`. This combinator takes two arguments: a `String` providing the text of the tag and the `Parser` for the structure enclosed between the tags. Its semantics are: recognize the 'open' tag s, then (combinator `<*>`) recognize the structure p, then (again `<*>`) parse the 'close' tag. The combinators `<*->`, `<$->` and `<-*>` combine parsers, but throw away the result at the side of the --symbol in their name. As a result of this the result of a call `taggedwith s p` returns only the result recognized by the call of p in its body.

```
    type Alg_List a b = ( a -> b -> b, b )

    type Alg_Table table rows row elems elem
      = ( rows  -> table, Alg_List row  rows
  5     , elems -> row  , Alg_List elem elems
        , (String -> elem, table -> elem) )

    taggedwith :: Eval a
                => String -> Parser Token a -> Parser Token a
 10 taggedwith s p =  topen s <-*> p <*-> tclose s
      where topen  s = pKey ("<")   <*-> pKey s <*-> pSym '>'
            tclose s = pKey ("</")  <*-> pKey s <*-> pSym '>'

    format_table :: Alg_Table table rows row elems elem
 15               -> Parser Token table
    format_table ( sem_table, sem_rows, sem_row
                 , sem_elems, (sem_selem,sem_telem) ) = pTable
      where
      pTable = sem_table <$> taggedwith "TABLE"
 20            (pFoldr sem_rows (taggedwith "TR"
                        ( sem_row <$>
                           pFoldr sem_elems (taggedwith "TD"
                                  (  sem_selem <$> pVarid
          <|> sem_telem <$> pTable
 25            )           )    ))          )
```

Listing 7: Parsing tables

```
    pFoldr :: Eq s => Alg_List a b -> Parser s a -> Parser s b
    pFoldr alg@(op,zero) p = pfm
      where pfm = op <$> p <*> pfm <|> succeed zero

  5 -- Some useful algebras
    init_list = ((:), [])
    max_alg   = (max, 0)   -- Take the max element; sizes are positive
    sum_alg   = ((+), 0)   -- Sum all elements
```

Listing 8: List manipulation

The Kleene * in two grammar rules of our Table_Formatting problem are realized by the combinator pFoldr (see listing 8). The first argument of pFoldr is a tuple of two values: (zero,op) :: Alg_List, an *algebra* that uniquely defines the homomorphism from the carrier set of the initial algebra to the carrier set of the argument algebra (in our case the type b). The second argument of pFoldr is a parser for p-structures. A parser pFoldr (op,zero) p recognises a sequence of p-structures, and foldrs the results using the binary operator op to combine results and using zero as its unit element; so pFoldr sum_alg p_Integer recognises a sequence of integers and returns their sum as a result, provided that pInteger recognises a single integer.

Finally we have a look at the function format_table. We see that it takes for each nonterminal of the describing grammar an algebra consisting of functions that describe how to construct the semantic value for a production out of the semantic values of the elements in its right hand side. From the type of Alg_Table we see that it takes a set of carrier types as argument. As a result the whole parser is polymorphic in all these domains: all it does is recognizing the structure of a table and composing the recognized elements once it is told how to compose them by the argument of type Alg_Table.

Exercise 1. A more traditional solution to linking the parsing phase with the semantic phase would have been to construct a tree first, that is subsequently mapped onto a final semantic domain using a catamorphism. Define appropriate data types, and the associated catamorphisms. How should the Alg_Table show up in your program?

Simulating structure walks: adding semantics By providing different definitions for the algebras passed to the pFoldr-calls and for the sem_antic functions we may compute quite different results. The set of definitions:

```
type Table = Rows
type Rows  = [ Row ]
type Row   = Elems
type Elems = [ Elem ]
data Elem  = SElem String | TElem Table

table = format_table (id,init_list,id,init_list,(SElem,TElem))
```

describes the data structure holding the table as the result of the parsing process. The type of the element to be returned by table is Table. It is already possible in the previous functions to see the role played by the semantic functions and the list algebras – figure 7(a). The latter apply functions to the collected elements, and the former provide intermediate computations such as transforming data types, collecting intermediate values and computing new values. In the following sections we will focus on the systematic description of these functions.

Walks, trees: where are they? In the previous section we have seen how we can define an algebra that describes the computation of the abstract syntax tree

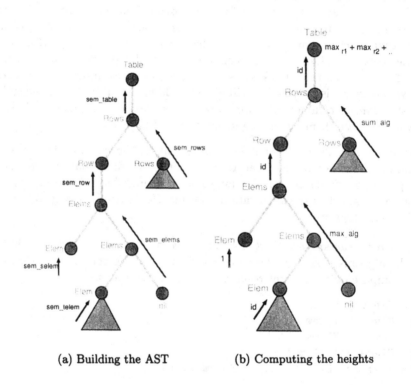

(a) Building the AST   (b) Computing the heights

Fig. 7. Computations over trees

itself: the *initial algebra*. For defining the semantics of such a tree we now have to define the catamorphism from the initial algebra (the abstract syntax trees) to some other algebra (the meaning). An interesting consequence of trees being initial is that this function is completely defined by the target-algebra. Expressed in computer science terms this is just saying that the structure of the recursion follows directly from the data type definition; a fact well known to (functional) programmers and attribute grammar system users.

A direct consequence of this is that it is possible to compute the meaning of a structure directly, without going through an explicit tree-form representation: instead of referring to the initial algebra (constructed from the data type constructors) we use the meaning-algebra (constructed from the semantic functions) whenever we are performing a reduction (i.e. would construct a tree-node) in the parsing process. The construction of the abstract syntax tree is fused with the catamophism giving a meaning to this tree, and thus the actual tree never comes into existence.

Computing Heights As a first step to a solution to the Table_Formatting problem we will focus on computing the height of the elements, the rows and the table itself. We will ignore the sizes taken by the dividing lines for a while. Figure 7(b) depicts an attribute grammar view of the solution. The height of an element is the height of a simple element, 1, or the height of a nested table. The height of a row is the maximum of the heights of the elements of the row, and the height of a table is the sum of the heights of all the rows. This computational structure is actually what `pFoldr` is capturing: roll over the elements of the list, taking every element into account, accumulating a result. Thus the list algebra, in the parser known as `sem_elems`, for computing the height of a row is `max_alg`.

The height of the table is the sum of the heights of the rows. Again we can use a list algebra to express that computation, thus for `sem_rows` we use `sum_alg`. The complete algebra for computing heights now is:

```
height_table = (id, sum_alg, id, max_alg, (const 1, id))
```

Note that `sem_table` and `sem_row` do not need special attention in this case: they only pass on their argument.

We observe the following relation between the set of functions defined and an attribute grammar: (a) the results of applying the semantic functions to the children nodes correspond to synthesized attributes and, (b) attribute computations are nicely described by algebras.

Computing the Widths At the table level, the computation of widths deserves a bit of attention. We will not be able to deduce any width of a column until we have recognized the last row of the table. But instead of keeping the widths of all the elements, we maintain a list with the maximum width found for each column. Whenever a complete new row has been recognized, the width of each element has to be compared with the thus far computed width of its corresponding column.

```
   width_table =  (sum, star max_alg, id, init_list, (length, id))

   star :: Alg_List a  b -> Alg_List [a] [b]
   star (op, zero) = (zipWith op, repeat zero)
5
   hw_table = ( id 'x' sum, sum_alg 'tuple_list' star max_alg
              , id 'x' id , max_alg 'tuple_list' init_list
              , ( (const 1) 'split' length , id 'x' id ) )

10 f   'x'  g = h where h (u,v) = (f u, g v)
   f 'split' g = h where h u    = (f u, g u)

   tuple_list :: Alg_List b a -> Alg_List b' a' -> Alg_List (b,b') (a,a')
   (f, e) 'tuple_list' (f', e')
15 = (\(x, x') (xs, xs') -> (f x xs, f' x' xs'), (e, e'))
```

Listing 9: Computing heights and widths

For this purpose we introduce the *star* combinator that lifts an algebra to the corresponding algebra on lists:

```
star :: Alg_List a  b -> Alg_List [a] [b]
star (op, zero) = (zipWith op, repeat zero)
```

The combinator `star` takes an algebra, and returns an algebra that has as carrier set lists of elements of the original algebra. In this way, once we have defined the algebra for computing a maximum, `max_alg`, we can define an algebra for computing the pairwise maxima of two lists: `star max_alg` and this is what we need to compute the widths at the table level.

Now we want to combine the computations of the height and the width. Again, thinking in an attribute grammar style, we need another synthesized attribute. Because functions can only return a single value, we have to pair both results (height and widths), and deliver them together. With a row we have associated the list of the widths of all its the elements: `init_list`.

Following our algebraic style of programming we define a *tupling* combinator that takes two algebras and returns an algebra that computes a pair of values. In this way it is possible to structure the computations even more. Note that the composition is at the semantic level and not only syntactic.

```
infixr 'tuple_list'
tuple_list :: Alg_List b a -> Alg_List b' a'
           -> Alg_List (b,b') (a,a')
(f, e) 'tuple_list' (f', e')
   = (\(x, x') (xs, xs') -> (f x xs, f' x' xs'), (e, e'))
```

Thus we use `max_alg 'tuple_list' list_init` for synthesizing the height of the row paired with the list of widths of the elements of the row. We do the same at the table level and obtain the algebra `sum_alg 'tuple_list' star max_alg`.

Finally, the result of the computation for a table must be a pair, but we obtain a list of widths from the application of pFoldr. Thus we need a further transformation id `'x' sum`. The *product* combinator x applies its argument functions to the corresponding left and right elements of the pair. The new version of the program is shown in listing 9.

Let us note that:

- we can compute several properties of a tree at the same time by tupling them
- computations for such tuples can be constructed out of computations for the elements of the tuples (`tuple_list`, `star`, `split` and `x`)
- the operators on algebras: composition and star, and split and product are independent of the problem at hand and could have been taken from a library
- these operators could have been automatically derived using the language PolyP

Exercise 2. Can you provide a tupling operator for table algebras?

Formatting Once we have computed the widths of all columns and the heights of all rows we can start to work on the formatting of the table. The approach will be very similar to the one taken in the Rep_Min problem. Instead of computing the formatted table directly we will compute a function that, once it gets passed the widths of the columns, builds the formatted table. Furthermore the computation of these functions will again be tupled with the computation for the widths and the heights. These table building functions will be constructed out of row-building functions that will construct a formatted row, once they get passed the height of that row and the widths of the columns.

To format the table we do the following: elements are made to be the top-left element of a quarter plane (we call them Boxes), extending to the east and the south, see figure 8. The table layout is constructed by placing these boxes beside and on top of each other. The code for the semantic functions and the algebras is shown in figure listing 10.

To simplify, we always place the element in the upper left corner of the box. Additional horizontal and vertical glue – blank text lines – are padded to the elements to fit in their actual layout space. All elements are furthermore equipped with a nice top left corner frame – delineating the quarter plane – as you can see in figure 8.

At the row level, elements are h_composed, laying out one row of the table. The composition is done as follows: concatenate the next text line from each element, until there are no more lines. Because all the elements in the row have been filled with vertical glue at the end, this process also creates blank spaces if the element is not large enough to fill the vertical space.

When the processing of a row has finished we shape the row horizontally. This is possible because the final height of the row is known,

```
layout_table
  = ( bot_right . mk_table
    , v_compose 'tuple_list' sum_alg 'tuple_list' star max_alg
    , \(fmtrow, hwds@(h, wds)) -> (fmtrow h, hwds)
5   , h_compose 'tuple_list' max_alg 'tuple_list' init_list
    , ( mk_box . ((:[]) 'split' (const 1) 'split' length)
      , mk_box
      )
    )
```

Listing 10: Computing the formatted table

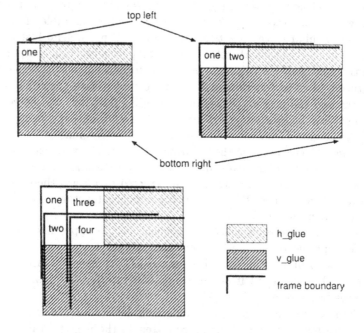

Fig. 8. Superposition of boxes

```
   mk_box             = to_box 'x' (+1) 'x' (+1)
   to_box t rh rw = map (take rw) . take rh . top_left . add_glue $ t
   top_left t     = map ('|':) (h_line:t)

 5 mk_table = \(fmttable, (h, wds)) -> (fmttable wds, (h, sum wds))
   bot_right (t,(h,w)) = (close_grid, (h + 1, w + 1))
     where close_grid = map (++"|") (t ++ [take w ('|':h_line)])

   h_compose = ( fork <||> decons <=>> zipWith (++), nil_table )
10 v_compose = ( lift (++)                          , nil_row   )

   nil_table _ _ = repeat ""
   nil_row   _   = []

15 h_glue         = repeat ' '
   v_glue         = repeat h_glue
   add_glue t     = map (++ h_glue) t ++ v_glue
   h_line         = repeat '-'
```

Listing 11: Functions for manipulating boxes

and can be passed on to all the boxes. This *surgery* is performed by \(fmtrow, hwds@(h, wds)) -> (fmtrow h, hwds). We have written this function in a pointwise style, in order to show how the flow of data proceeds.

At the table level, the rows already formatted are v_composed. This task is reduced to concatenating text lines. Finally, once all rows have been processed, the actual width of each column is known and thus, the table can be shaped vertically. This is done in mk_table. Finally the grid is closed, with bot_right placing the bottom and right lines, and correcting the actual size of the table. The implementation of box manipulation functions is given in listing 11.

Observe that the size of the boxes is flexible, but once we know the corresponding height and width, it is possible to actually obtain the nicely formatted table. Even without noticing, we also put the grid in the table, placing the elements besides and on top of each other. We only need to take care of closing the grid, and providing each element with a top-left grid.

The simplicity of h_compose and v_compose is suspicious. Let us take a look inside h_compose. In terms of text elements it's only string manipulation, but let us take the attribute grammar view. At the Elems level we have the situation depicted in figure 9(a): an Elems cons node takes two arguments, the height and a list of widths, and returns a formatted row, the layout of the element. The arguments are passed down to its children: the height is distributed as it is (it is a global value for the row), but the widths have to be split element by element. The synthesized attributes are combined together using the zipWith (++) (but in general any f). Thus the dataflow pattern in the leftmost graph in figure 9(a) is composed of three subgraphs: pass down a global value (fork), pass down and split a composed value (**decons** if the value is a list and we want to decompose a list into its head and tail), combine those subcomputations (**<||>**) and combine this with the upflowing part of the dataflow graph (**<=>>**), see figure 9(b).

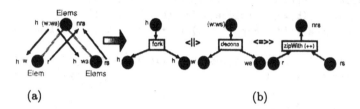

(a)   (b)

Fig. 9. Attribute computation: (a) example and (b) combining patterns

Once more, thanks to the abstraction and higher orderness of the language, these patterns can be abstracted and used in a compositional way to express a computation of **h_compose**. The code of these combinators is shown in listing 12.

We believe that this program clearly captures the notion of attribute grammar: a context-free grammar is represented by the use of parser combinators, while attributes and attribute computations are expressed in terms of algebras and parameterized functions. Note that there are no inherited attributes as such. We create partially parameterized functions and once we know the dependent value, we apply the function(s) to the value(s). Thus some attributes play a double role: they are synthesized (like the height of a row), but once their value has been computed they can be used in a subsequent computation; thus acting as inherited attributes.

Furthermore, the program can be generalized rather straightforwardly to a polytypic function [6] because the constructors are general. Although not presented here, the tupling operator **tuple_list** can be defined for any arbitrary data type constructor *f*.

As a final remark we notice that probably the hardest part of the derivation was the design of the combinators **<||>**, **<=>>**, **fork** and **decons**, and using them to construct the data-flow patterns of figure 9(a). On the one hand it is nice that we can define such patterns of passing values around by the introduction of extra combinators; on the other hand it is quite cumbersome to have to keep track of which element in the tuples represent what values.

2.3   Defining Catamorphisms

In previous subsections we have defined the catamorphisms needed for the data types involved explicitly. The question arises whether this can be done in a more generic way.

In the chapter on generic programming it has been shown how we can, given a functor, define the initial data type, corresponding to that functor. How to

```
   lift op f g = \x -> (f x) 'op' (g x)
   fork        = id   'split' id
   decons      = head 'split' tail

5 (<||>) :: (a->(b,c)) -> (d->(e,f)) -> a -> d -> ((b,e),(c,f))
  forkl <||> forkr
    = \inh_l inh_r -> let (inh_ll,inh_lr) = forkl inh_l
                          (inh_rl,inh_rr) = forkr inh_r
                      in  ((inh_ll,inh_rl),(inh_lr,inh_rr))
10
   (<=>>) :: (a -> d -> ((b,e),(c,f)))
          -> (g -> h -> k) -> (b -> e -> g) -> (c -> f -> h)
          -> a -> d -> k
   fork <=>> merge_op
15 = \fsyn_l fsyn_r -> \inh_l inh_r
      -> let ((inh_ll,inh_rl),(inh_lr,inh_rr)) = fork inh_l inh_r
             syn_l = fsyn_l inh_ll inh_rl
             syn_r = fsyn_r inh_lr inh_rr
         in  merge_op syn_l syn_r
```

Listing 12: Attribute computation combinators

define the catamophism corresponding to that functor in Haskell is by now well known: in listing 13 we provide the definitions taken from [14]. Note that if we take this approach we still have to indicate that a specific data type constructor is a functor, by defining the appropriate class instance. In the language PolyP it is no longer necessary to do this last step explicitly since there we can define the function cata once and for all as a polytypic function.

Unfortunately these approaches do not readily extend to the case where we have to deal with several mutually recursive data types, like the Table_Formatting problem. Although this is not a problem at all from a theoretical point of view, the actual coding is quite elaborate. In the next subsection we will show how to define two mutually recursive data types and we hope that from that it will be clear how to proceed in the general case.

Mutually Recursive Data Types As the running example we will take the definition of and the code generation for a small block-structured language. The language has two nonterminals: Expr and Decls. Since our language has two nonterminals, we want to define two mutually recursive data types and thus we start with the definition of a class Functor_2 for bi-functors (see listing 14). For getting hold of the joint fixpoint of two functors we define the data type constructor Rec_2, a straightforward extension of the Rec we have seen before. In listing 14 we have used two arguments, but in the most general case we would have n arguments, and by rotating the arguments one step at each next element

```
    data Rec f = In (f (Rec  f))

    out :: Rec f -> f (Rec f)
    out (In o) = o
5
    class Functor f where
      map :: (a -> b) -> (f a -> f b)

    cata :: Functor f => (f a -> a) -> Rec f -> a
10  cata phi = phi . map (cata phi) . out
```

Listing 13: Catamorphisms for a single recursive data type

```
    data Rec_2 f1 f2 = In_2 (f1 (Rec_2 f1 f2) (Rec_2 f2 f1))

    out_2 :: Rec_2 f -> f (Rec_2 f)
    out_2 (In_2 t) = t
5
    class Functor_2 f where
      map_2 :: (a1 -> b1, a2 -> b2) -> (f a1 a2 -> f b1 b2)

    cata_2 :: (Functor_2 f, Functor_2 g)
10          => ( f e d    -> e, g d e    -> d)
            -> ( Rec_2 f g -> e, Rec_2 g f -> d)
    cata_2 phis@(phi1, phi2) = (r1, r2)
      where r1 = phi1 . map_2 (r1, r2) . out_2
            r2 = phi2 . map_2 (r2, r1) . out_2
```

Listing 14: Catamorphisms for two recursive data types

```
    data Expr   e d  =  Con_Int   Int
                     |  Var       String
                     |  If        e e e
                     |  Apply     e e
5                    |  Where     e d
    data Decls d e  =  Dec       d String e
                     |  None


    type Expr_Algebra  e d = ( Int -> e          -- integer constant
10                           , String -> e       -- variable
                             , e -> e -> e -> e -- conditional expr.
                             , e -> e -> e       -- application
                             , e -> d -> e       -- where clause
                             )
15  type Decls_Algebra d e = ( d -> String -> e  -> d
                             , d
                             )
```

Listing 15: Bi-functors and its associated algebras

in the right and side of Rec_n they would all make it once to the first place in
the argument list of Rec_n.

Finally in listing 14 we define the corresponding mutually recursive bi-
catamorphism cata_2.

The Block-Structured Language Since our language has two nonterminals
we need two recursive data types, and thus define two bi-functors Expr and
Decls in listing 15. Having done this we may define the associated algebras
Expr_Algebra and Decls_Algebra.

Since we have taken a slightly different shape of our algebras in our definition of cata_2 we also introduce two functions that transform such a tupled representation of an algebra into functions with type Expr e d -> e and
Decls d e -> d:

```
expr_choose :: Expr_Algebra e d -> (Expr e d -> e)
expr_choose (f_Con_Int, f_Var, f_If, f_Apply, f_Where) e
    = case e of
        Con_Int  i        -> f_Con_Int i
        Var      s        -> f_Var s
        If ce te ee       -> f_If    ce te ee
        Apply    e1  e2   -> f_Apply e1 e2
        Where    e d      -> f_Where e d

decls_choose :: Decls_Algebra d e -> (Decls d e -> d)
decl_choose (f_Dec, f_None) d
```

```
   instance Functor_2 Expr where
      map_2 (ef, df) e = case e of
                         Con_Int  i       -> Con_Int i
                         Var      s       -> Var s
5                        If    ce te ee   -> If (ef ce) (ef te) (ef ee)
                         Apply f  arg     -> Apply (ef f) (ef arg)
                         Where body decl -> Where  (ef body)
                                                   (df decl)

10 instance Functor_2 Decls where
      map_2 (df, ef) d = case d of
                         Dec decls s e -> Dec (df decls) s (ef e)
                         None          -> None
```

Listing 16: Functor_2 instances

```
   = case d of
      Dec d s e -> f_Dec d s e
      None      -> f_None
```

When taking the combined fix-point of these functors the parameter e is going to be replaced by the type of an expression tree, and the parameter d by the list of declarations.

Having done this our next step is to make make the bi-functors Expr and Decls instance of the class Functor2. The definitions are shown in listing 16.

Code Generation Having set up all the above machinery all we have to do is to define the appropriate algebras. We will not go deeply into the kind of code to generate. The following should serve as a good enough description of what we want to achieve:

```
     expression         |         generated code
----------------------- | -------------------------------------
 if 3 then x else y      | Enter 2, Loadint 4,  Store (1,0),
 where x = 4             |          Loadint 5,  Store (1,1),
       y = 5             |          Loadint 3,  Brfalse  0,
                         |          Load (1,0), Bralways 1,
                         | Label 0, Load (1,1),
                         | Label 1,
                         | Leave 2
```

Notice that we need to introduce an environment that for each declared identifier keeps track of its lexical level and its displacement, and besides that we have to keep track of a label counter for compiling the conditional expressions. We first provide some auxiliary declarations:

```
type Index      =  Int
type Lex_level  =  Int
type Address    =  (Lex_level, Index)
type Env        =  String -> Address
type Lab        =  Int

data Code       =  Loadint  Int     |  Loadbool Bool
                |  Enter    Int     |  Leave    Int
                |  Brfalse  Lab     |  Bralways Lab
                |  Label    Lab
                |  Load     Address |  Store    Address
                |  Call
                deriving Show
```

Having done all this we can now define the two algebras. As the carrier set for the expressions we take functions mapping the cartesian product of an environment and a lexical level and a label counter onto the generated code and an updated label counter, whereas for the declarations we take functions mapping an environment/level pair and a label counter onto generated code, an integer counting the number of declarations contained in the list processed and an updated label counter. Now, once we have defined two appropriate algebras sl_expl and sl_decls (see listing 17) we can define our compiler by:

```
compile_expr = code
where
  (exprf, declf) = cata_2 (expr_choose sl_expr,decl_choose sl_decl)
  (code, _)      = exprf (null_env, 0) 0
```

2.4   Discussion

In this section we have treated three different algorithms: the Rep_Min problem, the Table_Formatting problem, and the definition of a small compiler for expressions. In the Rep_Min problem we have shown how we may construct circular programs. In the Table_Formatting problem we have shown how we may define algebra's in a step wise fashion and define special combinators to construct new algebra's out of other algebra's. Finally we have shown that we may define the concept of a catamorphism once and for all once we know with how many mutually recursive data types we have to deal with.

There is however also a somewhat sobering conclusion: although everything can be done in a very systematic way, it is still a lot of work. We identify the following problems:

1. when moving to higher order domains and composite results we have to keep track of which value is at which parameter position, or at which position in the resulting cartesian products.
2. extending the nonterminals with an extra alternative makes us go through all the data types, algebra's and instance declarations.

```
   sl_expr = ( \ i         -> \_        -> \lc -> ([Loadint i    ], lc)
             , \ s         -> \(env,_) -> \lc -> ([Load (env s)], lc)
             , \ ce te ee -> \ el       -> \lc
               -> let (cc, clc) = ce el (lc + 2)
5                      (tc, tlc) = te el clc
                       (ec, elc) = ee el tlc
                  in (     cc
                      ++ [Brfalse lc]
                      ++ tc
10                    ++ [Bralways (lc + 1)]
                      ++ [Label lc]
                      ++ ec
                      ++ [Label (lc + 1)]
                      , elc )
15            , \ e1 e2   -> \el -> \lc -> let (e1c, lc1) = e1 el lc
                                               (e2c, lc2) = e2 el lc1
                                           in  (e2c++e1c++[Call],lc2)
             , \ e d -> \(env,lev) lc ->
                  let (ec,elc)             = e (denv, lev+1) lc
20                    (dc,dnum,denv,dlc) = d (env , lev+1) elc
                  in  ( [Enter dnum]++dc ++ ec++[Leave dnum]
                      , dlc
                      )
             )
25 sl_decl = (\ d s e -> \el@(env,lev) lc
                  -> let (dc,dnum,denv,dlc) = d el lc
                         (ec, elc)    = e (denv,lev) dlc
                         nenv  = \ss -> if  s == ss
                                            then (lev,dnum)
30                                           else denv ss
                     in ( dc++ec++[Store (nenv s)]
                        , dnum+1
                        , nenv
                        , elc
35                      )
             ,        \(env,_)      lc -> ([], 0, env, lc)
             )
```

Listing 17: Algebras for compiling the expression language

3. the construction of the related catamorphisms is cumbersome, especially when we add another related data type. Furthermore the approach taken is unnecessarily complicated since it in principle deals with the case that each data type is reachable from all others in a set of mutually recursive data types. In general this will not be the case.

In the next section we will introduce special syntax in order to cope with these three problems. Unfortunately we will have to leave the semantic compositionality, and replace it with a syntactic one.

3 Attribute Grammars

In the previous section we have developed programs for the *Rep_Min* and *Table_Formatting* problems. In both cases we computed a tuple of values as the result of a catamorphism and at least one of the elements of those tuples was a function that at some point was applied to another element of the tuple. In the Rep_Min example the tree constructing function was applied to the computed minimal value, and in the Table_Formatting example we had two occurrences of this phenomenon: the row-constructing function was applied to the computed maximum height of the row, and the table constructing function was applied to the list of computed row widths.

Since this pattern is quite common and the composition and invention of all the algebras was not so straightforward, we will introduce an attribute grammar based notation, out of which we may easily generate equivalent Haskell code. The conclusion will be that we can design programs like the ones in the previous section by drawing pictures like the ones presented in the Rep_Min example. The price to be paid is that instead of having semantic compositionality, we have to fall back on syntactic compositionality provided by a preprocessor. Our current opinion however is that the advantages of our approach for developing combinator libraries by using a separate attribute grammar formalism allows transformations and ease of formulation that are hard to beat by an approach completely based on semantic composition.

We also hope to show that by taking the attribute grammar approach it will become much easier to extend the library or to make efficiency improvements. The next section, in which we develop a set of pretty printing combinators in a sequence of steps, is an example of the allowed flexibility. Since we anticipate that people will want to experiment with different implementations and designs we have tried to design our attribute grammar formalism in such a way that definitions can easily be changed and expanded without having to change the original program texts.

3.1 The Rep_Min Problem

In listing 18 we show the formulation of the Rep_Min problem, using our attribute grammar notation.

```
   DATA Tree
      | Leaf int: Int
      | Bin  left, right: Tree

 5 DATA Root | Root  tree: Tree

   -- Computation of the minimum value

   ATTR Tree [ -> m: Int ]
10 SEM Tree
      | Leaf LHS  .m     = int
      | Bin  LHS  .m     = "left_m 'min' right_m"

   ATTR Tree [ minval: Int <- ]
15 SEM Tree
      | Bin  left .minval = lhs_minval
             right.minval = lhs_minval

   -- Computation of the resulting tree
20
   ATTR Tree [ -> res: Tree ]
   SEM Tree
      | Leaf LHS  .res   = "Leaf lhs_minval"
      | Bin  LHS  .res   = "Bin left_res right_res"
25
   -- Use the computed minimal value

   ATTR Root [ -> res: Tree ]
   SEM Root
30    | Root tree .minval = tree_m
             LHS  .res    = tree_res
```

Listing 18: RepMin1.ag

The first two DATA declarations introduce the grammar corresponding to the structure of our problem. The ATTR declarations specify the inherited and synthesized attributes of the nonterminals. Attributes occurring before a <- are inherited attributes, corresponding to downward arrows in the pictures we have seen, and attributes following a -> are synthesized attributes, corresponding to the upgoing arrows in the pictures. Declarations between <- and -> introduce two attributes of the same name, one inherited and one synthesized. In the SEM parts we specify the way attributes are computed out of other attributes. The actual definitions are pieces of Haskell text, that are neither parsed nor typechecked, and are copied literally into the generated program. References to other attributes in such rules follow a naming convention: a synthesized attribute res of a child left is referred to as left_res, whereas an inherited attribute minval is referred to as lhs_minval, since it is an attribute of the nonterminal at the left hand side of the production. In each semantic rule we have to specify what nonterminal (SEM Tree), what alternative (|Leaf), what component of the production (LHS or left) and what attribute (.res) is specified by the rule.

If we put this text through our small system the code in listing 19 is generated.

Exercise 3. Use the parser combinators together with the generated file to construct a solution for the Rep_Min problem, that reads a tree from a file, and writes the result into another file.

One might wonder what progress has been made since both the input and the generated program are much longer than the original program in the previous section.

In the first place we have presented the input in the most elaborate form of our notation, thus making explicit all different components of the definition. Many abbreviations exist in order to cope with often occurring patterns of attribute use. A completely equivalent input is given in listing 20. Here we see that attributes may be declared together with the introduction of a new nonterminal, a new alternative or a new semantic rule. Furthermore many straightforward so-called *copy rules* can easily be inferred by the system. It is the extension of the notation that makes things really work well. So is the attribute minval automatically made available in all nodes of the tree by the rule that if both a child and a father node have an inherited attribute with the same name, it is automatically passed on from the father to the child if no semantic rule has been defined (actually the rules for doing so are a bit more complicated, but this description will do for the time being). This rule captures the pattern that is normally associated with a reader monad. This approach has the advantage that if we have several attributes following this pattern we do not have to introduce a new monad describing this joint passing around of values.

Furthermore there are a lot of small but convenient conventions; if an element in the right hand side of a production is not explicitly named, its name is constructed from the type by converting the first letter to lower case. As a consequence we do not have to be creative in inventing a name for the value at a Leaf, it is just called int.

```
module RepMin where
--------------------- Tree ------------------------
data Tree = Tree_Leaf Int| Tree_Bin Tree Tree
          deriving Show
5 -- semantic domains
type T_Tree =  Int ->(Tree,Int)
-- catas
sem_Tree (Tree_Leaf i) =  sem_Tree_Leaf  i
sem_Tree (Tree_Bin left right)
10 =  sem_Tree_Bin  (sem_Tree left)  (sem_Tree right)
-- funcs
sem_Tree_Leaf i lhs_minval =  ( (Leaf lhs_minval), int )
sem_Tree_Bin left right lhs_minval
 = let{ ( left_res, left_m )  = left lhs_minval
15  ;     ( right_res, right_m )  = right lhs_minval
    }in  ( (Bin left_res right_res), (left_m 'min' righth_m) )
--------------------- Root ------------------------
data Root = Root_Root Tree
          deriving Show
20 -- semantic domains
type T_Root =  Tree
-- catas
sem_Root (Root_Root tree) =  sem_Root_Root  (sem_Tree tree)
-- funcs
25 sem_Root_Root tree = let{ (tree_res, tree_m) = tree tree_m}in tree_res
```

Listing 19: RepMin

```
DATA Tree
  | Leaf Int
  | Bin  left, right: Tree

5 SEM Tree [ minval: Int <- -> m: Int  res: Tree ]
   | Leaf LHS.m   = int
             .res = "Leaf lhs_minval"
   | Bin  LHS.m   = "left_m 'min' righth_m"
             .res = "Bin left_res right_res"
10
  DATA Root [ -> res: Tree ] | Root Tree
  SEM  Root                  | Root tree.minval = tree_m
```

Listing 20: RepMin2.ag

```
   DATA Table   |  Table   Rows
   DATA Rows    |  Nil
                |  Cons    Row     Rows
   DATA Row     |  Row     Elems
 5 DATA Elems   |  Nil
                |  Cons    Elem    Elems
   DATA Elem    |  Str     String
                |  Tab     Table
```

Listing 21: TableData.ag

```
   --< TableData.ag
   ATTR Table  Row  Elem  [ -> mh : Int ]

   SEM Table
 5 | Table  LHS . mh = "rows_mh + 1"
   ATTR Rows  [ -> mh USE   "+"    "0": Int ]
   ATTR Elems [ -> mh USE "'max'" "0": Int ]
   SEM Elem
     | Str   LHS . mh = "2"
10   | Tab   LHS . mh = "table_mh + 1"
```

Listing 22: TableHeight.ag

3.2   The Table_Formatting Problem

In this section we will treat the Table_Formatting problem again, and do so
again in a number of steps. Remember that in the previous section, by combining
algebras we really had semantic compositionality: the algebras could be defined
and compiled separately only to be composed at the very last moment.

Since we are dealing with the generation of Haskell code (i.e. we use Haskell
instead of C++ as our "assembly" language), we do not have to adhere strictly to
the typing, naming and lexical rules of the language: we have much more freedom
in designing the attribute grammar formalism in such a way that we may express
ourselves in the most convenient way. To emphasize the compositional nature of
our approach we split up the attribute grammar in many separate pieces of text
that are to be combined by the system.

We start with the grammar in listing 21 that directly corresponds to the
type of the abstract syntax trees presented before. In the program in listing 22
we import the previous file (the line --< TableData.ag) and introduce for each
nonterminal a synthesized attribute containing its minimal height in the formatted table. In listing 23 this version is extended further with the attributes and
semantic functions for computing the minimal widths; note how the tupling is
now done implicitly by the system, and that we do not have to introduce special
combinators to merge the height and the widths algebras into a combined one.

```
--< TableHeight.ag

  SEM  Table  [ -> mws: Int ]
   |   Table  LHS .mws  = "lmw + 1"
5             LOC .lmw  = "sum rows_mws"
  SEM  Rows   [ -> mws: Rowwidths ]
   |   Nil    LHS .mws  = "repeat zero"
   |   Cons   LHS .mws  = "zipWith max row_mws rows_mws"
  ATTR Row    [ -> mws: Rowwidths ]
10 ATTR Elems  [ -> mws USE ":" "[]" : Rowwidths ]
  SEM  Elem   [ -> mws: Int ]
   |   Str    LHS .mws  = "length string + 1"
   |   Tab    LHS .mws  = "table_mws + 1"
  -->type Rowwidths = [Int]
```

Listing 23: TableWidths.ag

In listing 23 we see some other language elements. Lines preceded with --> are literally copied into the generated file. In this way additional Haskell functions and type definitions can be passed on to the generated program, thus obviating the need to edit the generated file to contain import .. lines. The semantic rule LOC.lmw = ... introduces a local attribute, that in the generated semantic function results in the declaration of a local variable lmw.

Furthermore it is possible to provide a binary operator and a unit element, together with the introduction of a synthesized attribute (see the USE ":" "[]" phrase in the introduction of attribute mws). If no semantic rule is given for this attribute the attributes of the children with the same name are combined using the binary operator, and if no such attributes exist the unit element is taken as its value. We go however a step beyond the kind of polytypism in PolyP since the composition here depends on the name of a part of the result of a child; something that cannot be expressed in the current version of PolyP.

In the next step the downwards distribution of the computed final heights and widths to the individual elements is described, so each element can be formatted according to the actual size it occupies in the formatted table (listing 24). Here the advantages of the attribute grammar based formulation show up most clearly: we do not have to invent combinators for combining subcomputations and all we have to do is to indicate how the computed heights and widths flow back into the abstract syntax tree. Finally we add the computation of the final formats, i.e. sequences of lines in listing 25.

In listing 25 we see another extension of the formalism: the EXT clause. The effect of this clause here is to extend the alternative Cons of nonterminal Elems with an extra element: top_Left : Top_Left. Although the nonterminal Top_Left has been introduced, it was not given productions and thus is interpreted as an external nonterminal. It does not show up as a parameter referring to a child in the generated semantic functions, but nevertheless a call is gen-

```
--< TableWidths.ag

  ATTR Elems  [ ah : Int <- ]
  SEM Row
5  | Row      elems . ah  = elems_mh

  ATTR Rows  Row  Elems [ aws : Rowwidths <- ]
  SEM Table
    | Table   rows  . aws = rows_mws
10 SEM Elems
    | Cons    elems . aws = "tail lhs_aws"
```

Listing 24: TableDistr.ag

```
--< TableDistr.ag

  SEM Table [ -> lines : Lines]
    | Table LHS .lines = "bot_right lmw rows_lines"
5 ATTR Rows [ -> lines USE "++" "[]" : Lines]
  ATTR Row  [ -> lines : Lines]
  SEM Elems [ -> lines : Lines]
    | Nil   LHS .lines = "repeat []"
    | Cons  LHS .lines = "zipWith (++) top_Left_ls elems_lines"
10          LOC .haws  = "head lhs_aws"
  SEM Elem  [ -> lines : Lines]
    | Str   LHS .lines = "[string]"

  -->type Lines = [String]
15
  DATA Top_Left [ haws elem_mws lhs_ah elem_mh elem_lines <- -> ls ]
  EXT Elems
    | Cons Top_Left
```

Listing 25: TableFormats.ag

```
     --< TableFormats.ag
     -->
     -->-- -------------------------------------------------------
     -->-- Additional layout functions ---------------------------
  5  -->
     -->sem_top_Left lines mh  ah  mw aw
     -->  =  ("|" ++ hor_line (aw - 1))
     -->  :  ["|" ++ l ++ hor_glue (aw-mw) | l <- lines]
     -->  ++ ["|" ++ vg | vg <- ver_glue (aw - 1) (ah-mh)]
 10  -->
     -->bot_right mw lines = [ l ++ "|"
     -->                        | l <- lines ++ ["|" ++ hor_line (mw - 1)]
     -->                        ]
     -->
 15  -->hor_glue h   = take h (repeat ' ')
     -->ver_glue h v = take v (repeat (hor_glue h))
     -->hor_line n   = take n (repeat '-')
     -->
     -->-- -------------------------------------------------------
 20  -->
```

Listing 26: TableFinal.ag

erated. In this way we may incorporate calls to external computations in the generated semantic functions.

We now come to a final convention: if an inherited attribute has been declared and in the rule an attribute with that name would be allowed as a semantic function such semantic functions are generated automatically. So in listing 25 we actually have inserted a call to an external function, passing on some of the available attributes. The final addition of some glue is given in listing 26.

3.3 Comparison with Monadic Approach

As mentioned before many have tried to employ monads for capturing often occurring patterns of parameter passing and use. Unfortunately monads do not compose well. Recognizing this problem we have, in our formalism, taken a purely syntactic approach.

Reader Monads correspond in our formalism to an inherited attribute that is automatically passed on to all the elements in the tree by the copy rule generation process, provided they have indicated their interest in that value by declaring an inherited attribute, and provided all their parent types have done so too. Thus parameterizing a whole computation by a global value is easily done. Furthermore this can be repeated as often as needed, so the effort for the programmer is almost nothing.

State Monads correspond to so-called chained attributes, i.e. pairs of an inherited and a synthesized attribute, that have the same name. In order to support the generation of the copy rules here too, we now explain the complete process underlying the copy rule generation. Each element in the right hand side of the production has a context that steers the generation of non-specified semantic functions. For each attribute **at** for which no function is defined we first check whether there exists an element **elem** that defines a synthesized attribute **def** such that **at = elem_def**; this includes the inherited attributes of the parent too (**lhs_def**). If this is the case, that value is taken. If not it is checked whether its left hand side neighbor **l** has a synthesized attribute with name **at**. If it does **l_at** is taken, and if not, the element one step further left is checked and so on. If nothing appropriate is found during this search finally the inherited attributes are checked. This rule also applies to the synthesized attributes of the left hand side, in which case the searching process starts at the last element of the right hand side.

So if we want to maintain e.g. a label counter, supplying new label numbers when generating code, we define the attribute **labels** to be both inherited and synthesized:

```
DATA Expr[<-labels: Int ->]
  | If ce,te,ee: Expr

SEM Expr
  | If ce.  labels = "lhs_labels +2"
```

In the generated code we now find:

```
sem_Expr_If ce te ee lhs_labels
 = let{ (ce_code, ce_labels)  = ce (lhs_labels +2)
    ;      (te_code, te_labels)  = te ce_labels
    ;      (ee_code, ee_labels)  = ee te_labels
    }in  ((ite_code ce_code te_code ee_code lhs_labels), ee_labels)
```

and we see that the **Labels**-value is nicely passed on. Again this can be done for many attributes at the same time, without having to worry about the composition of those instances.

Writer Monads somehow correspond to synthesized attributes that are composed with the **USE** clause.

4 Pretty Printing

In this section we attack the pretty-printing problem as described in [5,1]. Pretty-printing deals with representing tree-based structures in a width-bounded area in a top-down, left to right order, and in such a way that the logical structure of the tree is clearly represented in the layout. In this chapter we develop a set of combinators for describing such layouts.

Suppose we want to pretty-print an IF-THEN-ELSE-FI structure. We may display it with different layouts as depicted in figure 10(a). The layout chosen will normally depend on the page width. Thus, with page width at least 31, layout a. is preferred, between 30 and 17 b. is chosen and in the range from 16 to 10 c. wins. Any attempt however to display inside a page less than 10 characters wide is bound to fail.

```
a. IF c THEN t ELSE e FI     pp_ites c t e
b. IF c THEN t                 =    ifc >|<  thent >|< elsee  >|< fi
        ELSE e                      >^< ifc >|< (thent >-< elsee) >-< fi
   FI                              >^< ifc >-<  thent >-< elsee  >-< fi
c. IF c                     where ifc  = text "if"   >|< c
   THEN t                         thent = text "then" >|< t
   ELSE e                         elsee = text "else" >|< e
   FI                             fi    = text "fi"
```

(a) Possible layouts   (b) Specification

Fig. 10. Pretty-printing an IF-THEN-ELSE-FI structure

We define a layout to be *optimal* (nicest or prettiest) if it takes the least number of lines, while still not overflowing the right page margin. The examples in figure 10(a) are optimal for page widths 40, 28, and 15 respectively. Taking the layout b. with respect to a page width of 35 is thus considered non optimal.

Our approach is based on the relation between the height and the width of a layout: higher when elements cannot be placed next to each other horizontally because of the limited page width and wider otherwise. We prefer the wider solutions, since they will lead to a smaller overall height, as is evident in the examples of figure 10(a).

Since potentially many solutions have to be taken into account, this can be a cause of gross inefficiency. Fortunately we are saved by the fact that not all possible combinations have to be inspected. Of all the possible solutions with the same height, only a limited number of candidates has to be taken into account. Many combinations can be discarded from the overall computation by selecting only the narrowest solution for each height, and inspect only those candidate solutions that have at most the height of the final solution.

A possible description of the possible layouts is shown in figure 10(b).

A possible description of the possible layouts is shown in figure 10(b). The function **text** converts strings into layouts, >|< places its two arguments beside each other, >-< places them above each other and >^< combines two possible layouts. In addition to these combinators we also have **indent** that inserts a specific amount of white space in front of its argument and **empty** that represents the empty document and is a unit element for >-< and >|<. The effect of operations >|< and >-< is sketched in figure 11(a).

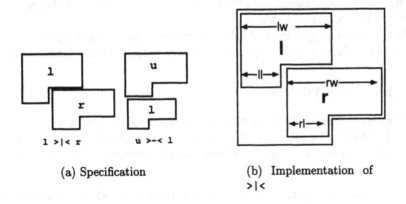

(a) Specification   (b) Implementation of
                                     >|<

Fig. 11. Pretty-printing operations

Before going into implementation details we want to fix the interface (or the
concrete grammar if you prefer) and the semantic domains involved:

```
infixr 2 >|<
infixr 1 >-<
infixr 0 >^<
```

```
empty  :: Formats
text   :: String  -> Formats
indent :: Int      -> Formats -> Formats
(>|<)  :: Formats -> Formats -> Formats
(>-<)  :: Formats -> Formats -> Formats
(>^<)  :: Formats -> Formats -> Formats
```

In the next sections we will, by improving on our search process, develop in-
creasingly sophisticated versions of these combinators.

4.1   The General Approach

We start out by defining a basic set of combinators based on the context-free
grammar of listing 27. We rely on the existence of a set of basic combinators that
generate alternative layouts as lists sorted by decreasing width and increasing
height, assuming that their arguments are sorted lists too. Take for example the
>|< combinator and assume

```
type Formats = [ Format ]
```

The combined solution is found by merging all lists that are obtained by putting
an element from the left argument list besides all elements of the right argument
list. Since we work in a lazy language the resulting list will be generated in an
incremental way as need arises. The other operations are implemented in an

analogous way. A detailed description of the implementation of the underlying basic machinery can be found in [9].

In the attribute grammar of listing 27 the specification of the pretty-printing operations is thus reduced to producing the appropriate basic function calls.

4.2 Improving Filtering

Since many potential candidates are taken into account, and every new choice point doubles the amount of work to be done, detecting solutions wider than the page width as early as possible will improve the efficiency of the process.

Filtering on the page width Our first filter is based in the idea of communicating to each node the page width, preventing candidates wider than the page width to be constructed. Adding this filter to our first program is trivial: declaring an extra inherited attribute for all nonterminals introduced thus far (i.e. including the pseudo nonterminals that stand for external function calls), as you can see in listing 28. [3]

Since we want to be able to work with many different versions of our basic combinators we indicate the system to prefix all generated calls with pw_ using the directive PRE pw.

A change in the underlying machinery is necessary because we now need to pass the width to be filtered on to the basic combinators, in which the actual combination process takes place. Take again the >|< operation depicted in figure 11(b). We now construct new solutions only when the width of the resulting layout (computed as ll + rw, where ll is the length of the last line of l and rw is the width of r) is less than the "global" page width pw.

Narrowing the Estimates Further Actually the page width may be seen as an upper bound on the space available to all nodes. We want to improve on this bound by taking the context of the node into account. Once we know for two nodes to be placed besides each other how much space each of them will take at least, and how much is available to both of them together, we may compute an estimate of how much space is at most available to each of them. The bound on the available space replaces the attribute pw and is called the frame. A frame contains two values: one describing the total width available for representing the text in the tree it is associated with and one for describing how much space is at most available to the last line of that text.

Now have a look at the example in figure 12, and assume a page width of 20. At the root node we start with $(20, 20)$, that is the bound on the total width and the length of the last line of the formats generated by that node.

Let us compute the frame of its left subtree b. Since the minimal width of the subtree c is 9, b has to fit inside a frame $(20, 11)$ (see figure 11(b)).

---

[3] One might compare this with the effort to convert the program into monadic form in order to use a reader monad.

```
   -- Context-free grammar
   DATA PP [ -> fmts : Formats ]
     | Empty
     | Text      String
5    | Indent    Int        PP
     | Beside    left,      right : PP
     | Above     upper,     lower : PP
     | Choice    opta,      optb  : PP

10 -- Calling external functions
   EXT PP
     | Empty     Empty_fmts    | Text     Text_fmts
     | Indent    Indent_fmts   | Beside   Beside_fmts
     | Above     Above_fmts    | Choice   Choice_fmts
15
   -- Introducing external functions
   DATA Empty_fmts  [                              -> fmts ]
   DATA Text_fmts   [ string              <- -> fmts ]
   DATA Indent_fmts [ pP_fmts, int        <- -> fmts ]
20 DATA Beside_fmts [ right_fmts, left_fmts  <- -> fmts ]
   DATA Above_fmts  [ lower_fmts, upper_fmts <- -> fmts ]
   DATA Choice_fmts [ optb_fmts, opta_fmts   <- -> fmts ]
   PRE sim

25 -- Display the solution found
   DATA Root [ -> fmts : Output ]
       | Best PP

   SEM Root
30   | Best LHS.fmts = "putStr . display best $ pP_fmts"

   -->type Output = IO ()
```

Listing 27: Simple pretty-printer (SPP.ag)

```
   --< SPP.ag

   ATTR PP Root [ pw : T_PW <- ]

5  ATTR Empty_fmts  Text_fmts  Indent_fmts
        Beside_fmts Above_fmts Choice_fmts [ lhs_pw <- ]

   PRE pw
```

Listing 28: Filtering with page width

Similar, since the end of the last line of the subtree b is at least 7 units from the left, the frame for the subtree c is (13,13). Since the frame (13,13) cannot accommodate the string **set of functions** the left alternative of the choice node c can be discarded locally, and thus will not be combined elsewhere with other candidates, only to be discarded as part of an impossible solution at the top of the computation.

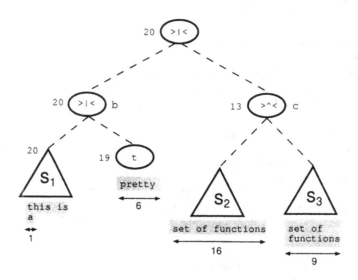

Fig. 12. The frame limit

In listing 29 we show how to compute the minimal space used by a node, that is needed to compute the frames for its fellow nodes. In figure 13(a) we depict the attribute computations involved in the operation >|<.

In listing 30 the semantic functions for passing frames downwards are shown, and an illustration of the data flow for the operation >|< is shown in figure 13(b). Recall that we do not have to code all data flows, only the relevant computations are made explicit. Copy rules involving passing information around are generated automatically as explained in chapter 3. Also note that at the top level we are initiating the attribute computations with the frame (lhs_pw,lhs_pw). Finally in listing 31 we add the synthesis of the formats and an attribute for handling error conditions.

Exercise 4. Note that up to now we do not need to compute the height of the document. Can you anticipate a situation where it is needed? Modify the program FRPP.ag so that the computation of heights is included.

Before starting to read the next section it is useful if you try to solve the following problem. The combinator hv :: Formats -> Formats -> Formats has the following behavior:

```
--< SPP.ag

    SEM PP [ -> minw  USE " 'max' " "0" : Int
                minll USE " 'max' " "0" : Int ]
5   | Text    LOC.minw  = "length string"
                LHS.minll = "minw"
    | Indent LHS.minw  = "int + pP_minw"
                  .minll = "int + pP_minll"
    | Beside LHS.minw  = "left_minw 'max' (left_minll + right_minw)"
10                .minll = "left_minll + right_minll"
    | Above  LHS.minll = "lower_minll"
    | Choice LHS.minw  = "opta_minw 'min' optb_minw"
                  .minll = "opta_minll 'min' optb_minll"
```

Listing 29: Computing min bounds: FRPP.ag

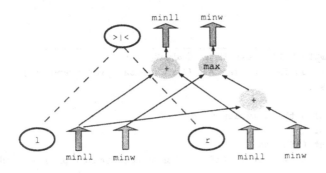

(a) Min limits for >|<

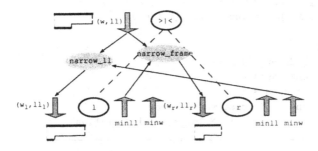

(b) Frame limits for >|<

Fig. 13. Computing the frame

```
   SEM PP [ frame : T_Frame <- ]
     | Indent pP   .frame = "narrow_frame int lhs_frame"
     | Beside left .frame = "narrow_ll right_minw lhs_frame"
              right.frame = "narrow_frame left_minll lhs_frame"
5
   SEM Root [ pw : T_PW <- ]
     | Best pP.frame = "(lhs_pw,lhs_pw)"

   -->narrow_frame i (s,l)  =  (s-i, l-i)
10 -->narrow_ll    i (s,l)  =  (s  , l-i)
```

Listing 30: Computing and communicating the frame: FRPP.ag(cont)

```
   ATTR Empty_fmts  Text_fmts  Indent_fmts
        Beside_fmts Above_fmts Choice_fmts [ lhs_frame <- ]
   PRE frame

5 -- Display the solution found
   SEM Root
     | Best LHS.fmts
               := "putStr (if null pP_error then display best pP_fmts
                                            else pP_error)"
10
   -- Error handling
   SEM PP [ -> error USE "++" "[]": T_Error ]
     | Indent  LHS.error = "err (int < 0) 1"

15 TXT err
   -->type T_Error = String
   -->err cond message
   -->  | not cond = ""
   -->  | cond     = case message of
20 -->                  1 -> "negative indentation"
```

Listing 31: Error and formats: FRPP.ag(end)

```
? render (hv (text "aaaa") (text "bbbb")) 15
aaaabbbb
? render (hv (text "aaaa") (text "bbbb")) 7
aaaa
bbbb
?
```

The combinator places its arguments either vertically or horizontally, depending on the available frame.

Note that the type of Formats in our latest version of the combinators is:

```
type T_Formats = (Int, Int) -> (Error,Minw,Minll,OrigFormats)
type Minw      = Int
type Minll     = Int
type Error     = String
```

where OrigFormats is the type of the elements manipulated by the underlying machinery.

Exercise 5. Write the combinator hv.

4.3   Loss of Sharing in Computations

You may have given the following solution in the last exercise:

```
hv a b  = a >|< b >^< a >-< b
```

Unfortunately you have in this way given an very inefficient solution too. Why the previous definition of hv does not solve our problem? Because the arguments, a and b, of the expression are not plain values, but functions to which secretly a frame is passed. Thus each occurrence of a and b in the body of hv leads to a separate computation. We have thus lost *sharing* as an unfortunate consequence of moving to a higher order domain.

In order to get back the situation in which the computations are shared we have now to collect all the arguments that are passed at the different occurrences of the same expression. Fortunately we have a pleasant *property of the filters and the generators*: the program is thus far constructed in such a way that *if we filter at some place with a value v and elsewhere with a value w, and v<w, then the solutions generated at the call with w may also be used at the place where the call with v is occurring.* So if we manage to collect all the arguments of places where the same expression is occurring, we may compute the maximal value of the argument, and perform the call only once.

The problem is solved with the introduction of the following two new combinators:

par acts as placeholder for a shared expression
apply binds the shared expression to their placetakers as a form of β-reduction

Given the new combinators we have to write the previous definition as:

```
    --< FRPP.ag

    DATA PPC [ -> fmts : Formats ]
      | Indent  Int     PPC
  5   | Beside  left , right: PPC
      | Above   upper, lower: PPC
      | Choice  opta , optb : PPC
      | Par

 10 DATA PP
      | Apply  PPC  PPList

    DATA PPList
      | Nil
 15   | Cons PP PPList
```

Listing 32: Extending the PP to PPC

```
hv a b  = (par >|< par >^< par >-< par) 'app' [a, b]
example = hv (text "hello") (text "world!")
```

Now, not even knowing the actual values of a or b, we can still construct efficient combinators for pretty-printing structures.

Extending the grammar with Par and Apply We introduce a different non-terminal in the grammar for those "complicated formats" as shown in listing 32. text and empty nodes are excluded since they can not contain placeholders.

For the implementation of the par and app we proceed as follows:

- Compute for each >-< and >|< nodes the number (numpars) of par occurrences in both its subtrees (figure 14(a) and listing 33)
- Compute the minimal sizes of the arguments (fillmins) and distribute this information over the tree, using the numpars computed in the first step (figure 14(b) and listing 34)
- Now all sizes of all leaves have become available, we may compute the minimal sizes (minll and minw) of all nodes (in listing 35), that in their turn may be used to
- Compute the frames for all nodes, that also will provide a frame to all the par nodes (in listing 35), which information (reqs) can be
- Collected, and compared on the way up (figure 15(a) and listing 33), and
- Be used at the right argument list of the app node to filter the list of solutions of the shared arguments, which
- Lists have to be passed down (fillfmts) and distributed over the tree (figure 15(b) and listing 34)
- When these solutions have reached their final destinations the original computation can take place (figure 16 and listing 36).

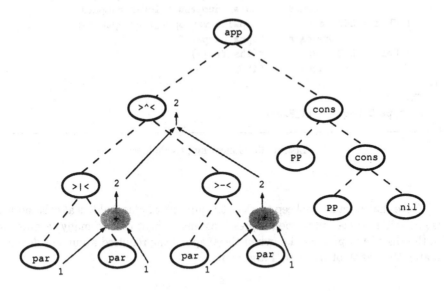

(a) Collect number of **par**

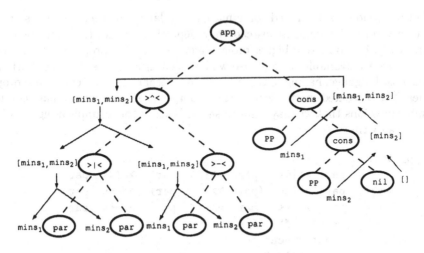

(b) Collect **fillmins** and distribute them

Fig. 14. Attribute computations with par and app

```
SEM PPC  [ -> reqs : T_Reqs  numpars : Int ]
   | Beside LHS.reqs      = "left_reqs ++ right_reqs"
                .numpars  = "left_numpars + right_numpars"
   | Above  LHS.reqs      = "upper_reqs ++ lower_reqs"
5               .numpars  = "upper_numpars + lower_numpars"
   | Choice LHS.reqs      = "zipWith max opta_reqs optb_reqs"
                .numpars  = "opta_numpars"
   | Par    LHS.reqs      = "[lhs_frame]"
                .numpars  = "1"
10
   TXT
   -->type T_Reqs  = [T_Frame]
```

Listing 33: Collecting placeholders

Note that because we keep track of the number of placeholders at each node it is possible to detect ill formed expressions: insufficient (or too many) arguments in the rhs of an **app** node, i.e. when the shape of the required argument does not match the shape of the actual argument.

4.4 Discussion

In this section we developed combinators for a language whose elements are not taken from a flat domain: instead they depend on values that are not known statically. By going to a higher-order domain not all the properties of first class elements are available (in our case we lost sharing). We lost thus support from the host language, having to reintroduce the mechanism to recover those properties. The presented mechanism is still incomplete, because we can have common subexpressions that we may want to share. Back to the example of figure 10, we now can write:

```
pp_ite c t e
   =         par  >>|<<   par  >>|<<  par   >>|<<  par
     >>^<<   par  >>|<<  (par  >>-<<  par)  >>-<<  par
     >>^<<   par  >>-<<   par  >>-<<  par   >>-<<  par
     >>$<   [ text "if"    >|< c
            , text "then" >|< t
            , text "else" >|< e
            , text "fi"
            ]
```

As we can see, there are still subexpressions that are combinations similar to the previous **hv** structure and we may want to share. A solution of this problem is to extend the combinator **app** to accept placeholders in the list of placetakers. This extension together with a complete mechanism for error manipulation is used in

```
   SEM PPC   [ fillfmts : T_Fills fillmins : T_Mins <- ]
     | Beside LOC  .e@(lfs,rfs) = "splitAt left_numpars lhs_fillfmts"
                   .m@(lfm,rfm) = "splitAt left_numpars lhs_fillmins"
              left .fillfmts = "lfs"
5                  .fillmins = "lfm"
              right.fillfmts = "rfs"
                   .fillmins = "rfm"
     | Above  LOC  .e@(ufs,lfs) = "splitAt upper_numpars lhs_fillfmts"
                   .m@(ufm,lfm) = "splitAt upper_numpars lhs_fillmins"
10            upper.fillfmts = "ufs"
                   .fillmins = "ufm"
              lower.fillfmts = "lfs"
                   .fillmins = "lfm"

15 SEM PP
     | Apply  pPC  . fillfmts = "pPList_fillfmts"
                   . fillmins = "pPList_fillmins"

   SEM PPList [  reqs : T_Reqs                              <-
20             -> fillfmts : T_Fills fillmins : T_Mins len : Int ]
     | Nil  LHS    . fillfmts = "[]"
                   . fillmins = "[]"
                   . len      = "0"
     | Cons pP     . frame    = "head lhs_reqs"
25         pPList  . reqs     = "tail lhs_reqs"
           LHS     . fillfmts = "(pP_error,pP_fmts ):pPList_fillfmts"
                   . fillmins = "(pP_minw ,pP_minll):pPList_fillmins"
                   . len      = "pPList_len + 1"

30 TXT
   -->type T_Fills = [(T_Error, Formats)]
   -->type T_Mins  = [(Int, Int)]
```

Listing 34: Collecting placetakers and distributing them

```
   SEM PPC [ frame: T_Frame <- ]
     | Indent pPC   . frame  = "narrow_frame int lhs_frame"
     | Beside left  . frame  = "narrow_ll right_minw lhs_frame"
               right . frame  = "narrow_frame left_minll lhs_frame"
5
   SEM PPC [ -> minw, minll: Int ]
     | Beside LHS   . minw   = "left_minw 'max' (left_minll + right_minw)"
                    . minll  = "left_minll + right_minll"
     | Above  LHS   . minw   = "upper_minw 'max' lower_minw"
10   | Choice LHS   . minw   = "opta_minw 'min' optb_minw"
                    . minll  = "opta_minll 'min' optb_minll"

   SEM PPC
     | Par    LOC   . m@(minw,minll) = "head lhs_fillmins"
```

Listing 35: Computing the minimal values

```
   SEM PPC
     | Indent LHS.fmts = "frame_indent_fmts lhs_frame int pPC_fmts"
     | Beside LHS.fmts = "frame_beside_fmts lhs_frame left_fmts right_fmts"
     | Above  LHS.fmts = "frame_above_fmts lhs_frame upper_fmts lower_fmts"
5  | Choice LHS.fmts = "frame_choice_fmts lhs_frame opta_fmts optb_fmts"
     | Par    LOC.e@(error,fmts) = "head lhs_fillfmts"

   SEM PPC [ -> error USE " ++ " "[]" : T_Error ]
     | Indent LHS . error = "err (int < 0) 1"
10   | Choice LHS . error = "err (length opta_reqs /= length optb_reqs) 3
                           ++ opta_error ++ optb_error"

   SEM PP | Apply  LHS . error = "err (pPList_len /= length pPC_reqs) 2"

15 TXT err
     -->                    2 -> "incomplete parameter list"
     -->                    3 -> "incomplete parameter list in choice"
```

Listing 36: Producing the final formats and error messages

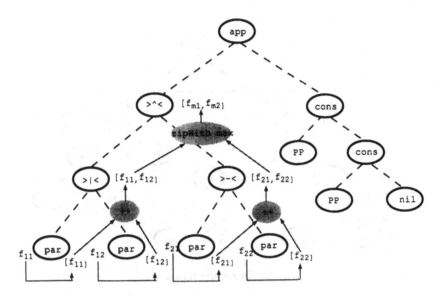

(a) Compute frames at par positions and collect them upwards

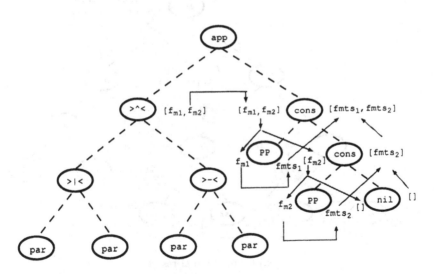

(b) Distribute frames and collect `fillfmts`

Fig. 15. Attribute computations with par and app (cont.)

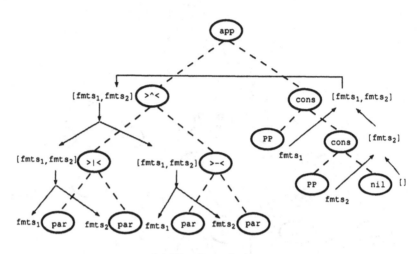

(a) Distribute formats

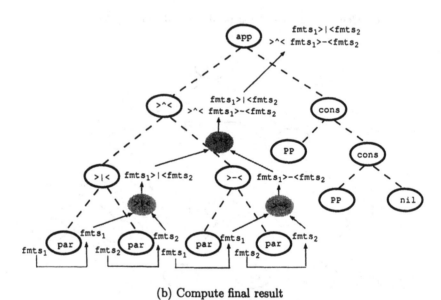

(b) Compute final result

Fig. 16. Attribute computations with par and app (final)

the actual version of our pretty printing combinator library.[4] We think it is a convincing example of the need of mechanical support for the implementation of advanced combinator languages. The attribute grammar paradigm has been indispensable in getting the correct implementation.

5   Strictification

5.1   Introduction

In a previous section we have remarked that it is always possible to combine a function `f:: a -> b` and a function `g:: c -> d` into a single function `fg:: (a, c) -> (b, d)` that has the combined effect. It is this fact that enables our small system to generate one large catamorphism walking over the tree "once", taking as its argument all inherited attributes and returning as its result all synthesized attributes. From a programmers point of view having this merging of all the separate functionalities into a single function makes it quite easy to refer in one computation to results computed in another computation. However one may wonder whether also the reverse transformation is possible and what it might be good for.

For attribute grammars there exists a long tradition in optimizing their implementations in order to achieve efficiencies similar to hand written compilers. In this section we will present some of the analyses and the results of these with respect to our pretty printing combinators. The work we present here is well known in the attribute grammar world, but translates nicely into a functional setting. The overall effect will be that instead of having a single large function that, lazily evaluated, manages to deal with dependencies from its results to its arguments, we will now construct a set of smaller functions that do not exhibit such behavior, and can thus be evaluated in a strict way. This implementation technique was chosen in the course of a project in which we wanted to evaluate attribute grammars in an incremental way, using function caching. For this function caching to work well we implemented the transformations needed to convert the program into strict functions, since the memoisation of lazy functions, albeit possible, is not what we want to use at a large scale.

5.2   Pretty Printing Combinators Strictified

If we look at the type of the `Tree` catamorphism generated for the Rep_Min problem we see that it returns as result a function that takes the computed minimal value as an argument and returns a tuple containing the minimal value and the new tree as a result, so its type is `Int->(Int,Tree)`. When analyzing the overall dependencies between the argument and the result of this function however we may deduce that actually the first component of the result does not depend on the argument in any computation higher up in the tree (only the production `Root` in our case). If we augment the type with arrows indicating this dependency we get its *flow type*, that we have given in figure 5.2.

---

[4] See the combinator's web site: `http://www.cs.uu.nl/groups/ST/Software`.

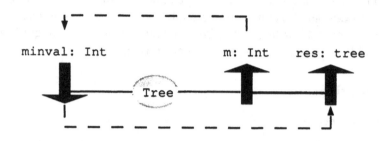

Fig. 17. Flow type of `Tree`

With the dashed arrow we indicate the dependencies occurring in the context in which the tree catamorphism is used. The trick in getting rid of these right-to-left dependencies, that demand lazy evaluation, is to split the function into two functions, as shown in figure 18. If we inspect the dependencies between the

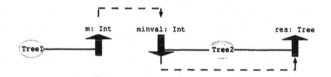

Fig. 18. Flow types of `Tree1` and `Tree2`

attributes in the pretty printing libraries (and this can be done automatically) we find the dependencies for the complicated pretty printing type PPC as shown in figure 19.

Initially we may compute the number of **par** occurrences (**numpars**), since this is a purely syntactical issue, and the number does not depend on any other attribute value. Next we can use this number to split the list of minimal sizes the fill-ins will have (**fillmins**) at the above and beside nodes. This constitutes a "second pass". Once all the sizes of the **par**s have become available we may now return the **minw** and **minll** attributes. They can in their turn be used to adjust the value with which the filtering has to be done (**frame**) when it is passed down the tree. Now it has become possible to collect the maximal sizes available for the corresponding **par** occurrences, that are collected, compared and returned in the synthesized attribute **reqs**. This will be used in the application node to compute the actual list of formats (**fillfmts**) to be used at the **par**-occurrences, and having available this we may at last construct the sought list of candidate

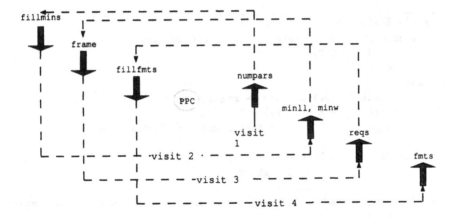

Fig. 19. Flow type of PPC

formats for each node in the tree. Although the constructor at each node is only inspected once in this process, thanks to the deforestated approach we have taken, we may say that the tree is "traversed" four times.

The code generated by the attribute grammar system LRC[5] for the combinator >-<, in the case children may contain par nodes, is given in listing 37. Each of the generated functions takes three kinds of arguments:

- values computed in previous visits and still needed in this or one of the later visits. These dependencies make the purely algebraic approach cumbersome to use when more and more computations get intertwined.
- functions constructed at earlier visits that encompass the rest of the work to be done at each of the children (if not completed). The subscripts refer to the visit number they stand for.
- inherited attributes that became available since the previous visit and that are enabling further computation in this visit.

6   Conclusions

In the beginning of this lecture we have argued that one should not take the step to designing a new language too easily, and in one of the later chapters we have introduced a new language ourselves for describing attribute grammars. The question that thus arises immediately is whether it would have been possible to describe this way of programming again by the introduction of a suitable set of combinators. Recently steps have been taken in pursuing this direction by Oege de Moor in Oxford based on the concept of extensible records. Although we think that our notation still has a lot to offer we hope it will be feasible with future versions of the Haskell type system to achieve the ease of formulation provided by our small system. Wouldn't it be nice if we could describe the threading

---

[5] http://www.cs.uu.nl/groups/ST/Software

```
   lambda_BesideC_1  left_1 right_1
  = ((lambda_BesideC_2  left_numpars right_numpars
        left_2 right_2)
     , numpars)
5    where
        (right_2,right_numpars) = right_1
        (left_2 ,left_numpars) = left_1
        numpars                 = left_numpars + right_numpars


10 lambda_BesideC_2  left_numpars right_numpars
                    left_2 right_2
                    fillsmins
   = ((lambda_BesideC_3  left_minll left_numpars right_minw right_numpars
         left_3 right_3)
15     , minll , minw)
     where
        left_fillsmins              = take left_numpars fillsmins
        (left_3,left_minll , left_minw) = left_2 left_fillsmins
        right_fillsmins             = drop right_numpars fillsmins
20      (right_3, right_minll , right_minw) = right_2 right_fillsmins
        minll = left_minll + right_minll
        minw  = max left_minw (left_minll + right_minw)


   lambda_BesideC_3  left_minll left_numpars right_minw right_numpars
25                   left_3 right_3
                     frame
   = ((lambda_BesideC_4  frame left_numpars right_numpars
         left_4 right_4) , reqs)
     where
30      left_frame            = narrow_ll right_minw frame
        (left_4,left_reqs)    = left_3 left_frame
        right_frame           = narrow_frame left_minll frame
        (right_4,right_reqs) = right_3 right_frame
        reqs                  = left_reqs + right_reqs
35
   lambda_BesideC_4  frame left_numpars right_numpars
                     left_4 right_4
                     fillsfmts
   = (fmts)
40   where
        left_fillsfmts = take left_numpars fillsfmts
        left_fmts      = left_4 left_fillsfmts
        right_fillsfmts = drop right_numpars fillsfmts
        right_fmts     = right_4 right_fillsfmts
45      fmts           = beside_fmts frame left_fmts right_fmts
```

Listing 37: Code generated by LRC for the combinator >-<

of an attribute by means of a function manipulating a grammatical structure, and wouldn't it even be nicer if we could have programs analyse themselves and transform themselves into the strict form as shown in the previous section, without having to go through a separate system.

For the time being we hope to have shown that thinking in terms of attribute grammars allows one to design new combinator languages in an incremental way, and to implement them in an efficient way. The pretty printing combinators have been a joy to study and implement and we hope that you agree with us.

Aknowledgements We want to thank all the people who have been working with us in recent years on the problems described. We want to thank especially Johan Jeuring, David Barton and Eelco Visser for providing comments on the paper and Oege de Moor, Ganesh Sittampalam and our students at Utrecht University for using the attribute grammar system.

References

1. Wadler P. A prettier printer. Available at: `http://cm.bell-labs.com/cm/cs/who/wadler/topics/recent.html`, March 1998.
2. Fokker J. Functional parsers. In Jeuring J. and Meijer E., editors, *Advanced Functional Programming*, number 925 in Lecture Notes in Computer Science, pages 1–52. Springer-Verlag, Berlin, 1995.
3. Hudak P. Haskore music tutorial. In Meijer E. Launchbury J. and Sheard T., editors, *Advanced Functional Programming: Second International School*, number 1129 in Lecture Notes in Computer Science, pages 38–67. Springer-Verlag, Berlin, 1996.
4. O. de Moor and R. Bird. *Algebra of Programming*. Prentice-Hall, London, 1997.
5. Hughes J. The design of a pretty-printing library. In Jeuring J. and Meijer E., editors, *Advanced Functional Programming*, number 925 in Lecture Notes in Computer Science, pages 53–96. Springer-Verlag, Berlin, 1995.
6. Jeuring J. and Jansson P. Polytypic programming. In Meijer E. Launchbury J. and Sheard T., editors, *Advanced Functional Programming: Second International School*, number 1129 in Lecture Notes in Computer Science, pages 68–114. Springer-Verlag, Berlin, 1996.
7. Kieburtz R. and Lewis J. Programming with algebras. In Jeuring J. and Meijer E., editors, *Advanced Functional Programming*, number 925 in Lecture Notes in Computer Science, pages 267–307. Springer-Verlag, Berlin, 1995.
8. S.D. Swierstra and O. de Moor. Virtual data structures. In Partsch H. Möller B. and Schuman S., editors, *Formal Program Development*, number 755 in Lecture Notes in Computer Science, pages 355–371. Springer-Verlag, Berlin, 1993.
9. Azero P. and Swierstra S.D. Optimal pretty-printing combinators. Available at: `http://www.cs.ruu.nl/groups/ST/Software/PP/`, April 1998.
10. Wadler P. Deforestation transforming programs to eliminate trees. *Theoretical Computer Science*, 73:231–48, 1990.
11. T. Johnsson. Attribute grammars as a functional programming paradigm. In G. Kahn, editor, *Functional Programming Languages and Computer Architecture*, volume 274 of *Lecture Notes in Computer Science*, pages 154–173. Springer-Verlag, September 1987.

12. Bird R. Using circular programs to eliminate multiple travesals of data. *Acta Informatica*, 21:239–50, 1984.
13. Swierstra S.D. and Duponcheel L.   Deterministic, error correcting combinator parsers. In Meijer E.and Sheard T. Launchbury J., editor, *Advanced Functional Programming: Second International School*, number 1129 in Lecture Notes in Computer Science, pages 184–207. Springer-Verlag, Berlin, 1996.
14. M. P. Jones. Functional programming with overloading and higher-order polymorphism. In Jeuring J. and Meijer E., editors, *Advanced Functional Programming*, number 925 in Lecture Notes in Computer Science, pages 97–136. Springer-Verlag, Berlin, 1995.
15. Fokkinga M. Meijer E. and Paterson R. Functional programming with bananas, lenses and barbed wire. In Hughes J., editor, *Proceedings of the 1991 ACM Conference on Functional Programming Languages and Computer Architecture*, number 523 in Lecture Notes in Computer Science, pages 124–44. Springer-Verlag, Berlin, 1991.
16. M. Kuiper and S. D. Swierstra. Using attribute grammars to derive efficient functional programs. In *Computing Science in the Netherlands CSN'87*, November 1987. `ftp://ftp.cs.ruu.nl/pub/RUU/CS/techreps/CS-1986/1986-16.ps.gz`.

Using MetaML: A Staged Programming Language

Tim Sheard

Oregon Graduate Institute

1 Why Staging?

The purpose of staged programming in general, and MetaML in particular, is to produce efficient programs. We wish to move beyond programs that compute the "correct" output, to those that also have better control over resources (both space and time). The mechanism for doing this is to use program annotations to control the order of evaluation of terms. It should come as no surprise to those who have studied the λ-calculus that the number of steps in a reduction is strongly influenced by the order of evaluation. Since the number of steps in a reduction relates strongly to the resources it consumes, controlling evaluation order gives programmers better control over resources consumed. MetaML allows programmers to move beyond a fixed evaluation strategy, and to specify precisely the desired evaluation order.

This provides a mechanism which allows general purpose programs (written in an interpretive style that eases both maintenance and construction) to perform without the interpretive overhead usually associated with such programs.

Much of the rivalry between lazy functional languages (such as Haskell) and strict functional languages (such as Standard ML) comes from the perceived superiority of one fixed evaluation order (outermost for lazy, innermost for strict) over another. But this perceived superiority is just that, *perceived*. Recent work, especially that of Chris Okasaki [8] on functional data structures, has shown that no single fixed evaluation order is superior in all cases.

There have been attempts at controlling evaluation order in the past. Strictness annotations in lazy languages temporarily employ an eager evaluation strategy, and constructs such as *force* and *delay* employ a lazy strategy in an strict language. It is also possible (in an strict language) to simulate laziness by using the delaying effect of lambda abstraction. For example, a typical simulation of lazy lists in a strict language might be defined as:

```
datatype 'a lazylist =
          lazyNil | lazyCons of 'a * (unit -> 'a lazylist);

fun count n = lazyCons(n, fn () => count (n+1))
```

Where the tail of a list is a function that forces the computation of the next element, but only when applied.

S.D. Swierstra et al. (Eds.): Advanced Functional Programming, LNCS 1608, pp. 207–239, 1999.
© Springer-Verlag Berlin Heidelberg 1999

The lambda expression, the basis of a language with first class functions, is both a blessing and a curse. It is a blessing since it allows us to build abstractions, which can be used many times. As illustrated, it allows programmers to construct lazy, infinite data structures even in a strict language, but it is a curse because it never allows computation under lambda until the lambda is applied. This profound limitation applies equally to lazy and strict languages. Sometimes computation under the lambda is exactly what is called for, yet we have no way of expressing this. I will try and illustrate this point below:

```
fun power n = (fn x => if n=0 then 1 else x * (power (n-1) x))
```

```
map (power 2) [1,2,3,4,5]
```

This defines a generic power function, and a small program where the power function is specialized to the square function (the exponent n is fixed at 2), and then this specialization is repeatedly applied many times by the map function.

The most efficient strategy is to unfold the definition of power once, but since the result of unfolding power 2 is a lambda no computation is really performed. Suppose we could direct which reductions were to be done, even under lambda. Then, by using the comments to choose which reduction step to employ, we proceed as follows

```
map (power 2) [1,2,3,4,5]
        (* unfold the definition *)
map (fn x => if 2=0 then 1 else x * (power (2-1) x)) [1,2,3,4,5]
        (* perform the if, under the lambda *)
map (fn x => x * (power (2-1) x)) [1,2,3,4,5]
        (* unfold power again *)
map (fn x => x * ((fn x => if 1=0 then 1 else x * (power (1-1) x)) x))
    [1,2,3,4,5]
        (* use the beta rule to apply the explicit lambda to x *)
map (fn x => x * (if 1=0 then 1 else x * (power (1-1) x))) [1,2,3,4,5]
        (* perform the if *)
map (fn x => x * (x * (power (1-1) x))) [1,2,3,4,5]
        (* unfold power again *)
map (fn x => x * (x * (fn x => if 0=0 then 1 else x *(power (0-1) x)) x))
    [1,2,3,4,5]
        (* use the beta rule to apply the explicit lambda to x *)
map (fn x => x * (x * (if 0=0 then 1 else x * (power (0-1) x))))
    [1,2,3,4,5]
        (* perform the if *)
map (fn x => x * (x * 1)) [1,2,3,4,5]
        (* apply the map *)
[1,4,9,16,25]
```

Only after completely unfolding the power function do we use the map function to repeatedly apply the squaring function. We could only unfold power by applying reduction rules under lambda. This saves the duplicated reductions which would unfold the power function each time power 2 is applied.

In MetaML we annotate a program to provide exactly this kind of knowledge. We use three annotations. One to delay the reduction of an expression, one to splice two delayed expressions together to build a larger delayed expression, and one to force a delayed expression to be reduced.

- We use brackets (< >) to surround expressions to indicate that reduction should *not* occur on the expression inside the brackets. We call such a delayed expression a piece of code. Brackets are the introduction rule for code.
- Inside brackets we use escape (˜) to relax the restriction that no reductions may occur brackets inside brackets. That is, only escaped expressions may be reduced inside brackets. This provides a mechanism to splice two pieces of code together to form a larger piece. Inside brackets, if an escaped expression reduces to a bracketed one, then both the escape and the inner bracket my be removed (e.g. < ... ˜ <e> ...> reduces to <... e ...>). This is the first elimination rule for code.
- Finally, we use run to remove outermost brackets. This forces a piece of code to be evaluated (run < e > reduces to e). This rule only applies when no escapes remain in the bracketed expression e. This is the second elimination rule for code

It is the first elimination rule for code (escape bracket cancellation) that makes MetaML so expressive. The escaped expression can be anywhere, even under a lambda! E.g. <fn x => ... ˜e ...> forces evaluation of e even though it would ordinarily be delayed until the lambda was applied. This is a very powerful and expressive construct as we shall see.

After all brackets have been eliminated the default evaluation strategy applies to the remaining term. With these annotations we rewrite the power example as follows:

```
fun power n =  fn x => if n=0
                       then <1>
                       else < ˜x * ˜(power (n-1) x) >)

map (run <fn z => ˜(power 2 <z>)>) [1,2,3,4,5]
```

This is just an annotated version of the original example (except that context requires the call to (power 2) to be eta-expanded).

Using (the default) strict[1] evaluation strategy, but following the order implied by the annotations (rather than using explicit comments to direct evaluation under lambda as in the previous example), we proceed:

```
map (run <fn z => ˜(power 2 <z>)>) [1,2,3,4,5]

map (run <fn z => ˜(if 2=0 then <1> else < ˜<z> * ˜(power (2-1) <z>) >)>)
    [1,2,3,4,5]
```

---

[1] by strict we mean a leftmost, innermost strategy

```
map (run <fn z => ~< ~<z> * ~(power (2-1) <z>) >>) [1,2,3,4,5]

map (run <fn z => ~< z * ~(power (2-1) <z>) >>) [1,2,3,4,5]

map (run <fn z => ~< z * ~(if 1=0 then <1>
                               else < ~<z> * ~(power (1-1) <z>) >) >>)
     [1,2,3,4,5]

map (run <fn z => ~< z * ~< ~<z> * ~(power (1-1) <z>) >>>) [1,2,3,4,5]

map (run <fn z => ~< z * ~< z * ~(power (1-1) <z>) >>>) [1,2,3,4,5]

map (run <fn z => ~< z * ~< z * ~(power 0 <z>) >>>) [1,2,3,4,5]

map (run <fn z => ~< z * ~< z * ~<1> >>>) [1,2,3,4,5]

map (run <fn z => ~< z * ~< z * 1 >>>) [1,2,3,4,5]

map (run <fn z => ~< z * z * 1 >>) [1,2,3,4,5]

map (run <fn z => z * z * 1 >) [1,2,3,4,5]

map (fn z => z * z * 1) [1,2,3,4,5]

[1,4,9,16,25]
```

This simple idea is the key to staged programming. It can have a profound effect on the way programs are constructed and used. The ability to direct reduction under a lambda makes this paradigm strictly more powerful than traditional paradigms with a single fixed evaluation strategy. The staged paradigm does not allow more programs to be expressed, but instead allows all programs to control their own evaluation order, and thus have more control over their resource consumption.

2   Relationship to Other Paradigms

MetaML is strongly related to several other programming paradigms. In particular lisp-like macros with eval, meta-programming, program generation, and partial evaluation.

Lisp-like macros. MetaML's three annotations, bracket, escape and run, are analagous to Lisp's back-quote, comma and eval. Brackets are similar to back-quote. Escape is similar to comma. Run is similar to eval in the empty environment. However, the analogy is not perfect. Lisp does not ensure that variables (atoms) occurring in a back-quoted expression are bound according to the rules of static scoping. For example '(plus 3 5) does not bind plus in the scope where the back-quoted term appears. This is an important feature of

MetaML. In addition, **Lisp** employs a dynamic typing discipline, while MetaML employs a static typing discipline, an important distinction.

Meta-programming. In MetaML a bracketed expression is considered a piece of code. We think of code as a data structure which can be manipulated like any other, but with the additional ability that it can be run.

Because a MetaML program manipulates programs (represented by code) MetaML is a meta-programming system. In MetaML both the meta-language (the language that describes the manipulations) and the object language (the language of the programs being manipulated) are the same: ML.

Program generation. One solution to inefficient interpretive programs is to write a program generator. Rather than write a general purpose but inefficient program, one writes a program generator that generates an efficient solution from a specification. This provides a natural staging to the solution. The use of the parser generator Yacc is an illustrative example. Rather than using a general purpose parsing program, we generate an efficient parser from a specification, i.e. a language grammar. MetaML provides a uniform environment for constructing program generators in a single paradigm. It provides an approach radically different from, and superior to, the ad-hoc "programs-as-strings" view that seems to predominate in most software generation systems.

Partial evaluation. Partial evaluation optimizes a program using a-priori information about some of that program's inputs. The goal is to identify and perform as many computations as possible in a program before run-time.

The most common type of partial evaluation, *Off-line* partial evaluation, has two distinct steps, *binding-time analysis* (BTA) and *specialization*. BTA determines which computations can be performed in an earlier stage given the names of inputs available before run-time (static inputs).

In essence, BTA performs automatic staging of the input program. After BTA, the actual values of the inputs are made available to the specializer. Following the annotations, the specializer either performs a computation, or produces text for inclusion in the output (*residual*) program.

The relationship between partial-evaluation and staged programming is that the intermediate data structure between the two steps is a *two-stage annotated program* [1], and that the specialization phase is the execution of the first stage in the two-stage annotated program produced by BTA.

3 Introducing MetaML

This section provides a gentle introduction to MetaML [12,6]. We designed MetaML as a meta-programming system, i.e. a system which is used to write programs (meta-programs) whose sole purpose is to build and manipulate other programs (object-programs). MetaML provides built-in support for a number of hard problems that repeatedly occur in meta-programming and generation systems. This support includes:

- A type system ensuring the well-formedness (type-safety) of object programs from a type analysis of the meta-program which produces them. This is crucial when debugging multi-stage programs because it reports type errors in the object-programs at the compile-time of the meta-programs, not when the object-programs are executed.
- The capability to use arbitrary values from the meta-program as constants in the generated program. This provides a solution to the *hygienic macro* problem in a typed language, i.e. it supports macro-like constructs which bind identifiers in the environment of definition, not in the environment of their expansion. This completely eliminates inadvertent "capture" problems, and is an implementation of static scoping in a staged language.
- The capability to display code. When debugging, it is important for users to observe the code produced by their programs. This implies a display mechanism (pretty-printer) for values of type code.
- The capability to perform "generation-time" optimization on generated code. Generated code is a first class piece of data and can be manipulated to effect optimizations etc.
- The capability to "execute" the code built for testing and prototyping purposes.

MetaML programs are simply ML programs which are annotated with staging operators. In the next section we describe each of the staging operators and introduce the MetaML language by using short, self-contained "sessions" of the actual implementation. MetaML uses a *read-typecheck-eval-print* top level loop. An expression is entered after the prompt (|-), it is type checked, evaluated, and then its name, value and type are printed.

3.1   The Bracket Operator: Building Pieces of Code

In MetaML, a stage-1 expression is denoted by enclosing it between meta-brackets. For instance, the pieces of code denoting the constant 23 is illustrated by the following MetaML session:

```
-| <23>;
val it = <23> : <int>
```

The expression <23> (pronounced "bracket 23") has type <int> (pronounced "code of int"). The types int and <int> are not the same. Trying to use <23> as an integer fails in the type checking stage, and the system complains:

```
-| <23> + 2;
Type Error:
  Cannot unify the types: in type application the type constructors
  do not match: int is not equal to <int>
 in expression: (<23>,2)
```

Consider the following example where length refers to a previously defined function.

```
-| <length [1,2]>;
val it = <%length [1,2]> : <int>
```

The % in the returned value indicates that `length` has been lifted from a value to a constant piece of code. We call this *lexical capture* of free variables or *cross stage persistence*. This is explained in more detail in section 3.5. Because in MetaML operators (such as + and *) are also identifiers, free occurrences of operators often appear with % in front of them when code is displayed.

Bracketed lambdas. Any expression can be delayed, including higher order (functional) expressions. Consider the examples:

```
-| val idCode = <fn x => x>;
val idCode = <fn a => a> : ['b].<'b -> 'b>
```

```
-| <fn n => n + 1>;
val it = <fn a => a %+ 1> : <int -> int>
```

`idCode` is the code representing a pure MetaML function, the type associated to `idCode` is `['b].<'b -> 'b>` which is a polymorphic piece of code with polymorphic[2] variable `'b`. Note that the display mechanism for code alpha-renames bound variables hence the (`fn a => a`). `<fn n => n + 1>` denotes the representation of a function. It is the encoding of the increment function over integers.

The *level* of any piece of code is the number of surrounding brackets minus the number of surrounding escapes. Simple values such as 13 and (`fn n => n+1`) are level-0 code. In `<fn n => n + 1>`, the function inside the brackets is level-1 code. Finally, in term `<fn n => <n + 1>>`, the sub-term `n + 1` is a level-2 piece of code.

```
-| <fn n => <n + 1>>;
val it = <fn a => <a %+ 1>> : <int -> <int>>
```

`<fn n => <n + 1>>` denotes a three stage program. In stage-0 it is simply a piece of data which represents a program (`<fn n => <n+1>>`). The result of running that program is a function that can be used in stage 1 (`fn n => <n+1>`). When applied to an integer that function produces another piece of code, which can be used in stage 2 (`<%n %+ 1>`).

3.2   The Escape Operator: Composing Pieces of Code

Bracketed expressions can be viewed as *delayed*, i.e. evaluation does not apply under brackets. However, it is often convenient to allow some reduction steps inside a large delayed expression while it is being constructed. MetaML allows one to *escape* from a delayed expression by prefixing a sub-expression within it with a tilde (~). Because tilde must only appear inside brackets, it can only be used at level 1 and higher. For instance, let us examine the function `pair` below:

---

[2] The treatment of polymorphism in MetaML is actually quite subtle, the full treatment of polymorphism is beyond the scope of this paper. See [6] for more details

```
-| fun pair x = <( ~x , ~x )>;
val pair = Fn : ['b].<'b> -> <('b * 'b)>
```

The function pair takes a piece of code (of type <'b>) as input, and produces a new piece of code (of type <('b * 'b)>). It transforms the input code x into the code of the pair (x, x). To do this we must "splice" x into the resulting code in two places. This is done by escaping the occurrences of x in the definition of pair.

When ~ e appears inside brackets at level 1, the system evaluates e to a piece of code <v>. Then v is spliced into the bracketed expression in the context where the original escaped expression occurred. This is the first elimination rule for code. It is an elimination rule since it shows how escape removes brackets.

The purpose of escape is to construct larger pieces of code by splicing smaller pieces of code together. Consider the function pair, which is used to construct new code from old:

```
-| (pair <17-4>);
val it = <(17 %- 4,17 %- 4)> : <(int * int)>
```

By using the first elimination rule for code (~<e> rewrites to e), this reduction proceeds as follows:

```
pair <17 %- 4>

<( ~<17 %- 4>, ~<17 %- 4> )>

<( 17 %- 4, 17 %- 4 )>
```

3.3   The Run Operator: Executing User-Constructed Code

The run operator is the explicit annotation used to indicate that it is now time to execute a delayed computation (i.e. a piece of code).

```
-| val z = <27 - 15>;
val z = <27 %- 15> : <int>

-| run z;
val it = 12 : int
```

The run operator allows us to reduce a piece of code to a value by executing the code. Computation is no longer deferred and the resulting value is a pure value. The second elimination rule for code (run <e> rewrites to e) can *only* be applied if e does not contain escaped expressions. If e does contain escaped expressions, they must be evaluated and then eliminated using the first elimination rule for code before the run elimination rule applies. This is an important rule, since it forces a piece of code to be "fully expanded" before it can be run.

```
run <1 + ~( (fn x => x) <2+3> )>
```

```
run <1 + ~( <2+3> ) >

run <1 + ~<2+3> >

run <1 + 2+3 >

1 + 2+3

6
```

N-stage code is executed by *N* applications of the run annotation.

```
-| val x = <fn n => <n + 1> >;
val x = <fn a => <a %+ 1> > : <int -> <int>>

-| val y = run x;
val y = fn : int -> <int>

-| val z = y 6;
val z = <%n %+ 1> : <int>

-| run z
val it = 7 : int
```

3.4 The Lift Operator: Another Way to Build Code

Similar to meta-brackets, lift transforms an expression into a piece of code.
But lift differs in that it reduces its input before delaying it. This is contrasted
in the examples below.

```
-| <4+1>;
val it = <4 %+ 1> : <int>      (*  no execution  *)

-| lift (4+1);                 (*  4+1 executed  *)
val it = <5> : <int>
```

Lift can be used to make the 2 stage example of the previous section more
comprehensible. By using lift in the second stage the bound variable n appears
as a literal constant (6 below) rather than a lexically captured constant (%n in
the previous example).

```
-| val x = <fn n => < ~(lift n) + 1> >;
val x = <fn a => <~(lift a) %+ 1> > : <int -> <int>>

-| val y = run x;
val y = fn : int -> <int>

-| val z = y 6;
val z = <6 %+ 1> : <int>
```

```
-| run z
val it = 7 : int
```

It should also be noted that lift can not be applied to a higher-order (i.e. functional) arguments, as it is undefined on them.

3.5   Lexical Capture of Free Variables: Constant Pieces of Code

As illustrated in the two stage example, it is often useful to construct code containing variables referring to values previously defined in an earlier stage. For example:

```
-| val n = 10;
val n = 10 : int

-| val codePair = <(n,3)>;
val codePair = <(%n,3)> : <(int * int)>
```

Here, the variable n is defined at stage 0, but inside codePair (where it occurs free), it is referenced at stage 1. At runtime, when the expression <(n,3)> is evaluated, the system has to compute a piece of code related to the *value of* n. This piece of code will be a constant, because n is known to be 10. We call this phenomenon *cross stage persistence*[12]. The pretty printer for code prints all lexically captured constants with the annotation %, followed by the name of the free variable whose value was used to construct the constant. All free variables (regardless of type) inside meta brackets construct these constants. This is the way functions are made into code.

Differences between lift and lexical capture. The lift operator cannot be used on functional values. This is because lift must construct an expression, which when evaluated returns the same result. For functions this is not always possible. With cross stage persistence we *can* lift a function into a piece of code. Cross stage persistence constructs a constant, which needs no evaluation when it is finally run. This allows us to construct code for functions.

```
-| val inc = fn a => a+1;
val inc = fn : int -> int

-| val encodeInc = <inc 5>;
val encodeInc = <%inc 5> : <int>

-| run encodeInc;
val it = 6 : int
```

We use lift when we want value in a previous stage to appear as a literal constant in the code representing a future stage.

4 Pattern Matching Against Code

Since code is just a data structure it is possible to pattern match against pieces of code. Code patterns are constructed by placing brackets around code. For example a pattern that matches the litteral 5 can be constructed by:

```
-| fun is5 <5> = true
   | is5 _ = false;
val is5 = fn   : <int> -> bool

-| is5 (lift (1+4));
val it = true   : bool

-| is5 <0>;
val it = false   : bool
```

The function is5 matches its argument to the constant pattern <5> if it succeeds it returns true else false.

Pattern variables in code patterns are indicated by escaping variables in the code pattern.

```
-| fun parts < ~x + ~y > = SOME(x,y)
   | parts _ = NONE;
val parts = fn   : <int> -> (<int> * <int>) option

-| parts <6 + 7>;
val it = SOME (<6>,<7>) : (<int> * <int>) option

-| parts <2>;
val it = NONE   : (<int> * <int>) option
```

The function parts matches its argument against the pattern < ~x + ~y >. If its argument is a piece of code which the is the addition of two sub terms, it binds the pattern variable x to the left subterm and the pattern variable y to the right subterm.

Code patterns which contain pieces of code with binding occurrences must use higher-order pattern variables. A higher-order pattern variable is indicated by an escaped application. This application must have a special form. It must be the application of a variable to arguments. This introduces a higher-order pattern variable. The arguments of the variable must be explicit bracketed variables, one for each variable bound in the code pattern at the context where the escaped application appears. For example consider the following patterns:

`<fn x => ~ (f <x>)>`	legal
`<fn x => ~ (f <2>)`	illegal, <2> is not a bracketed variable
`<fn x => ~ f>`	illegal, f, under lambda, is not applied to an argument
`<fn x => fn y => ~ (f <x>)>`	illegal, f not applied to all bound variables
`<fn (x,y) => ~ (f <x> <y>) + 1>`	legal

A higher order pattern variable is used like a function on the right hand side of a matching construct. For example a function which applies the rule that 0 is the identity of addition to the body of function is written as:

```
-| fun f <fn x => ~(g <x>) + 0> = <fn y => ~(g <y>)>
   | f x = x;
val f = Fn  : ['b].<'b -> int> -> <'b  -> int>

-| f <fn x => (x-4) + 0>;
val it = <(fn a => a %- 4)> : <int -> int>
```

In the next sections we give several substantial examples which illustrate program staging.

5   A Staged Term Rewriting System

One may think of a *term-rewriting system* as a set of directed rules. Each rule is made of a left-hand side and a right-hand side. Both the left-hand side and right-hand side of a rule are made of patterns. A pattern is a term with pattern matching variables as subterms.

A rule may be applied to a term t if a subterm s of t matches the left-hand side under some substitution σ. A rule is applied by replacing s with t', where t' is the result of applying the substitution σ to the right-hand side. We say "t *rewrites (in one step) to t'* ", and write $t \Rightarrow t'$. As an example, here are the rules for a Monoid [2]:

$$
\begin{array}{ll}
r_1: & x + 0 \to x \\
r_2: & 0 + x \to x \\
r_3: & x + (y + z) \to (x + y) + z
\end{array}
$$

Variables x, y, and z in the rules can each match any term. If a variable occurs more than once on the left-hand side of a rule, all occurrences must match identical terms.

Generally, the rules do not change over the life of the system. At the same time, the basic form of the matching function is a simultaneous traversal of a subject term and the left-hand side of the rule it is being matched against. This offers an opportunity for staging: We can "specialize" matching over the rules in a first stage, and eliminate the overhead of traversing the left-hand side of the rules. Not only that, but as we will see, we can also remove a significant amount of administrative computations involved in constructing and applying the substitution σ. One would expect that this would significantly speed up the rewriting system.

In our system we have both patterns (with variables) and terms (without variables) We capture this with the following data structures:

```
datatype 'a Structure =
  Op of ('a * string * 'a)     (* e.g. (1 + 5) *)
| Int of int;                  (* e.g. 5        *)

datatype term = Wrap of term Structure;

datatype pat =
  Var of string
| Term of pat Structure;
```

In the following algorithm it is necessary to compare two terms for equality if a pattern variable occurs more than once in the same pattern. Such a function is easy to write as a simultaneous traversal over two terms.

```
fun termeq (Wrap t1) (Wrap t2) =
case t1 of
  Op(m,s,n) =>
    (case t2 of Op(a,b,c) =>
       if s=b
         then (if termeq m a
                  then termeq n c
                  else false)
         else false
     | _ => false)
| Int n =>
    (case t2 of
       Int m => n=m
     | _ => false);
```

Because we are constructing a staged version of a pattern matcher, it is necessary to define a staged version of the substitution function. The subst function takes a substitution (binding variable names to code of terms) a pattern (containing variables) and produces the code of a term (without any variables). Since substitutions are implemented as lists, we need a auxillary function for looking things up in lists. The difference between this function and normal subsitution is that subst manipulates pieces of code (which will compute a term) rather than terms themselves.

```
fun find s [] = NONE
  | find s ((a,z)::xs) =
        if a=s then SOME z else find s xs

(* subst: (string * <term>) list  -> pat  -> <term> *)
fun subst sigma pat =
case pat of
  Var v =>
    (case find v sigma of
       SOME w => w)
| Term(Int i) => <Wrap(Int ~(lift i))>
```

```
| Term(Op(t1,s,t2)) =>
    <Wrap(Op (~(subst sigma t1),
              ~(lift s),
              ~(subst sigma t2)))>
```

Note the use of staging annotations to construct the code corresponding to the pattern.

A staged matcher takes a pattern and produces the code which matches a term against that pattern. The pattern is completely known, and the code produced depends upon the pattern. In the rewrite system the code we want to produce will build an instance of the right-hand side of a rule if the left-hand side matches the term. The instance depends upon the substitution built by the matching. Rather than returning a substitution (which is then applied to the right-hand side) the matching function is given a continuation which it should apply to the substitution. It is the continuation that builds the instance of the right-hand side, not the matching function.

```
type substitution = ((string * <term>) list) option;
type continuation = substitution -> <term>;

fun unWrap (Wrap x) = x;
fun unWrapCode <Wrap ~t> = t
  | unWrapCode e = <unWrap ~e>;

(* match: pat -> continuation -> substitution -> <term> -> <term>      *)
fun match pat    (* the pattern being matched, completely known        *)
          k      (* the continuation to build the code. Must be applied *)
                 (* to a substitution                                  *)
          msigma (* the substitution that is built when matching occurs *)
          term   (* code for the term being matched against the pattern *)
          =
case (msigma) of
   NONE => k NONE
 | SOME (sigma) =>
(case pat of
   Var u =>
     (case find u sigma of
        NONE =>
          k (SOME ((u,term) :: sigma))
      | SOME w =>
          <if termeq ~w ~term
              then ~(k (SOME sigma))
              else ~(k NONE)>)
 | Term(Int n) =>
     <case ~(unWrapCode term) of
        Int u => if u= ~(lift n)
                   then ~(k msigma)
                   else ~(k NONE)
      | _ => ~(k NONE)>
```

```
| Term(Op(p1,s1,p2)) =>
    <case ~(unWrapCode term) of
       Op(t1,s2,t2) =>
           if ~(lift s1) = s2
              then ~(match p1
                            (fn msig => match p2 k msig <t2>)
                            msigma
                            <t1>)
              else ~(k NONE)
       | _ => ~(k NONE)>
)
```

Rewriting builds the code of a term from a rule. We do this as follows:

```
fun rewrite (lhs,rhs) =
<fn (Wrap t) =>
   ~(match lhs
           (fn NONE => <Wrap t>          (* the initial continuation *)
            | SOME s => subst s rhs)
           (SOME [])
           <Wrap t>)>;
```

Note how we build a continuation to apply the substitution to the right-hand side of the rule, and pass it to the `match` function. If the continuation is ever passed the failure substitution (`NONE`) it simply returns the original term.

When we apply the `rewrite` function to a rule some code is constructed.

```
val r3 = (** (x + y) + z   =>  x + (y + z)  **)
  (Term(Op(Term (Op(Var "x","+",Var "y")), "+", Var "z")),
   Term(Op(Var "x","+",Term(Op(Var "y","+",Var "z")))));
```

```
-| rewrite r3;
val it =
<(fn Wrap a =>
     (case a of
        Op(d,c,b) =>
            if "+" %= c
               then (case %unWrap d of
                        Op(g,f,e) =>
                            if "+" %= f
                               then Wrap (Op(g,"+",Wrap (Op(e,"+",b))))
                               else Wrap a
                      | _ =>
                            Wrap a)
               else Wrap a
       | _ => Wrap a))>
 : <term  -> term >
```

6   Safe Reductions Under Brackets

The purpose of MetaML is to control evaluation order. The bracket annotation is the mechanism used to delay evaluation. It is used to say *"do not apply any reduction rules in this term until I say so"*. Even so, there *are* reduction rules that are safe to apply even inside brackets. These rules never change the semantics or the termination properties of term, or the order in which sub-terms are evaluated. The reason we wish to apply such rules is that they can significantly reduce the size and complexity of a piece of code without affecting any of its important properties. To write multi-stage programs effectively, one needs to observe the programs produced, and these programs should be as simple as possible. For this reason, it is important that code produced be as simple as possible.

6.1   Safe-Beta

There is one safe case which is particularly well known, namely instances of Plotkin's β_v rule [9]. Whenever an application is constructed where the function part is an explicit lambda abstraction, and the argument part is a value, then that application can be symbolicly beta reduced. In order to avoid duplicating code we restrict our safe-beta reductions to those terms where the argument is a constant or a variable (while Plotkin's β_v rule also allows the values to be lambda expressions). For example in:

```
val g = <fn x => x * 5>;
val h = <fn x => (~g x) - 2>;
```

The variable h evaluates to: `<fn d1 => (d1 * 5) - 2>` rather than `<fn d1 => ((fn d2 => d2 * 5) d1) - 2>`.

6.2   Safe-Eta

Another simple example is eta-reduction, i.e terms of the form: `(fn x => e x)` where e is a value (an explicit lambda or a variable) and x does not occur free in e. Such terms can be eta-reduced to e without changing their meaning or termination behavior. To see how this works in MetaML see the example below:

```
-| <fn f => (fn x => f x)>;
val it = <(fn a => a)> : ['b,'c].<('c  -> 'b ) -> 'c  -> 'b>

-| <fn (f,y) => (fn x => (f y) x)>;
val it = <(fn (b,a) => (fn c => b a c))> :
         ['b,'c,'d].<(('d  -> 'c  -> 'b ) * 'd ) -> 'c  -> 'b>
```

Notice how the eta-rule is applied in the first example, but not in the second. This is because the conditions for safety are not met (the function part is an application not a value) in the second example.

6.3 Safe-Let-Hoisting

Let-hoisting is illustrated by the following examples:

```
-| <let val x = (let val y = 5 in y+1 end) in x + 2 end>;
val it = <let val a = 5 val b = a %+ 1  in b %+ 2 end> : <int>

-| <let val y = 5 in let val x = y+1 in x+2 end end>;
val it = <let val a = 5 val b = a %+ 1  in b %+ 2 end> : <int>
```

Safe-beta, safe-eta, and safe-let-hoisting are instances of Wadler and Sabry's call-by-value equivalence rules [10]. Applying these rules makes it harder to understand *why* a particular program was generated, but in our experience, the resulting programs are smaller, simpler, and easier to understand. These advantages make this tradeoff worthwhile.

7 Non-standard Extensions

We built MetaML to investigate new paradigms of programming. As we used MetaML we discovered several simple extensions to ML in addition to the staging annotations that were quite useful. These extensions are not not original to MetaML. All are well thought-out ideas that have appeared in the literature, and several have appeared as features in other languages.

7.1 Higher Order Type Constructors

It is sometimes useful to define a parameterized type constructor, parameterized not just by a type, but by another type constructor. In MetaML this can be done by placing a kind annotation on the parameter that indicates it is a type constructor. For example consider the definition below for a tree of integers with an arbitrary branching factor:

```
datatype ('F : * -> * ) tree = tip of int | node of ('F tree) 'F;

datatype 'a binary = bin of 'a * 'a;
```

The branching factor of a `tree` is specified by the parameter 'F which is itself a type constructor. The notation: 'F : * -> * means 'F has kind "type to type", which means it is a type constructor taking one type (*) to another type (*).

For example the tree: `node(bin(tip 4, tip 7))` has type `binary tree`, and the tree constructed by: `node[tip 4, tip 0, tip 6]` has type `list tree`.

It is possible to define type constructors parameterized by several higher order type constructors by definitions of the form:
```
datatype ('F : * -> *, 'G: * -> *) T = ...
```
or by a type constructor that takes several arguments by a definition of the form:
```
datatype ('F : * -> * -> * ) S = ....
```

The postfix application (e.g. (int,string) T) of type constructors in ML causes a little subtlety. A unary type constructor can be constructed from a binary type constructor by partial application. But this requires some special syntax since in ML all arguments are "grouped together" inside parentheses. We think of the normal (parenthesized) notation of ML as a shorthand for our special syntax which allows partial application. Thus the normal ('a,'b,'c) T is a shorthand for the more verbose (but more flexible since it allows partial application) 'a ('b ('c T)).

For example by defining the binary type constructor state

```
datatype ('a,'b) state = St of ('a -> ('b * 'a));
```

we can construct an instance: node(St(fn x => (4,x))), which has type (int state) tree where the parameter to tree is a partial application of state

7.2   Local Polymorphism

It is often convenient to build records where a component of a record is a polymorphic function. This allows a limited form of "local polymorphism". By "local" we mean non-Hindley-Milner because all of the forall quantifications are not at the outermost level.

For example consider the specification of a list monoid as a record containing three polymorphic elements: an injection function, a plus function, and a zero element. In MetaML we specify this with an extension to the datatype definition which allows polymorphic record components:

```
datatype list_monoid = LM of
  { inject : ['a].'a -> 'a list,
    plus  : ['a]. 'a list -> 'a list -> 'a list,
    zero  : ['a].'a list
  };
```

The notation inject: ['a]. 'a -> 'a list declares that the inject component of the record must be a polymorphic function.

We could construct an instance of list_monoid by:

```
val lm1 = LM{inject = fn x => [x],
             plus  = fn x => fn y => x@y,
             zero  = []}
```

We can exploit the polymorphism of the record by using pattern matching:

```
fun f (LM{inject=inj, plus = sum, zero = z}) =
    (sum z (inj 2), sum (inj true) (inj false));
```

When applied to list_monoid we obtain:

```
-| f lm1;
val it = ([2],[true ,false ]) : (int list  * bool  list )
```

Note that the sum and inj functions are used polymorphically. Because of the explicit type annotations in the datatype declaration MetaML knows to generalize polymorphic names introduced by pattern matching and to enforce that construction of such records is only allowed on truly polymorphic objects. The effect of local polymorphism and higher order type constructors on the Hindley-Milner type inference system has been well studied[3,7].

7.3 Monads

A monad is a type constructor M (a type constructor is a function on types, which given a type produces a new type), and two polymorphic functions $unit : \,'a \to (\,'a\ M)$ and $bind: (\,'a\ M) \to (\,'a \to \,'b\ M) \to (\,'b\ M)$. The usual way to interpret an expression with type $'a\ M$ is as a computation which represents a potential action that also returns a value of type $'a$.

Actions might include things like performing I/O, updating a mutable variable, or raising an exception. It is possible to emulate such actions in a purely functional setting by explicitly threading "stores", "I/O streams", or "exception continuations" in and out of all computations. We sometimes call such an emulation the *reference implementation*, since it describes the actions in a purely functional manner, though it may be inefficient.

The two polymorphic functions *unit* and *bind* must meet the following three axioms:

(left id) $bind\ (unit\ x)\ (\lambda y.e[y]) = e[x/y]$

(right id) $bind\ e\ (\lambda y.unit\ y) = e$

(bind assoc) $bind\ (bind\ e\ (\lambda x.f[x]))\ (\lambda y.g[y]) = bind\ e\ (\lambda z.bind\ (f[z/x])(\lambda w.g[w/y]))$

where on the left side of an equation $e[x]$ indicates that e is an expression that contains occurrences of the free variable x, and on the right side of an equation $e[x/y]$ means substitute y for all free occurrences of x in e.

The monadic operators, *unit* and *bind*, are called the standard morphisms of the monad, and are used to create empty actions (*unit*), and sequence two actions (*bind*). A particular monad must also have non-standard morphisms that describe the primitive actions of the monad (like *fetch* the value from a variable and *update* a variable in the monad of mutable state).

A useful property of monads is that they encapsulate their actions in an abstract datatype (ADT), where the only access to the encapsulation is through *unit*, *bind*, and the non-standard morphisms. Like any ADT, it is possible to use different implementations without affecting the behavior of the system built on top of the ADT. Thus it is possible for a purely functional language to use a primitive implementation of a monad that actually side-effects the world[5], and for the applications built on top of this ADT to still appear purely functional. As long as the primitive implementation behaves like the reference implementation (that might passes stores etc.) everything works out.

Monads perform two useful functions. First, they abstract away all the "plumbing" that all the explicit threading implies, and second, they make explicit actions that can be used to effect the world.

7.4   Monads in MetaML

In MetaML a monad is a data structure encapsulating the type constructor M and the *unit* and *bind* functions[14].

```
datatype ('M : * -> * ) Monad = Mon of
   ( ['a]. 'a -> 'a 'M) * (['a,'b]. 'a 'M -> ('a -> 'b 'M) -> 'b 'M);
```

This definition uses two of the other non-standard extensions to ML. First, it declares that the argument ('M : * -> *) of the type constructor Monad is itself a unary type constructor. Second, it declares that the arguments to the constructor Mon must be polymorphic functions.

In MetaML, Monad is a first-class, although *pre-defined* type. In particular, there are two syntactic forms which are aware of the Monad datatype: Do and Return [5]. Both are parameterized by an expression of type 'M Monad. Users may freely construct their own monads, though they must be careful that their instantiation meets the monad axioms listed above.

Do is MetaML's interface to the monadic *bind* and Return is MetaML's interface to the monadic *unit*. In MetaML these are really nothing more than syntactic sugar for the following:

Syntactic Sugar		*Derived Form*
Do (Mon(unit,bind)) { x <- e; f }	=	bind e (fn x => f)
Return (Mon(unit,bind)) e	=	unit e

In addition the syntactic sugar of the Do allows a sequence of x_i <- e_i forms, and defines this as a nested sequence of Do's. For example:

```
Do m { x1 <- e1; x2 <- e2 ; x3 <- e3 ; e4 }   =
   Do m { x1 <- e1; Do m { x2 <- e2 ; Do m { x3 <- e3 ; e4 }}}
```

7.5   An Example Monad

A simple example is the intState monad which encapsulates read and write actions on a single, mutable, integer variable. We give a reference implementation which encodes the mutable integer value as an integer. This integer is threaded into and out of every computation. Read's will access the value, and Write's will pass out a new updated value.

```
datatype 'a St = St of (int -> ('a * int));
fun unSt (St f) = f;

(* unit : 'a -> St 'a *)
```

```
fun unit x = St(fn n => (x,n));

(* bind : (St 'a) -> ('a -> St 'b) -> (St 'b) *)
fun bind e f = St(fn n => let val (a,n') = (unSt e) n
                          in unSt(f a) n' end);

val intState : St Monad = Mon(unit,bind);
```

We encapsulate the type constructor of the monad as the algebraic datatype
St, the regular morphisms as functions over this datatype, and then encapsulate
them with the Mon data constructor.

The non-standard morphisms of the intState monad are the actions read
and write. Because there is only *one* variable they need not take a variable as
an argument.

```
(* read : int St *)
val read = St(fn n => (n,n));

(* write : int -> unit St *)
fun write n' = St(fn n => ( (), n' ));
```

It is interesting to unfold all these definitions by hand on a simple example:

```
Do intState { x <- read ; write (x+1) } =

Do (Mon(unit,bind)) { x <- read ; write (x+1) }  =

bind read (fn x => write (x+1))  =

St(fn n => let val (a,n') = (unSt read) n  in unSt(write (a+1)) n' end) =

St(fn n => let val (a,n') = (n,n)  in ( (), n'+1 ) end)
```

There are three important things to notice about this example. First, by
writing it in monadic style, the sequencing (the read *before* the write) is enforced
by the data dependencies of the result. Second, the "plumbing" of passing the
int valued state is completely abstracted away in the source. Third, it makes
the read and write "actions" that must be performed explicit.

7.6   Safe Monad-Law-Normalization Inside Brackets

Like safe-beta, safe-eta, and safe-let-hoisting the monad laws are reduction rules
that can safely be applied inside brackets without changing the evaluation order,
termination behaviour, or any other semantic property. We give several examples
below which illustrate the effect of monad law normalization on constructed code:

```
(* left id *)
-| <Do intState {x <- Return intState 5; Return intState x + 2}>;
```

```
val it = <Return %intState 5 %+ 2> : <int St>
```

```
(* right id *)
-| <fn e => Do intState { x <- e; Return intState x}>;
val it = <(fn a => a)> : ['b].<'b St -> 'b St>
```

When monadic code is constructed, the monad normalization laws are automatically applied in the MetaML interpreter.

8   From Interpetors to Compilers Using Staging

In this section, we construct a compiler by annotating a monadic interpretor for a small imperative *while-language*. We proceed in two steps. First, we introduce the language and its denotational semantics by giving a monadic interpreter as a one stage MetaML program. Second, we stage this interpreter by using a two stage MetaML program in order to produce a compiler.

8.1   The While-Language

In this section, we introduce a simple *while-language* composed from the syntactic elements: expressions (Exp) and commands (Com). In this simple language expressions are composed of integer constants, variables, and operators. A simple algebraic datatype to describe the abstract syntax of expressions is given in MetaML below:

```
datatype Exp =
  Constant of int            (*   5     *)
| Variable of string         (*   x     *)
| Minus of (Exp * Exp)       (*   x - 5 *)
| Greater of (Exp * Exp)     (*   x > 1 *)
| Times of (Exp * Exp) ;     (*   x * 4 *)
```

Commands include assignment, sequencing of commands, a conditional (*if* command), while loops, a print command, and a declaration which introduces new statically scoped variables. A declaration introduces a variable, provides an expression that defines its initial value, and limits its scope to the enclosing command. A simple algebraic datatype to describe the abstract syntax of commands is:

```
datatype Com =
  Assign of (string * Exp)          (* x := 1                    *)
| Seq of (Com * Com)                (* { x := 1; y := 2 }        *)
| Cond of (Exp * Com * Com)         (* if x then x := 1 else y := 1 *)
| While of (Exp * Com)              (* while x>0 do x := x - 1   *)
| Declare of (string * Exp * Com)   (* declare x = 1 in x := x - 1 *)
| Print of Exp;                     (* print x                   *)
```

A simple while-program in concrete syntax, such as

```
declare x = 150 in
  declare y = 200 in {while x > 0 do {x := x - 1; y := y - 1}; print y}
```

is encoded abstractly in these datatypes as follows:

```
val S1 =
Declare("x",Constant 150,
  Declare("y",Constant 200,
    Seq(While(Greater(Variable "x",Constant 0),
              Seq(Assign("x",Minus(Variable "x",Constant 1)),
                  Assign("y",Minus(Variable "y",Constant 1)))),
        Print(Variable "y"))));
```

8.2 The Structure of the Solution

Staging is an important technique for developing efficient programs, but it requires some forethought. To get the best results one should design algorithms with their staged solutions in mind.

The meaning of a while-program depends only on the meaning of its component expressions and commands. In the case of expressions, this meaning is a function from environments to integers. The environment is a mapping between names (which are introduced by Declare) and their values.

There are several ways that this mapping might be implemented. Since we intend to stage the interpreter, we break this mapping into two components. The first component, a list of names, will be completely known at compile-time. The second component, a list of integer values that behaves like a stack, will only be known at the run-time of the compiled program.

The functions that access this environment distribute their computation into two stages. First, determining at what location a name appears in the name list, and second, by accessing the correct integer from the stack at this location. In a more complicated compiler the mapping from names to locations would depend on more than just the declaration nesting depth, but the principle remains the same. Since every variable's location can be completely computed at compile-time, it is important that we do so, and that these locations appear as constants in the next stage.

Splitting the environment into two components is a standard technique (often called a binding time improvement) used by the partial evaluation community[4]. We capture this precisely by the following purely functional implementation.

```
type location = int;
type index = string list;
type stack = int list;

(* position : string -> index -> location *)
fun position name index =
    let fun pos n (nm::nms) = if name = nm then n else pos (n+1) nms
    in pos 1 index end;
```

```
(* fetch : location -> stack -> int *)
fun fetch n (v::vs) = if n = 1 then v else fetch (n-1) vs;
```

```
(* put: location -> int -> stack -> stack *)
fun put n x (v::vs) = if n = 1 then x::vs else v::(put (n-1) x vs);
```

The meaning of Com is a stack transformer and an output accumulator. It transforms one stack (holding the values of the variables in scope) into another stack (with presumably different values for the same variables) while accumulating the output printed by the program.

To produce a monadic interpreter we could define a monad which encapsulates the index, the stack, and the output accumulation. Because we intend to stage the interpreter we do not encapsulate the index in the monad. We want the monad to encapsulate only the dynamic part of the environment (the stack of values where each value is accessed by its position in the stack, and the output accumulation).

The monad we use is a combination of *monad of state* and the *monad of output*.

The part corresponding to the monad of state is similar to the monad described in section 7.5, except the mutable value is not an integer, but instead a vector of mutable integers that will be managed like a stack.

```
datatype 'a M = StOut of (int list -> ('a * int list * string));
fun unStOut (StOut f) = f;
fun unit x = StOut(fn n => (x,n,""));
fun bind e f = StOut(fn n => let val (a,n1,s1) = (unStOut e) n
                                 val (b,n2,s2) =  unStOut(f a) n1
                             in (b,n2,s1 ^ s2) end);
val mswo : M Monad = Mon(unit,bind); (* Monad of state with output *)
```

The non-standard morphisms must describe how the stack is extended (or shrunk) when new variables come into (or out of) scope; how the value of a particular variable is read or updated; and how the printed text is accumulated. Each can be thought of as an action on the stack of mutable variables, or an action on the print stream.

```
(* read : location -> int M *)
fun read i = StOut(fn ns => (fetch i ns,ns,""));
```

```
(* write : location -> int -> unit  M *)
fun write i v = StOut(fn ns =>( (), put i v ns, "" ));
```

```
(* push: int -> unit  M *)
fun push x = StOut(fn ns => ( (), x :: ns, ""));
```

```
(* pop : unit M *)
val pop = StOut(fn (n::ns) => ((), ns, ""));
```

```
(* output: int -> unit M *)
fun output n = StOut(fn ns => ( (), ns, (toString n)^" "));
```

8.3   Step 1: Monadic Interpreter

Because expressions do not alter the stack, or produce any output, we could give an evaluation function for expressions which is not monadic, or which uses a simpler monad than the monad defined above. We choose to use the monad of state with output throughout our implementation for two reasons. One, for simplicity of presentation, and two because if the while language semantics should evolve, using the same monad everywhere makes it easy to reuse the monadic evaluation function with few changes.

The only non-standard morphism evident in the `eval1` function is `read`, which describes how the value of a variable is obtained. The monadic interpretor for expressions takes an index mapping names to locations and returns a computation producing an integer.

```
(*  eval1: Exp -> index -> int M *)
fun eval1 exp index =
case exp of
  Constant n => Return mswo n
| Variable x => let val loc = position x index
                in read loc end
| Minus(x,y) =>
    Do mswo { a <- eval1 x index ;
              b <- eval1 y index;
              Return mswo (a - b) }
| Greater(x,y) =>
    Do mswo { a <- eval1 x index ;
              b <- eval1 y index;
              Return mswo (if a '>' b then 1 else 0) }
| Times(x,y) =>
    Do mswo { a <- eval1 x index ;
              b <- eval1 y index;
              Return mswo (a * b) };
```

The interpreter for `Com` uses the non-standard morphisms `write`, `push`, and `pop` to transform the stack and the morphism `output` to add to the output stream.

```
(* interpret1 : Com -> index -> unit M *)
fun interpret1 stmt index =
case stmt of
  Assign(name,e) =>
    let val loc = position name index
    in Do mswo { v <- eval1 e index ;  write loc v } end
| Seq(s1,s2) =>
    Do mswo { x <- interpret1 s1 index;
              y <- interpret1 s2 index;
              Return mswo () }
| Cond(e,s1,s2) =>
    Do mswo { x <- eval1 e index;
```

```
            if x=1
                then interpret1 s1 index
                else interpret1 s2 index }
| While(e,body) =>
  let fun loop () =
      Do mswo { v <- eval1 e index ;
                if v=0 then Return mswo ()
                        else Do mswo { interpret1 body index ;
                                       loop () } }
  in loop () end
| Declare(nm,e,stmt) =>
  Do mswo { v <- eval1 e index ;
            push v ;
            interpret1 stmt (nm::index);
            pop }
| Print e =>
  Do mswo { v <- eval1 e index;
            output v };
```

Although interpret1 is fairly standard, we feel that two things are worth pointing out. First, the clause for the Declare constructor, which calls push and pop, implicitly changes the size of the stack and explicitly changes the size of the index (nm: index), keeping the two in synch. It evaluates the initial value for a new variable, extends the index with the variables name, and the stack with its value, and then executes the body of the Declare. Afterwards it removes the binding from the stack (using pop), all the while implicitly threading the accumulated output. The mapping is in scope only for the body of the declaration.

Second, the clause for the While constructor introduces a local tail recursive function loop. This function emulates the body of the while. It is tempting to control the recursion introduced by the While by using the recursion of the interpret1 function itself by using a clause something like:

```
| While(e,body) =>
  Do mswo { v <- eval1 e index ;
            if v=0 then Return mswo ()
                    else Do mswo { interpret1 body index ;
                                   interpret1 (While(e,body)) index }
        }
```

Here, if the test of the loop is true, we run the body once (to transform the stack and accumulate output) and then repeat the whole loop again. This strategy, while correct, will have disastrous results when we stage the interpreter, as it will cause the first stage to loop infinitely.

There are two recursions going on here. First the unfolding of the finite data structure which encodes the program being compiled, and second, the recursion in the program being compiled. In an unstaged interpreter a single loop suffices. In a staged interpreter, both loops are necessary. In the first stage we only unfold the program being compiled and this must always terminate. Thus we must plan ahead as we follow our three step process. Nevertheless, despite the concessions we have made to staging, this interpreter is still clear, concise and describes the semantics of the while-language in a straight-forward manner.

8.4   Step 2: Staged Interpreter

To specialize the monadic interpreter to a given program we add two levels of staging annotations. The result of the first stage is the intermediate code, that if executed returns the value of the program. The use of the bracket annotation enables us to describe precisely the code that must be generated to run in the next stage. Escape annotations allow us to escape the recursive calls of the interpreter that are made when compiling a while-program.

```
(* eval2: Exp -> index -> <int M> *)
fun eval2 exp index =
case exp of
  Constant n => <Return mswo ~(lift n)>
| Variable x =>
  let val loc = position x index
  in <read ~(lift loc)> end
| Minus(x,y) =>
  <Do mswo { a <- ~(eval2 x index) ;
             b <- ~(eval2 y index);
             Return mswo (a - b) }>
| Greater(x,y) =>
  <Do mswo { a <- ~(eval2 x index) ;
             b <- ~(eval2 y index);
             Return mswo (if a '>' b then 1 else 0) }>
| Times(x,y) =>
  <Do mswo { a <- ~(eval2 x index) ;
             b <- ~(eval2 y index);
             Return mswo (a * b) }>;
```

The lift operator inserts the value of loc as the argument to the read action. The value of loc is known in the first-stage (compile-time), so it is transformed into a constant in the second-stage (run-time) by lift.

To understand why the escape operators are necessary, let us consider a simple example: eval2 (Minus(Constant 3,Constant 1)) []. We will unfold this example by hand below:

```
eval2 (Minus(Constant 3,Constant 1)) [] =

< Do mswo
    { a <- ~(eval2 (Constant 3) []);
      b <- ~(eval2 (Constant 1) []);
      Return mswo (a-b)} >              =
```

```
< Do mswo
    { a <- ~<Return mswo 3>;
      b <- ~<Return mswo 1>;
      Return mswo (a - b)} >                        =

< Do mswo
    { a <- Return mswo 3;
      b <- Return mswo 1;
      Return mswo (a - b)} >                        =

< Do %mswo
    { a <- Return %mswo 3;
      b <- Return %mswo 1;
      Return %mswo (a %- b)} >
```

Each recursive call produces a bracketed piece of code which is spliced into the larger piece being constructed. Recall that escapes may only appear at level-1 and higher. Splicing is axiomatized by the the first elimination rule for code: $\tilde{} <x> \longrightarrow x$, which applies only at level-1. The final step, where mswo and - become %mswo and %-, occurs because both are free variables and are lexically captured.

Interpreter for Commands. Staging the interpreter for commands proceeds in a similar manner:

```
(*  interpret2 : Com -> index ->  <unit M> *)
fun interpret2 stmt index =
case stmt of
  Assign(name,e) =>
  let val loc = position name index
  in <Do mswo { n <- ~(eval2 e index) ;
                write ~(lift loc) n }>
  end
| Seq(s1,s2) =>
  <Do mswo { x <- ~(interpret2 s1 index);
             y <- ~(interpret2 s2 index);
             Return mswo () }>
| Cond(e,s1,s2) =>
  <Do mswo { x <- ~(eval2 e index);
             if x=1
                then ~(interpret2 s1 index)
                else ~(interpret2 s2 index)}>
| While(e,body) =>
  <let fun loop () =
       Do mswo { v <- ~(eval2 e index);
                 if v=0
                    then Return mswo ()
                    else Do mswo { q <- ~(interpret2 body index); loop ()}
                }
```

```
      in loop () end>
| Declare(nm,e,stmt) =>
    <Do mswo { x <- ~(eval2 e index) ;
               push x ;
               ~(interpret2 stmt (nm::index)) ;
               pop }>
| Print e =>
    <Do mswo { x <- ~(eval2 e index) ;
               output x }>;
```

An example. The function `interpret2` generates a piece of code from a `Com` object. To illustrate this we apply it to the simple program: `declare x = 10 in { x := x - 1; print x }` and obtain:

```
<Do %mswo
    { a <- Return %mswo 10
    ; %push a
    ; Do %mswo
        { e <- Do %mswo
                   { d <- Do %mswo
                             { b <- %read 1
                             ; c <- Return %mswo 1
                             ; Return %mswo b %- c
                             }
                   ; %write 1 d
                   }
        ; g <- Do %mswo
                   { f <- %read 1
                   ; %output f
                   }
        ; Return %mswo ()
        }
    ; %pop
    }>
```

By applying the safe monad normalization laws while constructing the above program we obtain the more satisfying:

```
<Do %mswo
    { %push 10
    ; a <- %read 1
    ; b <- Return %mswo a %- 1
    ; c <- %write 1 b
    ; d <- %read 1
    ; e <- %output d
    ; Return %mswo ()
    ; %pop
    }>
```

The difference in the complexity of the two programs illustrates why program normalization is important if constructed programs are to be observed. In the MetaML implementation the normalization laws can be turned on and off. They are all on by default. The side effecting function `feature` can be used to control the normalization laws. `feature 0` displays the normalization modes, and `feature n` toggles the nth feature.

```
-| feature 0;
1 Safe-beta is on.
2 Safe-eta is on.
3 Let-hoisting is on.
4 Monad-law-normalization is on.
val it = false  : bool

-| feature 4;
Monad-law-normalization is off.
val it = false  : bool
```

9   Typing Staged Programs

In Figure 9 the derivation rules for typing a subset of MetaML are given. The interesting rules are **Br n** which addresses the typing of bracketed expressions, **Esc n+1** which addresses the typing of escaped expressions, and **Run n**. Note that **Br n** raises the level n of the term bracketed, and that **Esc n+1** only applies at levels 1 and higher. This ensures that escaped expressions only appear inside brackets.

9.1   Type Questions Still to be Addressed

The type system presented in Figure 9 represents the type system in the MetaML implementation. This type system has some drawbacks. In particular it types the program `<fn x => ~ (run <x>)>` which leads to a runtime error.

```
-| <fn x => ~(run <x>)>;
Error: The term:
x
in file 'top level' 18 - 19
variable bound in phase 1 used too early in phase 1
```

This is because the rule **Run n** removes brackets without lowering the level n. This is the normal course of affairs, and is the right thing to do, except if run is applied to a piece of code with free variables which are bound at a level higher than the level at which run is executed. This is the case for the example above because x is bound at level 1, and run is executed at level 0.

Designing a type system to keep track of this is quite hard. We have designed several type systems to invalidate such programs[11,13]. Unfortunately these systems either also throw away other good programs, or require elaborate annotations.

Domains and Relations

$$\begin{array}{ll}
\text{levels} & n \to 0 \mid 1 \mid n+1 \mid n+2 \mid \ldots \\
\text{integers} & i \to \ldots \mid -2 \mid -1 \mid 0 \mid 1 \mid 2 \mid \ldots \\
\text{types} & \tau \to \text{int} \mid \tau \to \tau \mid \langle \tau \rangle \mid \alpha \\
\text{terms} & e \to i \mid x \mid e\,e \mid \lambda x^\tau.e \mid \texttt{<}e\texttt{>} \mid \tilde{}e \mid \text{run}\, e \mid \uparrow v \\
\text{type environments} & \Delta \to \circ \mid \Delta, x \mapsto (\tau, \alpha)^n
\end{array}$$

$$\textbf{where } (\Delta, x \mapsto (\tau)^n)y \equiv$$
$$\text{if } x = y \text{ then } (\tau, \alpha)^n \text{ else } \Delta\, y$$

term typing *at level* n $\Delta \overset{n}{\vdash} e : \tau$

Static Semantics

Int n: $\Delta \overset{n}{\vdash} i : \text{int}$

Var: $\dfrac{\Delta\, x = (\tau)^i \quad i \le n}{\Delta \overset{n}{\vdash} x : \tau}$

Br n: $\dfrac{\Delta \overset{n+1}{\vdash} e : \tau}{\Delta \overset{n}{\vdash} \texttt{<}e\texttt{>} : \langle \tau \rangle}$

Esc n+1: $\dfrac{\Delta \overset{n}{\vdash} e : \langle \tau \rangle}{\Delta \overset{n+1}{\vdash} \tilde{}e : \tau}$

App n: $\dfrac{\Delta \overset{n}{\vdash} e_1 : \tau_1 \to \tau \quad \Delta \overset{n}{\vdash} e_2 : \tau_1}{\Delta \overset{n}{\vdash} e_1\, e_2 : \tau}$

Abs n: $\dfrac{\Delta, x \mapsto (\tau_1)^n \overset{n}{\vdash} e : \tau_2}{\Delta \overset{n}{\vdash} \lambda x^{\tau_1}.e : \tau_1 \to \tau_2}$

Run n: $\dfrac{\Delta \overset{n}{\vdash} e : \langle \tau \rangle}{\Delta \overset{n}{\vdash} \text{run}\, e : \tau}$

Fig. 1. The Static Semantics of MetaML

In the MetaML implementation we take the position that such errors are similar to errors such as taking the head or tail of an empty list: Typeable, but leading to a runtime error. Avoiding such errors are the responsibility of the programmer. We have written many staged programs and always avoided this error.

Research into improving the type system is an area of continued research.

10   Conclusion

A staged programming language gives the programmer a new paragdigm for constructing efficient programs. We have illustrated this by building staged programs for interpreters and polytypic programs.

We have also found that several other"advanced" features such as higher-order type constructors, local polymorphism, and monads have many uses.

We believe that languages with these features help programmers construct programs which are easier to maintain because they are generic, yet they are still efficient.

11   Exercises

- **Staged member function.** Write a staged membership function, where the list is known in the first stage, but the element being searched for is not known till the second phase. Experiment with the use of the lift annotation to make your generated code more readable.
- **3 level inner product function.** The inner product function can be staged in three stages. The 1 stage innner product function is given below.

```
fun inner_prod n x y =
if n = 0
   then 1
   else (nth n x)*(nth n y) + inner_prod (n-1) x y;
```

The three stage function is written to proceed as follows: In the first stage the arrival of the size of the vectors offers an opportunity to specialize the inner product function on that size, removing the overhead of looping over the body of the computation n times. The arrival of the first vector affords a second opportunity for specialization. If the inner product of that vector is to be taken many times with other vectors it can be specialized by removing the overhead of looking up the elements of the first vector each time. This is exactly the case when computing the multiplication of 2 matrixes. For each row in the first matrix, the dot product of that row will be taken for each column of the second. In addition the second stage affords the opportunity for additional optimization. Since the first vector is known multiplications by 1 or 0 can be elminated in the third stage.
- **Simple Compiler.** Define a language. Write an interpreter for the language. Stage the interpreter to construct a compiler.
- **Post code generation optimization.** Use the pattern matching for code feature of MetaML to construct a simple code optimization phase.

References

1. Charles Consel and Olivier Danvy. Tutorial notes on partial evaluation. In *20thACM Symposium on Principles of Programming Languages*, pages 493–501, January 1993.
2. Nachum Dershowitz. Computing with rewrite systems. *Information and Control*, 65:122–157, 1985.
3. Mark P. Jones. A system of constructor classes: Overloading and implicit higher-order polumorphism. In *FPCA'93: Conference on Functional Programming Languages and Computer Architecture, Copenhagen, Denmark*, pages 52–61, New York, June 1993. ACM Press.
4. Neil D. Jones, Carsten K. Gomard, and Peter Sestoft. *Partial Evaluation and Automatic Program Generation*. Series editor C. A. R. Hoare. Prentice Hall International, International Series in Computer Science, June 1993. ISBN number 0-13-020249-5 (pbk).
5. John Launchbury and Simon Peyton-Jones. Lazy functional state threads. In *PLDI'94: Programming Language Design and Implementation, Orlando, Florida*, pages 24–35, New York, June 1994. ACM Press.
6. Matthieu Martel and Tim Sheard. Introduction to multi-stage programming using metaml. Technical report, OGI, Portland, OR, September 1997.
7. Martin Odersky and Konstantin Läufer. Putting type annotations to work. In *Proc. 23rd ACM Symposium on Principles of Programming Languages*, pages 54–67, January 1996.
8. Chris Okasaki. *Purely Functional Data Structures*. Cambridge University Press, 1998.
9. G. D. Plotkin. Call-by-name, call-by-value- and the lambda-calculus. *Theoretical Computer Science*, 1:125–159, 1975.
10. Amr Sabry and Philip Wadler. A reflection on a call-by-value. *ACM Transactions on Programming Languages and Systems*, 19(6):916–941, November 1997.
11. Walid Taha, Zine-el-abidine Benaissa, and Tim Sheard. The essence of staged programming. Technical report, OGI, Portland, OR, December 1997.
12. Walid Taha and Tim Sheard. Multi-stage programming with explicit annotations. In *Proceedings of the ACM-SIGPLAN Symposium on Partial Evaluation and semantic based program manipulations PEPM'97, Amsterdam*, pages 203–217. ACM, 1997.
13. Walid Taha and Tim Sheard. Metaml: Multi-stage programming with explicit annotations. *Theoretical Computer Science*, To Appear.
14. Philip Wadler. Comprehending monads. *Proceedings of the ACM Symposium on Lisp and Functional Programming, Nice, France*, pages 61–78, June 1990.

Cayenne — A Language with Dependent Types

Lennart Augustsson

Department of Computing Sciences
Chalmers University of Technology
S-412 96 Göteborg, Sweden
augustss@cs.chalmers.se
http://www.cs.chalmers.se/~augustss

Abstract. Cayenne is a Haskell-like language. The main difference between Haskell and Cayenne is that Cayenne has dependent types, i.e., the *result type* of a function may depend on the *argument value*, and types of record components (which can be types or values) may depend on other components. Cayenne also combines the syntactic categories for value expressions and type expressions; thus reducing the number of language concepts.

Having dependent types and combined type and value expressions makes the language very powerful. It is powerful enough that a special module concept is unnecessary; ordinary records suffice. It is also powerful enough to encode predicate logic at the type level, allowing types to be used as specifications of programs. However, this power comes at a cost: type checking of Cayenne is undecidable. While this may appear to be a steep price to pay, it seems to work well in practice.

Keywords: Type systems, language design, dependent types, module systems

1   Introduction

Languages like Haskell [Hud92] and SML [MTH90] have type systems that are among the most advanced of any language. Despite this there are things that are inexpressible in these type systems. Dependent types, i.e., having types depend on values, increases the expressiveness of type systems and many of the problems of Hindley-Milner typing can be overcome.

Cayenne is a Haskell-like language that combines dependent types and first class types, i.e., types can be used like values. The syntax for value and type expressions is the same. Cayenne does not have a separate notion of modules; records are used as modules, this means that the language for combining modules is also the usual expression language. This is in contrast with Haskell and SML. Haskell has similar but different syntax for type and value expressions and definitions. SML has different syntax for value, type, and module expressions and definitions. It can be argued that they should look different, because they are different. But we want to argue the opposite, the facilities for the three types of expressions are similar, so why should they be different? In Cayenne they are

S.D. Swierstra et al. (Eds.): Advanced Functional Programming, LNCS 1608, pp. 240–267, 1999.

the same and exactly the same program constructs can be used on all levels, thus reducing the number of concepts that you need to master.

Although dependent types have been used before in proof systems, e.g., [CH88], to our knowledge this is the first time that the full power of dependent types has been integrated into a *programming language*.

We will now give some motivating examples, where we show problems in Haskell that are solved in Cayenne. The differences between Haskell and Cayenne will be explained as they occur.

1.1   The Type of `printf`

The C standard I/O library has a very useful function for doing output, namely printf. The function `printf` takes a formatting string as the first argument and then some additional arguments. The number of arguments and their types depends on the formatting string. It is simple to write a similar function in Haskell, but it will not type check.[1]

```
printf fmt = pr fmt "" where
  pr ""             res = res
  pr ('%':'d':cs) res =
      \ i -> pr cs (res ++ show (i::Int))
  pr ('%':'s':cs) res =
      \ s -> pr cs (res ++ s)
  pr ('%': c :cs) res =
      pr cs (res ++ [c])
  pr (c:cs)         res =
      pr cs (res ++ [c])
```

This is a very simplified version of printf, but as in the real version, the substring "%d" marks an integer argument and "%s" marks a string argument. The type of printf clearly varies with its first argument; e.g.,

```
printf "%d" :: Int -> String
printf "%s owes %d SEK to %s" ::
    String -> Int -> String -> String
```

As we can see, the function is easy to write and works perfectly, but cannot be given a type in Haskell.[2]

Cayenne solution The type of printf can easily be computed from the first argument. All we need to do is to write a function that computes the right type. The type of all types is called "#"[3] in Cayenne.

---

[1] The code given here is very inefficient, but that is easy to remedy.

[2] Olivier Danvy has recently shown, [Dan98], that functions similar to printf can be given a type with Hindley-Milner typing with a clever trick.

[3] We would like to use the more familiar notation "*" for the type of types. This might be possible, but it interacts badly with the use of "*" as an infix operator.

```
PrintfType :: String -> #
PrintfType ""              = String
PrintfType ('%':'d':cs) = Int    -> PrintfType cs
PrintfType ('%':'s':cs) = String -> PrintfType cs
PrintfType ('%': _ :cs) =          PrintfType cs
PrintfType ( _ :cs)     =          PrintfType cs

printf :: (fmt::String) -> PrintfType fmt
printf fmt = pr fmt ""

pr :: (fmt::String) -> String -> PrintfType fmt
pr ""           res = res
pr ('%':'d':cs) res =
    \ (i::Int)    -> pr cs (res ++ show i)
pr ('%':'s':cs) res =
    \ (s::String) -> pr cs (res ++ s)
pr ('%': c :cs) res =
    pr cs (res ++ [c])
pr (c:cs)       res =
    pr cs (res ++ [c])
```

The function PrintfType mimics the recursive structure of printf, but it computes the type instead of the value. E.g.,

PrintfType "%d" ⟼ Int -> String

The typing of printf is now

printf :: (fmt::String) -> PrintfType fmt

This example differs from Haskell in that the first argument (which has type String) has a name, fmt, which can be used in the type expression. A minor point to note is that λ-expressions in Cayenne have an explicit type on the bound variable, whereas they do not in Haskell.

Another example of a function with a dependent type can be found in appendix B.

1.2   The Set "package"

Record types in Haskell (and SML) can contain values, but not types; sometimes this can be inconvenient. To show an example of this we will use a simple set of integers. It should support creating the empty set, the singleton set, taking union, and testing for set membership. There are many possible ways to implement these sets and sometimes you want to have multiple implementations in a program and choose dynamically which one to use (e.g., depending on the use pattern). To be able to do this we would like to be able to store different set implementations in a data structure.

We would want to define the set type something like

```
data IntSet = IntSet {
    type T,
    empty :: T,
    singleton :: Int->T,
    union :: T->T->T,
    member :: Int->T->Bool
    }
```

Unfortunately, this is not possible since we cannot have a type in a record and the name T would also not be in scope. This kind of construct is only available at the module level in Haskell, but modules are definitely not first class objects in Haskell; there are no operations on modules except for the importation of them. SML allows this kind of definitions on the module level and has a rich language for combining them, but they are still not first class objects, so they cannot be put in a run-time data structure.[4]

Cayenne solution Cayenne records are different from Haskell records in several respects: Cayenne records are not data types, they can contain types, and when defining a record object the labels are bound within the record expression. The sig keyword starts a record type and the struct keyword starts a record value.

The IntSet type could be defined like this

```
type IntSet = sig
    type T
    empty :: T
    singleton :: Int->T
    union :: T->T->T
    member :: Int->T->Bool
```

An implementation could look like this

```
naûveSet :: IntSet
naûveSet = struct
    abstract type T = Int->Bool
    empty x = False
    singleton x x' = x == x'
    union s t x = s x || t x
    member x s = s x
```

This kind of record borrows features from Haskell modules, but they are still first class objects.

---

[4] It is not obvious that the first class modules proposed here extend easily to a language like SML that supports side effects.

1.3   The Eq Class

The Eq class in Haskell has the following definition:[5]

```
class Eq a where
    (==) :: a -> a -> Bool
```

This, quite correctly, states that (==) takes two arguments of the same type and returns a boolean, but surely this is not all we expect from an equality. We expect it to be a "real" equality, i.e., we most likely want it to be an equivalence relation.[6] The equivalence property of equality cannot be expressed in Haskell. The best we can do is to have it as a comment, and hope that each equality defined in the program is really an equivalence relation.

Cayenne solution Cayenne has no type classes so the Eq class problem must be reformulated slightly. A class definition in Haskell would correspond to a type definition of a record in Cayenne, and instance declarations in Haskell correspond to values of that type. All dictionaries will thus be passed explicity in Cayenne.

The Eq "class" in Cayenne would be

```
type Eq a = sig
    (==) :: a -> a -> Bool
```

To include an equivalence proof we must first have a way of expressing logical properties. This is, in fact, easy since Cayenne types can, through the Curry-Howard isomorphism, encode predicate calculus as types, see figure 1. Terms of the different types correspond to the proof of the corresponding properties. This is all well known from constructive type theory [NPS90], and well before that [How80].

Predicate calculus	Cayenne type
$\bot$	Absurd (or any empty type)
$\top$	any non-empty type
$x \lor y$	Either x y
$x \land y$	Pair x y
$\forall x \in A.P(x)$	$(x::A)$ -> $P(x)$
$\exists x \in A.P(x)$	$\{x::A;\ y::P(x)\}$

```
data Absurd =
data Pair x y = pair x y
data Either x y = Left x | Right y
```

Fig. 1. "Encoding" predicate logic as Cayenne types.

---

[5] It also has a definition of (/=), but it is of no use in this example so we disregard it.

[6] Or, even better, a congruence relation.

We encode the absurd proposition (i.e., falsity) by the empty type, and all types with elements encode truth. The dependent function type encodes universal quantification and records encode existential quantification. Proving a property correspond to finding an element (i.e., constructing a value) in a type. Since false logical statements correspond to the empty type we cannot find any values in them, but in (constructively) true logical statements we can.

One way of solving our problem in Cayenne is to extend the Eq type like this:

```
type Eq a = sig
    (==) :: a -> a -> Bool
    equiv :: Equiv (LiftBin (==))
```

LiftBin is a function that maps a binary operation yielding a Boolean into a corresponding relation. Equiv is a predicate on relations stating that the relation is an equivalence relation.

The following auxiliary definitions are used above. Further differences between Haskell and Cayenne appear below: type variables must be bound, but are often used as *hidden* arguments, introduced by the |-> function arrow, see section 3.1 for further discussion.

```
data Absurd =

data Truth = truth

Lift :: Bool -> #
Lift (False) = Absurd
Lift (True)  = Truth

LiftBin :: (a :: #) |-> (a -> a -> Bool) -> Rel a
LiftBin |a op = \ (x::a) -> \ (y::a) -> Lift (op x y)

type Rel a = a -> a -> #

Refl :: (a :: #) |-> Rel a -> #
Refl |a R = (x::a) -> x 'R' x

Symm :: (a :: #) |-> Rel a -> #
Symm |a R = (x::a) -> (y::a) -> x 'R' y -> y 'R' x

Trans :: (a :: #) |-> Rel a -> #
Trans |a R = (x::a) -> (y::a) -> (z::a) ->
    x 'R' y -> y 'R' z -> x 'R' z

Equiv :: (a :: #) |-> Rel a -> #
Equiv R = sig
    refl :: Refl R
    symm :: Symm R
    trans :: Trans R
```

Appendix A contains the complete code for this example with some instances.

2   Core Cayenne

Cayenne has three basic type forming constructs: dependent functions, data types (sums), and dependent records (products).[7] Core Cayenne is the subset of Cayenne that has no syntactic bells and whistles, just the basic constructs. We will start by looking at Core Cayenne and then at the various syntactic shorthands. The syntax of Core Cayenne is given in figure 2. The grammar disregards certain minor concrete syntax issues. There is no syntactic distinction between expressions and types in Cayenne, as is reflected in the grammar.

$$
\begin{array}{lll}
expr & ::= (\; varid :: type \;) \; \texttt{->} \; expr & \text{function type} \\
      & \texttt{\char`\\} \; (\; varid :: type \;) \; \texttt{->} \; expr & \lambda \text{ expression} \\
      & expr \; expr & \text{application} \\
      & \texttt{data} \; \{ \; conid \; \{ \; type \; \} \; | \; \} & \text{sum type} \\
      & conid \; \texttt{@} \; type & \text{constructor} \\
      & \texttt{case} \; varid \; \texttt{of} \; \{ \; arm \; \} :: type & \text{sum scrutinization} \\
      & \texttt{sig} \; \{ \; sign \; \} & \text{record type} \\
      & \texttt{struct} \; \{ \; defn \; \} & \text{record formation} \\
      & expr \; . \; lblid & \text{record selection} \\
      & id & \text{variable} \\
      & \texttt{\#}_n & \text{type of types} \\
arm & ::= (\; conid \; \{ \; varid \; \} \;) \; \texttt{->} \; expr \; ; & \\
      & varid \; \texttt{->} \; expr \; ; & \\
sign & ::= lblid :: type \; ; & \\
      & lblid :: type = expr \; ; & \\
defn & ::= vis \; lblid :: type = expr \; ; & \\
vis & ::= \texttt{private} - \texttt{public} \; abs & \\
abs & ::= \texttt{abstract} - \texttt{concrete} & \\
type & ::= expr & \\
varid & ::= id & \\
conid & ::= id & \\
lblid & ::= id &
\end{array}
$$

Fig. 2. Core Cayenne abstract syntax grammar. Metasyntax: { } are used to denote repetition of an arbitrary number of items.

2.1   Functions

Function expressions are written as λ-expressions. The bound variable must be given a type. The function type is written like the λ-expression, but without the leading "\".

---

[7] The terminology is a little confusing here, what in constructive type theory is usually called dependent products is called dependent functions in this paper and what in CTT is called dependent sums is called dependent records here. The latter terminology is more in the tradition of programming languages.

The big difference between the Cayenne function type and the Haskell function is that since the bound variable is available to the right of the arrow, the result type of a function may depend on the value of the argument.

Function application is written with juxtaposition as usual.

Example:
```
\ (x::Int) -> inc x
```
which has type
```
(x::Int) -> Int
```

2.2 Data Types

Unlike Haskell, a data type (sum type) does not have to be given a name; there is an expression that denotes each data type. E.g., "`data False | True`" is the type of booleans.

Constructors are written in a way that is very different from Haskell. The constructor names used in a data type expression have no name restrictions (unlike Haskell where they have to be capitalized) and need not be unique. Consequently, given only the name of a constructor it is impossible tell what type it constructs. Therefore, constructors are given with their types in Cayenne. E.g., "`True@(data False | True)`" is one of the constructors for the boolean type, or, if "`Bool`" has been defined, it can be written "`True@Bool`". Constructor names are not part of the usual name space; they can only occur in "`@`"-expressions and `case` expressions and in the latter the type that they construct can be deduced.

Case expressions in Core Cayenne look a little different from Haskell. Only simple patterns are allowed and all constructor patterns have to be parenthesised to distinguish them from variable patterns. Apart from the scrutinized variable and the case arms, the case expression also has a type attached. This type expression gives the type of the arms of the case expression. Note that this expression can contain the scrutinized variable so the type may depend on it. The reason for having this type is that with dependent types it is not in general possible to figure out the type of the case expression.

Example:
```
case l of
(Nil) -> True;
(Cons x xs) -> False;
   :: Bool
```
An example with a dependent type:
```
case l of
(True)  -> 1;
(False) -> "Hello";
   :: (case l of (True)  -> Int;
                 (False) -> String)
```

2.3   Records

The record type (product type) in Cayenne is the most complicated of the type formers. The reason for this is that records also serve the purpose of modules in most other languages.

A record type is written as `sig` followed by a signature for each component of the record. The signature normally gives only the type of the component, but it can also give the *value* of it. This feature is sometimes called a translucent sum, and is described in more detail in section 4.1.

A record is formed by the `struct` keyword followed by bindings for all the record components. Each binding gives the type and value of the component as well as its visibility. The names of the record components (the labels) are in scope within the record expression. This means that the bindings are mutually recursive.[8]

The visibility for a record component determines how it will show up in the type of the record. A `private` component does not show up at all in the type of the record, a `public abstract` component has only its type, and a `public concrete` component has both its type and value in the type of the record.

A record component, which occurs in (i.e., which is not `private`) the type of the record, can be extracted with the usual dot notation.

Examples:

```
struct
    private x :: Int = 1
    public abstract y :: Int = x+1
    public concrete z :: Int = x+2
```

has type

```
sig
    y :: Int
    z :: Int=3
```

Selection: `r.y + r.z`

2.4   The Type of Types

The type of types is $\#_1$, this type has type $\#_2$ which has type $\#_3$ etc. The reasons for using a stratified type system are twofold: first, using "# :: #" would, even in the absence of recursion, make the Cayenne type system unsound as a logic as it would allow Girard's paradox; second, the unstratified type system would make it impossible during type checking to determine if an expression corresponds to a type or a real value and it would be impossible to remove the types at runtime, see section 6.1.

Note that there is no elimination construct for the # type, i.e., no `casetype` construct. It would be possible and useful to have such a construct, but Cayenne currently lacks it, partly because having it would make it impossible to remove runtime type information, see 6.1.

---

[8] Though there are restrictions on how the recursion may occur in the signatures to ensure that the type can be viewed as a fixpoint of a Σ-type.

3 Full Cayenne

Using Core Cayenne would be feasible, but quite tedious, just like using the bare λ-calculus is. Cayenne has many syntactic constructs to make it more palatable and closer to an ordinary functional language.

3.1 Hidden Arguments

Many functions have type arguments that seem to serve no purpose, except to irritate the user. E.g.

```
if :: (a :: #) -> Bool -> a -> a -> a
```

for each use of if the type of the two branches must be given as the first argument.

To lessen this problem Cayenne uses a mechanism for leaving out certain arguments at the application site. However, the arguments still must be given when the function is defined. Hidden arguments introduce a new version of the function type, the function abstraction, and the function application.

The function arrow in both the type and abstraction notation is written |-> for hidden arguments. Application of a hidden argument uses infix |, but normally a hidden argument does not need to be given at all.

In function definitions the hidden arguments should not be present on the left hand side unless preceded by a |, i.e., the left hand side looks like an application.

Example:

```
if :: (a :: #) |-> Bool -> a -> a -> a
if (True)  x y = x
if (False) x y = y
```

This "if" function can the be used as "if True 1 2", or more explicitly "if |Int True 1 2".

The concept of hidden arguments is a syntactic device without any deep semantic properties. The function type for hidden arguments should not be viewed as a new type. It is completely compatible with the normal function type. It only serves as a marker to aid the insertion of the hidden arguments. This view of hidden arguments was presented in [ACN90] and later used in other systems like Lego, [LP92], where the concept was formalized. Similar mechanism exist e.g., in Quest, [Car94], and Russell, [BDD89].

The current implementation of hidden arguments is quite weak and cannot always find the hidden arguments even when it seems reasonable that it should. It can find a hidden argument if the variable (a in the example) occurs in a later argument type or the result type. In the future we will probably switch to a more powerful method that introduces metavariables (in the sense of logical frameworks) and tries to derive their values using more powerful methods such as unification.

3.2   Syntactic Sugar

This is a brief list of syntactic extensions that can be regarded as mere "sugar".

- If the variable bound in the function type does not occur anywhere it
  can be dropped and the function type is thus written as in Haskell. E.g.
  "(x::Int)->Int" can be written as "Int->Int" instead.
- Infix operators (with a fixed set of precedences) can be used. The same
  conventions as in Haskell are used.
- The patterns in case arms can be written in the normal Haskell style with
  nested patterns etc. The type part of case expression is only necessary if
  the type of the right hand sides depend on the scrutinized expression.
- public can be omitted, since it is the default. concrete is the default for
  type definitions, and abstract for other definitions.
- Function definitions can be written in the normal Haskell style with type
  signatures and pattern matching. E.g.,

```
last :: (a::#) |-> List a -> a =
    \ (a :: #) |-> \ (l::List a) ->
    case l of
    (x : (Nil)) -> x
    (x : xs) -> last xs
```

can be written

```
last :: (a::#) |-> List a -> a
last (x : (Nil)) = x
last (x : xs) = last xs
```

- If a definition is preceded by the keyword type it is assumed to have type
  # and all its arguments have default type #. E.g.
  `P :: # -> # = \ (a :: #) -> a->Bool`
  can be written
  `type P a = a->Bool`
- A data type definition can be written in the same way as in Haskell. This
  corresponds to several bindings. First one for the type itself, then one for
  each constructor in the type. E.g. the definition
  `data Maybe a = Nothing | Just a`
  corresponds to the definitions

```
Maybe :: # |-> # =
    \(a::#) |-> data Nothing | Just a
Nothing :: (a::#) |-> Maybe a =
    \(a::#) |-> Nothing@(Maybe a)
Just :: (a::#) |-> a -> Maybe a =
    \(a::#) |-> \(x::a) -> Just@(Maybe a) x
```

- Cayenne has a let expression that is like the Haskell let expression. This
  can be translated into a record expression.

- To make access to record components more convenient there is an **open** expression that "opens" a record and makes its components available. The **open** construct explicitly names the components that should be visible. E.g. "**open** movePoint d p **use** x, y **in** dist x y". The "open" expression can easily be translated to a "**let**" expression.
- A value of record type can be coerced to a value of a different record type if the result type is the same as the original except that it has fewer fields. The coercion is written "*expr* :: *type*" and translates to a let expression.
- Type signatures can be omitted in many places. Even if the basic rule is that all Cayenne definitions should have a type signature it is easy to relax this rule somewhat. With the relaxed rule Cayenne programs have about the same number of type signatures as the corresponding Haskell program would have and they place no big burden on the programmer.
- #$_1$ can be written as #.
- A Haskell-like "do" notation can be used for monads.
- The Haskell layout rule is used to avoid braces and semicolons. The keywords **case**, **do**, **let**, **sig**, and **struct** triggers it.

3.3 Modules

Cayenne does not really have any modules in the traditional sense, all it has is named expressions that exist in a global name space. Module names are distiguished by having a "$" in their names. The module name space can be viewed as hierarchical with "$" as the name separator (like how UNIX path names use "/" or how Java names use "."). Module identifiers can be used freely in expressions without any explicit import declaration (just as in Java).

A module definition looks like a simple definition except that it is preceeded by the keyword **module**. The type in the definition is not necessary and it can be left out. A module can also have **concrete** visibility. This plays the same role here as it does for records, i.e., you can make the value of a module known instead of only its type.

Some sample modules:

```
module foo$bar = struct
data Nat = Zero | Succ Nat

module foo$baz =
open System$Int use Int, (+) in
struct
inc :: Int -> Int
inc x = x+1
dec :: Int -> Int
dec x = x-1
```

Modules are the units of separate compilation. To compile a module, only the types of the modules it refers to need be known.

4   The Cayenne Type System

4.1   Translucent Sums

Many Haskell modules export types in a non-abstract way, i.e., the type is exported so that not only the name of the type, but also its constructors are known. E.g.

```
module Tree(Tree(..), depth) where
data Tree a = Leaf | Node (Tree a) a (Tree a)
depth :: Tree a -> Int
depth Leaf = 0
depth (Node l _ r) = 1 + (depth l `max` depth r)
```

If we try to write the corresponding Cayenne record we get

```
module ex$Tree = struct
data Tree a = Leaf | Node (Tree a) a (Tree a)
depth :: (a :: #) |-> Tree a -> Int
depth (Leaf) = 0
depth (Node l _ r) = 1 + (depth l `max` depth r)
```

which has type

```
sig
  Tree :: # -> #
  depth :: (a :: #) |-> Tree a -> Int
```

This is definitely not what we had in mind, because from this signature we can only see that Tree is a type constructor, but we cannot see its definition. We could try and remedy this by saying that to use a module, not only must its signature be known, but its actual value as well. This way, we would have the definition of Tree available. But this is also not what we intended, because this would reveal the definition of depth, which we may not want to reveal to users of the ex$Tree module.

For this reason we introduce the possibility for each record component to specify if it should be fully known or only known with its type. We then write[9]

```
module ex$Tree = struct
concrete
data Tree a = Leaf | Node (Tree a) a (Tree a)
abstract
depth :: (a :: #) |-> Tree -> Int
depth (Leaf) = 0
depth (Node l _ r) = 1 + (depth l `max` depth r)
```

---

[9] The abstract and concrete keywords are actually superfluous in this example because the default visibility is the same as those indicated by the keywords.

which has type

```
sig
  Tree :: # -> # =
     data Leaf | Node (Tree a) a (Tree a)
  Leaf :: (a::#) |-> Tree a =
     \ (a::#) |-> Leaf@(Tree a)
  Node :: (a::#) |-> Tree a -> a -> Tree a
            -> Tree a =
     \ (a::#) |-> \ (l::Tree a) -> \ (x::a) ->
     \ (r::Tree a) -> Node@(Tree a) l x y
  depth :: (a :: #) |-> Tree a -> Int
```

This is a very peculiar type because it not only specifies the types of the Tree, Leaf, and Node components, but also their exact values. Any record of this type will have a Tree etc. with exactly these values, whereas the value of depth may differ.

This idea comes from the type system for the SML module system where these types are called translucent sums, [Lil97], or the similar notion of singleton kinds. A similar construct is also present in Cardelli's Quest, where it is called manifest definitions, [Car94].

4.2   Typing and Evaluation Rules

The Cayenne typing rules are given in table 1 and table 2.

Some simplifications have been made to the typing rules for the purpose of presentation. In data type each constructor has exactly one argument which must be of value type. Furthermore, the order of the definitions in a struct/sig does not matter in real Cayenne, where as they do in the rules.

The stratification showed in the typing rules is also a simplification of the one used in Cayenne. The type of types as used in the rules is $\#_n$, but in actuality it is $\#_{n,m}$. The first subscript is derived as shown in the typing rules and the second we get by replacing min by max in the Prod rule. The reason for two subscripts is that the first number is necessary for getting the type erasure to be possible, and the second one is necessary if we want the logic to be sound (if recursion is removed).

The environment (or assumptions), Γ, in the typing rules may contain variables with their types, as is usually the case. But they may also contain variables with their types as well as their *values*. The reason for the values is that we sometimes need values to enable reductions during type checking. It is the Rec rule that introduces values into Γ.

The fact that Cayenne has dependent types shows up in a few places in the typing rules. In the App rule the term $f\ a$ has a type that may depend on x, so x is replaced with the actual value in B. Furthermore, in the Case rule in each arm the type of the arm may depend of the scrutinized variable so a substitution is performed here as well.

The translucent sums show up in the SelE rule where a term *e.l* can be reduced even if only the type of *e* is known. This reduction is only performed during type checking and never during normal reduction (execution).

Because of a lack of time, we have not yet proved essential theorems about the Cayenne type system, such as soundness and the subject reduction theorem. While we believe them to be true, and they have been proved similar systems, they have not proved for a system with dependent types and translucent sums.

The Cayenne evaluation rules, table 4, are unsurprising. Note that because definitions in a struct are recursive some care has to be exercised.

A problem with substitution Substitution in Core Cayenne as described by the rules in this section suffers from a problem: it does not really work; there are some unavoidable name clashes. We illustrate the problem with an example. To make the example shorter we omit types and use a let expression which could be translated to a record expression.

```
struct
    x = 1
    z = let y = x
        in  struct x = y
```

As we can easily see the z component of this record is a record with an x component with value 1. Let us apply the standard reduction rule for let, namely let $x = e$ in $e' \longmapsto e'[x \mapsto e]$.

```
struct
    x = 1
    z = struct x = x
```

This is clearly not the same value as we had before; the x has been captured when it should not be. Note that we cannot rename either of the two xs since the name of the labels appear in the type; renaming them would change the type.

This problem is annoying, but can be handled easily. All we need to do is to have two different names for all labels. One name is the label itself as it appears in the type and the other name is the name that is bound inside the record. The second name is not part of the type and can clearly be α-converted when necessary. To avoid cluttering the typing rules even more we will not introduce any notation for this in the rules, instead we assume that the problem can be handled if needed. A similar solution is used in [Bet98].

4.3   Type Checking

Type checking of Cayenne is basically simple, just because it is type checking rather than type deductions, like e.g. Haskell uses. Type checking proceeds in a single traversal of the syntax tree. On the way down the environment (Γ) is extended with the types (and sometimes values) of bound identifiers. Since Cayenne has explicit types the type of each bound identifier is known. On the

$$\frac{}{\Gamma \vdash \#_n \in \#_{n+1}} \text{ Star}$$

$$\frac{\Gamma \vdash A \in s}{\Gamma, x \in A \vdash x \in A} \text{ Var}$$

$$\frac{\Gamma \vdash A \in s \quad \Gamma, x \in A \vdash B \in t}{\Gamma \vdash (x::A)\text{->}B \in t} \text{ Pi}$$

$$\frac{\Gamma, x \in A \vdash b \in B \quad \Gamma \vdash (x::A)\text{->}B \in t}{\Gamma \vdash \backslash(x::A)\text{->}b \in (x::A)\text{->}B} \text{ Lam}$$

$$\frac{\Gamma \vdash f \in (x::A)\text{->}B \quad \Gamma \vdash a \in A}{\Gamma \vdash f\ a \in B[x \mapsto a]} \text{ App}$$

$$\frac{\Gamma \vdash A_1 \in \#_1 \quad \ldots \quad \Gamma \vdash A_n \in \#_1}{\Gamma \vdash \mathbf{data}\ C_1\ A_1 | \ldots | \ C_n\ A_n \in \#_1} \text{ Data}$$

$$\frac{\Gamma \vdash T \in \#_1}{\Gamma \vdash C_k @ T \in A_k\text{->}T} \text{ Con}$$
where $T \equiv \mathbf{data}\ C_1\ A_1 | \ldots | \ C_n\ A_n$

$$\frac{\begin{array}{c} \Gamma \vdash x \in \mathbf{data}\ C_1\ A_1 | \ldots | \ C_n\ A_n \\ \Gamma, x_1 \in A_1 \vdash e_1 \in A[x \mapsto C_1\ x_1] \\ \vdots \\ \Gamma, x_n \in A_n \vdash e_n \in A[x \mapsto C_n\ x_n] \end{array}}{\Gamma \vdash \mathbf{case}\ x\ \mathbf{of}\ \{\ C_1\ x_1\text{->}e_1; \ldots; C_n\ x_n\text{->}e_n\}::A \in A} \text{ Case}$$

$$\frac{\begin{array}{c} \Gamma \vdash A_1 \in \#_{u_1} \\ \Gamma, l_1 \in A_1 \vdash A_2 \in \#_{u_2} \\ \vdots \\ \Gamma, l_1 \in A_1, \cdots, l_{n-1} \in A_{n-1} \vdash A_n \in \#_{u_n} \\ \vdots \\ \Gamma, l_1 \in A_1, \cdots, l_n \in A_n \vdash e_j \in A_j \\ \vdots \end{array}}{\Gamma \vdash \mathbf{sig}\{\ l_1::\gamma_1; \ldots l_n::\gamma_n\} \in \#_{min\{u_i\}}} \text{ Prod}$$
where each γ_i is either A_i or "$A_i = e_j$"

Table 1. Core Cayenne typing rules

$$\frac{
\begin{array}{c}
\Gamma \vdash A_1 \in s_1 \\
\Gamma, \Delta \vdash e_1 \in A_1 \\
\Gamma, l_1 \in A_1 \vdash A_2 \in s_2 \\
\Gamma, \Delta \vdash e_2 \in A_2 \\
\vdots \\
\Gamma, l_1 \in A_1, \cdots, l_{n-1} \in A_{n-1} \vdash A_n \in s_n \\
\Gamma, \Delta \vdash e_n \in A_n
\end{array}
}{
\Gamma \vdash
\begin{array}{c}
\texttt{struct}\{\, p_1\, a_1\, l_1 :: A_1 \texttt{=} e_1;\ldots p_n\, a_n\, l_n :: A_n \texttt{=} e_n\} \\
\in \texttt{sig}\{\ldots l_i :: \gamma_i;\ldots\}
\end{array}
}\ \text{Rec}$$

$$\text{where } l_i \text{ is present iff } p_i = \texttt{public},$$
$$\gamma_i \text{ is ``} A_i = e_i \text{''} \text{ if } a_i = \texttt{concrete} \text{ otherwise } A_i$$
$$\Delta \equiv l_1 \in A_1 = e_1, \cdots, l_n \in A_n = e_n$$

$$\frac{\Gamma \vdash e \in \texttt{sig}\{\ldots l_i :: \gamma_i;\ldots\}}{\Gamma \vdash e.l_i \in A_i[\ldots, l_k \mapsto e.l_k, \ldots]}\ \text{Sel}$$

$$\frac{\Gamma \vdash a \in A \quad \Gamma \vdash B \in s \quad \Gamma \vdash A \approx B}{\Gamma \vdash a \in B}\ \text{Conv}$$

$$\frac{\Gamma \vdash A \in s \quad \Gamma \vdash \delta}{\Gamma, x \in A \vdash \delta}\ \text{Weak}$$

$$\frac{\Gamma \vdash a \in A \quad \Gamma, x \in A \vdash \delta}{\Gamma, x \in A = a \vdash \delta}\ \text{WeakE}$$

Table 2. Core Cayenne typing rules, continued

$$\frac{\Gamma \vdash a \in A \quad \Gamma \vdash b \in A \quad \Gamma \vdash a \approx b}{\Gamma \vdash C[a] \approx C[b]}\ \text{Congr}$$
$$\text{where } C[] \text{ is any context}$$

$$\frac{\Gamma \vdash a \in A \quad a \longmapsto b}{\Gamma \vdash a \approx b}\ \text{Red}$$

$$\frac{}{\Gamma, x \in A = e \vdash \Gamma \vdash x \approx e}\ \text{Lookup}$$

$$\frac{\Gamma \vdash e \in \texttt{sig}\{\ldots l_i :: A_i = e_i;\ldots\}}{\Gamma, l_1 \in A_1, \cdots, l_n \in A_n \vdash e.l_i \approx e_i}\ \text{SelE}$$

Table 3. Core Cayenne equality rules

$$(\text{``}x\!::\!t\text{->}f)e \longmapsto f[x \mapsto e]$$
$$e.l_k \longmapsto e_k[\ldots, l_k \mapsto e.l_k, \ldots]$$
$$\text{where } e \equiv \mathbf{struct}\{\ldots \mathtt{public}\, a_k\, l_k\!::\!t_k\!=\!e_k; \ldots\}$$
$$\mathbf{case}\; C_k @ t\, e \;\mathbf{of}\; \ldots\; C_k\, x_k\text{->}\, e_k; \ldots \longmapsto e_k[x_k \mapsto e]$$

Table 4. Core Cayenne evaluation rules

$$(\text{``}(x\!::\!t)\text{->}f)^* \to \text{``}x\text{->}f^*, \text{ if } t \in \#_1$$
$$(\text{``}(x\!::\!t)\text{->}f)^* \to f^*, \text{ if } t \notin \#_1$$
$$(f\, e)^* \to f^*\, e^*, \text{ if } e \in t \text{ and } t \in \#_1$$
$$(f\, e)^* \to f^*, \text{ if } e \in t \text{ and } t \notin \#_1$$
$$((x\!::\!t)\text{->}f)^* \to \bullet$$
$$\mathbf{struct}\{\, l_1\!::\!t_1\!=\!e_1; \ldots\, l_n\!::\!t_n\!=\!e_n\}^* \to \mathbf{struct}\{\ldots\, l_k\!=\!e_k^* \ldots\}, \text{ for those } l_k$$
$$\text{where } t_k \in \#_1$$
$$(e.l)^* \to e^*.l$$
$$\mathbf{sig}\{\; \ldots\; \}^* \to \bullet$$
$$(C@t)^* \to C$$
$$(\mathbf{case}\; e\; \mathbf{of}\; C_1\, x_1\text{->}\, e_1; \ldots\, C_n\, x_n\text{->}\, e_n)^* \to \mathbf{case}\; e^*\; \mathbf{of}\; C_1\text{->}\, e_1^*; \ldots\, C_n\text{->}\, e_n^*$$
$$\mathbf{data} \ldots\,^* \to \bullet$$
$$\#_n^* \to \bullet$$
$$x^* \to x, \text{ if } x \in t, t \in \#_1$$
$$x^* \to \bullet, \text{ if } x \in t, t \notin \#_1$$

Table 5. Type erasure transformation

$$(\text{``}x\text{->}f)e \mapsto f[x \mapsto e]$$
$$e.l_k \mapsto e_k[\ldots, l_k \mapsto e.l_k, \ldots]$$
$$\text{where } e \equiv \mathbf{struct}\{\ldots\, a_k\, l_k\!=\!e_k; \ldots\}$$
$$\mathbf{case}\; C_k\, e\; \mathbf{of}\; \ldots\; C_k\, x_k\text{->}\, e_k; \ldots \mapsto e_k[x_k \mapsto e]$$

Table 6. Core Cayenne typeless evaluation rules

way up the type of each subexpression can the be computed and checked. A complication arises when a typing rules has more than one occurence of a type, like A in the App rule in table 1. For these cases we need to check if the two types derived from the bottom up derivation are the same, and if they are not identical the Conv rule can be used to make them equal (assuming the program is type correct). For a strongly normalizing language without translucent types the Conv rule is uses $=_\beta$ for $\approx$. This relation is easy to implement; just compute the normal forms of the two types and compare those. Since Cayenne is not strongly normalizing this is not an option. The equivalence of two arbitrary expression is undecidable. For this reason, we can not implement anything but an approximation of the Conv rule and the equality rules (table 3). This is a tricky part of the Cayenne type checker since if the equivalence test is implemented in a naÔve way type checking can easily loop.

4.4   Undecidability in Practice

So type checking Cayenne is undecidable. This is unfortunate, but unavoidable for a language like Cayenne. How bad is it in practice to have an undecidable type checker? This question can only be answered by practical experiments. The Cayenne programs we have tried to date range from ordinary Haskell style programs, to programs using dependent types, to proofs of mathematical propositions. The total size of these programs are only a few thousand lines, but so far the experience shows that it works remarkably well.

Having undecidable type checking means that the type checker might loop. This is clearly not a user friendly type checker. So instead the implemented type checker has an upper bound on the number of reduction steps that it may perform. If this limit is exceeded the type checker will report this. Most of the type errors from the Cayenne compiler are similar to those that any other language would give. Very infrequently does the type checker report that it did not terminate within the prescribed number of steps. Most often, this is the result of a type error, but sometimes the type expression is just too complicated and the number of reduction steps must be increased (the number of reduction steps is a compiler flag).

The type checker can thus give one of three answers: type correct (meaning that the program will not go wrong when run), type incorrect, or "don't know"[10].

There are other languages with undecidable type checking, e.g., Quest [Car94] (which has a type system based on $F_{\omega<}$) and Gofer [Jon94], but it is usually more difficult to make these systems loop.

5   Cayenne as a Proof System

Since Cayenne has unrestricted recursion, this means that every type is inhabited by at least one element, namely $\perp$. Thus, proofs made in Cayenne cannot really

---

[10]   On a real machine Hindley-Milner type checking has the same problem, but the third alternative is usually spelled "Out of memory" instead.

be trusted as proofs, since any proposition can be proved by $\bot$. If proper checking is done, it is often[11] possible to ensure that a proof is valid, but no such checking is done at the moment.

Even if a proofs expressed in Cayenne cannot be trusted because they pass the type checker it is still valuable to have the encoding of predicate logic in the language. Firstly, it allows us to express properties about programs within the language even if we provide no proofs at all. It is better to have this ability within the language than to use comments or leave out those properties completely. Secondly, even if a proof cannot be trusted one can argue that a proof that has been checked, but may be $\bot$, is better than a proof that is not checked at all.

6 Implementation

Implementing Cayenne is fairly straight forward; it is like any other functional language. One decision that has to be made is what to do with types at runtime.

6.1 Erasing Types

Cayenne treats types like first class values. Does that mean that the types have to be present at run time, passed around as arguments, stored in data structures, etc? No, they do not. There is no language construct, e.g., **casetype**, that allows a ground value — which is all that can be observed in a program — to depend on a type. Hence, types do not have to be present at run time. Erasing types consists of removing all arguments and record components that have type $\#_n$ or are functions computing something of type $\#_n$. In [Car88] it is claimed that type erasing is not possible and that the distinction between compile-time and run-time is blurred with dependent types. We claim that this is not the case with the variant of dependent types used in Cayenne.

What we need to show is that evaluating an expression with types erased yields the same result as evaluating it with the types left in.

Definition An expression, e, has *value type* if $e \in t$ and $t \in \#_1$

Theorem If e has value type and $e \longmapsto^* v$ then $e^* \mapsto^* v^*$.

We first prove a useful lemma.

Lemma If e has value type, then e^* contains no $\bullet$.

Proof We assume that the expression to transform is of value type, and show that each invocation of the transformation on a subexpression is also on an expression of value type.

Cases A λ-expression "$(x::t)\text{->}f$ has type $(x::t)\text{->}r$, where r is the type of f. According to the assumption $(x::t)\text{->}r$ has type $\#_1$ and typing rule Pi shows that then r has type $\#_1$ as well. Thus the transformation of f is also on an expression of value type.

For an application $f\ e$, according to the definition of *, the transformation is only applied to e if it is of value type. f has type $(x::t)\text{->}r$ and $f\ e$ has type

---

[11] Not always, of course, since then we would have to solve the halting problem.

r, if r has type #$_1$ then, again according to typing rule Pi, $(x::t)$->r has type #$_1$, so the transformation of f fulfills the assumption.

The transformation cannot be applied to a function type since this does not have value type.

For a record value struct$\{ \dots \}$ the transformation is only applied to subexpressions of value type according to the definition of *.

If a record selection $e.l$ is of value type then the field l must be of value type. If one field of a record type type has type #$_1$ then the whole record type has type #$_1$ according to typing rule Prod (which takes the min of all the types), so the subexpression e (of $e.l$) must have value type.

The transformation cannot be applied to a sig$\{ \dots \}$ value since it is not of value type.

The lemma is trivially true for a contructor expression.

For a case expression the transformation is applied to the scrutinized expression, which is always of value type (typing rule Data) and to all the right hand sides. The right hand sides are of value type if the whole case expressions is.

The transformation cannot be applied to a data value since it is not of value type.

The transformation cannot be applied #$_1$ since it is not of value type.

The lemma is true for variables according to the definition of *.

Corollary A transformed expression of value type contains no variables that were not of value type in the original expression.

Proof Variables that are not of value types are translated to •, but there are no • in the expression, hence there can be such variables.

Lemma The substitution lemma states that type erasure commutes with substittion: $(e[x \mapsto t])^* = e^*[x \mapsto t^*]$.

Proof By structural induction over the expression syntax.

We can now return to proving the type erasure theorem. First we prove that if e has value type and $e \longmapsto f$ then $e^* \mapsto f^*$ or $e^* = f^*$. The theorem then follows simply by induction on the length of the reduction sequence.

The single step version of the theorem is proved by case analysis on the three different (typed) reduction kinds.

Cases If the reduction is $(\text{"}x::t\text{->}f)e \longmapsto f[x \mapsto e]$ then the translation of the redex is either $(\text{"}x\text{->}f^*)e^*$ in which case there is a corresponding untyped reduction step (according to the substitution lemma). Or the translation of the redex is f (if x and e do not have value type). In this case $f^* = f^*[x \mapsto e^*]*$ since x does not occur in f^* (according to the corollary).

If the reduction is a selection the selected label could either be left in the transformed struct or it could have been erased. But since the expression $e.l$ has value type this means that the label has value type and it must thus be left in the struct. There is then an exactly corresponding untyped reduction.

If the reduction is a case reduction there is an exactly corresponding untyped reduction.

QED

6.2 Keeping Types

By keeping types at runtime it is possible to do computations on types and base control decision on the dynamic type of values. With runtime types we could have a `casetype` language construct. Keeping types around at runtime have some advantages, like mostly tag-free garbage collection, as used in TIL, [TMC+96,Mor95].

6.3 The Current Implementation

The current implementation of Cayenne is written in Haskell and translates Cayenne to untyped LML. The compiler consists of about 5500 lines, a third of which is the actual type checker. The compiler parses Cayenne, does type checking and various other checks, erases types and then translates the resulting code into LML. The LML code is then compiled with the LML compiler, [AJ89], with type checking turned off. This works because the LML compiler does not rely on a the fact that the program is type correct in the Hindley-Milner type system; all the compiler assumes is that the program "makes sense".

A snapshot of the current implementation can be found on the Web at http://www.cs.chalmers.se/~augustss/cayenne/.

7   Related Work

There are many logical frameworks (proof checking systems) that are based on dependent types. Some examples, among many, are ALF [MN94,Nor93,ACN90], CoC [CH86,CH88], ELF [Pfe89,Fra91,HHP93], Lego [Pol94], and NuPRL [Con86]. All these systems are primarily designed for making (constructive) proofs even if many of them can also execute the resulting proofs or extract a program from them. Our approach is different in that we want to make a programming language, not a proof system, but of course there are big similarities.

There are few programming languages with dependent types. Cardelli's Quest, [Car94], have similarities with Cayenne, but the final version of Quest does not have the full dependency where types can depend on values. Russell, [BDD89], has dependent types, but the notion of type equality is "name equality" rather than the "structural equality" of Cayenne. Russell does not do full evaluation during type checking so it would not be able to do, e.g., the `printf` example. Russell also has a different notion of what a type is.

8   Future Work

There are many ways to continue the work on Cayenne and related languages. First, and foremost, is to gain more experience with a language with dependent types, both to see how dependent types can be used and to see how undecidable type checking works out.

Another interesting line of work is to make a partial evaluator for this kind of language. Since types and values are combined, a partial evaluator would serve both as a type specializer (as used in, e.g., [Aug93,PJ93]) and a traditional partial evaluator.

To make the record types more useful, subtyping could be added. Subtyping in the presence of dependent types has been studied in [Bet98].

As a proof of concept the Cayenne compiler should, of course, be rewritten in Cayenne.

9 Acknowledgments

A big thanks to Jessica for improving my English. The programming logic group at Chalmers has over the years provided me with enough background material to finally try to make a programming language with dependent types. A special thanks to Theirry Coquand for fruitful discussions and examples of how to write type checkers for dependent types. Thomas Johnsson, Niklas Röjemo and Dan Synek provided me with feedback on this paper as did the anonymous ICFP referees.

References

ACN90.   L. Augustsson, T. Coquand, and B. Nordström. A short description of Another Logical Framework. In *Proceedings of the First Workshop on Logical Frameworks, Antibes*, pages 39–42, 1990.

AJ89.   L. Augustsson and T. Johnsson. The Chalmers Lazy-ML Compiler. *The Computer Journal*, 32(2):127–141, 1989.

Aug93.   Lennart Augustsson. Implementing Haskell Overloading. In *Proc. 6th Int'l Conf. on Functional Programming Languages and Computer Architecture (FPCA'93)*, pages 65–73. ACM Press, June 1993.

BDD89.   H. Boehm, A. Demers, and J. Donahue. A Programmer's Introduction to Russell. Technical report, Cornell University, 1989.

Bet98.   Gustavo Betarte. *Dependent Record Types and Algebraic Structures in Type Theory*. PhD thesis, Department of Computing Science, University of Göteborg, Göteborg, Sweden, February 1998.

Car88.   Luca Cardelli. Phase Distinction in Type Theory. Research report, DEC SRC, 1988.

Car94.   Luca Cardelli. The Quest Language and System. Research report, DEC SRC, 1994.

CH86.   Thierry Coquand and Gérard Huet. The Calculus of Constructions. Technical Report 530, INRIA, Centre de Rocquencourt, 1986.

CH88.   Thierry Coquand and Gérard Huet. The Calculus of Constructions. *Information and Computation*, 76(2/3):95–120, 1988.

Con86.   R. L. Constable et al. *Implementing Mathematics with the NuPRL Proof Development System*. Prentice-Hall, Englewood Cliffs, NJ, 1986.

Dan98.   Olivier Danvy. Formatting Strings in ML. Technical Report RS-98-5, BRICS, Department of Computer SCience, University of Aarhus, Denmark, March 1998.

Fra91.   Logical Frameworks. Logic programming in the LF logical framework. In
            GÈrard Huet and Gordon Plotkin, editors, *LICS'89*, pages 149–181. Cam-
            bridge University Press, 1991.

HHP93.   Robert Harper, Furio Honsell, and Gordon Plotkin. A Framework for Defin-
            ing Logics. *JACM*, 40(1):143–184, 1993.

How80.   W. A. Howard. The formulae-as-types notion of construction. In J. P. Seldin
            and J. R. Hindley, editors, *To H.B. Curry: Essays on Combinatory Logic,
            Lambda Calculus and Formalism*, pages 479–490. Academic Press, London,
            1980.

Hud92.   Paul Hudak et al. *Report on the Programming Language Haskell: A Non-
            Strict, Purely Functional Language*, March 1992. Version 1.2. Also in Sigplan
            Notices, May 1992.

Jon94.   Mark P. Jones. The implementation of the Gofer functional programming
            system. Technical Report YALEU/DCS/RR-1030, Department of Com-
            puter Science, Yale University, New Haven, Connecticut, USA, May 1994,
            May 94.

Lil97.   Mark Lillibridge. *Translucent Sums: A Foundation for Higher-Order Mod-
            ule Systems*. PhD thesis, School of Computer Science, Carnegie Mellon
            University, May 1997. CMU-CS-97-122.

LP92.   Z. Luo and R. Pollack. LEGO Proof Development System: User's Manual.
            Technical report, LFCS Technical Report ECS-LFCS-92-211, 1992.

MN94.   Lena Magnusson and Bengt Nordström. The ALF proof editor and its proof
            engine. In *Types for Proofs and Programs*, LNCS, pages 213–237, Nijmegen,
            1994. Springer-Verlag.

Mor95.   Greg Morrisett. *Compiling with Types*. PhD thesis, Carnegie Mellon Uni-
            versity, 1995.

MTH90.   R. Milner, M. Tofte, and R. Harper. *The Definition of Standard ML*. MIT
            Press, 1990.

Nor93.   Bengt Nordström. The ALF proof editor. In *Proceedings 1993 Informal
            Proceedings of the Nijmegen workhop on Types for Proofs and Programs*,
            1993.

NPS90.   Bengt Nordström, Kent Petersson, and Jan M. Smith. *Programming in
            Martin-Löf's Type Theory. An Introduction*. Oxford University Press, 1990.

Pfe89.   Frank Pfenning. Elf: A language for logic definition and verified meta-
            programming. In *LICS'89*, pages 313–322. IEEE, June 1989.

PJ93.   John Peterson and Mark P. Jones. Implementing Type Classes. In *Proceed-
            ings of ACM SIGPLAN Symposium on Programming Language Design and
            Implementation*, June 1993.

Pol94.   Robert Pollack. *The Theory of Lego A Proof Checker for the Extended
            Calculus of Constructions*. PhD thesis, University of Edinburgh, 1994.

TMC+96.   David Tarditi, Greg Morrisett, Pery Cheng, Chris Stone, Robert Harper,
            and Peter Lee. TIL: A Type-directed Optimizing Compiler for ML. Techni-
            cal Report CMU-CS-96-108, School of Computer Science, Carnegie Mellon
            University, February 1996.

A   The Eq Class

```
module example$Eq =
#include Prelude
struct

data Absurd =

data Truth = truth

absurd :: (a :: #) |-> Absurd -> a
absurd i = case i of { }

type (<=>) a b = sig { impR :: a->b; impL :: b->a; }

concrete
Lift :: Bool -> #
Lift (False) = Absurd
Lift (True)  = Truth

concrete
LiftBin :: (a:: #) |-> (a -> a -> Bool) -> Rel a
LiftBin |a op = \(x::a) -> \(y::a) -> Lift (op x y)

type Rel a = a -> a -> #

concrete
Refl :: (a :: #) |-> Rel a -> #
Refl |a R = (x::a) -> x 'R' x

concrete
Symm :: (a :: #) |-> Rel a -> #
Symm |a R = (x,y::a) -> x 'R' y -> y 'R' x

concrete
Trans :: (a :: #) |-> Rel a -> #
Trans |a R = (x,y,z::a) -> x 'R' y -> y 'R' z -> x 'R' z

concrete
Equiv :: (a :: #) |-> Rel a -> #
Equiv R = sig
  refl :: Refl R
  symm :: Symm R
  trans :: Trans R

--------
-- The Eq "class", with equivalence proof
type Eq a = sig
  (==) :: a -> a -> Bool
  equiv :: Equiv (LiftBin (==))

--------
-- Equality on Unit
Eq_Unit :: Eq Unit
Eq_Unit = struct
```

```
  (==) (unit) (unit) = True

  equiv = struct
    refl (unit) = truth
    symm (unit) (unit) p = p
    trans (unit) (unit) (unit) p q = p


--------
-- Equality on Bool
Eq_Bool :: Eq Bool
Eq_Bool = struct
  (==) (False) (False) = True
  (==) (True)  (True)  = True
  (==) _        _      = False

  equiv = struct
    refl (False) = truth
    refl (True)  = truth
    symm (False) (False) p = p
    symm (False) (True)  p = absurd p
    symm (True)  (False) p = absurd p
    symm (True)  (True)  p = p
    trans (False) (False) (False) p q = q
    trans (False) (False) (True)  p q = absurd q
    trans (False) (True)  _       p q = absurd p
    trans (True)  (False) _       p q = absurd p
    trans (True)  (True)  (False) p q = absurd q
    trans (True)  (True)  (True)  p q = q


--------

private
liftAndL :: (x,y::Bool) ->
            Lift (x && y) -> Pair (Lift x) (Lift y)
liftAndL (False) _       a = absurd a
liftAndL (True)  (False) a = absurd a
liftAndL (True)  (True)  t = (t, t)

private
liftAndR :: (x,y::Bool) ->
            Pair (Lift x) (Lift y) -> Lift (x && y)
liftAndR (False) _       (a, _) = a
liftAndR (True)  (False) (_, a) = a
liftAndR (True)  (True)  (t, _) = t

private
isoEquiv :: (a :: #) |->
    (p, q :: Rel a) -> ((x, y :: a) ->
    p x y <=> q x y) -> Equiv p -> Equiv q
isoEquiv p q iso eqp = struct
  refl x = (iso x x).impR (eqp.refl x)
  symm x y lp =
    (iso y x).impR (eqp.symm x y ((iso x y).impL lp))
  trans x y z lp lq = (iso x z).impR
    (eqp.trans x y z ((iso x y).impL lp) ((iso y z).impL lq))
```

```
-- Equality on pairs.
Eq_Pair :: (a,b :: #) |-> Eq a -> Eq b -> Eq (Pair a b)
Eq_Pair eqa eqb = struct
  (==) (x, x') (y, y') = eqa.(==) x y && eqb.(==) x' y'

  private
  eq :: Pair a b -> Pair a b -> #
  eq (x, x') (y, y') =
    Pair (LiftBin eqa.(==) x y) (LiftBin eqb.(==) x' y')

  private
  eqEq :: (x,y::Pair a b) -> eq x y <=> Lift (x == y)
  eqEq (x, x') (y, y') = struct
    impR p = liftAndR (eqa.(==) x y) (eqb.(==) x' y') p
    impL p = liftAndL (eqa.(==) x y) (eqb.(==) x' y') p

  private
  equivEq :: Equiv eq
  equivEq = struct
    refl (x, x') = (eqa.equiv.refl x, eqb.equiv.refl x')
    symm (x, x') (y, y') (pxy, pxy') =
      (eqa.equiv.symm x y pxy, eqb.equiv.symm x' y' pxy')
    trans (x, x') (y, y') (z, z') (pxy, pxy') (pyz, pyz') =
      (eqa.equiv.trans x y z pxy pyz,
        eqb.equiv.trans x' y' z' pxy' pyz')

  equiv = isoEquiv eq (LiftBin (==)) eqEq equivEq
```

B   The Tautology Function

```
module example$taut =
#include Prelude
struct
data Nat = Zero | Succ Nat

concrete
TautArg :: Nat -> #
TautArg (Zero)   = Bool
TautArg (Succ m) = Bool->TautArg m

taut :: (n::Nat) -> TautArg n -> Bool
taut (Zero)   x = x
taut (Succ m) x = taut m (x True) && taut m (x False)


module example$tauttest =
#include Prelude
open example$taut use Nat, Zero, Succ, taut, TautArg in
```

```
let id :: Bool -> Bool
    id x = x

    implies :: Bool -> Bool -> Bool
    implies x y = not x || y

    equ :: Bool -> Bool -> Bool
    equ x y = implies x y || implies y x
in  do Monad_IO
        putStrLn (System$Bool.show (taut Zero True))
        putStrLn (System$Bool.show (taut (Succ Zero) id))
        putStrLn (System$Bool.show (taut (Succ (Succ Zero)) equ))
```

Haskell as an Automation Controller

Daan Leijen, Erik Meijer, and James Hook

Utrecht University
Department of Computer Science
{erik,daan}@cs.uu.nl

1 Introduction

Component-based programming and scripting support a style of rapid prototyping program development where reusable off-the-shelf software components are glued together to build new applications. One of the reasons of Visual Basic's popularity is its ability to script 'ready made' GUI components in a fancy development environment. Since all the hard work is done inside the components, not only professional programmers but also end-users are able to create non-trivial applications in a short period of time.

Visual Basic uses COM as the underlying component framework. COM is a language independent binary standard for implementing and using software components[2,1]. Vendors can use C++, Java, COBOL or any other language suited for the specific task to create COM components. The second ingredient that Visual Basic needs is the "glue" to compose different components together. ActiveX is a standard set of COM interfaces that specify how components can be composed and how they interact in an interactive and graphical environment [5,4]. The ActiveX interfaces deal with things as drawing, event notification and persistence. The language independence of COM allowed us to create a COM binding for Haskell [14,16,17,15,10]. Through this COM binding, we can take advantage of the enormous set of software components that is available to the Visual Basic programmer.

Of course Haskell in not the only possible alternative to Visual Basic. However most contemporary scripting languages such as ECMAScript, Perl, Tcl, etc. lack some of the essential properties of a truly high-level scripting language: *strong typing, parametric polymorphism* and *overloading* for flexibility of composition without sacrificing type safety, the unconditional principles of *abstraction, parameterization* and *correspondence* to exploit regularity and support reuse in the small, *lazyness* to hide non-termination effects and *monads* to hide other side-effects.

Many people consider monads and higher-order functions esoteric features, but they are essential to make objects and methods first-class values and thus composable and reusable. Strong typing catches many potential bugs at compile time; most modern scripting languages issue the bug at run-time at the client-site!

After a short introduction to Haskell, we start with a simple example that uses a standard COM component (section 3). In section 4, we explain the basics

S.D. Swierstra et al. (Eds.): Advanced Functional Programming, LNCS 1608, pp. 268–289, 1999.
© Springer-Verlag Berlin Heidelberg 1999

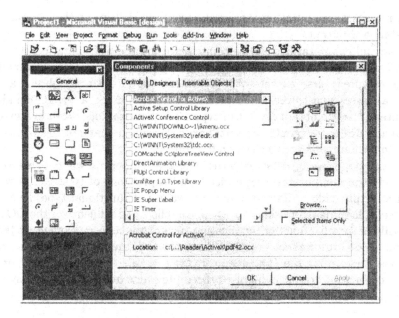

Fig. 1. Visual Basic uses ActiveX to script components

of COM and show how these concepts carry over to Haskell. Section 5 focuses on a special COM technology, called automation. After explaining how automation is used in Haskell, section 6 will discuss some advanced features and constraints of automation. The next section discusses a more involved example using automation and three COM components to create an interactive dictionary. Section 8 discusses various ways of exposing Haskell as a COM component and focuses on one of them; the Script Server interface. This interface is explained in the context of Haskell with some Visual Basic, DHTML and Java examples.

All the needed software and examples can be found at the *HaskellScript* web-site at **www.haskell.org/haskellscript**.

2   Minuscule Introduction to Haskell

When interacting with the outside world or accessing object models, we have to deal with side-effects. In Haskell [12], effectful computations live in the IO monad [11,7,6]. A value of type IO a is a *latently* effectful computation that, *when executed*, will produce a value of type a. The command getChar :: IO Char will read a character from the standard input when it is executed.

Like any other type, latently effectful computations are first class citizens that can be passed as arguments, stored in list, and returned as results. For example putChar :: Char -> IO () is a function that takes a character and then returns a computation that, when executed, will print that character on the standard output.

Effectful computations can be composed using the do{}-notation. The compound command do{ a <- ma; f a } :: IO b is a latent computation, that, when executed, first executes the command ma :: IO a to obtain a value a :: a, passes that to the action-producing function f :: a -> IO b and then executes (f a) to obtain a value of type IO b. For example, when executed the command do{ c <- getChar; putChar c } reads a character from the standard input and copies it to the standard output.

In this paper we adopt style conventions that emphasize when we are dealing with effectful computations. Specifically, all expressions of type IO are written with an explicit do{}. In the same vein, values of functional type a -> b are written as lambda-expressions \a -> b. To reflect the influence of the OO style, we will use postfix function application object#method = method object to mimic the object.method notation. Since methods are first class values, we can compose them using the (##) operator, f##g = \a -> do{ b <- f a; g b }. These conventions result in highly stylized programs from which it is easy to tell the type of an expression by looking at its syntactic shape.

3   Using COM Components

In this section we will show how we can use a COM component in Haskell. The Microsoft Agent Server is a COM component [3] that supports cartoon characters (Genie, Merlin, and Robby) that can talk, move, perform animations and even listen to commands. Agents can provide user-friendly user interaction in applications such as Word or Excel, or interactively guide users through an internet site.

Fig. 2. Three of the Agent characters

3.1   MS Agents in Haskell

The following example is a deluxe version of the mother of all examples; we will pop up the Genie character and have it say "Hello World!". In order to use the Agents, we must first import the module `AgentScript.hs`[1].

To create an instance of a COM component, we use the `coCreateObject` function. It takes the name of the component and the interface identifier (IID, see section 4.1) of the initial interface that we want to talk to:

```
server <- coCreateObject "Agent.Server" iidIAgent
```

Once we created an instance of the agent server and thus obtained a reference to the `IAgent` interface, we can use the methods of the `IAgent` interface. The `loadCharacter` method loads a fresh character from a specified animation file, while the `unloadCharacter` method discards the character.

```
loadCharacter   :: String -> IAgent a -> IO (IAgentCharacter ())
unloadCharacter :: IAgentCharacter b -> IAgent a -> IO ()
```

Note how the *self* argument is the last argument in Haskell. This allows us to use the (#) operator when calling the method:

```
genie <- server # loadCharacter "genie"
```

The `IAgentCharacter` interface has various method for animating the character:

```
showUp :: Int -> IAgentCharacter a -> IO ReqID
speak  :: String -> IAgentCharacter a -> IO ReqID
play   :: String -> IAgentCharacter a -> IO ReqID
hide   :: Int -> IAgentCharacter a -> IO ReqID
```

The server processes the animations asynchronously, so that we can have several characters acting in parallel. This enables our application code to continue while the method is completing. Each of the animations returns a request-id `ReqID` that uniquely identifies the command being executed. These request ids are used for synchronizing multiple parallel agents. For our simple example they can be ignored; the genie will show itself, greet the audience, speak a timeless sentence and disappear without interacting with other agents:

```
module AgentDemo where
import AgentScript

slow :: Int
slow = 0

main :: IO ()
main =
```

---

[1] This module is automatically generated, see section 5.4.

```
do{ server <- coCreateObject "Agent.Server" iidIAgent
  ; genie  <- server # loadCharacter "genie"
  ; genie  # showUp slow
  ; genie  # play "Greet"
  ; genie  # speak "Hello world!"
  ; genie  # hide slow
  ; server # unloadCharacter genie
  }
```

Since methods and properties of COM components are exposed as normal Haskell functions, a given interface can be seamlessly extended with new methods and properties. The syntax for calling new, compound methods is exactly the same as for primitive methods.

As an example, we will extend the characters repertoire with *smooth* animations. Besides animations like Greet, the characters also have a closing animations like GreetReturn. Such animation smoothly transitions the character back to its normal state.

```
smoothPlay :: String -> IO b -> IAgentCharacter a -> IO ReqID
smoothPlay = \anim -> \action -> \character ->
  do{ character # play anim
    ; action
    ; character # play (anim ++ "Return")
    }
```

```
nothing :: IO ()
nothing = do{ return () }
```

This newly defined method can be used in just the same way as 'primitive' methods:

```
genie # show
genie # smoothPlay "Greet" nothing
genie # speak "Hello World!"
genie # smoothPlay "Wave" nothing
genie # hide
```

In this simple example, we are already reaping the benefits of explicitly monadic functional programming by passing "latently effectfull computations" as values to other functions. Ultimately scripting languages describe IO behaviors. By having IO behaviors as first-class values, and not just the side effect of evaluation, we are able to support a compositional style of abstraction that is not possible in traditional scripting languages. This benefit of using Haskell as a scripting language is featured in earlier work, in which we develop parallel and sequential combinators for animation behaviors of Microsoft Agents [14].

Because all methods are first-class values, we can also define custom control structures. For example, Visual Basic language has the with keyword that allows the programmer to execute a list of methods on a single object:

```
With Genie
  .Show
  .Play "Greet"
End With
```

In Haskell, we can define a function ourselves with the same effect:

```
does :: object -> [(object -> IO a)] -> IO ()
```

Using this new function, we can rewrite the core of our example as:

```
genie 'does' [ showUp 0, play "Greet", speak "Hello", hide ]
```

3.2   Exercises

1. Load and run the agent example yourself[2].
2. Let Genie read the contents of a text-file instead of a fixed string.
3. Give a possible definition of the does function.

4   Essential COM

The only way to interact with a COM component is through one of its interfaces. Each interface is uniquely identified by its interface identifier (IID). This allows us to ask for a specific interface at run-time. In the previous example we used the IID of the IAgent interface (iidIAgent) as an argument to the coCreateObject function.

Every COM interface inherits from the IUnknown interface. The IUnknown interface has three methods: addRef, release and queryInterface. The first two methods manage the life-time of the component. A client never explicitly destroys a component; it will call release to indicate that, as far as it is concerned, the component may destroy itself. The component ultimately decides when it will commit suicide, presumably when its reference count drops to zero. In garbage collected languages like Haskell, the programmer never needs to worry about calling release or addRef since the garbage collector will take care of that.

The queryInterface method navigates between all the interfaces that the component supports. For example, we can ask an agent character if it also supports the IAgentBalloon interface:

```
balloon <- genie # queryInterface iidIAgentBalloon
```

If the call succeeds, balloon will be a new IAgentBalloon interface pointer on the character component.

---

[2] www.microsoft.com/msagent.

4.1 Interface Types

What would the type of `queryInterface` look like ? Its argument is an interface identifier and it returns a specific interface pointer with that interface ID; in other words, the return type is dependent on the value of its argument. In languages like C++ or Java, there is no way to express this dependency and hence `queryInterface` is untyped and a type cast is needed. For example, in C++ we would write:

```
IAgentCharacter* genie;
IAgentBalloon* balloon;
...
HRESULT hr;
hr = genie->QueryInterface( iidIAgentBalloon, (void**)balloon );
```

Luckily, we don't need the full generality of dependent types to assign a type to `queryInterface`. Parametric polymorphism can be used to create a typed connection between the passed IID and the returned interface. In some sense, `queryInterface` resembles a function like `head :: [a] -> a` where polymorphism ensures that the returned element is of the same type as the list elements. In the same way, we ensure that the returned interface is of the same type as the IID of the interface by parametrising the IID type with the resulting interface type:

```
queryInterface :: IID iface -> IUnknown a -> IO iface
```

The above type expresses that if we query with IID of an interface `iface`, we will have an interface `iface` as a result. The same trick can be used with the `coCreateObject` function that takes the interface ID of initial interface that we want to use. Actually, the type of both functions is less general since they can not return *any* interface, but only interfaces that inherit from `IUnknown` (since the garbage collector will call `release`). The real (and final) types are therefore:

```
queryInterface :: IID(IUnknown iface)
               -> IUnknown a
               -> IO (IUnknown iface)

coCreateObject :: String
               -> IID(IUnknown iface
               -> IO (IUnknown iface)
```

4.2 Inheritance

Surprisingly, polymorphism can also be used to express the inheritance relationship of COM interfaces.

A method like `queryInterface` should accept both `IUnknown`, `IDispatch` and `IAgentCharacter` interfaces (and in general any other interface inheriting from `IUnknown`) but a method as `Play` should only accept interfaces inheriting from `IAgentCharacter`. Haskell does not have subtyping, but it is possible to use polymorphism to model the inheritance relation.

The self argument in `queryInterface` has type `IUnknown a`, and the self argument in `play` has type `IAgent a`. Both interfaces are parametrised with a type variable. This type variable is used to encode the inheritance relation. For each interface we will have an abstract data type that identifies that interface:

```
data Dispatch a
data Agent a
data AgentCharacter a
```

The next step is to define type synonyms for each interface that use these abstract data types to encode the inheritance relation between them:

```
type IUnknown a          = ...
type IDispatch a         = IUnknown (Dispatch a)
type IAgent a            = IDispatch (Agent a)
type IAgentCharacter a   = IDispatch (AgentCharacter a)
```

That is, every interface pointer for an `IAgentCharacter` also is an interface pointer for an `IDispatch` or an `IUnknown`! We can thus use `queryInterface` on agent characters but we can't use `play` on `IUnknown` interfaces. We can now also understand the type for interface ID's:

```
iidIDispatch :: IID (IDispatch ())
iidIAgent    :: IID (IAgent ())
```

An `iidIAgent` is an interface ID for an `IAgent` exactly, expressed by instantiating the type parameter to `()`.

4.3   IDL

We are have been talking about interfaces all the time but how are interfaces actually specified? Normally, interfaces are defined using the interface description language (IDL). Another possibility is to ship the interface specification in a binary form, called a type library. The (freely available) `OleView` utility shows IDL information for most available components on the system.

As an example of IDL, we show part of the `IAgentCharacter` specification:

```
[ uuid(A7B93C8F-7B81-11D0-AC5F-00C04FD97575),
  dual, oleautomation
]
interface IAgentCharacter : IDispatch {
  HRESULT Play( [in] BSTR animation, [out] long* reqid);
  HRESULT Speak( [in] BSTR text, [out] long* reqid );
  ...
};
```

Everything between square brackets is an attribute. The [uuid] attribute specifies the IID of the IAgentCharacter interface. The interface has methods play and speak. Both return a HRESULT; COM's standard way of returning errors. HRESULT's do not show up in Haskell since they are automatically checked within the IO monad. Both return a request id (attribute [out]) and take a BSTR as an argument (attribute [in]). The BSTR type is a unicode string with length information. Haskell strings are translated to the BSTR layout when calling these functions. This process is called marshalling [16]. The dual and oleautomation attributes mark this interface as an *automation* interface. Before explaining how we can define Haskell functions that call the methods of the IAgentCharacter, we will first explain more about the automation technology.

5   Automation

At the most primitive level, calling methods on an interface is very much like calling a virtual method on a C++ object. While this is great for compiled code, it is not so good in an interpreted or highly dynamic environment. Interpreted languages need to be able to build method calls at run-time: dynamic binding. Automation is a technology that enables dynamic binding in COM. Any component that implements the IDispatch interface supports dynamic binding. The IDispatch interface implements four methods. Two of them allow a client to obtain type information about the interfaces of the component while the other two allow a client to dynamically construct a method call on the component.

Today, almost any COM component exposes its entire functionality through both pure COM interfaces and through an IDispatch interface (so called *dual* interfaces). Although Haskell can call both pure COM and automation interfaces, this article will focus on automation interfaces.

Languages supporting automation interfaces are so-called automation controllers. Haskell is an automation controller through the Automation module. This module contains all the functionality to make automation just as easy to use as in VB.

5.1   Using Automation

In Haskell, there is no (outside) difference between an automation and a COM call. Actually, the agent example uses automation when calling the agent interfaces. In the Agent IDL specification, the dual attribute tells that this interface can be both used as an automation interface and as a pure COM interface. The oleautomation tells the IDL processor to check for conformance with the automation calling requirements.

The methods of the Agent component are defined in Haskell with functions from the Automation module. It exports a set of functions that make it very easy to call methods on automation interfaces. The following sections show how these functions are used to define automation methods and properties in Haskell.

5.2   Methods

The Automation module exports a family of functions method_*n_m* that define automation methods that take n arguments and return m results (section 5.2 explains these functions in more detail).

For example, some methods of the agent component can be defined as:

```
play :: String -> IAgentCharacter a -> IO ReqID
play = \animation -> \agent ->
  do{ agent # method_1_1 "Play" animation }

moveTo :: Int -> Int -> IAgentCharacter a -> IO ReqID
moveTo = \x -> \y -> \agent ->
  do{ agent # method_2_1 "MoveTo" x y }
```

The first argument of a method_*n_m* function is the name of the method that we want to call.

Sometimes, the IDL specification also specifies a retval attribute besides an out attribute. In this case, we should use the function_*n_m* family to define the method. For example, the Play method *could* have been defined as:

```
HRESULT Play( [in] BSTR animation, [out,retval] long* reqid );
```

The play definition in Haskell would then be:

```
play :: String -> IAgentCharacter a -> IO ReqID
play = \animation -> \agent ->
  do{ agent # function_1_1 "Play" animation }
```

5.3   Properties

Besides methods, automation interfaces can also expose properties that can be read and sometimes written (when there is no readonly attribute). The propertyGet_*n* family defines property reads that can take n arguments. The propertySet_*n_m* family defines property writes that can take n arguments. For example, a selection in a Word document is represented by the ISelection interface. Among its properties are the font of the selection or the text in the selection:

```
[..., dual, oleautomation]
interface IDocument : IDispatch {
   [propget] ISelection* Selection;
   ...
};


[..., dual, oleautomation]
interface ISelection : IDispatch {
   [propget] BSTR   Text;
```

```
  [propget] IFont* Font;
  ...
};
```

In Haskell, we can define the properties of the ISelection interface as:

```
getText :: ISelection a -> IO String
getText = \selection ->
  do{ selection # propertyGet_0 "Text" }

setText :: String -> ISelection a -> IO ()
setText = \text -> \selection ->
  do{ selection # propertySet_1 "Text" text }

getFont :: ISelection a -> IO (IFont ())
getFont = \selection ->
  do{ selection # propertyGet_0 "Font" }

setFont :: IFont a -> ISelection b -> IO ()
setFont = \font -> \selection ->
  do{ selection # propertySet_1 "Font" font }
```

5.4 HaskellDirect

Although defining automation properties and methods by hand is fairly easy, it can be quite cumbersome to translate a substantial interface. In collaboration with Sigbjorn Finne and Simon Peyton-Jones, we have constructed an IDL compiler, called *HaskellDirect*[3] [16,17], that automatically generates appropriate interface, method and property definitions. *HaskellDirect* can also generate Haskell for pure COM interfaces and is able to package Haskell programs as COM components.

5.5 Exercises

1. Use the OleView[4] tool to view the type library for the Agent component.
2. Use OleView to generate IDL for JMail[5].

6   Advanced Automation

We have seen how the [oleautomation] attribute checks an interface for conformance with the automation requirements. This section describes the requirements of automation and some other automation attributes.

---

[3] http://www.dcs.gla.ac.uk/fp/software /hdirect/.
[4] www.microsoft.com/com/resource/oleview.asp.
[5] www.dimac.net.

6.1   Variants

The [oleautomation] attribute checks that only VARIANT's are used as argument or result. A VARIANT structure can contain a limited set of data types: *automation types*. The most important are integers, doubles, strings, interface pointers and arrays of variants.

In Haskell, constructor classes[18] are used to enforce the VARIANT contstraint on automation types. Every automation type is an instance of the Variant class. This class contains functions to marshal Haskell values to- and from VARIANT structures. By constraining automation arguments to the Variant class, the type checker will guarantee that no non-automation types are used as an argument.

$$
\overbrace{\qquad}^{n \geq 0} \qquad \overbrace{\qquad}^{m \geq 0}
$$

```
method_n_m :: (...,Variant a,...,...,Variant b,...)
              => String -> ... -> a -> ... -> IDispatch d
              -> IO (...,b,...)
```

$$
\overbrace{\qquad}^{n \geq 0} \qquad \overbrace{\qquad}^{m > 0}
$$

```
function_n_m :: (...,Variant a,...,...,Variant b,...)
                => String
                -> ... -> a -> ... -> IDispatch d
                -> IO (...,b,...)
```

$$
\overbrace{\qquad}^{n \geq 0}
$$

```
propertyGet_n :: (...,Variant a,...,Variant b)
                 => String
                 -> ... -> a -> ... -> IDispatch d -> IO b
```

$$
\overbrace{\qquad}^{n > 0}
$$

```
propertySet_n :: (...,Variant a,...)
                 => String
                 -> ... -> a -> ... -> IDispatch d -> IO ()
```

6.2   Optional Arguments

Automation supports optional arguments via the [optional] attribute. When the argument is left out, the object will choose some default value, which can be specified using the [default] attribute. In Haskell, optional arguments are always given, but have the Maybe type. This means that a programmer can either pass Nothing, or use the Just constructor to pass a value.

For example, the ADO framework, a COM interface on top of the standard ODBC database binding, defines the RecordSet interface:

```
[uuid(...),dual,oleautomation]
interface IRecordSet : IDispatch {
 void Move( [in] long NumRecords,
           [in, optional] VARIANT Start);
  ...
};
```

The Move method changes the current record. When the Start argument is not given, it simple moves NumRecords ahead. However, instead of counting from the current record, the Start argument can specify a (string) bookmark to count from or a number specifying the start or end of the recordset. This method is defined in Haskell as:

```
move :: Variant start => Int -> Maybe start -> IRecordSet a -> IO ()
move = \numrec -> \start -> \rs ->
   do{ rs # method_2_0 "Move" numrec start }
```

7   Advanced Example

In this section we will develop a more advanced example that explains the meaning of an English word. To achieve this it will use MS Word to retrieve the word, Internet Explorer to look up the meaning in an on-line dictionary and Agents to tell the meaning to the user.

As a first step, the agent character will say the selected word in an active MS Word document.

```
module ReadDoc where
import AgentScript

main =
  do{ server <- coCreateObject "Agent.Server" iidIAgent
    ; merlin <- server # loadCharacter "merlin"
    ; merlin 'does'
        [ showUp slow
        , smoothPlay "Greet" nothing
        , readSelection
        , smoothPlay "Wave" nothing
        , hide slow
        ]
```

The readSelection method connects to the currently running Word application using getActiveObject. The returned interface is the IDocument interface of the currently active document. To retrieve the selected text, we first read the Selection property that contains the active selection interface. The Text property of this interface returns the text as a string.

```
readSelection = \merlin ->
  do{ word <- getActiveObject "Word.Application"
    ; text  <- word # getSelection ## getText
    ; merlin # speak text
    }
```

Note how method calls are composed with the ## operator. Both getText and getSelection are defined in the Word97 module. However, since this module is so big, we define the two properties by hand:

```
getText :: IDispatch a -> IO String
getText = \selection ->
  do{ selection # propertyGet_0 "Text" }

getSelection :: IDispatch a -> IO (IDispatch ())
getSelection = \document ->
  do{ document # propertyGet_0 "Selection" }
```

7.1   Webster

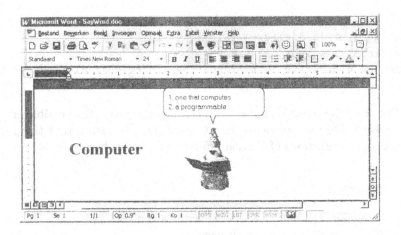

Fig. 3. Merlin tells the meaning of "computer"

We will now extend the previous program such that Merlin tells the *meaning* of a selected word instead of just repeating it. Merlin will retrieve the meaning of the word the Webster online dictionary using the Internet Explorer component to connect to the Webster web-site.

```
merlin # smoothPlay "Read"
              (do{ merlin # tellMeaning (words text) })
```

The `navigate` method of the browser opens an URL. This is used to execute a search on the Webster web-site. Using the `Document` property we get the interface of the returned HTML document. From this document we retrieve the HTML text with the `InnerText` property. The HTML source is than analysed and genie will speak all found meanings:

```
tellMeaning = \words -> \merlin ->
  case words of
    { [] -> do{ merlin # speak
```

```
                          "Sorry, you have to specify a valid word" }
    ; (word:ws)
        -> do{ ie <- coCreateObject
                          "InternetExplorer.Application"
                          iidIBrowser
            ; ie # queryWebster word
            ; txt <- ie # ( getDocument
                          ## getBody
                          ## getInnerText)
            ; merlin # speak (meanings txt)
            }
    }

queryWebster :: String -> IWindow -> IO ()
queryWebster = \word -> \ie ->
   do{ ie # navigate "http://www.m-w.com/cgi-bin/dictionary?va="
                     ++word }
```

The meanings function parses the HTML and extracts the possible meanings
of the word. We will not define this function here but state that the powerful
list processing functions of Haskell are very convenient here.

7.2 Exercises

1. Using the InnerText property, write a console application that renders
   user input directly in a web page.
2. Using a pretty printer and parser combinators, write a program that pretty
   prints some program text in a Word document.

8 Interacting with other Languages

In the previous sections we discussed how Haskell can use components. However, it is also possible to use Haskell from a component. We currently offer the
following choices:

- Using HaskellDirect we can generate the wrapper code that encapsulates
  a Haskell program as a COM component[17]. A client of the component
  never needs to know that the component is written in Haskell. This is
  a very attractive option that completely integrates Haskell with existing
  tools and languages.
- There is an ActiveX Script Engine for Hugs. Any language that implements these interfaces can be used to script any ActiveX Script Host.
  Examples of such hosts are the Internet Explorer, Windows 95/NT and
  Internet Information Server. With this scripting engine, Haskell can be
  used to do web page scripting, both on the server and client site[15].

- We have implemented an automation interface around the Hugs interpreter. Using this interface, other components can load and execute Haskell functions. The ActiveX Script Engine uses this interface internally to execute the Haskell code. In this article we will describe this interface and how it enables Haskell to be integrated with Visual Basic and Java programs.

8.1   The Script Server Interfaces

The interfaces that we implemented around the Hugs interpreter are called the *Script Server* interfaces. They basically represent the minimal functionality needed to program a language from an external application. Any language implementing those interfaces is called a *script server*. We designed the Script Server interface in a language neutral way, it can be implemented for any language; we are currently working on a script server implementation for the new Haskell run-time system[8] and even for general dynamic link libraries (DLL's). Since a Script Server is a COM component, it can also be used from any COM compliant language, like Visual Basic or Java.

A script is loaded with the LoadScript method. The source can be specified with a file path but also for example with an IStorage object. This feature is used in the ActiveX script engine to load a script that resides in memory. LoadScript returns an IScript interface.

```
[dual,oleautomation] interface IScriptServer : IDispatch
{
  HRESULT LoadScript( [in] VARIANT* source
                    , [out,retval] IScript** script );
};
```

Once we have obtained an IScript interface, we can use the Start method to execute the main function of the script.

```
[dual,oleautomation] interface IScript : IDispatch
{
  HRESULT Start         ( void );
  HRESULT AddHostItem   ( [in] BSTR name
                        , [in] IDispatch* item );
  HRESULT GetScriptItem( [in] BSTR name
                        , [out,retval] IScriptItem** item );
  HRESULT Expr          ( [in] BSTR expr
                        , [out,retval] IScriptItem** item );
};
```

For example, the following Visual Basic program starts the Haskell script server and runs the main function of a script:

```
Dim scriptServer as IScriptServer
Dim script       as IScript
```

```
Set scriptServer = CreateObject( "HugsScript" )
Set script       = scriptServer.LoadScript( "Test.hs" )
script.Start
```

8.2   Exporting Values from Haskell

Of course, we want to be able to call other functions than `main`. A client can get access to Haskell functions with the `GetScriptItem` method. Before a function in Haskell is visible to a client through `GetScriptItem`, it should be exposed using the `addScriptItem_n_m` function, where n is the number of arguments and m the number of results of the function. Since the function is exposed as an automation method, its arguments and results should be in the `Variant` class.

$$
\text{addScriptItem\_}n\text{\_}m :: (\overbrace{\ldots,\text{Variant } a,\ldots}^{n \geq 0},\overbrace{\ldots,\text{Variant } b,\ldots}^{m \geq 0})
$$
```
                          => String
                          -> (... -> a -> ... -> IO (...,b,...))
                          -> IO ()
```

For example, `getChar :: IO Char` is exported as:

```
main = do{ addScriptItem_0_1 "GetChar" getChar }
```

Note that a function like `length :: [a] -> Int` can only be exported by constraining its polymorphic type to a type that belongs to the `Variant` class:

```
strLen :: String -> Int
strLen = length
```

```
main    = do{addScriptItem "StrLen" (\s -> do{return (strLen s)}}}
```

When a client calls `GetScriptItem`, it obtains an `IScriptItem` interface to the exported Haskell function.

```
[dual,oleautomation] interface IScriptItem : IDispatch
{
  HRESULT Eval( [in] int numArgs,
                [in,sizeis(numArgs)] VARIANT* args,
                [out] VARIANT* result );
};
```

The `Eval` method calls the function and returns its results. The method takes the number of arguments, an array of arguments and a pointer to the result variant. However, this signature is only used with pure COM calls (i.e. C++). When automation is used, the `Eval` method simply takes a variable number of arguments[6]. This makes it much more convenient to use this interface from languages as Visual Basic or Java.

---

[6] This mechanism is implemented by intercepting an automation call at run-time and coercing the arguments to the `Eval` signature above.

8.3   Visual Basic and Haskell

Fig. 4. Computing the factorial with Haskell and VB.

As an example, we will create a hybrid program in Visual Basic and Haskell that computes the factorial of a number. Haskell is well suited to compute the factorial since it can use infinite precision integers to represent the possibly huge numbers. Visual Basic is well suited for programming the interface to the user since it has an excellent graphical environment where the interface can be 'drawn' by the programmer.

The front end is created in Visual Basic with a text input field, a button and a text field in which the result is displayed. The program will create an instance of the Haskell script server and will invoke the Haskell function Factorial on a button click and update the result field accordingly.

```
Dim Script As IScript

Private Sub Form_Load()
  Dim ScriptServer As IScriptServer
  Set ScriptServer = CreateObject("HugsScript")
  Set Script      = ScriptServer.LoadScript("FacDemo.hs")
  Script.Start
End Sub

Private Sub Button_Click()
  Set Fac = Script.GetScriptItem("Factorial")
  OutputBox.Caption = Fac.Eval(InputBox.Text)
End Sub
```

The Haskell program uses infinite precision Integer types to compute the factorial:

```
module FacDemo where
import HScript

main =
  do{ addScriptItem_1_1 "Factorial"
                      (\n -> do{return (factorial n)})
```

```
    }

factorial :: Integer -> Integer
factorial = \n ->
  case n of
    { 0    -> 1
    ; n    -> n * factorial (n-1)
    }
```

8.4   Importing Values into Haskell

In the previous example, we exposed Haskell values using `addScriptItem` and imported Haskell values using `GetScriptItem`. Dual, a client can expose values to Haskell using `AddHostItem`, which can be imported in Haskell using the `getHostItem` function.

The `AddHostItem` method takes an `IDispatch` interface and a name as an argument. For example, with clientside web scripting [15], Internet Explorer will call `AddHostItem` with the its current window interface and the name `"window"`. An embedded Haskell script will access this window interface by calling `getHostItem`. The functionality of the window can than be accessed from the script.

```
<HTML>
 <BODY>
  <SCRIPT LANGUAGE="HaskellScript">
  module Alert where
  import HtmlScript

  main = do{ window <- getHostItem "window"
           ; window # alert "An embedded Haskell script"
           }
  </SCRIPT>
 </BODY>
</HTML>
```

8.5   Handling Events

Besides exposing Haskell functions, we can also register Haskell functions as event handlers. The `onEvent_n_m` family of functions register a Haskell function, that takes n arguments and returns m results, as an event handler.

$$
\text{onEvent\_}n\text{\_}m :: \overbrace{(\ldots,\text{Variant a},\ldots,}^{n\geq 0}\overbrace{\ldots,\text{Variant b},\ldots)}^{m\geq 0}
$$
```
              => String
              -> (... -> a -> ... -> IO (...,b,...))
              -> IDispatch d -> IO ()
```

We can now redo the factorial example where we handle all events of the VB program in Haskell. All the application logic is moved to Haskell and VB is only used to draw the user interface. The VB program will create an instance of HugsScript, add the button, the input field and the result field to the script and run the main function.

```
Dim Script As IScript

Private Sub Form_Load()
  Dim Server As IScriptServer
  Set Server = CreateObject("HugsScript")
  Set Script = Server.LoadScript("FacDemo2.hs")
  Script.AddHostItem "button", Button
  Script.AddHostItem "output", OutputBox
  Script.AddHostItem "input", InputBox
  Script.Start
End Sub
```

The Haskell program installs an event handler for the button and simply returns. The `click` function is now automatically called when the user presses the button.

```
module FacDemo where

import HScript
import MSForms

main :: IO ()
main =
  do{ button <- getHostItem "button"
    ; button # onEvent_0_0 "Click" click
    ; return ()
    }

click :: IO ()
click =
  do{ input  <- getHostItem "input"
    ; output <- getHostItem "output"
    ; text   <- input # getText
    ; output # setCaption (show (factorial (read text)))
    }
```

The script server interface is used extensively in a front end to the Hawk system. Hawk is language to describe hardware circuits[13]. By using the Haskell script server, it is possible to *draw* hardware circuits in the Visio CAD/CAM application. The script server attaches events to the drawn Visio objects and automatically generates appropriate Hawk code.

8.6 Exercises

1. Import the Script Server type library in J++ and program a infinite precision calculator with Java and Haskell.
2. Implement a Tic-Tac-Toe game algorithm in Haskell ([9]) and construct the user interface with some other tool (for example, DHTML, Delphi or MFC).

9 Conclusions

We have shown how Haskell can be used as a scripting language for COM components. Before the use of monads, interaction with the outside world was difficult to achieve in a functional language; now we can not only *use* a functional language to interact with standard mass-market components, but it is even *advantageous* to do so. Although there are many scripting languages around, the use of a strongly typed, higher-order language makes scripting considerably safer and easier.

Acknowledgments

We would like to thank Sigbjorn Finne for continuous support and motivation to adapt the HaskellDirect compiler to our needs.

References

1. Microsoft. *The COM reference*. Microsoft Press, 1992.
2. Dale Rogerson. *Inside COM*. Microsoft Press, 1997.
3. Microsoft. *Programming Microsoft Agent*. Microsoft Press, 1997.
4. David Chappel. *Understanding ActiveX and OLE*. Microsoft Press, 1996.
5. Kraig Brockschmidt. *Inside Ole (second edition)*. Microsoft Press, 1995.
6. Philip Wadler. The essence of functional programming. *19'th Annual symposium on Principles of Programming Languages*, January 1992.
7. Simon Peyton Jones and John Launchbury. State in haskell. *Lisp and symbolic computation*, 8(4):293–341, 1995.
8. Simon Marlow and Simon Peyton Jones. The new ghc/hugs runtime system. http://research.microsoft.com/Users/simonpj/Papers/new-rts.ps.gz.
9. R. Bird and P. Wadler. *Introduction to Functional Programming*. Prentice Hall, 1988.
10. Daan Leijen. Functional Components, Using COM components in Haskell. Master's thesis, University of Amsterdam, August 1998. http://www.haskell.org/haskellscript.
11. Simon Peyton Jones and Philip Wadler. Imperative functional programming. *POPL*, 20:71–84, 1993.
12. John Peterson (editor). Report on the programming language haskell, version 1.4. Technical report, Yale university, http://www.haskell.org, April 1997.

13. John Matthews, Byron Cook and John Launchbury. Microprocessor specification in Hawk. *ICCL, Chicago, Illinois*, May 1998.
14. Simon Peyton-Jones, Erik Meijer and Daan Leijen. Scripting com components in haskell. *Fifth International Conference on Software Reuse, Victoria, BC, Canada*, June 1998.
15. Erik Meijer, Daan Leijen and James Hook. Client side web scripting with HaskellScript. *Practical Aspects of Declarative Languages, Austin, Texas*, January 1999.
16. Sigbjorn Finne, Daan Leijen, Simon Peyton Jones and Erik Meijer. H/direct, a binary language interface for haskell. *International Conference on Functional Programming, Baltimore*, September 1998.
17. Sigbjorn Finne, Daan Leijen, Simon Peyton Jones and Erik Meijer. Calling hell from heaven and heaven from hell; creating com components in haskell. *submitted to the International Conference on Functional Programming, Paris*, September 1999.
18. Mark P. Jones. A system of constructor classes: Overloading and implicit higher-order polymorphism. *FPCA '93: Conference on Functional Programming Languages and Computer Architecture, Copenhagen, Denmark*, pages 52–61, June 1993.

Springer
and the
environment

At Springer we firmly believe that an international science publisher has a special obligation to the environment, and our corporate policies consistently reflect this conviction.

We also expect our business partners – paper mills, printers, packaging manufacturers, etc. – to commit themselves to using materials and production processes that do not harm the environment. The paper in this book is made from low- or no-chlorine pulp and is acid free, in conformance with international standards for paper permanency.

Springer

Lecture Notes in Computer Science

For information about Vols. 1–1557
please contact your bookseller or Springer-Verlag

Vol. 1599: T. Ishida (Ed.), Multiagent Platforms. Proceedings, 1998. VIII, 187 pages. 1999. (Subseries LNAI).

Vol. 1601: J.-P. Katoen (Ed.), Formal Methods for Real-Time and Probabilistic Systems. Proceedings, 1999. X, 355 pages. 1999.

Vol. 1602: A. Sivasubramaniam, M. Lauria (Eds.), Network-Based Parallel Computing. Proceedings, 1999. VIII, 225 pages. 1999.

Vol. 1603: J. Vitek, C.D. Jensen (Eds.), Secure Internet Programming. X, 501 pages. 1999.

Vol. 1605: J. Billington, M. Diaz, G. Rozenberg (Eds.), Application of Petri Nets to Communication Networks. IX, 303 pages. 1999.

Vol. 1606: J. Mira, J.V. Sánchez-Andrés (Eds.), Foundations and Tools for Neural Modeling. Proceedings, Vol. I, 1999. XXIII, 865 pages. 1999.

Vol. 1607: J. Mira, J.V. Sánchez-Andrés (Eds.), Engineering Applications of Bio-Inspired Artificial Neural Networks. Proceedings, Vol. II, 1999. XXIII, 907 pages. 1999.

Vol. 1608: S. Doaitse Swierstra, P.R. Henriques, J.N. Oliveira (Eds.), Advanced Functional Programming. Proceedings, 1998. XII, 289 pages. 1999.

Vol. 1609: Z. W. Raś, A. Skowron (Eds.), Foundations of Intelligent Systems. Proceedings, 1999. XII, 676 pages. 1999. (Subseries LNAI).

Vol. 1610: G. Cornuéjols, R.E. Burkard, G.J. Woeginger (Eds.), Integer Programming and Combinatorial Optimization. Proceedings, 1999. IX, 453 pages. 1999.

Vol. 1611: I. Imam, Y. Kodratoff, A. El-Dessouki, M. Ali (Eds.), Multiple Approaches to Intelligent Systems. Proceedings, 1999. XIX, 899 pages. 1999. (Subseries LNAI).

Vol. 1612: R. Bergmann, S. Breen, M. Göker, M. Manago, S. Wess, Developing Industrial Case-Based Reasoning Applications. XX, 188 pages. 1999. (Subseries LNAI).

Vol. 1613: A. Kuba, M. Šámal, A. Todd-Pokropek (Eds.), Information Processing in Medical Imaging. Proceedings, 1999. XVII, 508 pages. 1999.

Vol. 1614: D.P. Huijsmans, A.W.M. Smeulders (Eds.), Visual Information and Information Systems. Proceedings, 1999. XVII, 827 pages. 1999.

Vol. 1615: C. Polychronopoulos, K. Joe, A. Fukuda, S. Tomita (Eds.), High Performance Computing. Proceedings, 1999. XIV, 408 pages. 1999.

Vol. 1617: N.V. Murray (Ed.), Automated Reasoning with Analytic Tableaux and Related Methods. Proceedings, 1999. X, 325 pages. 1999. (Subseries LNAI).

Vol. 1618: J. Bézivin, P.-A. Muller (Eds.), The Unified Modeling Language. Proceedings, 1998. IX, 443 pages. 1999.

Vol. 1619: M.T. Goodrich, C.C. McGeoch (Eds.), Algorithm Engineering and Experimentation. Proceedings, 1999. VIII, 349 pages. 1999.

Vol. 1620: W. Horn, Y. Shahar, G. Lindberg, S. Andreassen, J. Wyatt (Eds.), Artificial Intelligence in Medicine. Proceedings, 1999. XIII, 454 pages. 1999. (Subseries LNAI).

Vol. 1621: D. Fensel, R. Studer (Eds.), Knowledge Acquisition Modeling and Management. Proceedings, 1999. XI, 404 pages. 1999. (Subseries LNAI).

Vol. 1622: M. González Harbour, J.A. de la Puente (Eds.), Reliable Software Technologies – Ada-Europe'99. Proceedings, 1999. XIII, 451 pages. 1999.

Vol. 1625: B. Reusch (Ed.), Computational Intelligence. Proceedings, 1999. XIV, 710 pages. 1999.

Vol. 1626: M. Jarke, A. Oberweis (Eds.), Advanced Information Systems Engineering. Proceedings, 1999. XIV, 478 pages. 1999.

Vol. 1627: T. Asano, H. Imai, D.T. Lee, S.-i. Nakano, T. Tokuyama (Eds.), Computing and Combinatorics. Proceedings, 1999. XIV, 494 pages. 1999.

Col. 1628: R. Guerraoui (Ed.), ECOOP'99 - Object-Oriented Programming. Proceedings, 1999. XIII, 529 pages. 1999.

Vol. 1629: H. Leopold, N. García (Eds.), Multimedia Applications, Services and Techniques - ECMAST'99. Proceedings, 1999. XV, 574 pages. 1999.

Vol. 1631: P. Narendran, M. Rusinowitch (Eds.), Rewriting Techniques and Applications. Proceedings, 1999. XI, 397 pages. 1999.

Vol. 1632: H. Ganzinger (Ed.), Automated Deduction – Cade-16. Proceedings, 1999. XIV, 429 pages. 1999. (Subseries LNAI).

Vol. 1633: N. Halbwachs, D. Peled (Eds.), Computer Aided Verification. Proceedings, 1999. XII, 506 pages. 1999.

Vol. 1634: S. Džeroski, P. Flach (Eds.), Inductive Logic Programming. Proceedings, 1999. VIII, 303 pages. 1999. (Subseries LNAI).

Vol. 1636: L. Knudsen (Ed.), Fast Software Encryption. Proceedings, 1999. VIII, 317 pages. 1999.

Vol. 1638: A. Hunter, S. Parsons (Eds.), Symbolic and Quantitative Approaches to Reasoning and Uncertainty. Proceedings, 1999. IX, 397 pages. 1999. (Subseries LNAI).

Vol. 1639: S. Donatelli, J. Kleijn (Eds.), Application and Theory of Petri Nets 1999. Proceedings, 1999. VIII, 425 pages. 1999.

Vol. 1640: W. Tepfenhart, W. Cyre (Eds.), Conceptual Structures: Standards and Practices. Proceedings, 1999. XII, 515 pages. 1999. (Subseries LNAI).

Vol. 1643: J. Nešetřl (Ed.), Algoritms – ESA '99. Proceedings, 1999. XII, 552 pages. 1999.

Vol. 1644: J. Wiedermann, P. van Emde Boas, M. Nielsen (Eds.), Automata, Languages, and Programming. Proceedings, 1999. XIV, 720 pages. 1999.

Vol. 1649: R.Y. Pinter, S. Tsur (Eds.), Next Generation Information Technologies and Systems. Proceedings, 1999. IX, 327 pages. 1999.

Vol. 1650: K.-D. Althoff, R. Bergmann, L.K. Branting (Eds.), Case-Based Reasoning Research and Development. Proceedings, 1999. XII, 598 pages. 1999. (Subseries LNAI).

Vol. 1651: H. Güting, D. Papadias, F. Lochovsky (Eds.), Advances in Spatial Databases. Proceedings, 1999. XI, 371 pages. 1999.

Vol. 1653: S. Covaci (Ed.), Active Networks. Proceedings, 1999. XIII, 346 pages. 1999.